Every case of sanctification is unique – as unique as the holy man or woman at its centre. Yet at the same time the problem posed is a general one: how does an individual become a Saint? In this bold and pioneering study the author answers the question by providing a detailed analysis of the case of the late twelfth- and early thirteenth-century Byzantine holy man, the Cypriot Saint Neophytos the Recluse.

In this interdisciplinary analysis the author addresses three different but closely interconnected aspects of reality: the factual, the cultural and the personal. In so doing, she establishes events, names, dates, places; she examines aspects of the thoughts, mentalities, ideologies and other cultural processes at work in the society of which Neophytos was a member; and she focuses on the subjective realities of Neophytos the man: his surviving writings are considered together with the paintings in the caves of his monastery, to offer a rare insight into the thought-world of a Byzantine holy man. In placing Neophytos within the context both of Cypriot Orthodox society and of the wider Byzantine world, such matters are discussed as education, secular and ecclesiastical politics, the relationship between Constantinople and her provinces, and the effects on this relationship of the fall of the Queen City to the crusading armies in 1204.

The study traces the evolution of Neophytos' belief in his own sanctity and his idiosyncratic pursuit of self-sanctification, before it proceeds to reconstruct the long, complex and continuous interaction between Recluse and society – an interaction which culminated in his sanctification. This process is analysed on the basis of the surviving textual and pictorial evidence, but also in terms of social anthropology, sociology and psychoanalysis. The author's care in defining her terms throughout the book will ensure its accessibility both to the specialist and to the interested general reader.

The making of a Saint

The making of a Saint

The life, times and sanctification of Neophytos the Recluse

Catia Galatariotou

Honorary Research Associate
Department of Byzantine and Modern Greek
King's College London

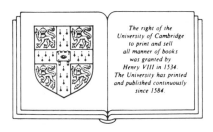

The right of the
University of Cambridge
to print and sell
all manner of books
was granted by
Henry VIII in 1534.
The University has printed
and published continuously
since 1584.

Cambridge University Press

Cambridge
New York   Port Chester
Melbourne   Sydney

Published by the Press Syndicate of the University of Cambridge
The Pitt Building, Trumpington Street, Cambridge CB2 1RP
40 West 20th Street, New York, NY 10011, USA
10 Stamford Road, Oakleigh, Melbourne 3166, Australia

First published 1991

Printed in Great Britain at
Redwood Press Limited, Melksham, Wiltshire

British Library cataloguing in publication data
Galatariotou, Catia
    The making of a Saint: the life, times and sanctification
    of Neophytos the Recluse.
    1. Byzantine Empire, History. Neophytos, Saint, the Recluse
    I. Title
    949.5

Library of Congress cataloguing in publication data
Galatariotou, Catia.
    The making of a Saint: the life, times, and sanctification of
    Neophytos the Recluse / Catia Galatariotou.
        p.   cm.
    Includes bibliographical references.
    ISBN 0 521 39035 4
    1. Neophytos, the Recluse, Saint, 1134–ca. 1214.   2. Christian
saints – Cyprus – Biography.   3. Recluses – Cyprus – Biography.
4. Sanctification – History of doctrines – Middle Ages, 600–1500.
5. Orthodox Eastern Church – Doctrines – History.   6. Byzantine
Empire – Social conditions.   7. Byzantine Empire –
History – 1081–1453.   8. Cyprus – Church history.   I. Title.
BX450.93.N46G35   1991
281.9′092 – dc20   90–43277 CIP
[B]

ISBN 0 521 39035 4 hardback

For Max

Contents

Part 4 Saint Neophytos the Recluse

Plates

All plates are reproduced by permission of Byzantine Visual Resources, © 1990, Dumbarton Oaks, Washington, DC.

Acknowledgments

Many of the central ideas in this book were first formulated in my doctoral thesis. I am grateful to Professor A. A. M. Bryer for his encouragement and the innumerable references with which he seasoned his supervision.

The dissertation was very extensively rewritten and expanded for this book. I am grateful to both Professor Judith Herrin and Dr Paul Magdalino for reading an advanced draft of the book. Their constructive criticism and many helpful suggestions saved this study from various pitfalls and led to a number of revisions.

I am especially grateful to my husband, Max Saunders, who spent long hours discussing with me theoretical and practical matters concerning this study, and became a sensitive and constructively critical last reader of the whole typescript. Above all, however, I am grateful for his support, encouragement, patience and good humour – all of which proved invaluable in seeing this book written, and its author surviving the inevitable frustrations of writing it.

Many other people provided help and support in many different ways and at various stages of my work. I am deeply grateful to Dr Jon Sklar. I would also like to thank, for many useful suggestions and bibliographical references, Professor Evelyne Patlagean, Professor Margaret Alexiou, Dr Chris Wickham, the Reverend Paul (Benediktos) Egglezakes, Dr Charles Stewart, Dr David Holton (the first four of whom read the dissertation, the last two a version of the book); Dr Aglaia Kasdagli, Dr John Haldon, Ms Katerina Krikos-Davis, Dr Robin Cormack, Dr Kostas Kyrris, Dr Athanasios Papageorgiou, Mr Valentino Joseph. Many thanks, too, to Ms Jenny Potts. Naturally, responsibility for the book's mistakes and weaknesses remains entirely mine.

This book was written at Selwyn College, Cambridge, and was the outcome of a Research Fellowship there. I am grateful to the Fellowship of the College, not least for electing a Byzantinist during difficult times, when academic institutions in this country were under pressure to turn away from so-called 'minority subjects'.

I thank the abbot and monks of the monastery of St Neophytos, in

Cyprus, for their gracious hospitality and for allowing me to use their library and the monastery's facilities at an early stage of my work.

Thanks are also due to the staff of a number of libraries: the University Libraries at Cambridge and Birmingham, the Bodleian at Oxford, the British Library in London, the *Bibliothèque Nationale* in Paris, the *Ethnikē Bibliothēkē* at Athens, the Patriarchal Library in Jerusalem, the *Phaneromenē* in Nicosia.

Last but not least, I am grateful to my family, and especially to my father, for support throughout many years of study and research.

Cambridge, May 1990

Abbreviations

AB	*Analecta Bollandiana*
ABαr	Ἀπόστολος Βαρνάβας (Nicosia)
AOL	*Archives de l'orient latin*
ASS	*Acta Sanctorum*
B	*Byzantion*
BAR	*British Archaeological Reports, International Series*
BCH	*Bulletin de correspondence héllenique*
BF	*Byzantinische Forschungen*
BHG	*Bibliotheca hagiographica graeca*
BMGS	*Byzantine and Modern Greek Studies*
BS	*Byzantinoslavica*
BZ	*Byzantinische Zeitschrift*
CB	*Corpus scriptorum historiae byzantinae, general ed. B. G. Niebuhr (Bonn, 1829–97).*
CH	*Church History*
DOP	*Dumbarton Oaks Papers*
DOS	*Dumbarton Oaks Studies*
EB	*Etudes byzantines (continued as REB)*
EEBS	Ἐπετηρίς Ἑταιρείας Βυζαντινῶν Σπουδῶν
EHR	*English Historical Review*
EIE	Ἐθνικόν Ἵδρυμα Ἐρευνῶν *(Athens)*
EKEE	Ἐπετηρίς Κέντρου Ἐπιστημονικῶν Ἐρευνῶν *(Nicosia)*
EO	*Echos d'Orient*
GRBS	*Greek, Roman and Byzantine Studies*
JEH	*Journal of Ecclesiastical History*
JHS	*Journal of Hellenic Studies*
JÖB	*Jarbuch der österreichischen Byzantinistik*
JÖBG	*Jahrbuch der österreichischen byzantinistischen Gesellschaft (continued as JÖB)*
JRS	*Journal of Roman Studies*
JTS	*Journal of Theological Studies*

ΚΣ	*Κυπριακαί Σπουδαί*
ΚΧ	*Κυπριακά Χρονικά*
MPG	J.-P. Migne, *Patrologia cursus completus: series graeco-latina* (161 vols., Paris, 1857–66)
MPL	J.-P. Migne, *Patrologia cursus completus: series latina* (221 vols., Paris, 1844–55)
NE	*Νέος Ἑλληνομνήμων*
OC	*Oriens christianus*
OCA	*Orientalia christiana analecta*
OS	*L'Orient syrien*
PEF	*Palestine Exploration Fund, Quarterly Statement*
ΠΚΣ	*Πρακτικά τοῦ Πρώτου Διεθνοῦς Κυπρολογικοῦ Συνεδρίου* (Nicosia, 1972)
PO	*Patrologia orientalis*
PP	*Past and Present*
RDAC	*Report of the Department of Antiquities, Cyprus*
REB	*Revue des études byzantines*
RHC, Occ.	*Recueil des historiens des croisades, historiens occidentaux* (4 vols., Paris, 1844, 1859, 1864, 1879; repr. Farnborough, 1967)
RHC, Or.	*Recueil des historiens des croisades, historiens orientaux* (5 vols., Paris, 1872, 1884, 1887, 1898; repr. Farnborough, 1967)
ROC	*Revue de l'orient chrétien*
TM	*Travaux et mémoires*
TU	*Texte und Untersuchungen zur Geschichte der altkirschlichen Literatur*
VV	*Vizantinijskij Vremennik*
ZRVI	*Zbornik Radova Vizantoloskog Instituta*

Introduction: aims and methods

The holy man was a feature of the Byzantine universe as indispensible as its emperor and its patriarchs. For centuries now the holy men and women of Byzantium have received the attention of generations of scholars who undertook the monumental task of editing and publishing the narrative accounts of Saints' *Lives* and *Miracles*. For far too long, however, no sustained effort was made to understand the links between the holy man and society, to comprehend the process of sanctification and to place it within a social context. It was only relatively recently, with the emergence of a serious interest in Byzantium's social and cultural history, that the importance of such an undertaking began to be appreciated. The seminal work of scholars such as Evelyne Patlagean and especially Peter Brown made it clear that we cannot hope adequately to comprehend Byzantine civilisation if we fail to take into account the interrelationship between Byzantine society and those of its members who ostensibly rejected it – its holy men and women.[1]

This study represents an attempt to comprehend this interrelationship. It presents an analysis of a Byzantine holy man within the society of his time, with specific reference to that most delicate of processes, the process of sanctification. In its analysis this study rests entirely on the premise that the process of becoming a Saint is one which – perhaps above all other social processes – underlies the inseparability of the individual from society: there is no Saint except for the one whom society has invested with sanctity. And since sanctification is a social process, human-made rather than God-sent, it is possible to chart out its various phases, to deconstruct it, to examine its consituent elements, to isolate the written and unwritten rules which define it in a given culture. In short, it is possible to analyse and understand sanctification – if sufficient information is at hand.

The last point is of crucial importance. Because the process of sanctification is an extremely complex one, even to begin to understand it we need to possess a great amount of information. And because this is a two-way, interactive process between a specific individual and the society in which he lived, our information must refer in detail both to the holy man and to the society in which he lived as a man and died as a Saint. Now, the second of

[1] E.g., Brown (1971b, 1976, 1981, 1982); Patlagean (1968, 1976, 1981b).

1

these requirements (information on the holy man's society) can be satisfied, in varying degrees, in the case of only relatively few Byzantine holy men – information on provincial life in particular being notoriously absent from Byzantine sources. Our first requirement is even more difficult to meet, for there is usually a complete absence of information of a detailed and personal nature concerning the holy man himself.

All of which leads us by contrast to the holy man at the centre of this study, Saint Neophytos the Recluse; and to the society of the island of Cyprus, where he lived and died (from 1134 until after 1214). Even though our knowledge of Neophytos' contemporary Cyprus remains tantalisingly incomplete, when the available historical information is pieced together it provides not only an outline of the general picture but also numerous and illuminating details. Equally important and much more rare is the nature of the information we have concerning the holy man himself. This is expressed through two different media: written texts, and painted images. Neophytos wrote extensively, and a very substantial part of his writings survives in manuscripts now resting on the shelves of various libraries in Europe and Jerusalem. What makes these writings extremely valuable for our present purposes is the great amount and the very personal nature of the information which Neophytos gives us about himself: it allows us to get to know him from very close quarters indeed. Further, a very substantial part of Neophytos' physical surroundings is still with us today, in the form of the painted caves of the troglodytic monastery which he founded. They too contain extremely valuable information concerning both Neophytos and his contemporary Cyprus. The written word and the painted image combine, in Neophytos' case, to form a bridge across the forbidding flow of time that separates us from him. They allow us a rare insight into the material and symbolic universe of a Byzantine man and his society; they permit us to retrace the long and complex interaction between this man and society – an interaction which was transformed into a process of sanctification.

By studying one specific example we can hope to deepen our understanding of sanctification as a general socio-historical process. This is not to claim that the present study presents in all its aspects a universally applicable 'model' for the process of sanctification in Byzantium. For one thing, Neophytos lived in an age which, within the confines and contradictions of its culture, permitted the expression of individualism to a remarkable extent.[2] Neophytos' individualism coloured everything about him, and this

---

[2] Kazhdan and Constable (1982: *passim*, esp. 34) ('individualism without freedom'); Kazhdan and Franklin (1984: *passim*); Kazhdan and Wharton Epstein (1985: *passim*, esp. 210ff.). The relevant findings of Kazhdan have been supported by those of other scholars. See, e.g., Magdalino (1984: esp. 62) ('the chronic individualism of Byzantine society'); Magdalino (1987); Mullett (1984: 173–4); Cormack (1984: 164). More recently, see the approach of Obolensky (1988: 45–82).

applies particularly to the process of sanctification evidenced in his case. But at any rate, it is, generally speaking, fruitless to search for a 'blueprint' for sanctification in Byzantium. First, because since the myth of a mono-lithic Byzantine culture has been, mercifully, well and truly buried (thanks – with respect especially to the eleventh and twelfth centuries – above all to the pioneering work of Alexander Kazhdan),[3] we have begun to perceive how many varied and widely divergent strands went into the cloth of the civilisation which we now call 'Byzantine'. It is true that to a certain extent this was a unified civilisation; but it is equally true that at any given time different classes and different groups within the empire manifested atti-tudes which were not just divergent but opposed and at times violently hostile to each other. It would therefore be naive to presume that what made a man holy for the Cypriots at a given point in time would necessarily equally satisfy the Constantinopolitan aristocrats, the common people of Athens, the Slav pastoralists or the Anatolian peasants. Indeed, one of the findings of this study is that even within the same small society of Orthodox Cyprus, the notion of having a local, living holy man underwent a dramatic transformation over a period of only a few years, changing from – at best – a vague desire, to an urgent need.

However, sanctification, in common with any other social process, con-tains an essential paradox. Each and every case of sanctification is as unique as the holy man or woman at its centre; as unique as the precise conjuncture of historical circumstances that shaped the society which acknowledged that man or woman as holy. But at the same time, the *problematic* which a case of sanctification poses is a general one. In this sense no case of sanctification, within the same or similar culture, is unique; and indeed parallels can be drawn from cultures otherwise quite divergent from each other. The characters, the settings, the costumes, are always different; the action does, always, vary; but the essential dynamic behind it does not. Every single case of sanctification presents us with an example which is both unique – in its specificities – *and* general, in that it is invariably the outcome of a continuous interaction between the holy man or woman and society. Thus it is that the specificity of Neophytos' case does not diminish its general relevance.

I have dealt with questions of methodological approach and definition in the main body of the text, whenever these were of specific, limited relevance. However, most of the theoretical and methodological concepts used are constantly present throughout this study, most frequently implicitly rather

---

[3] Especially through two fine books: Kazhdan and Franklin (1984) and Kazhdan and Wharton Epstein (1985). See also Kazhdan and Constable (1982).

than explicitly. In order to avoid repetition of references and definitions I decided to provide at this early stage a working definition of the terms and concepts used. The following paragraphs are intended to be of use not only in introductory terms but also in providing a specific point of reference for the reader to come back to later, should he or she feel unsure as to the meaning which a certain concept or term carries in this book. I hope that in return the reader may forgive me for the perhaps rather taxing conceptual and theoretical 'account' that follows immediately below, and which may well at this stage appear to be 'no more than theory'.

In understanding social processes – including sanctification – I found an extremely useful tool in Pierre Bourdieu's extended notion of the economic.[4] He understands symbolism to be as important as materialism in any given culture, and uses the term 'economic' to denote a series of calculations which encompass all goods, material *and* symbolic, which are considered to be rare and worthy of being sought after in a particular society. We usually have no problem in comprehending material capital. It is physically tangible, easily measurable, and we can quickly learn enough about a society to establish the relative value of a material commodity in it: a handful of golden coins held by a member of one society, a handful of eagle's feathers held by a member of another, will denote that each individual is wealthy in his or her respective community if what he or she possesses is considered to be precious and rare in that community. As such, possession of that commodity clearly confers material as well as symbolic power on its owner.

Symbolic capital is, by contrast, much more elusive. Symbolism works through evocation rather than (as a pure semiological approach would have it) through expressing specific 'meanings'.[5] Symbolism addresses emotions and thoughts by a process of associations whose topology of operation also encompasses the individual and collective unconscious. By its very nature it is therefore resistant to full and conscious articulation. It mocks especially our most commonly used, yet necessarily reductionist, means of communication: words, whether spoken or written, can only describe emotions and thoughts by approximation, since they themselves are symbols, ideograms representing commonly agreed upon – and therefore imprecise and generalised – notions. Yet we cannot cease from trying to understand symbolism, for even though its precise nature and dynamics appear to escape us, its effects cannot: daily we are startled by the power of its formative influence on human behaviour, individual and collective.

Our efforts to understand aspects at least of symbolism are mercifully not doomed to total failure: symbolic capital gives us a clue as to its nature

---

[4] Bourdieu (1977: esp. 177ff., and *passim*).   [5] Sperber (1975).

through the way it relates to material capital. As Pierre Bourdieu points out, despite their apparently totally different natures, material and symbolic capital relate to each other through being interconvertible.[6] This admits a limited 'translation' of symbolism into words, for it is precisely at the point of interconvertibility of symbolic into material capital that symbolism becomes 'speakable' and subject to a measure of conscious understanding and articulation. It is by taking into account this interconvertibility that we can appreciate both the extent of the power of symbolism and the rationality of the overall economic transaction involved in all social practices. For instance, it is partly because of this interconvertibility that Byzantine aristocrats spent vast amounts of material capital in founding and endowing monasteries; it is because of it that even the poorest peasant would offer a *tama* to a Saint,[7] or light a candle before an icon; it is because of it that people would turn their movable and immovable properties into testamentary gifts to their local church or monastery in order for their names to be commemorated and in the hope that their sins will be absolved after their deaths; it is because of it that ritual, that most glaring example of the perfect interconvertibility of material and symbolic capital, is always present, in all cultures, of all times.

The totality of the material and symbolic capital of a society comprises its 'culture'. Out of this totality, a society constructs a set of control mechanisms – plans, recipes, rules, instructions. These are used for the governing of its members' behaviour, and in order to bind them together in one coherent unit and to impart that unit with a collectively shared sense of identity. In using the term 'culture' I am thus also following Clifford Geertz in referring implicitly to these control mechanisms, rather than to complexes of behaviour patterns such as are expressed through customs, usages, traditions.[8]

I use 'ideology' in the sense of a set of conscious beliefs and practices, generated through the contradictions within the specific culture, part of which that ideology is; the latter's function being to mask those very contradictions that produce it.[9] Ideology is frequently – and perhaps most powerfully – expressed through symbolism, though the latter is in its turn convertible to material capital. I understand culture, ideology and symbolism as being inseparably interrelated, each reflecting and reproducing the other and each being affected by changes in one or more of the constituent elements of the other.

---

[6] Bourdieu (1977: esp. 178ff., and *passim*). [7] A *tama* is a votive offering.
[8] Geertz (1975: 3–54, esp. 44).
[9] Generally, Larrain (1979, 1983); also Lovell (1980); and especially within the Byzantine context, Haldon (1986).

I use the term 'factual reality' with reference to events whose physical occurrence is indisputable and subject to independent verification: the act of Neophytos' settlement at the *enkleistra*, for instance; the fact that a battle took place between the Byzantines and the Turks in Myriokephalon in 1176; or that Richard I of England conquered Cyprus in 1191. Within any given culture 'factual reality' is processed, as it were, through the system of ideologies in that culture, and what re-emerges after this largely unconscious process is a perceived 'reality' which is no longer 'factual reality' pure and simple, but a collectively held interpretation of it. In this sense the term 'reality' (as opposed to 'factual reality') describes essentially a product of culture.[10]

Further, of the many forms reality is capable of assuming, we shall also be concerned with the shape it might take on a purely individual level. At that subjective level, reality is a product both of culture and of the individual's personal idiom. This last term, 'personal idiom', I use to refer to that core of one's individuality which is totally personal to him or her. Constructed out of innate tendencies and moulded by subsequent early interactive experiences between the individual and his or her immediate environment, the personal idiom is as unique to that individual as his or her fingerprints. It forms the earliest part of an individual's psychological make-up, and it is responsible for those 'traits of character', as we commonly call them, which are unchangeable, intractable and which more than anything else make each individual a unique being. It would, however, be wrong to see the personal idiom as existing independently of cultural influences. The relationship between the two is subject to endless debate, but what remains indisputable is that the total personality of each individual (of which the personal idiom is only a part) also bears indelibly the added, very powerful formative effects of acculturation. These may not define the personal idiom, but they certainly influence in varying degrees the development of the rest of one's personality and provide the individual with the means of expression and communication which are essential if he or she is to become and remain a socialised being.[11]

Personal idiomatic expression, material and symbolic capital, culture, ideology, factual and perceived reality; the relationshsip between them: we must take account of all these factors to begin to comprehend the inherent economic rationality of individual acts and social processes. This is directly relevant to the subject of this book, since at its very core lies a particular type of social process, whose end results are commonly manifested in most – if not all – societies we know about. This is the process which culminates in a group of people (the whole of society or a group within it) investing one of its

[10] Berger and Luckmann (1967).   [11] Bollas (1989).

members with a status of positive difference, over and above the rest: he or she may be acknowledged as an exceptional leader, an extraordinarily wise person, a genius, a hero, a holy man or woman, a Saint. All such statuses tend – in very different degrees – to invest the acclaimed individual with what social anthropologists call 'interstitiality':[12] the individual is perceived as human, but has also been invested with some extraordinary, non-human or super-human powers and qualities, which in essence represent idealised and absolute versions of particularly highly considered moral qualities. The Saint is found at the pinnacle of such a scale of acclamations, since the Saint's interstitiality more directly than any other involves the divine: the Saint retains elements of his or her humanity, but has also come to partake of the divine. The process of achieving a status of positive difference involves continuous economic bargaining and exchange between an individual and society, continuous investment of material and symbolic capital between the two, which culminates in society granting to the individual a status (in the case under discussion here, that of sanctity) in return for something that individual offers it. That 'something' is a 'commodity' which is considered to be sufficiently precious and necessary for society to receive it and to bestow in return a comparably precious status on this one of its members.

Within this context, this study attempts to answer a twofold question: what was the 'commodity' which Neophytos offered to the Orthodox society of Cyprus; and why was it considered by the members of that society to be so precious and so necessary that they should receive it with an appreciation deep enough to be expressed in their investiture of Neophytos with sanctity?

As is probably already apparent from the preceding paragraphs, in attempting to answer this question I have followed no 'given' theoretical credo. In working through Neophytos' writings I preferred to allow myself to be led by the source material, to follow the course which it, through the information it yielded, appeared to be charting, rather than to follow any predetermined theoretical framework. I have thus pursued a study which, though firmly based on Neophytos' writings and other – mainly Byzantine –

---

12 Social anthropologists describe as 'interstitial beings' those partaking of more than one cultural category or state, and who are declared by society to be dangerous, powerful, holy. According to Mary Douglas, who first discussed the concept, interstitiality or ambiguity is based on a system of binary opposites created between the natural and the human-made. Subsequent social anthropological work, however, points out that all types of ambiguity are culturally constructed, human-made opposites creating an abnormality in order that it should fulfil a certain function. See Douglas (1969, 1973); Tambiah (1969); Bulmer (1967); and for an application of interstitiality in a social–historical context see Beard (1980).

sources, is also interdisciplinary in character, using theoretical and non-theoretical material from disciplines other than history (as this has been delineated by traditional scholarship) whenever these appeared to provide valid insight into the available source material.

If I have behaved in my methodological approach in an 'eclectic' way, it is not because I am unaware of the dangers of eclecticism. It is simply because I find its dangers avoidable at best, and at worst potentially much less harmful than those involved in the total commitment to either one given theoretical formulation, or to the so-called 'non-theoretical' approach.[13] Each of these two approaches tends to present itself not as an interpretation of history (which is what every work of historiography inevitably is) but as the Truth. The great danger of the former approach is that it lures its follower to dogmatism, and to the pursuit thereafter not of historical understanding but of validation of a given set of theoretical propositions through the editing of historical information. In this lies also its main redeeming feature: because it reveals its theoretical basis, it allows at least the critical reader to know where the bias lies in the particular interpretation of history he or she is reading. No such margin exists in works of historiography that declare themselves to be 'non-theoretical' (itself a fiction, since no individual reacts to entirely 'objective' conditions, but only to practical and subjective interpretations he or she produces out of these conditions). The great danger of this approach is that by remaining silent as to its premises, it pretends that they do not exist; it envelops itself in the fallacy of its 'objectivity' and thus remains unaware that it is as interpretative, as editorial and as subjective as any other approach. The bias of the unspoken theoretical framework may thus more easily elude both the writer and the reader.

Even though I find a theoretical approach preferable to a 'non-theoretical' one, I chose not to work within one single theoretical framework of the many already in existence, but to use instead aspects of a number of theories, from a number of fields. This was because I have searched but found no single theoretical formulation that successfully and fully accounts for the individual, society and the relationship between the two. If one such all-encompassing theoretical formula existed, I would have instantly embraced it with pleasure, gratitude and an enormous sense of relief. However, the genius capable of such total and absolute understanding has not yet appeared amongst us. Nor do I have any great hope that such a

---

[13] For a discussion of theoretical and 'non-theoretical' approaches with specific reference to Byzantine historiography, see Haldon (1984–5); within a wider theoretical and social anthropological context see Bourdieu's attacks on the more rigid forms of functionalism, structuralism, objectivism, Marxist economism and semiology: Bourdieu (1977: esp. 115, 177, 179, 188, and *passim* by implication).

Messiah will appear in truth (as opposed to his or her own phantasy, and that of his or her adherents). Individuals, societies and relationships are far too complicated and far too fluid for any single theory to explain fully any one of the three, let alone all three together. However, general patterns of the forces at work both on the individual and on the collective level do emerge; and our theories are based on the observation and analysis of these patterns. Occasionally, the results of research in different fields of enquiry clearly show that *some* researchers have gained a measure of understanding of *some aspects* of the total picture. We can – indeed, perhaps I should say 'we must' – use such relevant insights to try and gain a better, fuller understanding of history. At the same time, we must never forget the limitations of theory: at best, our theories are only a means of understanding by comparison and approximation. I can think of few things more sterile and narcissistic than to believe in them totally; and of few things more dishonest and dangerous than to cut our evidence to suit our theories rather than to test the latter against the former.

My understanding of sanctification as a two-way process is reflected in the way the material in this book has been organised. Part 1 introduces Neophytos and eleventh- to thirteenth-century Cyprus. Part 2 focuses on the holy man himself. It presents expressions of Neophytos' personal idiom, as evidenced in his surviving manuscripts and the paintings of his caves; it seeks to establish his conception of sanctity and his pursuit of it through a complicated – and not necessarily always consciously deliberate – process of self-sanctification. Part 3 attempts to examine the relationship between the Recluse and the Orthodox society of Cyprus which invested him with sanctity. At the same time I have tried to place both Neophytos and Cyprus within the wider context of contemporary Byzantium by drawing parallels where parallels could be drawn, and by pointing out contrasts where these were in evidence. Part 4 recapitulates and interprets the evidence presented earlier, and presents the conclusions of this study.

The source material for this book consists basically of Neophytos' surviving manuscripts – some 1,000 folios, still mostly unpublished, which appear to represent about half of Neophytos' literary output. The Appendix provides a 'guide' to the Recluse's writings, as well as an essential tool for tracing the citations to his works in this book. The general literary and wider cultural influences on Neophytos' work as a writer are examined in Part 1, to be compared later in the book with the further, highly individualistic uses to which Neophytos put his sources.

I have translated and paraphrased Neophytic passages extensively, but refrained from editing as yet unpublished passages to which reference is made in this book: a number of scholars have already undertaken the edition and publication of Neophytos' unpublished manuscripts, and it now appears that it will not be too long before their efforts bear tangible fruit.[14]

Transliteration was, as always, a nearly insoluble problem. In common with other Byzantinists I had to devise my own 'system' in the end. By and large I have preferred direct transliteration of Greek names rather than use of their Latin or any other equivalent (Neophytos and not Neophytus; Eustathios and not Eustathius or Eustace; Alexios Komnēnos and not Alexius Comnenus); even though I found it almost always preferable to change, for example, Ioannis to John and Kyrillos to Cyril, since the latter is in common English usage.

My attempt to reach an understanding of Neophytos' case of sanctification took the form of an exploration of three different but interconnected levels of reality: the factual, the cultural and the personal. At the first level, the aim of this study was to establish elements of factual reality; at the second, to understand relevant aspects of the thoughts, mentalities and cultural processes at work in the society of which Neophytos was a member; at the third, to reconstruct expressions of the personal idiom of the holy man at the centre of this study. The challenge was to try and investigate each level without losing sight of the other two. Compartmentalisation, however, was of course inevitable: frequently, the interconnections had to remain implicit, in suspension until the concluding Part 4, where I attempted to bring them all explicitly together. Whether with the final page this journey of exploration reached its end, or whether it was worth making at all, is, as always, a matter for the reader to decide.

---

[14] Mr B. Egglezakes is working on an edition of Neophytos' *Interpretation of the Commandments* (*Cod. Coisl. Gr. 287*); Mr S. Chatzistilles is working on the *Book of Fifty Chapters* (*Cod. Athen. 522*) and on the *Homilies* contained in *Cod. Lesb. Leim. 2*; and Mr G. Christodoulou intends to edit the *Catecheseis* (personal communications of Mr Egglezakes, Mr Chatzistilles and Mr Christodoulou).

Part 1

The life and times of Neophytos the Recluse

1 The life of Neophytos

What we know of Neophytos' life comes from the Recluse himself. The following outline of the main events of his life has been culled from his writings.[1] It is presented below in an introductory form which is short and completely uncritical: I have reserved detailed references, critical commentary and analysis for later.

Neophytos was born in 1134 in the Cypriot mountain village of Lefkara, which is situated on the southern slopes of the Troodos mountain range.[2] He was one of eight siblings. His parents were almost certainly farmers: Neophytos' knowledge of vineyard tending, of which he was in later years very proud, evidently dated from the days before he left his village. It is difficult to know whether he came from a particularly pious family or whether it was his example that members of his family followed: we know that one of his brothers, named John, joined the monastery of St John Chrysostom at Koutsovendēs and rose through its ranks to become its abbot; and Neophytos' mother died as a nun under the assumed name of Eudoxia.

By the time Neophytos had reached the age of eighteen he was convinced of the vanity of the worldly life and he longed to escape it and to devote himself to God. He kept his thoughts to himself, however, and so when his parents arranged a marriage for him they knew nothing of their son's secret desires. Seven months after the contracts of marriage had been signed, and while the preparations for the wedding were well under way, Neophytos vanished from the village. Scandalised relatives, friends and neighbours combed the island for two months until they tracked the fugitive down: he had fled to the monastery of St John Chrysostom at Koutsovendēs, on the southern slopes of the Kerynia mountain range. Neophytos was brought back to Lefkara, where he fought hard and eventually succeeded in getting the contracts of marriage dissolved. He returned to the monastery of

[1] Autobiographical passages are found in the *Typikon*, the *Hexaēmeros*, *Panegyric 20*, *Sign of God*, *Letter 1*. For tracing all of Neophytos' works cited in this book, consult the Appendix.
[2] By slight contrast to Neophytos' testimony, popular tradition locates his birth-place at the settlement of Katō Drys, near the village of Lefkara.

Koutsovendēs where, with tears of joy in his eyes, he was tonsured a monk in 1152.

The young novice was first appointed to tend the vineyards of the monastery, a task which he performed for five years. It was during this time that he learned how to read and write – for he was completely illiterate when he entered the monastery. His newly acquired literacy led to his appointment as assistant sacristan, a post which he held for the next two years. He had by then decided that he wanted to abandon the communal life of the monastery and to become a hermit; but he was prohibited from doing so by his abbot, who considered Neophytos far too young and inexperienced for the rigours of the solitary life.

In 1158 Neophytos set off for a pilgrimage to the Holy Land, hoping also to come across a hermit who would permit him to stay with him as his disciple. He travelled up and down Palestine for six months, but his efforts were in vain. He became depressed, until a vision directed him to leave Palestine. This he did, returning to Cyprus and to the monastery of Koutsovendēs.

Neophytos' wish to embrace the solitary life was as firm as ever, but so was also his abbot's resolution to oppose it. Undeterred, Neophytos decided to try his luck out of Cyprus once more. He decided to take to the sea again, this time in a different direction: he would try to join the monks and solitaries on Mount Latros, near Miletus in Asia Minor. He arrived at the port of Paphos, fare-money in hand, ready to board a ship bound for the holy Mount. His plans were frustrated yet again, this time even more cruelly: arrested by the coastal guards, who mistook him for a fugitive, Neophytos was imprisoned for a day and a night in the castle of Paphos. He was then released, but not before the guards robbed him of his precious two coins – his fare-money and his only means of leaving the island. Neophytos wandered out of the town of Paphos, into the hinterland and up the mountains, until he eventually came across a cave in a ravine situated in a mountain valley about six miles north-north-east of the town.

Neophytos first came across this cave on 24 June, feast-day of the Nativity of St John the Baptist. The year was 1159, and Neophytos was twenty-five years old. He searched the neighbouring area in case he found a better spot, but by September he was satisfied that this cave was the place best suited for his purposes. He set down to work for a whole year, widening the natural cave, removing the insecure parts in it, excavating in its innermost parts a tomb, and setting up an altar. His work came to an end on 14 September 1160, feast-day of the Exaltation of the Holy Cross. From then on this cave became Neophytos' *enkleistra* ('place of seclusion'), in which he lived as an *enkleistos*, that is to say a recluse (literally, 'one who is

1 The monastery of St Neophytos. General view from the east, facing the structures of the Enkleistra. On the right-hand side can be seen various monastic buildings of later date, including the *katholikon* (which is a domed basilica in the 'Franco-Byzantine' style).

enclosed'). It seems that Neophytos left the ravine only once, in 1165, for an apparently brief and successful search for a particle of the Holy Cross.

Some time after Neophytos had settled in his cell his fame spread further than the immediately neighbouring villages and reached the town of Paphos and the ears of its new bishop, Basil Kinnamos. Bishop Basil persuaded the Recluse to be tonsured a priest and to take up one disciple, and it was thus that in 1170 Neophytos' initial total solitude was compromised. Subsequently, more monks joined this first disciple and a monastic community in the form of a *lavra* sprang up around the cell of the Recluse, who was now also abbot of the monastery.[3] More cells were excavated along the face of the

[3] The term *lavra* denotes a form of monasticism which has been described as 'hybrid' because it combines elements of the solitary and the communal way of life. A monastic community of the latter type (a *koinobion*) existed in its most usual form within a number of built structures, where a number of monks lived, ate, attended church services and sustained their community through working together. By contrast, in a *lavra* a number of monks lived as solitaries in individual cells or caves, preferably at some distance from each other; but they also gathered together, usually weekly, in a communally held church and kitchen–refectory. See Chitty (1977: 14–16, 20–33); Ward and Russell (1981: xx, 7, 8, 106). The *lavriot* type of monasticism came into existence during the very early days of Christian monasticism. Its continued existence in the middle Byzantine period is well attested, and indeed it appears to have expanded in the tenth and eleventh centuries: Papachryssanthou (1973); Morris (1985).

2 The cliff of the Enkleistra, seen from the east. The ravine at the foot of the cliff was originally much deeper (about 32 m instead of today's nearly 18 m). The arcade in front of the surviving caves was erected during structural repairs carried out by the Cypriot Department of Antiquities in 1963 and 1964.

cliff, and one of them was consecrated as the church of the Holy Cross. The monastery became commonly known as that of the Enkleistra.[4] In 1183 the walls of the main cells of the troglodytic community were decorated with paintings, and a second cycle was executed *c.* 1200.

In 1177 the Recluse provided his monastery with a Charter of Foundation (*Typikon*).[5] Amongst other rules, he laid down that only a small number of monks should be admitted to the monastery. This document does not survive, but Neophytos' revised *Typikon* of 1214 does. In it Neophytos says that he was pressed by certain people to raise the numbers of the monks in the Enkleistra 'even up to twenty-five'. He consented instead to admitting only up to eighteen monks, opposing the admission of more because he believed that a great number of brothers spells trouble for the community. Neophytos also opposed the acquisition of property by the monastery for many years. Following the Latin occupation of Cyprus in 1191, however,

[4] See plates 1, 2, 3. Henceforward I shall use *enkleistra* to refer to Neophytos' cell, and Enkleistra to refer to his monastery.
[5] On Byzantine monastic *Typika* and for the relevant bibliography see most recently Galatariotou (1987a; 1988).

3 Cell, looking west. This was the first cell which Neophytos excavated, and which also contains his tomb chamber (see plates 12 and 13). The Recluse completed his excavation of the cell in 1160 and lived in it until 1197, when he moved to the 'upper *enkleistra*'. The picture shows the desk of Neophytos (see also plate 4) and behind it a bench which most probably also served as the bed of the Recluse.

the Enkleistra fell upon hard times, and Neophytos was forced to permit the acquisition of some property (a small plot of arable land, a vineyard, a moderate amount of cattle) to make ends meet.

By 1197 Neophytos felt increasingly that he was being unduly troubled by visitors who flocked to his cell to see him. The 63-year-old Recluse decided to move higher up the cliff, and he set upon excavating a cell above his first *enkleistra*. He succeeded at length in creating a new cell (the 'upper *enkleistra*'), in which he was to retire for the rest of his life. No sooner had he finished digging than he had to set out to work again, for he suddenly realised that his new cell had no privy. He decided to dig along the face of the cliff and to contrive his privy at a spot further south. While working, Neophytos met with an accident: a 2 metre long stone fell on him, immobilising him at the end of the precipice with his left leg hanging down it. There he remained, crying out for help, until some monks came to his rescue. The Recluse, who escaped unharmed (except for a cut on his little finger), believed that the whole incident was caused by the devil and that his escape from death was due to a miraculous divine intervention. Neophytos wrote extensively about this event, which was the most important of his later life.

We do not know the exact time of Neophytos' death. Popular tradition places his death on 12 April, but does not specify the year. The Recluse was certainly alive in May 1214, when he signed his revised *Typikon* and appointed his nephew Esaias as his successor *enkleistos* and abbot of the Enkleistra. Considering that Neophytos was eighty years old at the time and that no dated later writings of his survive, it is commonly assumed that he died not long after 1214.

2 The literary and wider cultural context of Neophytos' writings

The very titles of Neophytos' works as he listed them in his *Typikon* (and as they appear, with commentary, in the Appendix to this book) indicate the wide and perhaps unexpected variety of the Recluse's interests. He was a writer of *Catecheiseis* and *Panegyrics*, a hagiographer, a composer of epigrams and hymns, an interpreter of the Scriptures, an avid letter writer, a poet, an administrator who did not neglect to furnish his monastery with a *Typikon*; and the reference to one of his now lost books, which he tantalisingly described as 'referring to the last forty and fifty years', may imply that he also concerned himself with historiography – in which case the loss of this book is particularly regrettable.[1] Reading his works, we also encounter an autobiographer of sorts (as will become apparent especially in Part 2) and an almost journalistic reporter of historical events as well as of expressions of popular culture. The social–historical aspect of his writings makes Neophytos one of our very few Byzantine provincial witnesses.

Neophytos' writings are also of considerable interest to the linguistic historian. The Recluse composed some of the earliest surviving 'politic' verse in demotic.[2] In almost all of his surviving works he tried to write in more 'elevated' Greek. He remained very weak in diction until the end of his life but apart from this his attempt to write in learned, ecclesiastical Greek was surprisingly successful – especially considering his illiteracy until the age of eighteen and his total lack of formal schooling. Neophytos bitterly regretted his lack of formal tutoring;[3] yet had he been taught how to master absolutely the art of writing in elevated Greek, his writings would have lost a lot of their linguistic interest, which stems from the Recluse's inevitable occasional slips into words and syntactical forms directly referring to the spoken Greek Cypriot dialect. And just as the lack of formal education adds to the linguistic interest of Neophytos' works, the same factor may also account for some of the more interesting characteristics of Neophytos' style of writing. The freshness, directness, impetuosity, sudden changes of

---

[1] *Typikon*, 83.16–31. See generally the Appendix to this book; and see plate 4.
[2] Beaton (1980: 77–8); Jeffreys (1974: 160).
[3] For a discussion of which see ch. 6, pp. 153–7, 160.

19

4 Cell. The desk of Neophytos.

subject-matter, personal reminiscences and comments which are, strictly speaking, out of place (suddenly appearing, for instance, in the course of a *Panegyric*); all these and other similar characteristics would have irritated a highly educated Byzantine, but they are a blessing for us. A lot of extremely valuable information concerning Neophytos' inner, as well as his external, world is contained in precisely such 'diversions' and 'irrelevancies'. These the rigours of formal education could possibly have eliminated, to the gain of 'high style' and to the loss of the future historian.[4]

In terms of content, Neophytos' writings reflect in many ways his highly idiosyncratic and complex personality, and we shall indeed be looking at them from this angle in the course of this book. It is all the more important, therefore, to be also aware of the common Byzantine cultural heritage out of which the Recluse's works were – up to a point – shaped. The aim of the following introductory remarks is not to provide an analysis of each and every writing of the Recluse (this would have required another volume), but simply to acknowledge the importance of the literary and wider cultural context into which Neophytos' writings were steeped; to indicate the – frequently insoluble – problems his work presents when examined within this context; and to describe the sources which Neophytos used.

Neophytos the writer drew information and inspiration from two vast pools of written and unwritten material.

The written sources

It is obviously impossible to reconstitute exactly what Neophytos had read in his cell. A general idea of the kind of literature he was acquainted with can be gained from a perusal of the manuscripts once belonging to the Enkleistra, at least thirty of which have survived.[5] Of these I exclude for our purposes all the manuscripts which are of a date later than Neophytos' lifetime, and those that contain Neophytos' own works.[6]

---

[4] This is not to say that individuality and concern with everyday life and the ordinary world necessarily went with a low level of education. On the contrary, two of the innovatory aspects of twelfth- and early thirteenth-century literature were the emphatic emergence of individualism and (contrary to Cyril Mango's assertions that 'Byzantine literary works tend to be divorced from the realities of their own time') precisely a concern with everyday life; both being usually – though not exclusively – expressed in 'high' style. See Mango (1975b); Hunger (1968); Beck (1974); Kazhdan and Constable (1982: ch. 5); Kazhdan and Franklin (1984); Kazhdan and Wharton Epstein (1985: esp. 210ff.); Magdalino (1987).

[5] See the list of manuscripts of Cypriot provenance given by Darrouzès (1950); Tsiknopoulos (1954h: ης ff.; 1958). See also Mango and Hawkins (1966: 128). The information concerning Cypriot manuscripts which appears in the discussion below has been culled from Darrouzès (1949: 56–68; 1950; 1957); Devreese (1945); Turyn (1964); Astruc and Concasty (1960); Omont (1896); Tsiknopoulos (1954h, 1958).

[6] I am also not taking into account *Cod. Coisl. 301*, which contains an *Evangeliarion* written for a *metochion* of the Enkleistra. See later, pp. 175–6.

Seven of the manuscripts we are left with were definitely owned and read by Neophytos, since they contain his autograph notes or corrections: *Cod. Coisl. 71* contains extracts and précis of *Homilies* by St John Chrysostom on Matthew, Luke and John; *Cod. Coisl. 245* contains twenty-two *Homilies* of St John Chrysostom, letters by the same, a *Homily* of Ephraim and a *Life* of the same by Gregory of Nyssa: *Cod. Coisl. 256* contains ascetic Chapters of Antiochos the Monk and St John's *Apocalypse*;[7] *Cod. Paris. 576* contains *Homilies* of Gregory of Nanzianzos with some explanatory comments by Nikētas of Serres; *Cod. Paris. 691* contains *Homilies* of St John Chrysostom; *Cod. Paris. 1454* is a *Metaphrastēs* of September, containing, obviously, Saints' *Lives*; *Cod. Paris. 1492* also contains *Lives* – including one of St Mamas' – and various *Homilies*.

It is very likely that in addition to the above the following manuscripts were also present in the Enkleistra during Neophytos' lifetime: *Cod. Coisl. 80*, containing an *Interpretation of the Psalms* by Theodoret of Cyrre and short extracts from *Homilies* and commentaries of Church Fathers, including John Chrysostom, Cyril of Alexandria, Gregory of Nyssa, Gregory of Nanzianzos and Origen. (I think it very likely that Neophytos was acquainted with this manuscript, because the folios used as *garde* were torn from a November *Metaphrastes*, the rest of the folios of which same *Metaphrastes* were used as *garde* for *Cod. Coisl. 71*. It appears, therefore, that both these manuscripts were bound at the same time by the same person; and, since one of these manuscripts bears Neophytos' autograph words, it is reasonable to assume that both were owned and read by him.) *Cod. Paris. 1461* contains Saints' *Lives*. It bears signatures which appear to be similar to those found in the *Cod. Paris. 1189* and the *Cod. Paris. 1492* (the first containing Neophytos' *Panegyrics*, the second his autograph notes), and so it probably – though not certainly – also counted among Neophytos' books. Again, *Cod. Paris. 1470*, containing Saints' *Lives*, bears signatures comparable to those in the *Cod. Paris. 1461*, and it is probable – though again not certain – that it too belonged to Neophytos. If it did, then probably so did the *Cod. Paris. 1476*, for it was copied by the same person who copied the *Paris. 1470*. It contains *Homilies* and a tract on the Forty Martyrs. Finally, *Cod. Paris. 524* contains a note which appears to be in Neophytos' handwriting.

There are some other manuscripts which may also have been read by Neophytos. These were written before, or contemporaneously with, Neophytos' life, and once belonged to the Enkleistra, but their date of acquisition by the monastery remains uncertain. They are as follows: *Cod.*

---

[7] This appears to be the manuscript to which Neophytos refers in his *Interpretation of the Apocalypse*: Egglezakes (1975–7: 76–7).

Coisl. 53 (containing works of Gregory of Nanzianzos, including *apologias*, laudatory works, theological and dogmatic tracts and passages against heretics and about martyrs); *Cod. Coisl 65* (*Homilies* Thirty-three to Sixty-seven of St John Chrysostom on *Genesis*); *Cod. Coisl. 227* (*Catecheseis* of Cyril of Jerusalem); *Cod. Coisl. 266* (various works of Maximos: letters, theological tracts, *Hypomneseis*, commentaries, *Homilies*); *Cod. Paris. 605* (*Homilies* of St John Chrysostom on *Genesis*; this manuscript was read by a certain Theodoulos, probably at the Enkleistra, a reader also of *Cod. Coisl. 227*); *Cod. Paris. 914* (Fathers' *Lives* and *Apophthegmata*, ascetic Chapters, extracts from Moschos' *Leimon*, *Homilies* of Marcian and Basil); *Cod. Paris. 1106* (*Homilies* of John Damaskēnos, funerary oration of Gregory of Nyssa for Meletios of Antioch).

The evidence presented above clearly suggests that Neophytos' literary culture was entirely based on ecclesiastical literature, and that within that it was confined to a limited, routine patristic, ascetic and hagiographical content.[8] However, we know that the Recluse read more than what was held in his monastic library: he borrowed books from the libraries of other monasteries, of bishoprics and of rich households; and even though such further readings would not have altered the basic character of his literary culture, it is nevertheless important to note that on at least one occasion Neophytos records having read a chronicle (probably the *Chronographia* of Theophanēs); and twice he refers to Eusebius' *Ecclesiastical History* and, through it, to Josephus.[9] Relatively limited though it was, Neophytos put the literature he read to good use: he enriched his vocabulary from it; he learned what a *Panegyric*, an *Enkōmion*, a sermon, an *Interpretation* or a *Typikon* looked like, what kind of documents they were and how they were meant to be written; and he used this knowledge to shape his own works. Below, I shall point out briefly the three most frequent ways in which the Recluse's literary culture is reflected in his writings; and the complicated way in which Neophytos handled his written sources – for one thing which he appears never to have done was simply to copy them, unaltered.

Biblical quotations

Neophytos acquired very intimate knowledge of the Bible and especially of the Gospel texts. He seems to have had an almost photographic memory of

---

[8] See e.g. Mango and Hawkins (1966: 128).
[9] *Cod. 13, Andros, Panegyric 3*, 355.127–356.141. Cf. Theophanēs, I, 472.23–473.4, 475.10f.; and see Egglezakes (1979–80: 53–6). For Neophytos' habit of borrowing books see later, pp. 158–9. For references to Eusebius' *Ecclesiastical History* see *Cod. 13, Andros, Panegyric 1*, 322.48–9 (for Josephus see *ibid.*, 323.92–3); *Panegyric in Cod. Paris. Gr.395*, 348.151–3 (for Eusebius and Josephus); and see Tsiknopoulos (1969b:327, 351).

the Gospels, and many of his passages read like *centos* of quotations from them. This does not prejudice the originality of Neophytos' own work, for it is obvious that the Recluse was purposefully eclectic in his selection of references. As he himself wrote: 'Infinite . . . are the sayings of the Holy Ghost in the Scriptures; and having chosen a few out of many, I shall embellish with them – as with divine pearls and precious stones – this present *Homily* [of mine].'[10] It is worth keeping in mind this passage of Neophytos', for it refers to one of the ways in which the Recluse used his written sources: out of a vast number of passages he chose to reproduce only some, and, as we shall see later, he did so purposefully, selecting those which could be useful in supporting an argument which he was pursuing.

Conventional literary figures and rhetorical clichés

An example of these is provided by the expressions of humility and worthlessness on the hagiographer's part. Long before Neophytos' time this had been established as one of the oldest and perhaps most frequently encountered Byzantine literary-conventional figures.[11] And since the hagiographers habitually protested their worthlessness before they nevertheless proceeded to write a Saint's *Life*, it is not surprising that another literary convention was established side by side with the one just mentioned: the hagiographer conventionally apologised for his writing and presented his justifications for it. Most frequently, the writer claimed that he wrote the Saint's *Life* so that it would be recorded for posterity and saved from oblivion; that he did so in the hope that others may derive spiritual benefit through familiarising themselves with the good example offered by the Saint's *Life*; that he did not want God to find him wanting in the execution of his duty as a Christian.[12] Neophytos used both these related conventions extensively.[13]

---

[10] *Panegyric* 6, Egglezakes (1979–80: 45–6).

[11] In Saints' *Lives* such expressions are most commonly found at the beginning and/or at the end of the text. Out of a vast number of examples see, e.g., Ancient *Life* of St Alypios, 167.23–32; *Life* of St Daniel, 1.11–2.7; *Life* of St Sabas, 85.16, 85.20, 86.11; Leontios' *Life* of St John the Almsgiver, 345.8.

[12] E.g., *Life* of St Daniel, 1.11–2.7; *Life* of St Sabas, 85.20–86.6, 86.11–16; Anonymous *Life* of St John the Almsgiver, 19.3–16; Metaphrastic *Life* of St John the Almsgiver, 108.7–16; Leontios' *Life* of St John the Almsgiver, 344.50–72, also 347.5–10. Leontios of Neapolis adds as a further reason for writing the *Life* to be his wish to write – by contrast to Moschos' and Sōphronios' *Life* of St John – in 'low' style and in simple language so that even the unlearned and the illiterate will understand and derive benefit from it.

[13] For a few examples from Neophytos see *Panegyric* 5, 163.9–30 (para. 2) (he writes so that the information will not be forgotten); *Panegyric* 29, 148.21–149.2 (he writes for the benefit of those who may listen). For more examples see later, pp. 116–18, 120–4.

Again, Neophytos was utilising well-established literary conventions in his invocations to the Saint whose *Life* he was writing to intervene in favour of the monks of the monastery;[14] or when he pointed out that he was putting in writing information exactly as he had received it from an eye-witness.[15] There is no reason to disbelieve the Recluse in the latter case, but it is interesting to note that even in the making of these claims Neophytos moved within the context of well-established literary traditions.[16]

Hagiography

Neophytos drew extensively from earlier *Lives* and *Enkōmia* of Saints. However, in his use of hagiographical material he was, as always, eclectic; he frequently handled his sources in quite an arbitrary way; and he followed no specific or consistent rules of methodology. Indeed, in one passage he asked Christ not to hold Neophytos' way of treating a source against him, but to show forgiveness 'if I omit something for the sake of brevity, or if I change something for the sake of clarity, or if I interpret something for the sake of clearer understanding'.[17] The Recluse almost never named the written sources which he so liberally handled, and, indeed, at times it is difficult to know whether he had used a written source at all. Occasionally, however, he hinted in the title of a *Panegyric* that he had drawn information from a written – though unnamed – source, by describing his own work as presenting an abridged version of a *Life*, or selections from a Saint's *Miracles*.[18] Our ignorance of the precise source which Neophytos had used for a *Panegyric* of his, coupled with the arbitrary way in which he used his written sources, frequently makes the search for these sources extremely problematic.

Thus, for example, it is obvious that Neophytos used the *Synaxaria* for his references to the great 'classical' earthquakes (which the Orthodox

[14] Compare, e.g., Ancient *Life* of St Alypios, 168.8–9; Neophytos' *Panegyric 23*, fol. 180α.

[15] Leontios of Neapolis provided a classic example of this when he stated that he had noted down Mēnas' narrative 'word by word' – a claim which scholars have long recognised to represent a literary fiction: Leontios' *Life* of St John the Almsgiver, 345.108–347.197; and see Gelzer (1893: xiv); Festugière (1974: 15). Cyril of Skythopolis claimed that he noted down the stories concerning St Sabas as he collected them from the Saint's disciples and monks in his own monastery, eighty years after St Sabas' death; and that he recorded with precision names, dates and places so that his account would be convincing and true: *Life* of St Sabas, 86.5–11, 86.22–4.

[16] These are only a few examples of the many conventional literary figures and rhetorical clichés which Neophytos reproduced in his writings. Cf., e.g. the description of hermits living 'in deserts and mountains and in caves and in the holes of the earth' (Metaphrastic *Life* of Alypios, 170.4–7), with Neophytos' very similar phrase: *Panegyric 14*, 200.16–201.3.

[17] *Panegyric 9*, 87.14–19.

[18] See, e.g., the titles of *Panegyrics* 11, 13, 20, 29. I exclude the obvious instances of the Recluse explicitly referring to his source because he is interpreting it.

Church commemorates on 26 October) in his *Panegyric* concerning earthquakes. Yet one of the earthquakes he mentions (on 9 December) is not found in the *Synaxaria*;[19] and he mentions only the earthquakes found in the *Synaxaria* between 25 September and 26 January, omitting the earthquakes of 16 March and 16 August. We do not know whether Neophytos used a *Synaxarion* which only noted the earthquakes which he also mentions; or whether, as H. Delehaye suggests, the Recluse simply did not bother to extend his researches for his *Panegyric* beyond the first semester of the year in the *Synaxaria*.[20]

Neophytos always tried to keep his hagiographical works brief. It must be remembered that his Saints' *Lives* appear within the context of *Panegyrics*, in other words as works to be read out to an audience, and they therefore had to be kept within manageable proportions.[21] But when the Recluse presents a *Life* in an abridged form, it is usually not clear whether he had used an already abridged *Life* as a source; or whether he used his own skills to abridge a full *Life* by condensing certain passages and by omitting others altogether. Such a question mark hangs, for instance, over his abridged rendering of the many legends connected with the lives and adventures of Sts Andronikos and Athanasia.[22] Another example is presented by Neophytos' abridged *Life* of St Hilariōn. Diverse Greek texts of this *Life* appear in the *mēnologia*, all deriving ultimately from St Jerome's famous *Vita Hilarionis*.[23] For his *Panegyric* Neophytos appears exclusively to have used a favourite source of his, the Metaphrastēs; and he appears to have produced an abridged version by simply omitting large parts of the Metaphrastic *Life*.[24] Alternatively, of course, Neophytos may have used as a source an already abridged *Life* which itself had followed the Metaphrastic version very closely.[25]

The dangers of making any assumptions concerning the identity of the precise sources used by Neophytos can be illustrated by a comparison of Neophytos' *Panegyric* for St Alypios with two other surviving – and earlier – *Lives* of the Saint: the Ancient and the Metaphrastic. There are many similarities between these three texts, and it is indeed in itself interesting to see the same incident, with many of its details identical, assuming three

[19] *Panegyric 16, Synax. Eccl. CP*, 79, 117, 166, 308, 380, 425.
[20] Delehaye (1907: 288–9).
[21] Neophytos also knew that the longer the speech the less attentive the audience became: see later, p. 164.
[22] *Panegyric 11.* The legends of Sts Andronikos and Athanasia were well known and very popular long before Neophytos' times. See Clugnet (1900: 370–87, 401–6).
[23] For the Greek version of St Hilarion's *Life* see Van den Ven (1901: 142–61); Oldfather (1943: 306–448).
[24] See Oldfather (1943: 406–7).
[25] *Panegyric 13.* It is strange that, as Delehaye noted, none of the Cypriot legends linked with the same Saint found their way into Neophytos' *Panegyric*: Delehaye (1907: 286).

different linguistic and stylistic expressions.[26] Neophytos' language is, inevitably, the least 'learned', despite his constant attempts to elevate it to a 'high' style.[27] The other great difference between the three *Lives* is one of length: the Ancient *Life* runs to 721 edited lines, the Metaphrastic to 610, Neophytos' to only 233. At first glance, Neophytos appears to have used the Metaphrastic *Life* and to have abridged it by using two devices: first, by condensing a scene, so that it is reproduced with all its essential details intact but in far fewer words[28] (occasionally the compression is extreme[29]); second, by completely omitting passages which tend to refer to incidents of secondary importance to the main plot, and whose omission does not therefore affect the internal coherence and consistency of Neophytos' narrative.[30]

[26] Cf., e.g., the dream of St Alypios' pregnant mother (Ancient *Life* of St Alypios, 148.22–149.5; Metaphrastic *Life* of St Alypios, 170.27–171.13; Neophytos' *Panegyric* 22, 188.21–8); St Alypios' confiding of his plans only to his mother, her acceptance of his decision with fortitude and the tearful parting embrace between the two (Ancient *Life* of St Alypios, 151.5–152.2; Metaphrastic *Life* of St Alypios, 173.23–174.21; *Panegyric* 22, 189.9–32); St Alypios' request of a mallet from his mother, with which he destroys the roof of his cage, his mother's despair at her son's extreme ascetic measures, their discussion about it and the mother's change of heart (Ancient *Life* of St Alypios, 159.22–160.11; Metaphrastic *Life* of St Alypios, 181.3–22; *Panegyric* 22, 191.16–32).

[27] E.g., St Alypios' fight with the demons and especially his words to them: Ancient *Life* of St Alypios, 158.31–159.20, esp. 159.4–15; Metaphrastic *Life* of St Alypios, 179.33–181.3, esp. 180.22–32; Neophytos' *Panegyric* 22, 190.18–191.15, esp. 191.7–13.

[28] Cf., e.g., the description of St Alypios' struggles on the column before he demolishes the roof of his cage: Ancient *Life* of St Alypios, 157.30–159.21 (sixty lines); Metaphrastic *Life* of St Alypios, 179.16–181.3 (fifty-four lines); Neophytos' *Panegyric* 22, 190.18–191.15 (thirty-three lines).

[29] E.g., the Ancient *Life* describes in great detail how the bishop of Adrianople frustrated St Alypios' efforts to become a hermit on a nearby mountain by blocking the source of water which St Alypios had discovered there after a vision: Ancient *Life* of St Alypios, 152.21–153.11. The Metaphrastic *Life* (174.32–175.22) is almost equally detailed, following the Ancient *Life* very closely. By contrast Neophytos' reference to the incident is almost laconic: *Panegyric* 22, 190.6–9.

[30] Neophytos omits, e.g., St Alypios' escorting his local bishop – on his way to Constantinople – to Chalcedon, where St Euphēmia appeared in a dream, and instructed St Alypios to return to his country; the Saint did so, having first built a church for St Euphēmia (Ancient *Life* of St Alypios, 155.5–156.15; Metaphrastic *Life* of St Alypios, 177.22–178.8). The Recluse does not mention that two monasteries were built near the Saint's column, one for men and one for women. He mentions only the women's monastery, which is also clearly the most important in the other *Lives* (Ancient *Life* of St Alypios, 161.16–162.32; Metaphrastic *Life* of St Alypios, 182.19–183.7; *Panegyric* 22, 192.3–18). Nor does he mention St Alypios leading prayers seven times a day, joined by the nuns, monks and the *enkleistoi* near his column (Ancient *Life* of St Alypios, 163.19–164.4; Metaphrastic *Life* of St Alypios, 183.28–184.13). The absence of the *enkleistoi* – who include a woman – from Neophytos' account is particularly striking (Ancient *Life* of St Alypios, 161.10–15, 163.30–1; Metaphrastic *Life* of St Alypios, 182.13–19, 184.5–6). He does not mention either Euphēmia the *enkleistē* or Euboula, the first abbess for the women's monastery (Ancient *Life* of St Alypios, 161.10–25; Metaphrastic *Life* of St Alypios, 182.13–26); he omits the scenes of the crowds who gathered to lament for the Saint's death and to touch his body (Ancient *Life* of St Alypios, 168.23–30; Metaphrastic *Life* of St Alypios, 187.12–22); and he does not refer to a posthumous miracle mentioned in both the other *Lives* (Ancient *Life* of St Alypios, 168.31–169.1; Metaphrastic *Life* of St Alypios, 187.23–9).

But Neophytos' *Life* of St Alypios is also different in ways which may suggest that Neophytos used a source other than the Metaphrastic *Life*, rather than (as H. Delehaye perhaps rashly concludes) that the Recluse's text has 'errors':[31] Mary appears in Neophytos' text as the maternal aunt of St Alypios and not as his sister;[32] according to Neophytos, St Alypios died at the age of one hundred, having spent sixty years on the column, during thirteen of which he lay on his side because he was semi-paralysed, whereas according to the Ancient and the Metaphrastic versions the Saint died aged eighty-five, having spent sixty-seven years on the column, during fourteen of which he lay on his side.[33] Unless we allow for the possibility that Neophytos used neither of these previous *Lives* as they have come down to us, it is difficult to account for the omission of a reference to the *enkleistoi* who, according to the other *Lives*, took up residence near St Alypios' column.[34] It is more reasonable to suppose that Neophytos, who consistently and proudly signed his writings as an *enkleistos*, failed to mention the presence of other *enkleistoi* because he knew nothing about them, rather than to assume that he considered the information irrelevant. It looks, therefore, as if the mere presence of a Metaphrastic *Life*, which Neophytos' text appears to be following quite closely, does not in itself afford conclusive proof that he did indeed use it: he may have used instead an already abridged *Life*, which was itself based on the Metaphrastic.

Other *Panegyrics* present similar problems. For his *Panegyric* for St Sabas, for example, Neophytos may or may not have used the obvious source, the *Life* by Cyril of Skythopolis. A number of incidents and details are shared by Neophytos' and Cyril's texts;[35] but a number of others are

---

[31] Delehaye (1923: lxxxi).

[32] *Panegyric 22*, 192.3–4; Ancient *Life* of St Alypios, 161.26; Metaphrastic *Life* of St Alypios, 182.27–38.

[33] *Panegyric 22*, 193.10–17; cf. Ancient *Life* of St Alypios, 167.7–8, 167.28–168.2; Metaphrastic *Life* of St Alypios, 186.12–34.

[34] Ancient *Life* of St Alypios, 161.10–15, 163.30–1; Metaphrastic *Life* of St Alypios, 182.13–19, 184.5–6. Delehaye's unsubstantiated suggestion that Neophytos may have used an abridged *Life* as a source appears therefore to be supported by internal textual evidence: Delehaye (1923: lxxxi).

[35] E.g., the names of St Sabas' parents (John and Sophia), his place of birth (Cappadocia), the name of the emperor (Theodosios) (*Life* of St Sabas, 86.22–87.9; Neophytos' *Panegyric 23*, fol. 174α); St Sabas' ten-year stay in a monastery following his meeting with St Euthymios (*Life* of St Sabas, 93.12; *Panegyric 23*, fol. 174β); the Saint's five-year stay in a cave as a hermit (*Life* of St Sabas, 99.5; *Panegyric 23*, fol. 175β); St Sabas accepting disciples when he became forty-five years of age (*Life* of St Sabas, 99.10; *Panegyric 23*, fol. 175β); his monastery having seventy monks and later 150 (*Life* of St Sabas, 100.5–102.9; *Panegyric 23*, fols. 175β–176α); St Sabas' death on 5 December, when he was ninety-four years old (*Life* of St Sabas, 183.5–6; 183.17; *Panegyric 23*, fols. 178β–179α).

different.[36] The length of the two works is very different, Cyril having set out to write a full *Life* in fastidious detail,[37] Neophytos having produced only a short version as part of a *Panegyric*. Indeed, Neophytos' version is at times abridged in an extreme way (for instance, he brings together in one short passage two separate and very long passages in Cyril's account).[38] Again, even though all the miracles referred to by Neophytos are found in more detailed form in Cyril's *Life* of St Sabas, yet Neophytos' text quickly abandons the order in which the passages appear in Cyril's text.[39] We cannot be certain as to whether Neophytos used Cyril's text, re-editing the material drastically; or whether he used a different text, a perhaps already abridged and re-edited version of Cyril's work. The only thing of which we can be certain is that Neophytos did use a written source.

The same can be said of a number of Neophytos' *Enkōmia*. It is clear that for some of them he relied exclusively on his own powers of imagination, but for others he relied also on written sources. An example of the first

[36] According to Cyril of Skythopolis, St Sabas stayed in a monastery for ten years before he went to Jerusalem; according to Neophytos he did so for eight years (*Life* of St Sabas, 90.16–25; Neophytos' *Panegyric 23*, fol. 174β). In his narration of one miracle Cyril refers to starving Saracens, Neophytos to Ismailites (*Life* of St Sabas, 96.12–97.2; *Panegyric 23*, fol. 175α); in another, Cyril has St Sabas pursued by six Saracens, Neophytos by five Hagarens (*Life* of St Sabas, 97.3–21; *Panegyric 23*, fols. 175α–β); in another story Cyril refers to four Saracens, Neophytos to four Hagarens (*Life* of St Sabas, 98.21–99.4; *Panegyric 23*, fol. 175β).

[37] *Life* of St Sabas, 86.22–3.

[38] These concern St Sabas' two visits to Constantinople, his meetings with the emperors Anastasios and Justinian and his struggles against the heretices in the City: *Life* of St Sabas, 139.20–147.2; 171.26–179.25; *Panegyric 23*, fols. 176β–177α.

[39] Cf. in terms of length and order of appearance: *Life* of St Sabas, 90.15–90.4; Neophytos' *Panegyric 23*, fol. 174β (St Sabas emerges unharmed from a furnace). *Life* of St Sabas, 96.12–97.2; *Panegyric 23*, fol. 175α (St Sabas saves starving Ismailites/Hagarens). *Life* of St Sabas, 97.3–21; *Panegyric 23*, fols. 175α–β (St Sabas and the monk Anthos are pursued by six Saracens/five Hagarens, until the earth swallows one of them and the rest flee). *Life* of St Sabas, 97.22–98.20; *Panegyric 23*, fol. 175β (St Sabas finds a cave after a vision and settles there). *Life* of St Sabas, 98.21–99.4; *Panegyric 23*, fol. 175β (four Saracens/Hagarens enter the Saint's cave to rob him, but end up giving him food instead). *Life* of St Sabas, 101.6–19; *Panegyric 23*, fol. 176α (miraculous appearance of water for the Saint's monastery). *Life* of St Sabas, 101.20–102.7; *Panegyric 23*, fol. 176α (vision of a column of fire leads to the discovery of an underground church). *Life* of St Sabas, 107.8–22; *Panegyric 23*, fol. 177β (St Sabas saves disciple Agapētos from a lion). *Life* of St Sabas, 110.1–111.10; *Panegyric 23*, fol. 177β (demons expelled from Kastellion). *Life* of St Sabas, 118.27–119.14; *Panegyric 23*, fol. 178α (St Sabas converses with a lion in a cave). *Life* of St Sabas, 119.20–120.3; *Panegyric 23*, fol. 178α (two lions let go of two bandits after the latter mention St Sabas). *Life* of St Sabas, 133.7–134.7; *Panegyric 23*, fol. 177β (monk Anthimos' holiness revealed after his death). *Life* of St Sabas, 138.19–26; *Panegyric 23*, fol. 178α (St Sabas removes thorn from lion's foot, after which the lion follows him everywhere). *Life* of St Sabas, 163.14–164.10; *Panegyric 23*, fol. 177α (the Saint cures a woman of interminable bleeding). *Life* of St Sabas, 164.11–28; *Panegyric 23*, fol. 177α (St Sabas expels demon from young woman). *Life* of St Sabas, 167.4–24; *Panegyric 23*, fols. 178α–β (St Sabas' prayers bring rain during a draught). *Life* of St Sabas, 184.21–185.16; *Panegyric 23*, fol. 179α (posthumous miracle of St Sabas, involving Romylos. This is the only posthumous miracle which Neophytos also mentions: cf. *Life* of St Sabas, 185.17ff.).

appears in the *Panegyric* for St John the Almsgiver, where, following his *Life* of the Saint, the Recluse describes what next appears in his text as 'some insignificant *enkōmia* of my very own'.[40] An example of the second is provided by Neophytos' *Enkōmion* of St Dēmētrios, for which he used extensively the well-known second version of the *martyrion* of St Dēmētrios.[41]

Occasionally Neophytos combined information from a number of different written sources. A hint of such a collation of written material appears in his *Panegyric* for St Gennadios, where the Recluse says that he used information from 'some brief commemorative notes'.[42] It is indeed obvious to the reader of the *Panegyric* that parts of it are drawn from different texts, of diverse provenance and value.[43] This work can be divided into five parts, following its Prologue. The first part establishes the chronology (the Patriarch is described as a contemporary of emperor Leo the Great, St Daniel the Stylite, St Andrew the Fool and the heretical emperor Anastasios); it describes St Gennadios' rise to the Patriarchal throne of Constantinople and the exact period of his tenure (thirteen years and two months); it establishes the Saint's position in the line of succession to the throne (eighth after St John Chrysostom); and the names of his predecessors.[44] In the second part Neophytos reproduces the only writing of Gennadios which has survived in various versions – his Synodical letter.[45] In the fifth part (whose end is missing) Neophytos refers to emperor Anastasios and narrates a number of stories connected with his reign and death.[46]

It is clear that the brief sources which Neophytos says he consulted are related to these three parts. But the problem of identifying these sources is a particularly difficult one, not least because Neophytos' *Life* of St Gennadios is the only surviving hagiography of this Saint.[47] For instance, even though Gennadios' Synodical letter appears in Neophytos' text in its entirety, yet it does not fully agree with any of the other surviving versions of it.[48] Does this indicate that Neophytos reworked it? Or did he consult a now lost source? Problems of a similar nature arise in respect of the first and fifth parts of the *Panegyric*. H. Delehaye points out that the *Life* of St Daniel the Stylite mentions St Gennadios and that the *Life* of St Andrew the Fool (which does

---

[40] *Panegyric 29*, 157.31–4.   [41] *Panegyric 15*; *Martyrion* of St Dēmētrios.

[42] Ἐκ τινῶν βραχέων ὑπομνημάτων: *Panegyric 30*, 221.25–6.

[43] Delehaye (1907: 294–7).   [44] *Panegyric 30*, 221.27–222.18.

[45] *Ibid.*, 222.18–223.35.

[46] *Ibid.*, 227.30–228.34. We shall return to the third and fourth parts of the *Panegyric* in the discussion of Neophytos' unwritten sources, below.

[47] Neophytos' *Panegyric* also clarifies the otherwise obscure date of death of the Saint by fixing it on 20 November. See *ASS*. Aug., V, 148–55. Earlier *Synaxaria* proposed either 20 November or 25 August (*Synax. Eccl. CP*, 240, 924); later ones proposed yet another date: 17 November (*ibid.*, 233).

[48] Pitra (1868: II, 183–7).

not refer to the Patriarch) mentions emperor Leo. He suggests that the Recluse put information from the two together to establish his chronology for St Gennadios; and that for the line of succession on the Patriarchal throne, the precise period of Gennadios' Patriarchate, and the stories in the fifth part (concerning emperor Anastasios) Neophytos used *Chronicles* like Nikēphoros'.[49] Neophytos may well have used Saints' *Lives* to draw information concerning St Gennadios; and it is certainly true that, as was pointed out earlier, at least on one occasion he explicitly stated that he drew information for a *Panegyric* from 'one of the books of the chronographers' which specifically referred to 'emperors and Patriarchs'.[50] However, Flavios (whose name figures in the *Chronicles*) is missing from the Recluse's Patriarchal list; and it thus still seems possible that Neophytos simply used an abridged *Life* of St Gennadios and perhaps another source (since in his title he refers to a number of sources), both of which have since been lost.

Neophytos' *Panegyric* for St John the Almsgiver provides another example of the numerous problems which Neophytos' use of written sources presents. Neophytos states in this *Panegyric* that he will present an abridged *Life*, from 'the *Life*' of the Saint.[51] We know of at least four *Lives* of St John the Almsgiver, the earliest of which has been lost: this was the first *Life*, written in the late sixth or early seventh century by the contemporaries of the Saint, John Moschos (C. 550–619) and Sōphronios the Sophist (C. 560–619).[52] The seventh century bishop Leontios of Neapolis in Cyprus wrote another *Life*, which he described as complementary to the earlier one.[53] He refers only to incidents which occurred after St John's rise to the Patriarchal throne of Alexandria, and which are omitted in the earlier *Life*.[54] Later, an unknown author appears to have salvaged part of the first *Life* and to have used it to produce a compilation: the first fifteen chapters of this 'full' Anonymous *Life* are based on Moschos' and Sophrōnios' account, and the rest on Leontios'.[55] Later still, the Metaphrastēs produced his own *Life* of St John: he drew from the Anonymous for the first six chapters, and used exclusively Leontios for the rest.[56]

[49] Delehaye (1907: 294–5).   [50] See above, especially note 9 in ch. 2, p. 23.

[51] Ἐκ τοῦ βίου αὐτοῦ συλλογὴ εὔληπτος ἅμα καὶ σύντομος: *Panegyric* 29, 148.3.

[52] Delehaye (1927: 5–7); Festugière (1974: 263–7).

[53] Τὰ λειπόμενα τοῦ βίου: *ibid.*, 343.1–.3. Leontios died during the reign of Constance (642–68): *ibid.*, 1–2; Gelzer (1893: x). On Leontios' linguistically remarkable hagiographies, see Festugière (1974: Introduction); Delehaye (1927: 5–9); Baynes (1955: 230–9).

[54] Leontios' *Life* of St John the Almsgiver, 347.2–11.

[55] How closely the Anonymous followed the now lost *Life* in his first fifteen chapters we cannot, of course, know. See generally Delehaye (1927: 5–9); Festugière (1974: Introduction and 266–7).

[56] Gelzer (1893: 108–12) edits the part of the Metaphrastic *Life* which is not based on Leontios' *Life*, i.e. the Metaphrastēs' first six chapters.

Neophytos' *Life* of St John the Almsgiver (contained in his *Panegyric* for the Saint) can be divided in two parts, following the Prologue. The first concerns St John's life before he became Patriarch of Alexandria. Regarding this part of the Saint's life, all three works (the Anonymous, the Metaphrastic and Neophytos') agree on basic details.[57] Neophytos, as usual, abridges by omitting certain incidents which both other authors mention, and by condensing others.[58] At first sight therefore it seems that Neophytos used either of these two *Lives* for the first part of his own *Life* or John, and internal evidence suggests that the Metaphrastic *Life* is the most likely candidate.[59] But the evidence is inconclusive, for Neophytos introduces details which are found in neither of the other two *Lives*: he gives us the number of children which St John fathered;[60] and the name of his mother.[61] There are a number of possible explanations for these additions: for example, that the Recluse used a source since lost; or that he followed the Metaphrastic *Life* but introduced details from popular legends – which must have been in circulation in Cyprus, since St John the Almsgiver was a Cypriot Saint. The name of the mother also invites speculation. Neophytos calls her 'Eukosmia'. The other sources provide no name, but the Metaphrastēs describes her as a *kosmia* ('modest') woman.[62] Did Neophytos simply turn this adjective to its closest possible proper name? Did he read a source in which the name was mentioned? Or was the name preserved in popular legends? If the latter is true, then it is possible that it is the Metaphrastēs who carries a corrupt echo of the name, in the form of an adjective.

[57] All three agree that John was born in Cyprus, of illustrious parents; that he was married against his wishes and in obedience to his parents'; that he wanted to continue practising celibacy and consummated his marriage only after pressure; that he fathered children, and they and his wife subsequently died; that emperor Hērakleios appointed him patriarch of Alexandria after the persistent advice of the patrician Nikētas and the people of Alexandria: *Panegyric 29*, 149.6–31; Anonymous *Life* of St John the Almsgiver, 19–22; Metaphrastic *Life* of St John the Almsgiver, 108.19–112.27.

[58] Neophytos omits, e.g., St John's struggles against the heretics and his strong and effective support of the Orthodox faith – due to which the seven Orthodox churches of Alexandria were multiplied to seventy; and St John's support of the Christians who fled Syria because of the Persian invasions: Anonymous *Life* of St John the Almsgiver, 21–22; Metaphrastic *Life* of St John the Almsgiver, 110.22–111.10, 112.4–27. Neophytos' narrative is much briefer and less detailed: cf., e.g., his references to the pressure which was exercised so as to persuade the Saint to consummate his marriage: Anonymous *Life* of St John the Almsgiver, 20; Metaphrastic *Life* of St John the Almsgiver, 109.6–23; *Panegyric 29*, 149.10–18.

[59] Note, e.g., the likening of St John to the river Nile in the passage referring to his philanthropic activities of setting up hostels, hospitals, soup kitchens and maternity wards for the poor: *Panegyric 29*, 149.26–38; Metaphrastic *Life* of St John the Almsgiver, 111.15–31. See also the discussion concerning the name of the Saint's mother, below.

[60] Two: *Panegyric 29*, 149.13.   [61] Eukosmia: *ibid.*, 149.9.

[62] Metaphrastic *Life* of St John the Almsgiver, 108.22. The Anonymous uses instead the adjective *euklēria* with reference to St John's mother: Anonymous *Life* of St John the Almsgiver, 20.2.

The speculation ends with the first part of Neophytos' *Life* of St John. For the second and by far largest part Neophytos, as much as the Metaphrastēs or the Anonymous, followed Leontios' *Life* exclusively and very closely. The Recluse follows Leontios with striking exactitude, reproducing a number of episodes in every precise detail, and following Leontios' text almost line by line – though reproducing it in his own words.[63] The sequence of stories also follows the sequence in Leontios' *Life*.[64] The Recluse acknowledged fully this wholesale 'borrowing' at the end of his *Life* of St John: 'Having taken these from your divine and glorious *Life* – not in bits but in whole chapters, nor [secretly] like a thief but openly having collected them – I was then moved to add to them also a few insignificant *enkōmia* of my very own.'[65]

There are two major differences between Leontios' and Neophytos' *Life* of St John: they concern, as usual, the language and the length.[66] In his short first part of the *Life* Neophytos omitted and condensed from – possibly – the Metaphrastic *Life*. In the second part he achieved brevity by omission of chapters (or occasionally parts of chapters) from Leontios' *Life*. Clearly, since Neophytos was writing a *Panegyric* he would have to be relatively brief in his reference to the Saint's *Life*. But what motivations lay behind Neophytos' choice of which chapters or passages to omit remains an

---

[63] Cf., e.g., the details (including the numerical references) in the following passages: Leontios' *Life* of St John the Almsgiver, 347–8; *Panegyric 29*, 150.5–13. Leontios' *Life* of St John the Almsgiver, 353–4; *Panegyric 29*, 151.23–152.18. Leontios' *Life* of St John the Almsgiver, 355–6; *Panegyric 29*, 152.19–153.1. Leontios' *Life* of St John the Almsgiver, 356–7; *Panegyric 29*, 153.2–30. Leontios' *Life* of St John the Almsgiver, 378–80; *Panegyric 29*, 155.6–36. Leontios' *Life* of St John the Almsgiver, 404–5; *Panegyric 29*, 156.37–157.9. Exceptionally, Neophytos' numbers diverge slightly from Leontios', e.g. Leontios' *Life* of St John the Almsgiver, 357–9 (150 litres of gold); *Panegyric 29*, 153.31–154.15 (180 litres of gold). Leontios' *Life* of St John the Almsgiver, 380–1 (1,400 litres of gold); *Panegyric 29*, 155.36–156.20 (1,300 litres of gold).

[64] The following chapters in Leontios' *Life* of St John the Almsgiver are reproduced by Neophytos: ch. 1, 347–8 (cf. *Panegyric 29*, 150.5–13); part of ch. 6, 351.19–352 (*Panegyric 29*, 150.14–151.13); ch. 7, 352–3 (*Panegyric 29*, 151.14–22); ch. 8, 353–4 (*Panegyric 29*, 151.23–152.18); ch. 9, 355–6 (*Panegyric 29*, 152.19–153.1); ch. 10, 356–7 (*Panegyric 29*, 153.2–30); ch. 11, 357–9 (*Panegyric 29*, 153.31–154.15); ch. 14. 362–3 (*Panegyric 29*, 154.16–30); ch. 19, 366–7 (*Panegyric 29*, 154.31–155.5); ch. 27, 378–80 (*Panegyric 29*, 155.6–36); ch. 28, 380–1 (*Panegyric 29*, 155.36–156.20); ch. 52, 402–3 (*Panegyric 29*, 156.21–36); ch. 57, 404–5 (*Panegyric 29*, 156.37–157.9); ch. 58, 405 (*Panegyric 29*, 157.10–24 – here Neophytos' narrative diverges slightly from Leontios': for once, Neophytos is more detailed); part of ch. 60, 408–9 (*Panegyric 29*, 157.25–30).

[65] *Panegyric 29*, 157.31–4.

[66] Neophytos' capacity to reproduce exactly the same passage but in his own words is very impressive. The passages in which the two texts are linguistically extremely close are very few, short and consist mainly of quotations: cf., e.g., Leontios' *Life* of St John the Almsgiver, 347.25–6; *Panegyric 29*, 150.6–7. Leontios' *Life* of St John the Almsgiver, 356.10–11; *Panegyric 29*, 153.5–7. Leontios' *Life* of St John the Almsgiver, 363.36–7; *Panegyric 29*, 154.24–5.

interesting question, and comparative study of the two *Lives* provides only part of the answer: the reasons – conscious or unconscious – for excluding some chapters remain unclear;[67] but with regard to other excluded chapters certain patterns emerge which suggest the possible motivations behind their omission. First, Neophytos omitted chapters which are very long, possibly for this very reason.[68] Second, he excluded passages which contained specific historical (political or ecclesiastical) references. He did not thus refer to St John's struggles against specific heretics in Alexandria; or to the Persian invasions and their devastating effect on the Christians in Syria and Jerusalem.[69] The Recluse may have excluded such references because he considered them outdated and therefore irrelevant; or perhaps, in a *Panegyric* written after the fall of Cyprus in 1191 and of Constantinople in 1204, the Recluse may have thought it unwise to provide his already demoralised audience with further examples of crushing defeats suffered by the Orthodox.[70] Third, Neophytos tended to avoid passages which refer to disputes within the Orthodox Church; to quarrels between the Patriarch and lay people; to portrayals of priests, monks and nuns as morally imperfect or as persons who were accused, amongst other things, of sexual misconduct – despite their final repentance or the eventual revelation of the accused's innocence.[71] In other words, Neophytos omitted examples of behaviour by members of the Church which was – or which could be misinterpreted as being – unedifying. He may have done so in his desire not to scandalise his readers or listeners, or not to provide material for destructive speculation on the part of the more sceptical amongst them; but above all perhaps his omission of this last 'category' of passages may have been due to a combination of his sense of purity (which he felt should characterise his writings) and of his strong sense of duty concerning the moral state of his audience. As he himself wrote: 'I do not wish to put down in writing [matters which are] ... blasphemous and shameful, for such matters are impure and unlawful and capable of causing great harm to those who may encounter them.'[72]

---

[67] Barring the dubious possibility of pure coincidence, I could find no obvious motivation for excluding the following chapters from Leontios' *Life* of St John the Almsgiver: chs. 2–5, 17, 22, 23, 25, 29–36, 39–48, 56, 59, part of 60 (408.1–26).

[68] E.g., the story of Peter: Leontios' *Life* of St John the Almsgiver, chs. 20–1. The same applies for ch. 38.

[69] Metaphrastic *Life* of St John the Almsgiver, 110.22–111.10, 112.4–27; Leontios' *Life* of St John the Almsgiver, 350.1–351.16 (from ch. 6: a particularly telling example since Neophytos excluded from this chapter only the passage referring to the Persian invasions), chs. 18, 24, 37, 49.

[70] Concerning Neophytos' reaction to the political and ecclesiastical problems of the empire see later, esp. chs. 9 and 10.

[71] Leontios' *Life* of St John the Almsgiver, chs. 12, 13, 15, 16, 23, 38, 50, 51.

[72] *Panegyric* 5, 170.18–20.

The unwritten sources

Neophytos used information culled from three different, though frequently overlapping, unwritten sources. First, he wrote about events which formed part of his own personal experience. The general historical element in such accounts is strong; the autobiographical is even stronger.[73] Second, he recorded information which had been orally transmitted to him by his visitors.[74] Third, he drew from popular culture in the way in which it was expressed through legends, moral codes, beliefs, rituals, songs, poems, etc. Echoes of these appear in his writings: in the descriptions, for example, of the celebrations of a wedding feast; of childbirth and breastfeeding; of women's ritual laments for the dead, of which, in registering his strong disapproval, he gave a very vivid description.[75] Similarly, he referred to the Cypriot peasant songs of the quick, improvised question-and-answer type which are known as *chattista*, and added his own contribution to the *genre*;[76] and he recorded popular beliefs concerning widely varied subjects: from what happens to a man's soul at the time of death, to what it is exactly that the earth stands on.[77] He also used extensively – and especially in his hagiographical works – elements of popular culture which he believed to be historically significant and true.

In this last case, it is at times difficult to distinguish clearly between those parts of a Neophytic Saint's *Life* which are drawn from popular legends, those which are drawn from a written source and those which are invented by the writer himself, who is not only very unforthcoming but even at times misleading regarding the provenance of his information. An example is provided by Neophytos' *Panegyric* for St Diomēdēs, written to celebrate the feast-day of the Saint, on 8 October. On that day the *Synaxaria* record the name of the 'holy martyr Diomēdēs of Leukoupolis'.[78] Careful reading of the *Panegyric*, however, reveals that Neophytos refers to another Diomēdēs: not the martyr but an '*hosios* and miracle worker' Diomēdēs 'the Young'.[79] Neophytos writes that when a monk from the monastery of this St Diomēdēs left Cyprus and went to Constantinople to commission an icon of the Saint, the painter told the monk that he could paint the icon of St Diomēdēs 'the martyr', 'but an *hosios* Diomēdēs I neither know nor can

[73] See later, esp. *Part II* for autobiographical information and *Part III* for wider historical information.

[74] See later, esp. pp. 170, 188–9, 196.

[75] Respectively, *Cod. Athen. 522*, fols. 405β–406α, p. 294.10–20, *Cod. Coisl. Gr. 287*, fols. 89α, 90α (wedding celebrations); *Cod. Lesb. Leim. 2*, fols. 263α (*Homily 2*) (childbirth), 297α–β (*Homily 4*) (breastfeeding); *Cod. Athen. 522*, fols. 36α–β, p. 131 (ritual laments).

[76] *Cod. Athen. 522*, fols., 43β–45β; and see Beaton (1980) 77–8, 201–2; Petropoulos (1954).

[77] *Cod. Paris. Gr. 1189*, fols. 152α–β (*Panegyric 19*) (time of death); *Cod. Paris. Gr. 1189*, fols. 49β–50β (*Panegyric 8*) (earth's foundations).

[78] *Synax. Eccl. CP*, 171.   [79] *ASS*, Aug., III, 278.

depict in painting'. It took the miraculous appearance of the Saint in the painter's dream before the latter could reproduce the image in painting.[80]

The story illustrates the purely local character of the cult of this Cypriot Saint. There is no question of a written *Life* of St Diomēdēs the Young preceding Neophytos' account of his life in the homonymous *Panegyric*; and Neophytos' account bears all the hallmarks of an oral account: there are very few details concerning the Saint's life; only few and vague historical references (to the fourth-century bishop Triphyllios of Lefkoupolis; and echoes of unspecified Arab occupations of the island); and Neophytos concentrates, by contrast, on the miracles of the Saint, which are narrated in vivid detail and at great length. The Recluse claimed two 'sources' for this *Panegyric*. Regarding the more recent miracles of the Saint, he writes that he got his information from an eye-witness, the priest of the church of the Saint, who had also commissioned the *Panegyric* – though he does not tell us whether or to what extent he then embellished the priest's account.[81] For the largest part of the *Panegyric* (St Diomēdēs' *Life* and ancient miracles) Neophytos claims divine revelation.[82] What the Recluse does not mention is the richest of his sources, for it is fairly obvious that for the largest part of the *Panegyric* Neophytos drew from the popular legends surrounding the cult of St Diomēdēs the Young.[83] Again, we do not know to what extent his own considerable powers of imagination contributed to altering these legends.

Neophytos' two *Panegyrics* for the Cypriot brother Saints Arkadios and Theosebios are also to a large extent based on popular legends. The two *Lives* repeat, rather than complement, each other, and the absence of historical detail is even more pronounced than in the case of the *Life* of St Diomēdēs, so that even though we are given the names of two bishops of Arsinoē (Nikōn and Aristōn) as predecessors of Arkadios', we have no idea as to where to place them chronologically.[84] If Neophytos used a written source at all (none has survived), then it must have been a very brief and poor source. On the contrary, both *Panegyrics* contain passages narrated in such a detailed and lively manner as strongly to suggest that he is telling already well-known popular stories connected with the cult of these two Saints.[85] H. Delehaye thought that the very detailed and vivid nature of the

---

[80] *Panegyric 17*, 215.23–216.16.
[81] *Ibid.*, 216.16–27.   [82] *Ibid.*, 218.30–219.21.
[83] Machairas also refers to St Diomēdēs as a disciple of Triphyllios; and to a miracle involving Saracens similar to the one found in Neophytos' *Panegyric*: Machairas, I, 34, para. 35. See generally Delehaye (1907: 289–90).
[84] *Panegyrics 12, 14*; *Panegyric 14*, 203.1–4, 203.31–5.
[85] E.g., the description of St Theosebios' death, the discovery of his corpse and the role of the Saint's dog in this discovery, the vision through which the Saint demands to be buried at the spot where he was found: *Panegyric 12*, 191.26–193.19.

narrative may suggest that very recent popular memories were involved. But another view would be that the absence of chronological detail suggests the very opposite (the eradication of datable detail through the passage of a long period of time) and that the passage of time may in fact help to create more, rather than less, detailed descriptions of an event.[86] What appears at any rate to be clear is that Neophytos drew his information from popular culture, through legends whether of old or recent creation.

Neophytos drew from this same source information not only regarding Cypriot Saints but also non-Cypriot ones who either died on the island or enjoyed a particularly popular cult there. Such examples are given, respectively, by the *Panegyrics* for St Gennadios and St Polychronios. As I mentioned earlier, the *Panegyric* for St Gennadios can be divided into five parts, following the Prologue. There is no doubt that Neophytos used written sources for the first, second and fifth part, as we saw. In the fourth part the Recluse poses and ponders over the question of why the Saint's relics had not been transferred to Constantinople, as was the case with other Saints' relics; and he proceeds to give his answer.[87] It is obvious that in this part Neophytos expressed thoughts entirely personal to him, drawn from no written source: he makes this even more clear by using twice the phrase 'it seems to me that'.[88]

In the third part of the *Panegyric* Neophytos refers to the closing period of St Gennadios' life. He describes the Saint's secret escapade from Constantinople when, accompanied by the monk Neilos, Gennadios travelled *incognito* to the Holy Land and then to Cyprus. Neophytos describes the events that led to his death on the island, the miracles performed during and after it and which revealed his holy status and his burial at a miraculously revealed spot.[89] There can be little doubt that for this part of the *Panegyric* Neophytos drew upon local popular legends. The narrative is, as is usual in such cases, long, detailed and very lively; in mood it is strikingly reminiscent of other Neophytic narratives based on popular legends, such as the ones I referred to earlier; and certain elements in it are particularly frequently encountered in folk stories and legends: such as the miraculous appearance and disappearance of a river, or the miraculous revelation of the place of burial because of the coffin suddenly becoming so heavy as to be unmovable.[90] This third part, which is also the longest of the *Panegyric*, reverberates with echoes of popular legends and of a popular cult of St Gennadios on the island.

[86] Delehaye's other suggestion – that Neophytos is relying purely on his powers of imagination – is even less satisfactory (Delehaye 1907: 285).

[87] According to Neophytos it was the Saint's wish that his relics should remain in Cyprus, so as to prove that it is not the place but the manner of death that matters: *Panegyric 30*, 227.17–29.

[88] *Ibid.*, 227.17, 227.20.   [89] *Ibid.*, 224.1–227.16.   [90] See Delehaye (1906: 35).

St Polychronios did not die in Cyprus, but he enjoyed a very popular cult there. The legends concerning St Polychronios are many and very confused.[91] Neophytos had certainly consulted at least one written source, the *Synaxaria*, where the feast-day of St Polychronios is accompanied by a short note on his life.[92] Neophytos' narrative, however, diverges from them: the Recluse makes no mention of St Polychronios' father's name (Bardanios in the *Synaxaria*), or to the presence of the Saint at the Council of Nicaea. On the other hand, Neophytos writes that 'some say' that St Polychronios became a Patriarch – which the *Synaxaria* do not mention;[93] and he is unique among the Greek hagiographers of St Polychronios in mentioning ten companions of the Saint: according to the Neophytic *Life*, the Saint leaves his country accompanied by these ten men, who are described as vineyard tenders, are individually named and are eventually martyred together with Polychronios.[94] Further, Neophytos refers to two feast-days of the Saint and his companions, on 7 October and on 17 February. No trace of the last is found in the *Synaxaria*.[95]

It seems that Neophytos once again drew upon popular legends. We know that one Polychronios, bishop of Babylon, was martyred for refusing to venerate a statue of Saturn.[96] The legends that sprang up in Syria around his martyrdom mention that he was executed on 17 February (the second feast-day which Neophytos, alone amongst the Saint's Greek hagiographers, mentions), and that he was joined by several others in his martyrdom. The names of these co-martyrs are exactly the same as those which the companions in Neophytos' account have, with the more Arabic-sounding names having been 'hellenised'.[97] It seems clear that the Syriac legends of this St Polychronios, already attested by the fourth century, reached Cyprus, possibly through the Nestorians on the island. The list of names was preserved (either in popular memory or perhaps in a brief written list), but the legends were stripped of their Oriental elements, to resurface in a different dress, attached to the homonymous Orthodox Saint. Neophytos drew from this apparently purely local Cypriot oral *mélange* of legends connected with the cult of St Polychronios.[98]

---

[91] See Delehaye (1907: 282–4); Crabbe (1981).   [92] *Synax. Eccl. CP*, 117.

[93] *Panegyric 10*, 176.24–5.   [94] *Ibid.*, 175.37–176.6, 176.34–177.18.

[95] *Ibid.*, 177.11–14. Note that the Latin version refers to St Polychronios on 17 February: Crabbe (1981: 148, 154).

[96] Fiey (1966: 133–45).

[97] 'Abdios' and 'Semnios' for the Syriac 'Abdon' and 'Sennen': *Panegyric 10*, 176.2–3; Fiey (1966: 133–45).

[98] It has been suggested that the companions of St Polychronios in Neophytos' *Panegyric* were 'borrowed' by him from the Latin acts or from a Greek version of the Latin *Passion*: Crabbe (1981). The first seems an implausible proposition; the second is possible, though it is still purely speculative, since we know of no such Greek version of the Latin *Passion*. It would be more plausible perhaps to attribute the curious coincidence of dates (the Latin *Passion* also refers to 17 February) to a common original source.

On other occasions Neophytos became not the hagiographer but simply the recorder of names of Cypriot Saints, historical evidence of whose cults has not otherwise survived. These include the local bishop and martyr Konōn, contemporary of the apostles;[99] and the local *anargyros* medical St Hermolaos.[100] The Recluse also put in writing current creations of popular culture. Such an example is provided by the stories which he recorded in the course of his discussion of the incorruptibility of the body and blood of Christ in the eucharist.[101] He narrated at least three accounts which purported to prove the miraculous transformation of the wine and bread into – literally – flesh and blood. The beginning of this part of the narrative is missing. The first incident is recorded to have happened in a village or place called Arabandas, apparently near Neophytos' native village of Lefkara,[102] in a church of St Marina. The second incident was told to Neophytos by the monk Leontios, and it also appears to have taken place in Cyprus. The third incident, narrated by another monk, took place in the monastery of St Euthymios in Jerusalem.[103] Stories similar to the ones recorded by Neophytos also circulated in other parts of the empire at the time, obviously a by-product of the dispute.[104]

The examples of Neophytos drawing from the reservoirs of personal experience (his own or others') and of collective memory and popular culture can be multiplied almost indefinitely. They are found in all of Neophytos' surviving writings, and extensive reference will be made to them, directly or indirectly, later.

[99] *Panegyric 12*, 185.34–186.8. There is an unedited legend on which certain *Synaxaria* depend (6 March): *Synax. Eccl. CP*, 514, 996. See Delehaye (1907: 261, 285).

[100] *Panegyric 18*, fol. 140β. The other *anargyroi* (meaning 'unpaid') Saints mentioned by Neophytos are: Kosmas and Damian (fols. 139β-141α), John and Kyrros (fol. 140β) and Panteleēmōn (fol. 141α). They are well known to the Synaxarists: see *Synax. Eccl. CP*, 144, 791. The *Synaxaria* record Saints bearing the name of Hermolaos but none of them is identical to Neophytos' St Hermolaos, since none is related to either the *anargyroi* or to Cyprus: *Synax. Eccl. CP*, 321, 843. Delehaye (1907: 290).

[101] *Panegyric 25*, 8.13–9.11.

[102] *Panegyric 25*, 8.13–14. The loss of the beginning of the story – just before fol. 200 – makes the reading uncertain.

[103] *Ibid.*, 8.13–9.5.

[104] Similar recorded stories include the story of the miracle which St Arsenios performed in order to convince an unbelieving Jew; another miracle which the protagonist of the dispute, Michael Glykas, narrates; the story narrated by Anastasios of Sinai in the *Hodēgos*: respectively, *MPL*, 73, col. 978; Glykas, *Aporiai*, II, 376; *MPG*, 89, cols. 296–305 (ch. 23). See generally Jugie (1949: 6, note 2).

3 Cyprus in the eleventh, twelfth and early thirteenth centuries[1]

Cyprus was a province of Rome when the Roman Empire was divided into an eastern and a western part. As the two moved slowly but inexorably apart, Cyprus, which had naturally fallen into the orbit of the eastern part, became a part of Byzantium, the Empire of New Rome. The island remained a Byzantine province until the mid-seventh century, when the rapid expansion of the Arabs put an end to this relatively peaceful period. The first recorded Arab raid of Cyprus occurred in 648/9: the Arab fleet under Muawiya, emir of Syria, destroyed the town of Constantia and imposed an annual tribute on the Cypriots. We know very little about the island's history over the next three centuries. Such information as survived these 'dark' years suggests that Cyprus, caught in the struggle between Byzantium and the Arabs, belonged to neither, except for relatively small periods of time. Instead, the island paid tribute (or taxes) sometimes to one of the two and sometimes to both powers, was used by both as a military base and was repeatedly raided by the Arabs for alleged breaches of its obligations towards them.[2] Cyprus became an integral part of Byzantium again in 965, when it was reclaimed for the empire by Nikēphoros Phōkas in the process of the late tenth-century Byzantine military expansion. The re-establishment of Byzantine rule on the island and the beginning of its second Byzantine period are mentioned only laconically in the sources, and subsequently Cyprus practically disappears from them: we revert to a period of darkness as far as our knowledge of it goes, especially since the lack of written information is accompanied by the general absence of monuments from the period.[3] Both become much more abundant with the eleventh and especially the twelfth centuries.

[1] Hill (1948–52, I: 257ff.; II), remains the best introduction to the history of Cyprus in medieval times. The collection of source material concerning eleventh- to thirteenth-century Cyprus produced by the Greek National Centre for Research ('Εθνικόν 'Ιδρυμα 'Ερευνῶν) in Athens is an extremely useful tool for historical research on the period.

[2] Hill (1948–52, I: 257ff.); Jenkins (1953); Dikigoropoulos (1956, 1958); Papageorgiou (1964); Papadopoulos (1976); Oikonomakes (1972, 1984).

[3] Lemerle (1972). For examples of tenth- and eleventh-century mural decoration in Cyprus see Papageorgiou (1974).

Before the close of the eleventh century Cyprus emerges twice in the sources in connection with revolts carried out by its governors. The first of these was the revolt of Theophilos Erōtikos, who had been appointed governor of Cyprus in 1140. It appears that he decided to take advantage of the confusion created by the dethronement of emperor Michael V Kalaphatēs in 1042, by rebelling against Constantinople. The new emperor, Constantine IX Monomachos, lost no time in dealing with the rebel. An expedition against him, led by Constantine Chage, was rewarded with quick and easy victory. Theophilos Erōtikos was arrested and sent to Constantinople, where his properties were confiscated and his punishment was completed with public ridicule: he was exhibited at the races in the Hippodrome, dressed in woman's clothes. This relatively light punishment indicates that the authorities in Constantinople did not consider the rebellion to have posed a serious threat.[4]

Some fifty years later (in 1092) another governor of Cyprus, Rapsomatēs, led another rebellion. This was an altogether much more serious affair than that of Erōtikos'. Rapsomatēs' rebellion coincided – most probably not at all accidentally – with the revolt of Karykēs, governor of Crete, and the occupation of Aegean islands (Mytilenē, Chios, Klazomenai and others) by Tzachas, the Turkish emir of Smyrna. A detailed account of the revolt survives from the pen of princess Anna Komnēna. Her father, emperor Alexios I Komnēnos (1081–1118), dispatched his brother-in-law caesar John Doukas and Manuel Boutoumitēs to suppress the rebellion. John Doukas recovered the Aegean islands and proceeded to put an end to the revolt of Karykēs, who was murdered by the Cretans. He then arrived in Cyprus, landed at Kerynia, attacked and quickly took the town. Rapsomatēs moved with his army to a fortified position on the hills opposite Kerynia; but he was no match for John Doukas, if we are to believe the eloquent but obviously biased Anna Komnēna. She describes Rapsomatēs as a feeble and indecisive man: he had jut a few days earlier held a sword in his hands for the first time; he barely knew how to mount a horse; he procrastinated for far too long. When he finally decided to move against Doukas, a large part of his army (a few hundred soldiers) deserted him and joined other Cypriots who had already gone over to Doukas' camp. Rapsomatēs fled. He tried to reach Nemesos, hoping to board a ship for Syria, but, hotly pursued by Boutoumitēs, he changed his course and sought refuge at

---

[4] Kedrēnos-Skylitzēs, II, 549.16–550.5; Glykas, 594.20–595.3; Zonaras, Dind ed. IV, 162, *CB* III, 624.1–8; Sathas, II, ξγ. See generally, Hill (1948–52, I: 296–7). See also later, pp. 197–9.

the chapel of the Holy Cross in the monastery of Stavrovouni. Boutoumitēs arrested him there and delivered him to John Doukas. Order was restored from Lefkōsia.[5]

Constantinople was able to suppress both of these eleventh-century revolts, but less than a hundred years later it proved incapable of meeting the challenge posed to its authority by the revolt of Isaac Komnēnos. This adventurer, great-nephew of emperor Manuel I Komnēnos, arrived in Cyprus and presented the Cypriots with forged letters of his appointment as governor of the island. Once in power, he declared Cyprus independent from Constantinople and ruled it from 1184 until 1191, issuing his own coins.[6] Emperor Isaac Angelos made one serious attempt to remove the rebel from power in 1186, by dispatching against him an expeditionary force consisting of seventy longships led by John Kontostephanos and troops under Alexios Komnēnos. Isaac enlisted the help of the Sicilian admiral Margarito, and the emperor's forces suffered a complete and humiliating defeat.

All surviving accounts of Isaac Komnēnos are entirely unfavourable. Nikētas Chōniatēs, the chief Byzantine authority on Isaac's revolt in Cyprus, describes him as a man constantly gripped by uncontrollable outbursts of violent anger. Concerning his rule of Cyprus, and comparing him to the bloodstained emperor Andronikos I Komnēnos (1183–5), Chōniatēs writes:

He exposed himself as a tyrant, revealing the cruelty which he nurtured and behaving savagely towards the inhabitants. Such was the disposition of this Isaac that he so far exceeded Andronikos in obdurateness and implacability as the latter diametrically surpassed those who were most notorious tyrants as the most ruthless men who ever lived. Once he felt secure in his rule, he did not cease from perpetrating countless wicked deeds against the inhabitants of the island. He defiled himself by committing unjustifiable murders by the hour and became the maimer of human bodies, inflicting, like some instrument of disaster, penalties and punishments that led to death. The hideous and accursed lecher illicitly defiled marriage beds and despoiled virgins.

---

[5] *Alexiad*, II, 162.10–164.22; Glykas, 620.7–621.4 (he confuses Crete for Cyprus); Zonaras, Dind ed. IV, 239, *CB* III, 736.16–737.18; Sathas, II, ξδ'–ξζ'; Hill (1940–52, I: 297–9). See also Beaton (1986), who compares Anna Komnēna's account of the revolt of Rapsomatēs with modern Greek folk songs on the theme of revolt against a king, in which the hero is punished by having his eyes stitched up; and suggests that Anna's source belonged to the mythological discourse of popular oral tradition to which the fate of a real, minor personage had become attached.

[6] No contemporary mentions that Isaac struck his own coins but a number of types, representing all major denominations except the gold *hyperpyron*, have been convincingly attributed to him: Hendy (1969: 140–2, 148; 1981: 69).

Chōniatēs also describes Isaac's cruel treatment of the island's rich.[7] Of the western chroniclers, the author of the *Itinerarium* describes Isaac as 'most wicked of all bad men, and surpassing Judas in treachery and Gyenelon in treason; he wantonly persecuted all who professed the Christian religion. He was said to be a friend of Saladin, and it was reported that they had drunk each other's blood.' And Benedict of Peterborough paints a picture of Isaac as a psychopathic monster: he killed his wife and his only son because the latter confessed to liking the Latins; he ordered painters to depict his achievements on the walls of churches, where he also put up gold and silver statues of himself; he forced people to worship him as he sat at the place of the Cross before the altar, on Good Friday, during which he ate meat and ordered people to do likewise.[8] Such accounts must be treated with caution, since both Byzantine and western writers had every reason to want to discredit Isaac. But even allowing for exaggeration, the numerous reports of Isaac's rule of Cyprus show him to have been the cruellest scourge Cyprus ever had – and Neophytos' evidence, as we shall see later, supports this impression.[9]

Following his 1186 victory over the Byzantine forces, Isaac's authority remained unchallenged until he lost his throne and the island to Richard the Lionheart, in the course of the Third Crusade. The fall of Cyprus to the Crusaders has been recorded by many writers, in detail which is great but also unusually discordant. It is, however, clear that Richard arrived in Cyprus on 6 May 1191, and that Isaac surrendered at the end of the same month, having fought at least two battles, at Kolossi and at Trimithoussia. Richard sailed away from Nemesos on 5 June 1191, leaving Richard de Camville and Robert de Turnham as justiciars and sheriffs of the island.[10] Shortly afterwards, a rebellion broke out, centred on the mountainous districts of the south-west of the island (presumably not very far from the monastery of the Enkleistra). The rebels proclaimed a Greek monk, reputedly a relative of Isaac Komnēnos', emperor of Cyprus. The revolt was easily crushed by Robert de Turnham, who arrested the 'emperor' and hanged him.[11]

---

[7] Chōniatēs, *Historia*, I, 290.12–293.88, 340.38–43, 369.74–370.12, 463.78–465.17; translation (from I, 291.39–48) from Magoulias (1984: 161). Concerning Isaac's treatment of the rich in Cyprus see later, pp. 199–200.

[8] Benedict of Peterborough, I, 261–2; *Itinerarium*, 182–3, translated in Mogabgab (1941, I: 5.

[9] For Neophytos' reaction see later, pp. 199–200, 211–13. The image of Isaac as an evil ruler remained imprinted on Cypriot collective memory. The fifteenth-century chronicler Leontios Machairas calls him 'a whoremonger': Machairas, I, 8. 40–1. See generally Hill (1948–52, I: 312–14); Hackett (1901: 55–8, 60). Also Ahrweiler (1966a: 244); Brand (1968: 55–6, 124, 172).

[10] Mas Latrie, *Histoire*, II, 19–23, discusses the discrepant versions. See generally Hill (1948–52, I: 314–21); Hackett (1901: 59–64); Setton (1969–85, II: 61–4).

[11] Generally Hill (1972, II: 34); Hackett (1901: 64–5).

Richard decided to get rid of Cyprus, which he never seems to have intended to keep anyway (he never called himself king of Cyprus). He sold his troublesome possession to the Order of the Templars for 100,000 gold dinars. The Order paid part of this sum (40,000 dinars) and sent a few knights under Arnaut de Bouchart to Cyprus. The Templars quickly became hated on the island, not least because they imposed extra taxes on the local markets, partly, apparently, in order to raise the money which they still owed Richard. Another rebellion broke out, this time in Lefkōsia. Bouchart barricaded himself in the castle of the town, together with his small army: fourteen monks with their horses, twenty-nine other mounted men and seventy-four foot-soldiers. On Easter Sunday, 6 April 1192, Bouchart surprised his besiegers when he and his men sallied forth from the castle. The Templars carried out an indiscriminate massacre in Lefkōsia and pillaged the town and villages. The terrified population fled to the mountains. The rebellion was drowned in blood, but the Templars evidently realised that it was too dangerous for them to remain on the island. They left, returning Cyprus to Richard, who turned it over, at a price, to Guy de Lusignan, the deposed king of Jerusalem.[12] Guy did homage to Richard, who granted the island to him as a fief for his lifetime.

Guy de Lusignan arrived in Cyprus in May 1192. His reign was brief (May 1192–April 1194) but during it the foundations of the Latin kingdom were laid. A feudal western social system was, in effect, transplanted to Cyprus. New settlers flocked to the island, and some five hundred fiefs were disposed to about three hundred knights and two hundred *sergents à cheval*, besides grants of lands to commoners. The institution of the Haute Cour (the assembly of knights which acted as the court for the nobles) and the Basse Cour (the assembly of bourgeois notables, equally competent for their peers) were directly transplanted from the Latin kingdom of Jerusalem. Guy was succeeded by his brother Aimery de Lusignan, Constable of Jerusalem (1194–1205), during whose reign the Latin Church was firmly established in what now became the Latin Kingdom of Cyprus. Following a Bull of pope Celestine III (dated 20 February 1196) a Latin archdiocese was created in Lefkōsia and three suffragan bishoprics at Paphos, Nemesos and Ammochōstos. It is also to Aimery's reign that internal evidence dates the

[12] Hill (1972, II: 31–8); Hackett (1901: 65–6). According to Neophytos, the price paid by Guy was 200,000 pounds of gold: *Letter 4*, 12.11–12. Memories of the Templars as tyrannical oppressors remained embedded in folk memory. An example is provided by the legend according to which the castle of Buffavento was built by a noble Cypriot woman as a haven from the Templars who tyrannised the island for a year: Mariti, I, 135–6, translated by Cobham (1909: 58).

compilation of the earliest portion of the *Assizes of Jerusalem* (the law book of the kingdom of Jerusalem and Cyprus), namely the *Livre au Roi*. Aimery was succeeded by Hugh I de Lusignan (1205–18). In 1217 Hugh led a Cypriot contingent to the Fifth Crusade, in Syria, and died suddenly in Tripoli on 10 January 1218. Henry I (1218–43) became the fourth in a long line of Lusignan kings: the Latin kingdom of Cyprus was to survive for nearly three hundred years (1192–1489) before the island came under the rule of Venice.[13]

Interwoven with information concerning these political unheavals, our sources also provide scattered pieces of evidence concerning the internal conditions in Cyprus.

During its second Byzantine period, and in common with the rest of Orthodox Byzantium, the two essential institutions on the island were the Church and (through its provincial administrative machinery) the state. The Church had already proved the more resilient and at times the more important of the two: it had survived the long years between the first and the second Byzantine period of Cyprus, during which it alone gave the Christian Orthodox inhabitants a measure of stability, continuity and cultural identity. It was to play the same role again later, when Cyprus ceased to be a part of the Byzantine Empire.

The Orthodox Church of Cyprus was not subject to any Patriarchate. It was independent and self-governing, having secured its Autocephalous status in the reign of emperor Zēnon (*c.* 488).[14] The Cypriot Church never officially lost this status. It has, however, been suggested that the deterioration of internal conditions on the island during the Arab interregnum led the island's Church to seek help from the Patriarchate of Constantinople; and that the latter proceeded to exercise increasingly greater supervision over the Cypriot Church until (before the end of the eighth century) Cyprus had become *de facto* a subject of the Patriarchate of Constantinople.[15] This suggestion is supported only by circumstantial and inconclusive evidence, but it deserves serious consideration. It certainly places into a comprehensible context an otherwise inexplicable fact: namely, that during the second Byzantine period of Cyprus ecclesiastical leaders on the island were

---

[13] Generally Hill (1972, I: 11–83).
[14] On the Autocephalous status of the Church of Cyprus see Dikigoropoulos (1965–6: esp. 253–63); Mitsides (1976); Konidares (1943; 1972: esp. 101–20); Panayiotakos (1959); Hackett (1901: chs. 1 and 5); Efthimiou (1987: 32–5).
[15] Konidares (1934, 1943). The suggestion has been refuted by Dikigoropoulos (1965–6). For the most recent relevant discussion see Efthimiou (1987: 34–5).

at least occasionally appointed from Constantinople. Such was the case with Nicholas Mouzalōn, who arrived in Cyprus as archbishop in 1107, during the reign of Alexios I Komnēnos (1081–1118).[16] John Krētikos also came to Cyprus as archbishop in 1152, evidently appointed by Manuel I Komnēnos (1143–80).[17] It is interesting to note that the same emperor is depicted in the *Life* of St Leontios of Jerusalem offering to the Saint the archbishopric of Cyprus, amongst others.[18] Lower down the hierarchical scale, the bishop of Paphos, Basil Kinnamos, appears also to have been a Constantinopolitan appointment, again during the reign of Manuel I Komnēnos. It is at this stage impossible to know whether such appointments were invited and welcomed by the Orthodox Church of Cyprus or whether they were felt to be intrusive – whether they reflected, in other words, the close links between Cyprus and Constantinople (especially, it would appear, in the Komnēnian period), or simply the island's total subordination to the Queen City and to its emperor's will.

In terms of civil and military administration Cyprus was governed by officials who, at the highest level, were appointed from Constantinople. A characteristic feature of Byzantine provincial administration – especially from the mid-eleventh century onwards – was the sharp separation of the military from the judicial authority in the provinces, with military matters and supreme power vested in the governor (*doux* or *katepanō*). Cyprus was also administered in this manner. We note, for instance, that in 1092 emperor Alexios I Komnēnos appointed Eumathios Philokalēs as governor and military commander (*doux, stratopedarchēs*), and Kalliparios as judge and assessor of taxes (*kritēs, exisotēs*) of the island.[19]

The surviving scattered and, for the most part, chronologically undefined references to Byzantine governors of Cyprus allow us to draw up the following list: Theophilos Erōtikos (1040–2/3), Nikēphoros Botaneiatēs (*c.* 1065), one Michael (some time in the eleventh century), Rapsomatēs (?–1092), Eumathios Philokalēs (twice: 1092–*c.* 1102; *c.* 1110 until before 1118), Constantine Euphorbēnos Katakalōn (1102–8/9), Constantine Kamytzēs (possibly *c.* 1110), Leo Nikeritēs (some time between 1107–11 or after 1118), another Constantine (?–1136–?), John Komnēnos (?–1155/6), Alexios Kassianos (some time between 1152 and *c.* 1176), Alexios Doukas Bryennios (?–1161–?), Andronikos Synadēnos, another Michael (some time

---

[16] Mouzalōn, 119. On Mouzalōn in Cyprus see later, pp. 192–3, 197–8.
[17] On John Krētikos in Cyprus see Chatzipsaltes (1955; 1988: 349–51); for a seal attributed to John as Archbishop of Cyprus see Laurent (1965, II: 313).
[18] *Life* of St Leontios of Jerusalem, 412–14. And see below, p. 215.
[19] *Alexiad*, II, 164.11–19. See Ahrweiler (1960a: 46–52, 67–86); Hill (1948–52, I: 259–60, 295ff.); Hendy (1985: 430); and see below, pp. 198–9.

in the twelfth century), Elpidios Brachamios (also in the twelfth century).[20] Leaving aside the governors of whom we know nothing other than their first name, it appears from this incomplete list that from the late eleventh century, and particularly following Rapsomatēs' revolt in 1092, almost all the men appointed as governors of Cyprus were members of prominent Byzantine families; at least a number of whom are known to have counted among the most trusted and powerful servants of the emperor.[21]

The careful choice of men of very high calibre for the post of governor reflected the increased interest of Constantinople in Cyprus in the late eleventh and the twelfth centuries. This was an interest due, at least to a large extent, to the strategic importance which the island, because of its geographical position, acquired in the wake of the Crusades and especially following the establishment of the Latin Kingdom of Jerusalem. Within this context Cyprus emerges repeatedly in the sources: the island became a convenient base for military operations in the area; an important reprovisioning centre for the Byzantine and western Crusading armies; a relatively safe place for refugees and exiles of war; a convenient meeting place for negotiations between warring factions. Thus, we know that in 1097 Symeon II, the exiled patriarch of Jerusalem, lived in Cyprus and sent provisions from there to the Crusaders who were besieging Antioch;[22] and that on 19 August of the same year a Byzantine fleet from Cyprus attacked Laodicaea.[23] A year later, when the Byzantine armies withdrew from the siege of Antioch, they went to Cyprus;[24] while the western Crusading armies also used the ports of Cyprus, amongst others, to withdraw to during the siege.[25] A reference to the island about a century later indicates that it could offer relative safety to Muslims, too: following the fall of Beirut to the Crusaders in 1110, the emir of Beyrout fled to Cyprus, where he was later joined by

---

[20] Our only source of information that Alexios Kassianos was governor of Cyprus is Neophytos, according to whom Alexios Kassianos was *doux* at the same time that John Krētikos was archbishop of Cyprus: *Panegyric* 25, 8. Alexios also appears in Kinnamos, as governor of Seleukeia, *c.* 1155: Kinnamos, 179.10–180.3, also 268.10–21. He must not be confused with Alexios Doukas (Bryennios) of our list of governors above, who was probably the grandson of Anna Komnēna: see Polemes (1968: no. 80). John Krētikos was archbishop of Cyprus from 1152 until *c.* 1170: Jugie (1949: 7). On Byzantine governors of Cyprus see Zakynthinos (1941: 268–70); Mango (1976a: 7); Chatzipsaltes (1988: 345–9). Concerning Eumathios Philokalēs and Constantine Kamytzēs see later, pp. 193–4, 196–7.

[21] As already observed by other scholars, see, e.g., Mango (1976a: 7).

[22] Alberti Aquensis, *Historia*, 489.

[23] Kemal-ed-Din, 578.

[24] Alberti Aquensis, *Historia*, 417; *Alexiad*, III, 20.24–21.1; Raymond of Aguilers, 255. See also *EIE* (1982), no. 12.

[25] Baldrici, *Historia*, 45, var. 13; Guiberti, *Gesta*, 176; *Histoire Anonyme*, 80. More citations in *EIE* (1982), no. 13.

other inhabitants of the city, who brought with them the Muslims' possessions.[26]

Anna Komnēna's references to Cyprus in this context are also indicative of the various uses which the island was put to in pursuit of Byzantium's military and diplomatic aims. The princess tells us that in September 1099 the Byzantine ambassadors and duke Landulf met in Cyprus to discuss peace proposals concerning Bohemund I of Antioch; and that Manuel Boutoumitēs was subsequently dispatched from Cyprus to Laodicaea for negotiations with Bohemund. When these proved unsuccessful, Boutoumitēs returned to Cyprus, and the Byzantine fleet stationed there left the island and returned to Constantinople.[27] In October 1102 Alexios I Komnēnos ordered the *doux* of Cyprus, Eumathios Philokalēs, to send builders and building materials from Cyprus to Tripoli 'for the building of a small town' (Mont Pèlerin).[28] In 1103/4 the emperor ordered Manuel Boutoumitēs to transfer his troops from Attaleia to Cyprus.[29] In 1111/12 Alexios sent Boutoumitēs and another, Latin-speaking, Byzantine, to Tripoli. On their way they called at Cyprus, from where they took money and ships. The threats uttered by Alexios' ambassadors in Tripoli underscore the importance of Cyprus as a reprovisioning centre: Pons (son of Bertrand, count of Tripoli) and the Latin bishop of Tripoli were told that unless they returned the money which the Byzantines had entrusted to them earlier, the *doux* of Cyprus would be ordered to cut off their food supplies, with the result that they would be 'consumed with famine'.[30]

The *Alexiad* naturally refers only to events of the late eleventh and early twelfth centuries, but we can safely assume that Cyprus continued to serve the empire in the same way until Isaac Komnēnos arrived on the island; and we know that it was used in a like manner by the Latins after 1191.[31]

Despite the military importance of Cyprus in this period, the island appears to have been only partially fortified. There were certainly three strong castles during the second Byzantine period: St Hilariōn, Buffavento and Kantara. Alexios I Komnēnos ordered defensive works to be carried out on the island after the suppression of Rapsomatēs' revolt in 1092;[32] and these three castles, all situated on the Kerynia mountain range, provided northern Cyprus with a chain of defence which was clearly meant to repel invaders from its northern shores. The intention might also have been to

---

[26] Alberti Aquensis, *Historia*, 670–1.   [27] *Alexiad*, III, 44.18–45.18.
[28] *Ibid.*, 35.14–.18.   [29] *Ibid.*, 40.24–41.5.   [30] *Ibid.*, 148.14–153.26.
[31] Cyprus was the centre of Crusader operations in the Levant for another century: see Hill (1972, II: 38–189, and *passim*).
[32] *Alexiad*, II, 164.10–19.

safeguard communications between the island and the rest of Byzantium: the only good port on northern Cyprus, that of Kerynia, was also the one closest to the other lands of the empire and the sources repeatedly refer to its use by representatives of the emperor, whether in war or in peace.[33]

There is very little evidence regarding the fortification of towns, but such as there is suggests that they were not strongly fortified. The coastal towns of Kerynia and Paphos were perhaps better protected than the rest. Kerynia had a castle, to which Isaac Komnēnos sent his wife and his daughter for safety in 1191 – which may imply that the castle was reasonably well fortified.[34] Wilbrand of Oldenburg, who visited the island in 1211, described Kerynia as a small but walled town, with a castle with towers.[35] His evidence, however, must be treated with caution as regards the Byzantine provenance of the fortifications he saw in Cyprus: Estienne de Lusignan tells us that Guy and Aimery de Lusignan (1192–4 and 1194–1205) carried out works on the island's fortresses.[36] Sections of the Byzantine castle of Kerynia and its small church of St George of the Castle (dated to the Komnēnian period) survive, but they provide little evidence since they are incorporated, together with Lusignan sections, in a predominantly Venetian, sixteenth-century reconstruction.[37]

Paphos also had a castle, as Neophytos knew only too well: he was imprisoned in it for a day and a night in 1159.[38] The castle appears to have been situated at the harbour: Neophytos refers to a church of the Virgin Limeniotissa ('of the Harbour'), which stood inside the castle.[39] A bishop of Iceland who called at Paphos at about the year 1150 reported that a detachment of Varangians garrisoned the port;[40] presumably they were housed in the castle. This must be the structure referred to by Roger of Hoveden as the 'castellum quod dicitur Baffes' which was held by Isaac's supporters in 1191 before it surrendered to Richard.[41] A. H. S. Megaw has recently

---

[33] E.g., *ibid.*, 162.20–1 (John Doukas lands at Kerynia to quash Rapsomatēs' rebellion); III, 41.12–19 (Kantakouzēnos arrives at Kerynia as envoy of Alexios I Komnēnos from Constantinople).

[34] Benedict of Peterborough, II, 167, transl. in Cobham (1908: 8); Cont. of William of Tyre, III, 592; *Itinerarium*, 201–2, translated in Mogabgab (1941, I: 14); Roger of Hoveden, 110, transl. in Mogabgab (1943, II: 52); and see also *Eracles*, 165–9. On Isaac and his daughter see Rudt de Collenberg (1968).

[35] Wilbrand of Oldenburg, 181, translated in Cobham (1908: 13).

[36] Lusignan, *Chorograffia*, 50.

[37] On the castle of Kerynia see Megaw (1954: esp. 175; 1961; 1974: 81); and also Megaw in Setton (1969–85, IV: 196–207). For further bibliography see *EIE* (1982) nos. 113, 114.

[38] *Typikon*, 76.19–26.   [39] *Panegyric 16*, 211.

[40] Nicholas of Thingeyrar, 408; and see Megaw (1988: 147).

[41] Roger of Hoveden, III, 111, translated in Mogabgab (1943, II: 52). The castle of Saranda Kolones at Paphos is now known to be not of Byzantine but of Crusader origin, dating at the earliest from the late twelfth century. See Megaw (1972a); Rosser (1985).

suggested that the fortifications of Paphos were substantial, consisting not only of this harbour castle but also of a sea-wall lining the waterfront, and possibly also of an inland land wall.[42]

Our meagre evidence suggests that the other towns were very lightly fortified. Lefkōsia is a case in point. The town appears to have been the capital by 1092: Anna Komnēna's account of the rebellion of Rapsomatēs leaves little doubt that it was the power centre of the island; and we note that in 1155/6 the *doux* of Cyprus, John Komnēnos, stayed in Lefkōsia during Renaud de Châtillon's raid on Cyprus.[43] What little knowledge of Byzantine Lefkōsia we have betrays its pretentions as a capital town and hints at how powerful a point of cultural reference Constantinople was: Lefkōsia's main street was called the *mesē*; there was a church of the Hagia Sophia; another of the Panagia Hodēgētria; and a monastery of St George of Mangana – all 'borrowed' from Constantinople.[44] Yet even though Lefkōsia had a castle, it appears to have been a very weak one: Anna Komnēna implies that in 1092 the town was not defensible against a small expeditionary force; one hundred years later the Templars who took refuge in the castle of Lefkōsia found it difficult to defend themselves even though they were besieged by no more than a crowd; and in 1211 Wilbrand of Oldenburg noted that the Lusignans had 'just now' built 'a strong castle' in a town described as having 'no fortifications'.[45] On the site of the old Byzantine castle they erected the church of St Clair *Castigliotissa*.[46]

Anna Komnēna implies that in 1092 Nemesos was no more defensible than Lefkōsia was. The town had some fortification in the twelfth century (possibly built or improved under Alexios I Komnēnos' programme of fortification), but this appears to have been slight. We are thus told that in 1191 Richard the Lionheart established his camp outside the walls of Nemesos; but also that, faced with the possibility of a Crusader attack on the town, Isaac Komnēnos had to order its evacuation and to improvise defences.[47] In 1211 Wilbrand of Oldenburg found that Nemesos was 'but slightly fortified' even though it had a busy port. He observed the same of Ammochōstos.[48]

The existence of three strong castles on the Kerynia mountain range, of possibly substantial harbour castles in the towns of Kerynia and Paphos and

[42] Megaw (1988).
[43] For Rapsomatēs see *Alexiad*, II, 162.10–164.22; for the raid of Renaud de Châtillon see below, pp. 187–8.
[44] Megaw (1974: 80).
[45] Respectively, *Alexiad*, II, 162.23–6, 163.24–8, 164.6–9; Mas Latrie, *Histoire*, I, 32–3; Wilbrand of Oldenburg, 181, translated in Cobham (1908: 14).
[46] Enlart, II, 518, translated in Hunt (1987: 387); Hill (1972, II: 14).
[47] Mas Latrie, *Histoire*, II, 19–21; Hill (1948–52, I: 318).
[48] Wilbrand of Oldenburg, 181, translated in Cobham (1908: 14), Hill (1948–52, I: 317; II, 15–16).

of very light fortifications in the other towns (Lefkōsia, Nemesos and Ammochōstos) would in itself not be sufficient to protect Cyprus from invaders. More defensive structures, but also a strong permanent army, were required – and the latter Cyprus certainly did not have. This is apparent from the accounts of raids carried out against it. The island was evidently considered easy prey by raiders, and the raids recorded (by Neophytos among others[49]) must represent only the most serious of those suffered. Pirates were never far from the island's shores: Constantine Manassēs, who visited Cyprus in 1161/2, likened it to a prison from which escape was difficult because the waters around it were thick with pirates.[50]

The raids became particularly devastating by the mid-twelfth century. One of the best recorded is the 1155/6 raid of Renaud de Châtillon. Renaud had been initially used by emperor Manuel I Komnēnos against the Armenian prince Thoros II (1145–68), but after the battle of Alexandretta Renaud made peace with Thoros. Accompanied by the Armenian prince or – more likely – supported by a contingent of his army, Renaud decided to turn against Cyprus for reasons which (greed apart) are not entirely clear. An unkept promise of Manuel's to pay Renaud a large amount of money appears to have been the most likely excuse behind the raid; though the Armenian (but not the Syriac) version of Michael the Syrian cites as other possible reasons rumours that the Greeks in Cyprus were maltreating the Latins, or that they were inciting the Turks to kill the Armenians. Whatever the reasons, Renaud prepared for an expedition against Cyprus. The govenor of the island at the time was John Komnēnos. According to some sources, the *doux* and his right hand man, Michael Branas, were warned of the impending attack, probably by Latin travellers from Antioch; yet they only managed to gather as much of an army as they could scrape together in great haste. John stayed in Lefkōsia and Branas went to the coast where, according to John Kinnamos, he had some initial success against the invaders. But it was not long before Branas retreated. Renaud pressed on to Lefkōsia without much difficulty. He captured both the governor and Branas and proceeded to devastate the island. The extent of the outrages perpetrated by the invaders shocked not only Byzantine but also western writers. According to the horrified recorders the invaders burned towns and churches, slaughtered and mutilated the inhabitants (including priests), carried away as much plunder as they could and forced the Cypriots to pay a huge ransom, having taken hostage lay and ecclesiastical dignitaries. The

---

[49] See later, pp. 187–8.   [50] Manassēs, 346.153–347.186.

raid excited such universal horror partly because it was carried out mainly by Christians. William of Tyre called it a piacular crime.[51]

Only about two years later (in 1158) the Egyptian fleet undertook a number of expeditions against Cyprus. They returned with many prisoners, including one described as 'the brother of the count, king of the island of Cyprus'. This was the governor of the island, who was treated with respect and was sent back to Constantinople.[52] The 1160 negotiations between emperor Manuel I Komnēnos and Raymond III of Antioch, count of Tripoli, for the hand of Raymond's sister Melissenda, formed the background of another raid on Cyprus. Manuel allowed the negotiations to continue for more than a year, but in July 1161 he suddenly married Marie, daughter of Constance, princess of Antioch. In an act of vengeance, Raymond turned over to pirates the ships which had been prepared to take his sister to Constantinople as a bride, and commissioned them to raid the lands of the emperor of Byzantium. Cyprus was one of their targets, and its governor (Alexios Doukas) was yet again unable to stop the indiscriminate slaying, looting and burning that took place.[53] Finally, in 1191, either just before Richard's arrival or coinciding with it, some Frankish renegades carried out a lightning raid. They took with them to Laodicaea the entire congregation of a church (twenty-seven women) and enough booty for each pirate to receive a share of 4,000 pieces of silver.[54]

The accounts of these raids provide evidence for the defencelessness of Cyprus and the inability of its military governors to protect it – or indeed to protect themselves; but they also bear witness to the existence of wealth on the island. Indeed, in the Middle Byzantine period Cyprus was considered to be a lucrative possession. In 1097 Radulfo Cadomensi described it as 'most wealthy' (*Cyprus opulentissima*).[55] Earlier than that Mukaddasi, writing in 985, alluded to some of the ways in which wealth was generated when he referred to 'the great quantities of merchandise, stuffs, and goods, which are produced there'.[56] Sugar was amongst these 'stuffs and goods': the production of sugar, which became very important in the Lusignan period, was already under way in the tenth century.[57] In the 1070s Kekaumenos referred to Cyprus as one of the areas which, together with Crete, the

---

[51] Kinnamos, 178.3–179.3; William of Tyre, I.2, 834–5. See Hill (1948–52, I: 306–8); also Hackett (1901: 63–4); Chalandon (1912: 437ff.); Ahrweiler (1966a: 234–5).

[52] See Hill (1940–52, I: 308).

[53] In his account of the raid Constantine Manassēs gives us the name of Alexios Doukas (*Doukoblastos*) as κυριαρχῶν Κυπρίων: Manassēs, 343.36–344.88, 336.57–8. See Hill (1948–52, I: 311); and Horna (1904: 315ff.) for the negotiations for the hand of Melissenda.

[54] Hill (I: 314–15).   [55] *Gesta Tancredi*, 647.

[56] Mukaddasi, 82, translated in Cobham (1908: 5).

[57] The sugar cane arrived in Cyprus from India via Egypt in the tenth century: Aristeidou (1980; 1983: 33–44; 1984).

Cyclades and the coastland of Asia Minor, produced wheat, barley, pulse, cheese, wine, meat, olive oil.[58] The island's timber resources may have provided another source of revenue, despite the severe deforestation of the plains caused by centuries of exploitation and the acute conflict between goat grazing and forestry: in the twelfth century Edrisi refers to Cyprus' timber and copper resources; while the supplies which Richard the Lionheart dispatched from the island to Syria, laden in five ships, included wood.[59] Finally, as we shall see presently, trade was an important – if not the most important – generator of wealth.

It is clear that substantial amounts of money could be raised quite quickly on the island: raiders would not otherwise have demanded enormous ransoms for their hostages, nor would their demands have been met. Again, when the Holy Sepulchre was threatened by the Arabs in 1099, it was to Cyprus that the Latin patriarch of Jerusalem, Anoul de Roeux went to collect the money required to save it;[60] while, as we saw earlier, in 1111/12 Manuel Boutoumitēs stopped at Cyprus to take money, as well as ships, on his way to Tripoli.

The amounts of tax collected from Cyprus also suggest that the island was relatively wealthy. Kekaumenos referred to Cyprus in the 1170s as yielding very considerable revenues; and by the end of the twelfth century these appear to have amounted to about 50,000 *hyperpyra*.[61] This high yield is implied in Cyprus' emergence in the sources on two occasions in the twelfth century. In 1142 emperor John II Komnēnos (1118–43) considered giving Cyprus, together with Cilicia, Antioch and Attaleia, to his youngest son, Manuel, as an 'appanage', a possession.[62] Later (*c.* 1166), upon dispatching his cousin Andronikos Komnēnos as governor to Cilicia, emperor Manuel I Komnēnos gave him a large sum in gold and, in order to meet heavy expenses, the tax yield of Cyprus. Andronikos was under orders to terminate the Armenian revolt of Thoros in Cilicia, and it seems clear that the money from Cyprus was to be used for expenses incurred for this specific purpose.[63]

The great booty which raiders and Richard the Lionheart seized in Cyprus, the enormous ransoms paid by the Cypriots and the high tax yield recorded under Byzantine rule cannot be attributed exclusively to the

---

[58] Kekaumenos, *Stratēgikon*, Litavrin ed., 292.28–294.6; Kekaumenos, *Logos Nouthetētikos*, 102.12–17.

[59] Edrisi, II, 130. Hendy (1985: 60); Hill (I: 7, 10, 156, 174; II: 31).

[60] William of Tyre, I.1, 314, 359.

[61] See note 58 above; and generally Hendy (1985: 132, 173, 598–9); Mango (1976a: 10).

[62] *Eis klēron*: Kinnamos, I, 22.22–23.3.See Hendy (1985: 132); Hill (1948–52, I: 305).

[63] Kinnamos, 250.1–5; Chōniatēs, *Historia*, 137.89–138.1. The two grants are different in character: the first is clearly an 'appanage', the second is strictly speaking not: Hendy (1985: 132–3); cf. Ahrweiler (1966a: 218, note 4).

ruthlesness of the invaders or of the Byzantine tax collectors; but must be placed within the context of a relatively vibrant economy. The wealth of the island during the eleventh and twelfth centuries seems to have been due to an economic – and possibly also demographic – growth. This took place in the Byzantine Empire as a whole during this period, as Michael Hendy has consistently and convincingly argued, and as the findings of Alan Harvey's study of the economy of the period also clearly indicate.[64] Further evidence indicating economic expansion during this period comes from scattered references to the island's ports and to trade.

The coastal towns of Kerynia, Nemesos, Ammochōstos and Paphos had ports which were by all accounts busy. Part of the traffic was generated by travellers in transit, especially pilgrims to the Holy Land, whose numbers increased enormously with the beginning of the Crusades and the establishment of Latin kingdoms in the Levant. Travellers and pilgrims who are known to have called at Cyprus include St Lietbert, archbishop of Cambrai, who stopped there on his way to the Holy Land and was arrested by the *katepanō* of the island (1055); William of Tyre, who called at Cyprus on his way from Constantinople to the Syrian port of St Symeon (1066); the Anglo-Saxon Sæwulf, who called at Paphos (1102); Welf, duke of Bavaria, who died and was buried in Paphos on his return from Jerusalem (1102/3); Eric the Good, king of Denmark, who also died in Paphos on his return from the Holy Land and was buried at the cathedral of the town (1103); the Russian abbot Daniel, who paid a long visit to the island (1113–15); Henry VII, king of France, who called at Limassol (1149); a bishop from Iceland, who stopped at Paphos (1150); Benjamin of Tudela (1170); Narsēs, later archbishop of Tarsos, who came to the island to join an Orthodox monastery (some time between 1172 and 1179); St Kendeas and his companions, who arrived at Paphos from Palestine (1187); St Constantine and his companions, who also left Palestine in the same year on a ship bound for Paphos.[65] It is evident from the above that the port of Paphos was particularly busy with pilgrims. By contrast, Kerynia appears to have been particularly used by travellers from Constantinople: the Byzantine fleet dispatched to quash the rebellious Rapsomatēs used it; as did imperial ambassadors in

---

[64] Hendy (1970: on Cyprus, esp. 47; 1985), Harvey (1989: on Cyprus, esp. 223, 244–5); for the view that the eleventh and twelfth centuries were marked by an economic and demographic expansion in Byzantium in general see Hendy (1970: 31–52; 1985; 1989: esp. II and III), Harvey (1989; 1982–3).

[65] The most comprehensive list of sources is in *EIE* (1982), nos. 2 (St Lietbert), 3 (William of Tyre), 348 (Sæwulf), 349 (Welf), 350 (Eric the Good), 281 (Henry VII), 31 (Daniel), 43 (Benjamin of Tudela), 42 (Narsēs), 357 (St Kendeas), 358 (St Constantine); see also Megaw (1988: 147) (bishop of Iceland). For the specific dating of Benjamin of Tudela's visit to Cyprus (to 1170) see Prawer (1988: 192–4).

more peaceful times.[66] Fleets from Byzantium and the west also used the ports of Cyprus for military operations in the Levant, as we saw earlier.

Above all, however, the Cypriot ports were used for trade. Even in times of war in the neighbouring areas traders in Cyprus profited, since the Byzantine and western armies not only stored provisions on the island but also bought them there. During the siege of Antioch, for example, William of Tyre tells us that Greeks and Armenians from Cyprus, Rhodes and other islands, and from the shores of Asia Minor, carried and sold foodstuffs to the Crusaders (1098); the same historian and Raymond of Aguilers mention Cyprus as one of the Greek islands from which Genoese, Venetian and Greek ships carried foodstuffs for the reprovisioning of the Crusaders (1099). Raymond of Aguilers also tells us that in 1098 envoys from Mamistra were sent to Cyprus to buy provisions.[67]

Whether in times of war or peace, the geographical position of Cyprus ensured a continuous flow of trade. This became much stronger in the eleventh and twelfth centuries, as evidenced by the establishment of foreign trade colonies on the island in this period. Trade routes linked Cyprus with the rest of Byzantium, but also with other lands. Trade was brisk between Cyprus and southern Asia Minor: the eleventh-century seal of one Leontios, '*kommerkiarios* of Cyprus and Attaleia' hints at the trade links between the two; and the very lively communication between Cyprus and the Armenian kingdom of Cilicia (established in the eleventh century) may have led to Armenian traders settling in Cyprus.[68] Relations between Cyprus and Syria and Palestine had for centuries been very close, and they may have led to the establishment of trading colonies in Cyprus. Mukaddasi wrote in 985 that Cyprus 'offers the Muslims many advantages in their trade thither'.[69] Jews were also attracted to the island, and an important Jewish settlement had occurred by 1170.[70]

Trade routes also linked the island increasingly with the west, especially with Venice and, almost certainly, with Genoa and Pisa. The most important trade colonies seem to have been the western ones. Contemporary witnesses tend to refer to the westerners on the island indiscriminately as 'Latins', and as such they make a few fleeting appearances in the sources:

---

[66] See e.g. *Alexiad*, II, 162.20–1; III, 41.12–19.

[67] William of Tyre, I.1, 248–9, 310; Raymond of Aguilers, 255, 274, 290.

[68] Schlumberger (1884b: 436–8); Hill (1948–52, I: 281: II, 2–3).

[69] Mukaddasi, 82, also translated in Cobham (1908: 5). In the tenth century the country with which Cyprus was most closely connected was Palestine, if we are to judge from the movement of manuscripts which were written in or passed through Cyprus. This indicates at least close relations between Orthodox monasteries in Cyprus and Palestine: Darrouzès (1957: 132–3).

[70] Benjamin of Tudela, 14–15, translated also in Cobham (1908: 5), and in Sharf (1971: 138); Hill (1972, II: 2, 4–5); Prawer (1988: 192–4).

Michael the Syrian, as was mentioned earlier, cited rumours of their ill-treatment by the Greeks in Cyprus in 1155/6; we know that the Latin merchants who lived in Nemesos welcomed Richard the Lionheart in 1191.[71] The absence of specific information on the numbers and provenance of the western colonies is general but not absolute: Camera mentions Amalfitan trade colonies on the island in 1168;[72] and there is much more information concerning the Venetian presence in Cyprus.

The seventeenth-century Venetian author Giovanni Francesco Loredano claimed that Venetians had settled on the island at the end of the eleventh century, when the fleet of doge Vitale Michiel called at Cyprus on its way to the Holy Land[73] – a claim which has been dismissed as improbable.[74] It is at any rate clear that Venetian traders settled in Cyprus in the twelfth century. In 1126 John II Komnēnos gave Venetian merchants the right to trade tax-free in Crete and Cyprus, thus extending the right which Alexios I Komnēnos had given them in 1082 in respect of Byzantine ports in Greece and Asia Minor. In October 1147 Manuel I Komnēnos renewed these privileges.[75] We know that a Venetian colony was installed on the island in that same year. This was not the first Venetian base, and, indeed, by the time of Richard the Lionheart's arrival there appear to have been at least three Venetian communities on the island.

The largest and probably the oldest was in Nemesos. Already in 1139 a document records that the Venetian trader Domenico Rossani withdrew from the trading company which he had formed with one Angelo Agnello in Nemesos.[76] And a list of Venetian landed properties in Cyprus, dated between 1236 and 1247, makes it clear that at that time the Venetians were primarily concentrated in Nemesos, and that this permanently settled community had been preceded by an earlier one already established there in the previous century.[77] (Venetians must have therefore counted among the unspecified Latins who welcomed the king of England in 1191.) According to the same document, the next major concentration of Venetians was in Lefkōsia. Since Lefkōsia is situated in the middle of the island we would not, perhaps, have expected this community to have also been preceded by a

[71] Hill (1948–52, I: 306 note 2, 318).
[72] Camera, 206. See also Mas Latrie, *Histoire*, II, 4, note 2.
[73] Loredano, 9–10.   [74] Jacoby (1977: esp. 164).
[75] Tafel and Thomas (1856, no. 51: 124 for the chrysobull of John Komnēnos); Dölger, *Regesten*, II, nos. 1365, 1356 (for Manuel Komnēnos). For the most recent commentary see Nicol (1988: 59–62, 77–81, 85–6), who points out (81) that the 1126 chrysobull did not itself extend the Venetians' rights to Crete and Cyprus, but that these were conceded shortly afterwards. See also Harvey (1989: 223).
[76] Morozzo della Rocca and Lombardo (1940, I: 77–8 (no. 74)); Lanfranchi (1968: 405–6).
[77] The document has been edited by Thomas (1878) and more recently with commentary by Papadopoulou (1983). I use the latter edition.

trade colony from the previous century; yet there were Venetians already settled there before 1191, according to a document sent by the Venetian Senate to the king of Cyprus, Henry II, in 1302.[78] The document refers to the Venetian communities of Nemesos and Lefkōsia as the two oldest Venetian settlements in Cyprus, dating from Byzantine times: *a tempore grecorum*. Further, another Venetian trade colony existed in Cyprus in the twelfth century, in the town of Paphos. According to a document of 1143 the Venetian Giovanni Montanario and other traders, who had called at Paphos on their way from Acra to Constantinople, were witnesses to a payment which took place at the port of Paphos.[79] According to another document, in 1173 one Pietro Rambaldo, from Venice, entrusted seventy-one coins (*byzantii stavarati*) to one Gionavvi Menculo, from Paphos, in the presence of another Venetian, named Fatius Totulo. A subsequent document (of 1201) specifies the relationship between Menculo, who was still in Paphos, and Rambaldo (Rambaldo was Menculo's nephew and partner), and records the dissolution of their partnership.[80]

The material presented above concerning trade and wealth in Cyprus clearly indicates that the eleventh, and especially the twelfth, century was a period of economic growth. At the same time another, great, expansion took place on the island. Away from the hustle and bustle of the traders and the ports, the quiet world of monks and monasteries expanded greatly.

The late eleventh and especially the twelfth centuries comprise the 'golden age' of Cypriot Orthodox monasticism. Old monasteries, such as that of the Holy Cross at Stavrovouni, flourished, and many important new ones were founded.[81] Our evidence shows the increasingly frequent foundation, endowment and decoration of monasteries and churches, and the phenomenon is directly connected to increased patronage. Amongst these monuments and churches we find the most important of such monuments on the island: St Nicholas of the Roof at Kakopetria (founded probably in the early eleventh century and decorated in the eleventh and twelfth centuries); the Virgin of Alypou (founded and decorated some time before 1091); the Virgin of Kykko (founded, according to tradition, in or shortly after 1092): St John Chrysostom at Koutsovendēs (expanded and decorated some time after 1092 and before 1118); the Virgin of Asinou (founded and decorated in 1105/6); the Virgin Amasgou at Monagri (founded in the early

---

[78] Mas Latrie, *Nouvelles preuves*, 46–8.
[79] Morozzo della Rocca and Lombardo (1940, I, 85–6 (no. 82)).
[80] *Ibid.*, 444–5 (nos. 455, 454).
[81] St Helena is traditionally associated with the foundation of the monastery at Stavrovouni, which boasted part of the Holy Cross as a relic. The Russian abbot Daniel visited it in 1106/7. According to tradition, the foundation of the monastery of St Nicholas of the Cats at Akrōtēri, associated with the rebel governor Kalokairos, also dates from the reign of Constantine the Great. See Hackett (1901: 439–51, 358–60 respectively).

twelfth century and decorated in the early and late twelfth century); the Virgin Theotokos at Trikōmo (decorated in the early twelfth century); the Virgin Apsinthiotissa near Sykhari (founded and decorated in the early twelfth century); the Virgin of Machairas (endowed richly by emperors Manuel I Komnēnos, Isaac II Angelos and Alexios III Angelos); the Virgin Chryssorogiatissa on mount Roia (founded, according to tradition, in 1152); the Holy Apostles at Perakhōrio (decorated some time between 1160 and 1180); the Enkleistra (decorated in 1183 and c. 1200); St Mamas in Morphou (traditionally dated to c. 1190); the Virgin of Arakou at Lagoudera (decorated in 1192); Christ Antiphonitēs near Kalogrea (founded and decorated in the late twelfth century); Panagia Aphendrika near the monastery of Koutsovendēs (decorated in the late twelfth century); the Virgin Trooditissa on mount Troodos (founded, according to tradition, c. 1200).[82]

Some of these monuments also contain the most brilliant examples of Byzantine painted decoration on the island. Of the sophisticated style of painting associated with the Komnēnian period our earliest surviving Cypriot example comes from the church of the Holy Trinity at the monastery of Koutsovendēs, followed by the paintings at Asinou and culminating in the paintings at Lagoudera.[83] In parallel, a different, more traditional style continued to be employed, such as we encounter, for example, in the 1183 painted decoration of the Enkleistra. This period of painting of the highest quality came to an abrupt end with the establishment of the Lusignans on the island in 1192.[84] The monastery of the Enkleistra provides a striking example of pre- and post-1192 art in the respectively dated cycles of

---

[82] Generally Stylianou and Stylianou (1985); also Hackett (1901; 329–62); Hill (1948–52, I: 302–3, 308–11); and see Kazhdan and Wharton Epstein (1985: 86–92) on eleventh- and twelfth-century monasticism in general and (88–9) on the monastery of St John Crysostom at Koutsovendēs in particular.

[83] For a survey of monumental painting in Cyprus in the Komnēnian period see Megaw (1964). See also Stylianou and Stylianou (1985: respectively 456–62, 114–40, 157–85); and for more specialised information, Mango and Hawkins (1964); Winfield and Hawkins (1967); Winfield (1971a, 1971b, 1972); Megaw (1972b); Mouriki (1980–1: esp. 98ff.). It has recently been suggested that the splendid frescoes of the period had their counterpart in high-quality illuminated liturgical manuscripts, Cyprus being the centre of production of the so-called 'Family 2400' group of manuscripts: see especially Weyl Carr (1982, 1989); also Canard (1981); Browning (1989: 121–2). By contrast, however, Gamillscheg provides evidence that these manuscripts were produced at the monastery of Prodromou-Petras, at Constantinople: Gamillscheg (1987).

[84] The only securely dated thirteenth-century decoration is that of the church of Moutoullas (of 1280): see Mouriki (1984). Other churches containing murals attributed to the thirteenth century include the underground cave church of St Solomōnē (Paphos), the church of St John Lampadistēs (Kalopanayiotēs), St Nicholas of the Roof (Kakopetria), St Marina (Rizokarpaso), St Sergios (Neta), Virgin Angeloktistos (Kiti), Archangel Michael (Lefkara): see Papageorgiou (1972).

paintings adorning its walls.[85] In architecture too, the new, eleventh-century novelty of the so-called 'église à trompes d'angle' also appeared in Cyprus.[86] There was a close connection between art and architecture in Cyprus and in Constantinople.[87]

The late eleventh- and twelfth-century increase in patronage in Cyprus has yet to be fully explained and understood. According to Cyril Mango, the increased patronage and the appointment of illustrious men as governors of Cyprus are interrelated, and are both due to the strategic importance which the island acquired, especially after the establishment of the Latin kingdom of Jerusalem.[88] Michael Hendy presents a different explanation: he understands the phenomenon of increased patronage as related not so much to the island's military importance as rather to the economic expansion which took place there.[89] The two views are not necessarily mutually exclusive: they must be seen as complementary rather than as contradictory, although the 'military significance' theory is clearly of only secondary importance: it does not explain why military governors took an especially active interest in patronising monasteries and churches in Cyprus; nor does it account for the fact that governors and other high officials are known to have patronised only a few of the surviving monuments. Indeed, as Michael Hendy points out, the majority of cases involved not public and imperial but private and aristocratic benefactions: most patrons came from the wealthier sectors of the local population.[90]

This last point helps us also to put into perspective the extent of the economic expansion and wealth in Cyprus. This is reflected in the extent of patronage. The latter was greatly increased and became very widespread but it never became exceedingly lavish. All the surviving churches of the second Byzantine period of Cyprus are of small dimensions and simplicity of build; and even though sometimes very expensive colours were used in their painted decorations, not one single example of mosaic decoration – which was by far the more expensive – survives. This contrasts sharply with the first Byzantine period of Cyprus, which bequeathed us three examples

---

[85] Mango and Hawkins (1966); Winfield (1972). Other churches containing mural decoration attributed to the twelfth century are Panagia Amasgou at Monagri, St Herakleidios at the monastery of St John Lampadistēs, Archangel Michael at Lefkara, Christ Antiphonitēs at Kalogrea, Panagia Theotokos at Trikōmo, St Solomonē at Paphos, St Antony at Kellia: see Stylianou and Stylianou (1985: respectively 238–45, 292–320, 447–50, 469–85, 49–50, 433–7). See more specifically Boyd (1974); Hatfield Young (1978); Winfield (1971a, 1971b).

[86] This was definitely a Constantinopolitan innovation, according to Mango (1976b: esp. 358ff.).

[87] Megaw (1974).   [88] Mango (1976a: 5, 7).

[89] Hendy (1970: 47); and see the bibliography in note 64 above.

[90] See also Wharton (1988: 68).

of rich mosaic decoration in the churches of Panagia Kanakaria at Lythrankomē, Panagia Angeloktistos at Kiti and Panagia Kyra at Livadia (all apparently dating to the sixth century).[91] We must thus be careful not to exaggerate the true proportions of the economic growth on the island in the last two centuries of Byzantine rule, and we must remember that our terms are always comparative: the economic expansion and wealth was very substantial, compared with the situation before it, and considering that the island was but a province of Constantinople.

It is also important to recognise that wealth was extremely unevenly distributed. Of the inhabitants of the towns clearly a considerable proportion benefited from the economic expansion – certainly, the foreigners of the trade colonies and the members of the local Cypriot ruling class. We do not know what proportion of the population lived in the towns (Mukaddasi described them in 985 as 'populous', and we can assume that they expanded in the late eleventh and twelfth centuries as a result of the upsurge in trade).[92] But without doubt the majority of the population did not live in towns, and they had no – or no substantial – share of the benefits of the economic expansion. The relatively vibrant economy of the late eleventh and twelfth centuries existed despite – or indeed partly perhaps because of – a measure of economic oppression suffered by the predominantly peasant population. This was an oppression which, as we shall see, greatly worried and angered Neophytos.

It has been estimated that by the eleventh century the population of Cyprus was between 60,000 and 75,000. This figure must be treated with caution. First, because it is based on an eighth- and ninth-century figure, derived from the amount of tax (7,000 or 7,200 dinars) collected from Cyprus by the Arabs; second, because even as an eighth- and ninth-century figure its credibility is in dispute.[93] Concerning the ethnic and religious composition of this population during the second Byzantine period of Cyprus, there is no doubt that the vast majority were Greek Orthodox. The remaining minority of Cyprus' inhabitants represented a veritable mosaic of ethnically, religiously and linguistically different peoples. The opening years of Lusignan rule brought about a very substantial alteration in the composition and the numbers of these non-Greek, non-Orthodox minorities. Within the short reign of Guy de Lusignan a very substantial number of immigrants arrived from Palestine, Syria and Cilician Armenia

[91] Megaw and Hawkins (1977); Stylianou and Stylianou (1985: 43–52).
[92] Mukaddasi, 82, also translated in Cobham (1908: 5). See also Mango (1976a: 11).
[93] Hill rejects it as 'ridiculously small', while Mango considers it to be a reasonable figure: Mango (1976a: 5, and note 6); Hill (1948–52, I: 257).

to be given fiefs by Guy.[94] These were followed by other, successive waves of immigration. The most substantial of the earliest of such waves occurred in the second half of the thirteenth century, when the closing years and the fall of the Latin states of the Levant provoked a massive exodus to Cyprus of very great numbers of refugees. Amongst them were Latins, Syrians and Jews. Of the traders, the Genoese (who were given privileges in 1218 by Alice, Queen of Cyprus) and the Venetians (the recipients of privileges in the thirteenth century) also multiplied on the island.[95]

The scarcity of evidence, and the changes brought about after 1192, preclude a detailed and full account of the composition of the population of Cyprus during its last Byzantine period; but the scattered pieces of information which we have refer to a number, at least, of the groups composing the heterogeneous population of the island.

In the closing centuries of Byzantine rule, most of the non-Greek, non-Orthodox Cypriots were Armenian. There were Armenian settlements on the island as early as the sixth century. In the eleventh and twelfth centuries the numbers of Armenians on the island expanded. I have already referred to the possibility of Armenian emigrations to Cyprus in these centuries. Further, we know that in 1136/7 the whole population of Tell Hamdun in Little Armenia was transplanted to Cyprus by emperor John Komnēnos; and that a good proportion of the soldiers brought to Cyprus in the twelfth century were also Armenian, some or all of whom may have settled on the island.[96] References to Armenians in Cyprus in the twelfth and the early thirteenth century give the impression of a firmly settled and very large sect: as was mentioned earlier, the Armenian version of Michael the Syrian cites rumours that the Greeks in Cyprus were encouraging the Turks to massacre the Armenians in 1155/6; according to Benedict of Peterborough the army of Isaac Komnēnos which fought the Crusaders in 1191 was composed of Greeks and Armenians; and Wilbrand of Oldenburg, who visited Cyprus in 1211, refers to its non-Latin inhabitants as 'Greeks and Armenians'.[97]

I have already referred to the presence of westerners on the island and to their expanding numbers in the twelfth century. In the same century there were also sufficient numbers of Jews in Cyprus to sustain two different

[94] The new settlers were people from all walks of life. A contemporary writer complained that even poor cobblers, masons and public scribes were suddenly turned into land owners: Cont. William of Tyre, in Mas Latrie, *Histoire*, I, 43–4; *Eracles*, 192–3. See Hackett (1901: 70–1); Hill (1972, II: 39–40).

[95] Jacoby (1977).

[96] Hill (1948–52, I: 281, 305; II, 2–3); Kyrris (1970); Charanis (1972: 25–6).

[97] Benedict of Peterborough, II, 164, 172, translated in Cobham (1908: 7, 9); and see also Roger of Hoveden, III, 116; Wilbrand of Oldenburg, 180, translated in Cobham (1908: 13). See Hill (1948–52, I: 306, note 2).

religious sects (the Orthodox Rabbanitic and the 'heretical', so-called Kaphrosein or Cyprian Jews), as Benjamin of Tudela noted on his visit to the island in 1170.[98] There is some evidence that Turks also lived in Cyprus in the twelfth century: the Armenian version of Michael the Syrian mentions them with reference to 1155/6, as we saw earlier. Among the Byzantine soldiers sent to the island in the twelfth century there was a contingent of Tourkopouloi (Turks who had been baptised as Christians while in the Byzantine imperial service), and some or all of them seem to have settled in Cyprus: Benedict of Peterborough refers to 400 Tourkopouloi horsemen in Isaac Komnēnos' army in 1191.[99] Of a very different disposition were the few Georgians who also lived in Cyprus at the time: they manned at least one monastery, whose ruins have recently been identified some 7 kilometres east of the Bay of Chrysochou. The monastery is certainly attested in the twelfth century, when Queen Thamar (1184–1213) restored it; and it has been suggested that it was in continuous existence at least since the end of the tenth century. There is no evidence that the Georgian presence on the island extended beyond the monastic walls.[100]

There is circumstantial evidence to the effect that Muslim Arabs lived in Cyprus.[101] It is reasonable to assume that a number of them must have settled on the island in the course of so many centuries of close contact, and especially since between the first and second Byzantine period of Cyprus the Arabs occasionally occupied the island for varying periods of time: there is, for example, fairly clear evidence that in the seventh century a very large Arab garrison (the number given is 12,000 men) stayed on the island for about thirty years at a stretch.[102] It is also worth remembering that the *tekke* of Um-Harram (Hala Sultan *tekke*) near Larnaka was one of the holy places which every Muslim was expected to visit as a pilgrim, ranking only fourth in importance after Mecca, Medina and Jerusalem. Traditionally believed to have been built at the place where Um-Harram died in 649, the *tekke* is

[98] Benjamin of Tudela, 14–15, translated in Cobham (1908: 5) and in Sharf (1971: 138); and see Prawer (1988: 192–4) for Benjamin's date of visit.

[99] Benedict of Peterborough, II, 165, translated in Cobham (1908: 7); and see also Roger of Hoveden, III, 109. On the practice of baptising Turks who were in the imperial service (evidenced from the twelfth century) and on Tourkopouloi generally see Vryonis (1971a: 265–6, 441–2); and – also for bibliography – Jacoby (1974: 231, 232 and note 90, 259 and note 253).

[100] It appears almost certain that the Georgians came to the island from northern Syria, and more precisely from the western vicinities of Antioch, where there were at least thirteen Georgian monasteries between the end of the eleventh and the thirteenth century. On their presence in Cyprus see Djobadze (1984).

[101] On the Arabs in Cyprus see generally Hill (1948–52, I: 285; II: 1); and more specifically the bibliography in ch. 3, note 2, above, p. 40.

[102] Papageorgiou (1964).

next mentioned in the sources by Cornelis van Bruyn who visited it in 1683. There is no evidence that it ceased to function as a place of pilgrimage for Muslims in the intervening period, and its existence may have been accompanied by an Arab settlement.[103] Stronger evidence for the settlement of considerable numbers of Arabs on the island is provided by the existence of toponymics – still in use today – of clearly Arab origin (such as 'Kome Kebir' and 'Kantara'); and also by popular memory: in the sixteenth century Estienne de Lusignan claims that there used to be a *djami* in Lefkōsia 'built at the times when the Saracens occupied this island, for fifteen years, during the reign of Charlemagne'.[104] If there were Arabs already settled in Cyprus by the beginning of its second Byzantine period, they may well have expanded because of trade and of generally friendly relations: I have already mentioned Mukaddasi's reference, in 985, to the advantages which Cyprus offered for Muslim traders;[105] and the emir of Beyrout and his people's flight to Cyprus in 1110.

Many Syrians lived on the island in the early Byzantine period (there was a Monophysite community on the island in the seventh century) and there is no evidence that they left in the intervening period.[106] Certainly, under the Lusignans they formed a sufficiently large and important sect to be granted special privileges, but it is difficult to tell whether most of them were descendants of much earlier immigrants or whether they were post-1192 arrivals.[107] The same goes for the Jacobite and Nestorian presence on the island. Evidence concerning the seventh and the eighth centuries clearly suggests that there were considerable numbers of Jacobites in Cyprus, since there were Jacobite bishops. But the Jacobites and the Nestorians re-emerge in the sources only in 1222 when, together with the Syrians, they were ordered by pope Honorius III to obey the Latin bishop of Lefkōsia.[108]

Concerning the presence of Maronites on the island before the Lusignan period, a lot of inferences have been drawn out of a rather puzzling little dossier of information. Scholars have pondered over four references in marginal notes found in manuscripts. According to general scholarly agreement the notes are dated to, respectively, 1120/1, 1140/1, 1153/4 and 1238/9. They refer to a monastery of St John of 'Kuzaband' or 'Kusbandu', in Cyprus, as subject to the Maronite patriarch of Lebanon, the earliest two

---

[103] Van Bruyn, bet. 373–88, transl. in Cobham (1908: 240). See Aristeidou (1982).
[104] Lusignan, *Description*, 31vo.
[105] Mukaddasi, 82, translated also in Cobham (1908: 5).
[106] Sacopoulo (1975) 79ff.; also Mango (1976a: 3–4); Herrin (1987: 206).
[107] See Hill (1972, II: 1–2).   [108] *Ibid.*, 4.

of the notes recording the appointments by the patriarch of two monks as abbots of the monastery.[109]

Sir George Hill identifies this monastery as that of St John Chrysostom at Koutsovendēs, and considers the appointment of Maronite abbots there as 'evidence for the influx of Maronites at this time' in Cyprus. Cyril Mango agrees with the identification, and further points out that 'not a hint' is found in the writings of Neophytos (who was a young novice at the monastery of St John Chrysostom from 1152 until 1158) 'that he was living in a non-Greek or partly non-Greek community'; 'that at the very same time and indeed very soon after its foundation this monastery was subject to the Maronite patriarch of Lebanon, who appointed the abbot, and that some at least of the monks were reading the Scriptures in Arabic'.[110]

The evidence is, however, much more problematic than would appear from the above interpretations. The dating itself is unclear, partly because the four manuscript notes are, in fact, double-dated to, respectively, 1432 'according to the Greek calendar' and 1121; 1452 (Greek) and 1141; 1465 (Greek) and 1154; 1550 (Greek) and 1239.[111] The interpretation of these dates is not without controversy. The general view, represented by Hill, is that they correspond to the twelfth- and the thirteenth-century dates; but Tsiknopoulos argues plausibly – though ultimately does not prove – that they refer to the fifteenth and sixteenth centuries.[112]

If we accept Hill's dating, what is very difficult is to believe that Maronite abbots were appointed in 1120/1 and 1140/1 at that same monastery of St John Chrysostom in which Neophytos was a novice. We know that the monastery received the aristocratic patronage of the Byzantine *doux* of the island, Eumathios Philokalēs, some time after 1092 and before 1118.[113] We

---

[109] The references are found in marginal dated notes in the *Cod. Vat. Syr. 118* and in the Rabula Gospels (*Laurent. Plut. I. 56*). The first, third and fourth of these notes have been translated by Leroy (1964: 235, 146, notes 1, 2); for the second see Assemani, 1/3 (1759: 114–15); Leroy (1964: 235, note 2). See also Frangiskos (1989: 24–5, 94–100); Tsiknopoulos (1959: 49–54).

[110] Respectively, Hill (1948–52, I: 305); Mango (1976a: 6).

[111] This is the generally accepted reading. By contrast, according to Foradari, the 'Greek' dates correspond to the earlier, not the later set of dates: Foradari, in Frangiskos (1989: 24–5). The confusion over the notes is partly due to the fact that the original text is now very difficult to read, and Assemani's rendering of the second note in Latin is partly unintelligible: see Hill (1940–52, I: 305, note 1).

[112] Hill (1940–52, I: 305 and note 1); Tsiknopoulos (1959: 49–54); also Frangiskos (1989: 94–100, 9–106 *passim*). Tsiknopoulos argues that it is quite plausible that in the fifteenth and sixteenth century Maronite abbots were appointed at the Orthodox monastery of St John Chrysostom at Koutsovendēs. He sees this as yet another act of Latin intrusion in the affairs of the Cypriot Orthodox Church and monasticism, and points out that at that time the Maronites dominated the area and were much privileged by the Latin rulers of Cyprus. Note that the list of Maronite bishops in medieval Cyprus which can be drawn from documented references is chronologically restricted to between 1357 and 1516: Frangiskos (1989: 25, 113).

[113] Mango and Hawkins (1964: 335–9).

have no reason for suspecting that Eumathios Philokalēs was anything but Orthodox, or that he would have patronised anything other than an Orthodox monastery. When Neophytos arrived there in 1158, he clearly arrived at an Orthodox monastery, whose abbot at the time, Maximos, was succeeded *c.* 1158 by Euphrosynos and *c.* 1211 by Neophytos' brother, John.[114] Can we seriously consider that during the most powerful period of Cypriot Orthodox monasticism an important and by all accounts flourishing Orthodox monastery, which received the patronage of the Byzantine governor of the island, became a Maronite monastery dependant on the patriarchs of Lebanon for its abbots in 1120/1 and 1140/1; and that it had reverted back to Orthodox rule by 1158, when Neophytos arrived there? Alternatively, is it at all possible that we are dealing with a double monastery (Orthodox and Maronite) which had both Orthodox and Maronite abbots, the latter being subject to the Maronite Patriarchate of Lebanon; and would a powerful Orthodox monastery ever have allowed such an arrangement, especially in view of the fact that, according to the marginal notes, the Maronite monks there counted not more than four souls at best?

Let us reconsider the evidence. If we accept that the dates refer to the twelfth and thirteenth centuries, then there seems to be only one plausible interpretation: that we are dealing not with one but with two monasteries. For a start, there is no evidence that the Maronites are referring to a monastery of St John Chrysostom: the notes simply mention a monastery of St John of 'Kuzaband' or 'Kusbandu'. In fact, it is not even absolutely certain that 'Kuzaband' and 'Kusbandu' are alternative renderings of 'Koutsovendēs', although there is a clear similarity, and the possibility is made stronger by the (at least subsequent) concentration of Maronites in the area. 'Koutsovendēs', however, is a toponymic. It refers to the geographical area in which stood the Orthodox monastery of St John Chrysostom ('of Koutsovendēs', so as to locate it and possibly to distinguish it from another monastery or monasteries dedicated to the same Saint elsewhere on the island).[115] A mile south of this monastery stood the village of Koutsovendēs;

---

[114] Tsiknopoulos (1959: 49–54).

[115] Moutoullas provides a parallel example. The church of the Virgin there is known as that of the Panagia of Moutoullas (founded in 1280). According to a supplicatory inscription its founder was John Moutoullas and his wife Eirēnē. The same man had earlier recorded his name (and his wife's) in the same church as John Yerakoullas. The village where the church is situated is now known as Moutoullas; and there is a neighbouring village of Yerakes. It is not known whether John took his surname from the village of Yerakes and then, settling in Moutoullas, changed it to that; or whether the name of a local powerful family became attached to the village and the church. We do not know, in other words, whether the inscription refers to 'John, son of Yerakoullas', or to 'John, of the village of Yerakes' (and subsequently 'of Moutoullas'). Papageorgiou convincingly argues for the latter. At any rate, this example clearly illustrates the interchangeability of toponymics and surnames. See Papageorgiou (1975: 50–1, note 1); Mouriki (1984: 172–3); Stylianou and Stylianou (1985: 323–30, esp. 323–5); also Papageorgiou (1972). As to the possible meaning of *koutsovendēs* see later, p. 194.

and somewhere nearby there may well have also stood a Maronite monastery, subject to the Maronite patriarchs of Lebanon, and dedicated to (the same or a different) St John. The absence of the ruins of such a monastery need not puzzle us: the marginal notes testify that the Maronite community consisted of three or four monks, and their buildings must have been correspondingly humble. We have no evidence that such a monastery – if it existed there – had anything whatever to do with the Orthodox monastery in the same area. In short, the evidence permits the drawing of none of the inferences which Hill and especially Mango have drawn. The Maronite references testify only that: (1) there was a Maronite monastery of St John in Cyprus, in which the Maronite patriarchs of Lebanon appointed at least two abbots, in 1120/1 and in 1140/1 (or – the possibility exists – in 1431 and in 1451); (2) that this monastery may have been situated in the same area in which the Orthodox monastery of St John Chrysostom stood: namely, the area known as that of Koutsovendēs. The presence of a community of three or four monks and the appointment of two abbots hardly suggest in themselves an influx of Maronites on the island; and it seems reasonable to suggest that if Neophytos never mentioned Arabic-speaking Maronite monks and abbots in the monastery in which he was a monk, it is because there were none.

There is thus no clear evidence of a Maronite community in Cyprus prior to the establishment of the Latin kingdom, although the possibility of the existence of a small Maronite community prior to 1192 is quite likely.[116] By contrast, there is clear evidence of the presence of very considerable numbers of Maronites after 1192. In the late Lusignan period they occupied some thirty villages and they were the most numerous sect after the Greeks, according to Estienne de Lusignan.[117]

Until further research brings to light more information, we must remain content with this necessarily incomplete account of the composition of the population of Cyprus in the eleventh, twelfth and early thirteenth centuries. Even this account, however, gives a taste of the diversity of religions, languages and ethnicities which were encountered in Cyprus prior to 1192. It is clear that alongside the Greek Orthodox majority there co-existed a sizeable minority, whose numbers became greater and its composition more diverse in the eleventh and especially the twelfth centuries. It included Armenians, Jews, Latins, Turks, a few Georgians, very probably Syrian

---

[116] For the most recent discussion and bibliography concerning possible Maronite migrations to Cyprus prior to 1192 see Frangiskos (1989: 19–26).

[117] Lusignan, *Chorograffia*, 346; Lusignan, *Description*, 73. This appears to contradict other information, referred to earlier, according to which the Armenians were the most numerous after the Greeks; but it must be remembered that the evidence regarding the Armenians refers to the Early Lusignan period. See Hill (1972, II: 3–4).

and Palestine Arabs, and Maronites. A further and much more substantial demographic change was brought about following the establishment of the Lusignans in Cyprus.

As the above general introductory sketch suggests, by the early thirteenth century the situation in Cyprus was radically different from that prevailing in the eleventh and the better part of the twelfth century. Neophytos had been born in relatively peaceful times, in the Byzantine province of Cyprus. By the time of his death the third – if not the fourth – member of the house of Lusignan had already ascended the throne of the Latin kingdom of Cyprus. In between, the Recluse's life spanned one of the most dramatic periods in the history of the island. To bear witness to such a period of great upheavals and transformations was a privilege which, as we shall see, Neophytos found both deeply painful and irresistibly challenging.

Part 2

The process of self-sanctification

Part 2 comprises an attempt to reconstruct and analyse the process of self-sanctification which Neophytos followed. The information concerning this process has been pieced together from the physical remains of the Recluse's legacy (his manuscripts, and the structures and paintings of his caves), and it bears witness to a complex and highly idiosyncratic aspect of his personality. This does not refer to Neophytos' wish to be a Saint, for there is nothing exceptional or surprising in such a wish: whether he lived in a *koinobion* or a *lavra*, as an *hēsychastēs* on a column or enclosed in a cave or a cell, the achievement of closeness (*parrēsia*) to God was the stated aim of every monk, the target of all his efforts, the conscious aim of his entire way of life.[1] What is exceptional is to encounter from close quarters a Byzantine man who turned his wish to become a Saint into reality (in the sense that he and his society came to believe that he was a Saint) partly by following a process of self-sanctification.

Neophytos' was a complicated personality, and this is reflected in the way in which he pursued self-sanctification. He did not, for instance, follow the way in which his near-contemporary, Nikēphoros Blemmydēs, had tried to invest himself with sanctity. Blemmydēs did so in a very direct way, writing two autobiographies which were obviously – and no doubt consciously – intended to be his own Saint's *Life*.[2] Neophytos was far more subtle, perhaps because a lot of the time he was far less consciously deliberate, in the depiction of his own sanctity. Part of Neophytos' power lies in that he never tells the reader that he is a Saint. Instead, he leads the reader to reach this conclusion as though it were an inescapable one. The bulk of the evidence of Neophytos' process of self-sanctification comes from asides, hints, parallels; from brief details concerning his life, from sentences suddenly stopped in half. By contrast to Nikēphoros Blemmydēs, the Recluse's statements concerning his own sanctity are not contained in any one single document, are never fully explicit, are not very long. It is only through close and careful examination of his writings, and through following the glimpses of Neophytos' changing attitude towards himself over the years, that we find the evidence of the Recluse's growing belief in his own sanctity and of his public propagation of it.

It is important for the purposes of our discussion to establish first what Neophytos understood by 'sanctity'. The bulk of our information concerning Neophytos' conception of sanctity comes from his hagiographical writings. These represent a considerable part of his total literary output, as a glance at the Appendix will indicate. Neophytos' hagiography was firmly rooted in well-established cultural and specific literary traditions, as we have already seen. Naturally enough, however, the Recluse did not use all of the many and varied existing hagiographical traditions, but drew from only parts of a vast body of available material. It is precisely this element of choice which allows us, through studying Neophytos' writings, to gain an insight into his own conception of sanctity.

In attempting to reconstruct Neophytos' conception of sanctity I found the

---

[1] For the terms *koinobion* and *lavra* see ch. 1, note 3. *Hēsychia* means, literally, 'quiet'. In the context of asceticism, the term is used to describe a state of contemplation, inner recollection and prayer in private and in silence. The term was also put to other uses, which do not concern us here. For the term's many meanings and for the fourteenth-century theological dispute known as the Hesychast Controversy, see Meyendorff (1974), Ware (1980: 70–81), Hussey (1986: 257–60).

[2] Munitiz (1981).

application of a type of structuralist analysis to his hagiographical writings particularly useful. It is true that the use of structuralism in historiography has come under fire. Simply put, the main criticism against it is that it takes no account of the dimension of time, being synchronic rather than diachronic; that it may thus be a good tool for descriptive purposes but that it fails to account for the crucial historical dynamic element of change.[3] Here, however, I am not aiming at a study of the changes of a model of sanctity through the centuries; and even though elements of such a comparative study will inevitably appear in the course of the discussion, nevertheless the causes, the dynamic behind these changes, is a matter which – important though it undoubtedly is in itself – is irrelevant for our present purposes. I am aiming rather at a description of the mental categories of sanctity in the mind of one particular person, a description arrived at through the examination of his hagiographical writings, which span a period of about forty years and which reveal a conception of sanctity that remained unchanged.[4] It is the analysis of the essentially static thought patterns of a specific individual that I want to effect and use in the course and for the purposes of the argument pursued.

In describing earlier the analysis which follows as 'a type of structuralist analysis', I meant to acknowledge the debt which it ultimately owes to structuralism, as well as the limited extent to which it is related to it: it is a by-product rather than a direct application of what now might be termed 'Orthodox' structuralism.[5] Now that the dust of the debate over structuralism has settled down, we are no longer justified in succumbing to the temptation of throwing the baby out with the bath-water – the bath-water being the all too glaringly exposed limitations of structuralism; the baby being the very considerable extent to which structuralism did succeed in opening up new possibilities for insight into thought patterns. This, surely, is the most enduring and valuable legacy of structuralist thought and method. Naturally, the ways in which it is understood and applied have become, with time, as diverse as also increasingly distant from 'Orthodox' structuralism.[6] The ultimate debt, however, remains and, just because 'structuralism' has become already an 'unfashionable' term, we should not shy from acknowledging it, especially when, as in the case under discussion here, an analysis which ultimately, if distantly, derives from structuralist thought and method provides a useful methodological tool.

The obvious limitations of the source material also mitigated in favour of the choice of this methodology: Neophytos writes of sanctity only indirectly, through his hagiography (that is to say, through stories of or about the lives of Saints), avoiding any philosophical or theological discussion of sanctity or sanctification. For the Recluse sanctity was composed of a number of given factors, and it is these 'given' elements, this 'given' structure that forms the basis of his hagiographical narratives and of his conception of sanctity.

---

[3] With specific reference to Byzantine historiography, see Haldon (1981: esp. 210–11); for a wider social anthropological critique, see Bourdieu (1977: esp. 115).

[4] Our earliest datable manuscript has a *terminus post quem* of 1170; our latest securely dated manuscript is of 1214: see Appendix.

[5] See generally Lévi-Strauss (1949; 1972: esp. chs. 1, 11, 12, 15).

[6] Within the context of Byzantine historiography especially noted are aspects of the work of Evelyne Patlagean (e.g. 1977 and her collected articles in 1981a). For other works which contain elements of or were influenced by insights from work in the field of social (structural) anthropology, see e.g. Brown (1971a, 1971b, 1973); Cameron (1978).

Reading through Neophytos' *Lives*, *enkōmia* or descriptions of Saints, perhaps their most striking feature is the diversity of their composition, description and characterisation. At the same time, however, close and careful reading of these writings reveals a number of common themes. These are not always present in all of Neophytos' Saints' stories, but they are shared by a sufficient number of them to form clearly recognisable patterns. And even though each theme or pattern appears in each story in a slightly different form, it nevertheless retains in substance the same essential identity from story to story. These hagiographical themes, taken together, form the main structure around which the tale of the world and the holy man in it is spun. They reveal the structure of the relationship between that man and the world; and it is the terms of this relationship which define the man as a holy man.[7]

In examining the structure of Neophytos' hagiographical narratives from a thematic point of view my aim was to remove the specificities unique to each story, and to focus on its basic internal structural elements. Then, to compose one single such structure, made up of all the elements existing in common in Neophytos' Saints' stories. What we end up with is the underlying structure, the basic indispensable foundations, on which each and every story of sanctity was, in Neophytos' mind, built. Only having achieved this, can we understand Neophytos' conception of sanctity: what he recognised as holy, what elements in a man's or woman's life he considered as evidential material for a case of sanctity. Having thus gained an insight into what the Recluse understood by 'sanctity', I shall proceed to examine another aspect of Neophytos' thought process: how his belief in his own sanctity grew; how he proceeded to imbue his own life's story with the same structural characteristics of sanctity which he himself had used to give flesh and blood to his own Saints' stories; and what part the structures and the paintings of the Enkleistra played in Neophytos' process of self-sanctification.

---

[7] See also Patlagean (1968: 111).

4   Neophytos' conception of sanctity

The world renounced: *Anachōrēsis*

Despite the relative paucity and the lack of uniformity of available material, scholars have tentatively identified certain trends in Orthodox hagiography over the centuries. One of these concerns the theme of *anachōrēsis*. The term *anachōrēsis* describes the concept of withdrawal (literally 'departure') from the world. By an act of *anachōrēsis* a person physically moved away from human society and into the wilderness and loneliness of the desert. This physical departure also signified in the most visible manner possible an emotional renunciation of the world. The anchorite endeavoured not only to refute civilised society but also to refute – to a point as close to negating as possible – his own body through leading a life of solitude, strict material austerity, prayer and contemplation. The ultimate aim was to reach a state of intimacy with, closeness to, God (*parrēsia*). The single act of *anachōrēsis* stood as a recognised rite of passage: it transformed the status of a man, from that of a civilian, a member of civilised society, into that of an anchorite, a person who had renounced the world to live outside it, recalling and aspiring to reach the state of Adam's existence before the Fall: outside the boundaries of civilised society and into those of a life of direct communion with nature and as direct a communion with God as was humanly possible. In the very early days of Christianity the life of the anchorite was conceived of as an entirely individual matter, and in this sense there is no doubt that the earliest type of Christian monk was the hermit.[1] Within the very first centuries of Christianity, communal forms of monasticism also developed. But whether a monk joined a *koinobion*, became a member of a *lavra*, attached himself to an anchorite or set up entirely on his own as a hermit, he still shared in common with every other monk the single initial act of *anachōrēsis* and the ongoing commitment to it.[2]

It is hardly surprising, therefore, that *anachōrēsis* is undoubtedly the most frequently shared theme in all Saints' *Lives*, Neophytic or not. The flight

[1] Chitty (1977: 2–6).
[2] See ch. 1, note 3, for brief discussion of the terms *koinobion* and *lavra*.

into the desert (recalling Christ's withdrawal into the desert, and St John the Baptist's before him), so important an ingredient in early Saints' *Lives*, was gradually and increasingly altered to a flight from the world to a monastery which was still conceived of as 'the desert'. This substitution of monastery for (actual) desert appears already in the sixth century, in the *Lives* of monks of Palestine composed by Cyril of Skythopolis, and in the *Lives* of the ancient stylites.³ It becomes much more frequent in the *Lives* of ninth- to eleventh-century Saints, with only rare examples of a Saint beginning his ascetic life by direct withdrawal into the desert (such as that of St Peter of Atroa). Far more frequently, the Saint withdraws into the desert after an initial period in a monastery; but further, on a number of occasions he may never withdraw into the desert at all, but only to a monastery.⁴

In the eleventh-century flight from the world continued to be a favourite hagiographical *topos* and it was by then set very definitely within the context of entry into monasticism. Thus, for example, St Symeōn the New Theologian leaves a promising career in the imperial service when he is about twenty-eight years old, to enter the monastery of Stoudion; St Lazaros the Galesiot follows his uncle in the monastery of Kalathōn after having attained some education; while St Cyril Phileōtēs' departure from the world is peculiarly gradual: he withdraws into and then comes out of monasteries, until his commitment to *anachōrēsis* takes a permanent form when he retires in a monastery founded by his brother.⁵

The theme of flight from the world into a monastery continued to be present in the relatively few Saints' *Lives* which were produced in the twelfth century: St Christodoulos of Patmos fled to a monastery on Olympos in Bithynia after his parents, who wished to keep him in secular society, betrothed him to a girl against his will.⁶ St Meletios the Younger left home when he was fifteen (according to the account of his life given by Nicholas of

³ See Patlagean (1968: 115–16 and 121). Withdrawal into a monastery instead of into the actual desert was, of course, not a totally universal pattern: both St Daniel the Stylite and St Symeōn the Stylite first embraced the monastic life and only subsequently became hermits. *Life* of St Daniel, 4.12–27.16; *Life* of St Symeōn, 3.4ff.; see also Delehaye (1923: xxv–xxvi).
⁴ Cyril of Skythopolis, 13.9–16.24 (*Life* of Euthymios), 87.19–88.1, 90.5–92.16, 93.20–94.12, 95.6–11 (*Life* of St Sabas), 204.14–209.16 (*Life* of St John the Hēsychastēs), 224.1–225.26 (*Life* of Kyriakos), 236.14–237.10 (*Life* of St Theodosios), 242.6–17 (*Life* of St Theognios), 243.22–244.7 (*Life* of Abraamios). See also Delehaye (1923); and Patlagean (1981b: esp. 93–5).
⁵ See respectively *Life* of St Symeōn the New Theologian, 4–8, paras. 3, 4; *Life* of St Lazaros; *Life* of St Cyril Phileōtēs, 106–9, ch. 22; 57, ch. 5ff. Most of the eleventh- to thirteenth-century Saint's *Lives* are definitely set within the monastic walls throughout the Saint's life. See, e.g., the *Lives* of Sts Symeōn the New Theologian, Meletios the Younger, Hilariōn of Moglena, Meletios the Confessor, or even Cyril Phileōtēs who also eventually follows a strictly monastic life. On eleventh-century sanctity see generally Morris (1981: esp. 44–5).
⁶ *Life* of St Christodoulos of Patmos, paras. 4, 5; and see Branouse (1966: 51).

Methōnē) or sixteen (according to the *Life* by Theodore Prodromos) and entered a monastery. Both his hagiographers depict Meletios fleeing from his parents' plans of marrying him off.[7] St Leontios of Jerusalem leaves home and directs his steps towards Constantinople. He becomes a monk before he enters the City.[8] The same theme also appears in the *Lives* of St Cyprian of Calabria, St Hilariōn of Moglena (who leaves home and enters a monastery at eighteen); and also of two St Gregories, the one an ascetic near Nicomēdia, the other a bishop of Assos in the Troad, both of whom possibly (but not certainly) lived in the twelfth century.[9] The theme of flight into a monastery is also present in the even sparser early thirteenth-century hagiography – in the *Life* of Nikēphoros Blemmydēs, for instance, who became a deacon when he was twenty-eight and was tonsured a monk ten years later.[10] The theme is also certainly present in the more abundant late thirteenth-, fourteenth- and fifteenth-century Saints' *Lives*. An example of the latter is presented by the *Life* of St Meletios the Confessor, who leaves home as a young man, following a vision, and enters a monastery in Palestine.[11]

In Neophytic hagiographical narratives the theme of *anachōrēsis* assumes two forms: its original form, in the sense of a move away from the world; and another, of a subsequent flight, from fame.

In the case of flight from the world Neophytos often follows the pattern (usual by the twelfth century) of withdrawal into a monastery, which is sometimes followed by a later withdrawal into total solitude. Thus Sts Andronikos and Athanasia, having experienced marriage and parenthood, leave their home for a pilgrimage to the Holy Land, which culminates in their decision to leave the world altogether and adopt the monastic life.[12] St Hilariōn leaves his home and unchristian parents and enters a monastery at the age of fifteen.[13] St Sabas leaves home and becomes a monk at the even earlier age of ten. He stays in the monastery for eight years until, following a vision, his abbot allows him to leave the community and to visit the Holy Land. There he stays in another monastery for ten years before he becomes an hesychast. St Sabas stays in the desert for four years, then settles in a cave

---

[7] *Life* of St Meletios the Younger, 3, 42–3, 45. See also Papadopoulos (1935).
[8] *Life* of St Leontios of Jerusalem, 381–3.
[9] See respectively: *Life* of St Cyprian of Calabria; *Life* of St Hilariōn of Moglena, and Turdeanu (1947: 83); *Life* of St Gregory, 506.81–96; *Life* of St Gregory of Assos, 18–19. On these twelfth-century Saints see Magdalino (1981: esp. 52–4).
[10] *Life* of Nikēphoros Blemmydēs, 8, para. 12.1–20; 21, para. 37.6–17.
[11] *Life* of St Meletios the Confessor, esp. 609–11. See generally Laiou-Thomadakis (1980). All sixteen Saints to whom Laiou refers were monastic Saints.
[12] *Cod. Paris. Gr. 1189*, fols. 81β–82α (*Panegyric 11*).
[13] *Panegyric 13*, 138.16–27.

for another five years, living on his own until he is joined by disciples and a *lavra* grows around his cave to house as many as 150 monks.[14]

On other occasions Neophytos follows the earlier hagiographical model of flight from the world into the (actual) desert rather than into the monastery. An obvious example of this is presented by the Recluse's references to the life of St John the Baptist, who lived in the desert since childhood.[15] Other examples include St John Chrysostom, who withdrew into a cave after twelve years as a priest and stayed there for three years, until he was brought out to become a patriarch.[16] St Alypios, too, became consumed with a desire to leave the world while he was a priest. His plans of going to the Holy Land to become an ascetic there were frustrated by his bishop, who caught up with him on his way and brought him back. St Alypios' second effort, however, proved successful: he withdrew into a narrow cell for two years and then became a stylite for the rest of his life.[17]

The hagiographical theme of withdrawal into a monastery followed by a subsequent withdrawal into a desert, was well established by the time Neophytos came to contribute to the *genre*. It first appears with regularity in Saints' *Lives* from the ninth to the eleventh century; in the *Lives*, for example, of St Constantine of Synnada, St Euthymios the Younger, St Paul the Younger, St Michael Maleinos, St Luke the Younger.[18] It has been suggested that the difficulties which arose between Sts Constantine of Synnada, Paul or Luke the Younger and their respective abbots (who resist their desire to withdraw from the monastery into the desert) signify the tension between the tradition of withdrawal into solitude as opposed to withdrawal into a monastery.[19] This is a tension also expressed in Neophytos' story of St Alypios. Often, and increasingly as the time passed, the objection to the Saint's flight comes from his family. In eleventh-century *Lives* the description of the Saint's family's efforts to find the run-away and to persuade him to abandon his plans of leaving the world becomes a *topos*.[20] One such example from the eleventh century is provided by the *Life* of St Symeōn the New Theologian: amidst tearful embraces, his father tries to convince him to abandon his plans of joining a monastery; and he tries again later, when St Symeōn is already a monk.[21] In the twelfth century, the *Life*

---

[14] *Cod. Paris. Gr. 1189*, fols. 174β–175α, 175β, 176α (*Panegyric 23*).
[15] *Cod. Lesb. Leim. 2*, fol. 311a (*Homily 6*).
[16] *Panegyric 20*, 10.6–34.
[17] *Panegyric 22*, 189.6–15, 189.30–9, 190.5–34.
[18] See respectively: *Life* of St Constantine of Synnada; *Life* of St Euthymios the Younger, 174.2–178.18, and cf. Papachrysanthou (1975: 22–31); *Life* of St Paul the Younger, 106.11–110.8; *Life* of St Michael Maleinos, 558–9, paras. 12, 13; *Life* of St Luke the Younger, 86.18–87.28, 91.23–92.14.
[19] Patlagean (1981b: 93).   [20] Morris (1981: 45).
[21] *Life* of St Symeōn the New Theologian, 14–16, para. 8; 26, para. 17.

of Christodoulos of Patmos depicts his parents betrothing him against his will in order to stop him from entering a monastery.[22]

In Neophytos' hagiography the theme of flight from the world also assumes other variants. St Gennadios, for example, flees not from home but from the patriarchal throne, motivated by a desire not to meet his death (whose imminent coming was revealed to him by God) in a city ruled by a heretical emperor. He secretly departs from Constantinople for the Holy Land, subsequently reaching Cyprus, where he dies.[23] St Mamas' flight from the world is aided by God in a way which is more direct than in other cases: having been arrested and tortured by the emperor Aurelian for his Christian faith, St Mamas is thrown in the sea to drown. An angel rescues him and transports him to a mountain, where St Mamas begins to live alone, far from the world and in the company of animals.[24] In the case of Saints who never undertook a clear act of physical *anachōrēsis*, the element of withdrawal from the world is still often present in the form of secret escapades in solitary places. There the holy man, unknown to the world, prays, fasts and keeps vigils. Thus, St Theosebios would pretend to take his sheep for grazing in order to spend days alone in a cave, glorifying God.[25] Similarly, his bishop brother St Arkadios practised secret 'flights' both before and after he became a bishop.[26]

Apart from moving away from the world, the theme of flight also appears in Neophytos' writings in the form of a subsequent flight from fame. This, again, is no innovation of Neophytos'. An early Christian example of a Saint whose fame attracted followers despite his wishes is that of St Euthymios of Palestine. He lived as a solitary and wished to continue living thus but his fame attracted followers until eventually a *lavra* grew around him.[27] Closer to Neophytos' times, in the eleventh century, St Lazaros the Galesiot left the column which he had occupied for eleven years and moved to another, higher up the ravine, in order to avoid visitors and to be alone in his struggles against demons.[28] The general idea is that once the holy man acquires fame he finds himself besieged by people who want to receive the beneficial effects of his holiness by becoming disciples or by asking him for

---

[22] *Life* of St Christodoulos of Patmos, para. 4; and see also Branouse (1966: 51). St Meletios also flees from home after parental plans to marry him off: *Life* of St Meletios the Younger, 15, 42–3, 45.

[23] *Panegyric 30*, 224.11–225.8. Foresight of the time of death by the Saint is a theme well established by early hagiography. It is, of course, related to the notion of predestination, constantly present in Orthodox teaching under guise of God's foreknowledge of the moment of death. By contrast to other hagiographical themes, it persisted after the ninth century. See Patlagean (1981b: 92–3; 1968: 116).

[24] *Panegyric 2*, 134.21–135.2.   [25] *Panegyric 12*, 191.20–5.

[26] *Panegyric 14*, 205.5–10.   [27] Chitty (1928: esp. 135).

[28] *Life* of St Lazaros, c. 43; and see Delehaye (1923: cvi–cxvi).

advice or cure. Often, therefore, he tries to flee, because of modesty and dislike of fame, as well as because he feels distracted from *hēsychia*. The *Lives* of Sts Christodoulos of Patmos (twelfth century), Meletios the Younger and Meletios the Confessor (thirteenth century) are amongst those providing examples of such flights from fame.[29]

Similarly, in Neophytos' stories, St Polychronios leaves his country when, following a miracle, people begin to honour him as a holy man.[30] St Alypios, disturbed by the people attracted to him on account of his fame, leaves the cell where he had stayed for two years, and 'flees' to the top of a column so as to be left alone.[31] St Sabas finds that the *lavra* which sprang around his cave is too crowded and noisy a place for him, and he leaves, wandering in the desert, founding monasteries everywhere he goes, only to leave those too.[32] But no other Neophytic story illustrates how seriously a holy man can become trapped, even imprisoned, in his fame, than that of St Hilariōn. Disturbed by the multitude of people who flock to see him, St Hilariōn decides that he wants to leave his monastery and to withdraw into *hēsychia*. The reaction of his monks when they get wind of his plans is to keep constant vigils over him, day and night, so that he would not be able to slip out of the monastery in secret. Eventually, St Hilariōn finds himself besieged 'by the whole of Palestine', which gathered, begging him not to leave. Faced with what amounted to physical imprisonment, St Hilariōn initiates a hunger strike, refusing to receive any food or drink. After seven days the crowd and the monks, fearing that he might die, reluctantly agree to let him go. However, St Hilariōn quickly discovers that his fame follows him everywhere, and he has to keep constantly on the move in order to avoid 'both the disturbance of the people and the honour which they paid him'. He leaves and goes to another desert, from where again he soon has to depart for the same reason. His constant travels in search of *hēsychia* takes him to Sicily and then to Cyprus, only to see the same story repeating itself. In Cyprus he has to leave Paphos, where he initially stayed, and withdraw to a mountain which is described as high and difficult of access. Even there, people follow him. St Hilariōn finds *hēsychia* only in death.[33]

The underlying implication in this theme of flight from fame is that sanctity cannot be hidden: 'Just as the sinners are found out even if they do

---

[29] *Life* of St Christodoulos of Patmos, para. 10, and see also Branouse (1966: 60); *Life* of St Meletios the Younger, 17; *Life* of St Meletios the Confessor (particularly rich in such examples) 612, 614, 615.

[30] *Panegyric 10*, 175.30–2.   [31] *Panegyric 22*, 190.26–34.

[32] *Cod. Paris. Gr. 1189*, fols. 176α–β (*Panegyric 23*).

[33] *Panegyric 13*, 143.9–145.9.

not wish to be, so too the righteous ones are revealed even if they do not wish to be', Neophytos writes, referring to St Arkadios.[34] And just as St Arkadios finds it impossible to conceal his sanctity, so too St Polychronios flees to Constantinople, where nobody knows him, only to discover that he is recognised as a holy man there too.[35]

The achievement of sanctity

In early (fifth- to seventh-century) hagiography the achievement of sanctity is clearly marked by the beginning of performance of miracles. This occurs when the holy man breaks his self-imposed exile in the desert to take up again some social links with the world.[36] By the twelfth century there appears to be no frequent expression of a specific point in the narrative when a man becomes a holy man. In some post-ninth-century *Lives* such a point is hinted at rather than clearly stated. For example, St Symeōn's *Life* describes him as receiving the grace of the Holy Ghost, following which he lives in a state of perpetual spiritual concentration (*katanyxis*) and acquires spiritual wisdom and knowledge.[37] St Leontios of Jerusalem also acquires spiritual wisdom (*gnōsis*) after a vision; and in the *Life* of St Cyril Phileōtēs descriptions of miracles performed by him follow a reference to his decision to sever the last remaining links with his family.[38]

Certainly, in a few of Neophytos' Saints' *Lives* the narrative clearly indicates such a point. For St Mamas it comes when, saved from the depths of the sea by an angel, he is transported to a mountain. There 'by the Lord's command, he is given a rod and a Gospel, and he becomes the shepherd of wild beasts'. It is after this point that he begins to perform miracles.[39] St Polychronios lives a life of fasting and prayer until God, responding to his prayers, creates a source of water for the use of St Polychronios and his oxen. This is the turning point in St Polychronios' life, after which he achieves fame as a holy man.[40] The turning point for St John Chrysostom is also clearly defined by the visitation of an angel while he is in a monastery in Antioch. The angel announces to him that he is destined to preach the word of God. 'It was then, holy one, that you were enriched with the gift of miracles', writes Neophytos.[41]

---

[34] *Panegyric 14*, 200.22–4. [35] *Panegyric 10*, 175.30–176.19.
[36] Patlagean (1968: 116).
[37] *Life* of St Symeōn the New Theologian, 28–30, para. 19.
[38] *Life* of St Leontios of Jerusalem, 392; *Life* of St Cyril Phileōtēs, 136, para. 12ff.
[39] *Panegyric 2*, 134.34–135.2.
[40] *Panegyric 10*, 175.19–32. [41] *Panegyric 20*, 18.11–16.

These, however, are the only cases in Neophytos' hagiographical narratives in which we find some clear reference to a passage into sanctity. No such point can be found, for example, in the story of Sts Andronikos and Athanasia, except where we read that this saintly married couple became famous 'not only because of their virtue . . . but also because of the source of miracles' which followed their second, celibate, cohabitation.[42] In a similarly vague way, St Arkadios is described as having reached a state of holiness following time spent 'hiding in mountains and in caves and in the holes of the earth, fasting, keeping vigils and praying'.[43]

Frequently, however, Neophytos sees sanctity as not simply a state reached at a vague point during a life of abstinence, but further, as a manifestation of God's grace bestowed on a man even before that man acted in any way to achieve it. There is, in other words, a sense of predestination, a choice by God of a number of men to become vehicles of His grace, sometimes, indeed, even before they are born. Recreating this theme (which is ubiquitous in all hagiography) Neophytos hails Sts Mamas, Diomēdēs and Nicholas as men thus designated to be holy, and describes St Alypios' mother having a prophetic dream while pregnant, revealing to her that her son would achieve greatness.[44] Other Saints (Polychronios, Sabas, Nicholas again) are declared to have been chosen by God as soon as they were born (ek prōtēs balbidos);[45] or from a very early age: at the age of ten for St Sabas, twelve for St Diomēdēs, fifteen for St Hilariōn, 'from childhood' for St John the Baptist.[46] When St Hilariōn leaves home at the age of fifteen and visits the Great Antony, the latter realises upon seeing him that the boy is chosen by God and tonsures him a monk within two days.[47] St Sabas demonstrates his great future at the age of ten when, already a monk, he follows strict rules of ascesis and decides to abstain from ever eating apples, since they remind him of the Fall.[48] St Nicholas is revealed to be a chosen one when, as soon as he is born, he stands on his own feet for two hours, and then practises abstinence from food, receiving milk only in the evenings of Wednesdays and Fridays.[49]

[42] Cod. Paris. Gr. 1189, fol. 83α (Panegyric 11).
[43] Panegyric 14, 200.16–201.3. The phrase is a conventional literary figure. See, e.g., Metaphrastic Life of St Alypios, 170.4–17; and pp. 24–5 above.
[44] Respectively, Panegyric 2, 136.37–40; Panegyric 17, 213.3–8; Panegyric 24, 393.28–32; Panegyric 22, 188.21–31.
[45] Respectively, Panegyric 10, 177.32–3; Cod. Paris. Gr. 1189, fol. 179α (Panegyric 23); Panegyric 24, 393.20–1.
[46] Respectively, Cod. Paris Gr. 1189, fol. 174α (Panegyric 23); Panegyric 17, 213.3–8; Panegyric 13, 138.16–27; Cod. Lesb. Leim. 2, fol. 311α (Homily 6).
[47] Panegyric 13, 138.16–27.
[48] Cod. Paris. Gr. 1189, fol. 174β (Panegyric 23). Ascesis literally means 'exercise', 'training', 'practice'; and by extension denotes the various practices exercised in pursuit of the ideal of negation of the body and the self, leading towards a state of spiritual perfection.
[49] Panegyric 24, 393.32–394.6.

Miraculous events preceding and during childhood provide a theme which persisted throughout Byzantine hagiography. In ninth- to eleventh-century *Lives*, for instance, it is exemplified by cases of long periods of sterility which end when, following prayers, the mother of the Saint becomes pregnant. This was the case, for example, of the ninth-century Saint Peter of Atroa.[50] It is a theme which faithfully follows earlier models of sanctity, established in the fourth to the seventh century. Post-ninth-century hagiography continued to provide examples of divine signs at birth: visions, for instance, received by various persons at the birth of the Saint, revealing the latter's status; or prophetic dreams seen by the Saint's pregnant mother – a situation identical to that of Alypios'.[51] More generally, the theme of miraculous events during the Saint's childhood is a common one throughout Byzantine hagiography. It is a theme found, for example, both in early *Lives* and in the thirteenth-century auto-hagiographical account of Blemmydēs: his mother has visions of angels clothing the infant; the latter refuses to be suckled by anyone other than his mother.[52] By contrast, wisdom at an early age, rendering the child intellectually closer to old age rather than to childhood, is a theme which appears to have developed after the ninth century. So that Neophytos, for example, writes that St Euthymios called St Sabas a 'child–old-man' (*paidogeronta*); and it is in pursuing this same theme that Nikēphoros Blemmydēs claims that as a child he never used bad language, never lied, always liked going to church, never kissed a woman, and hurled stones at anyone who dared jokingly to mention marriage to him.[53]

Predestination never formed part of the official doctrine of the Orthodox Church, but it was both a constant motif in Orthodox teaching under guise of God's foreknowledge of human action and, in a fatalistic sense, deeply embedded in popular culture.[54] It is also present in less obvious but equally important instances in Neophytic Saints' stories. In a number of cases it is clear that God Himself led a man to the acquisition of sanctity. For instance,

---

[50] *Life* of St Peter of Atroa, 69–71, para. 2; and cf. *Life* of St Stephen the Younger, 1073–7.

[51] See Patlagean (1981b: 92; 1968: 115–16).

[52] *Life* of Nikēphoros Blemmydēs, 48, para. 3.3–18. See Munitiz (1981: 166). For other examples, see *Life* of St Symeōn the New Theologian, 34.7–8; *Life* of St Meletios the Younger, 2; *Life* of St Hilariōn of Moglena, and Turdeanu (1947: 82–3) (prophetic dream preceded his birth); *Life* of St Meletios the Confessor, 584, 609 (prophetic dream).

[53] Respectively, *Cod. Paris. Gr. 1189*, fol. 174β (*Panegyric 23*); *Life* of Nikēphoros Blemmydēs, 48, para. 3.18–21, para. 4.1–7. See generally Patlagean (1981b: 92).

[54] Predestination continues to be part of Greek popular culture, in the form, e.g., of the belief that everything that will happen to one is ultimately 'written' by God, or that the infant is visited by the three fates (*moirai*) on the third night after its birth: the *moirai* write down his or her fate, and what they decree is unalterable. See, for the *moirai* Krikos-Davis (1982); and for personifications also of Destiny or Luck in Sarakatsan, Greek and Greek-Cypriot culture, Campbell (1964: 329–30); Blum and Blum (1970: 100, nos. 19, 20); Dawkins (1953: 458–65).

the crucial meeting of Sts Andronikos and Athanasia (which ends in their second, celibate, cohabitation after twelve years of separation, and their subsequent achievement of sanctity) takes place when, unknown to each other, they both set off from their respective monasteries 'moved by the Holy Ghost' (*pneumatokinētos*) and meet 'through some inexpressible providence'.[55] Similarly, following a vision, St Sabas sets out 'moved by God' (*theokinētos*) from the monastery where he had stayed for eight years to go on a pilgrimage to the Holy Land. After four years in the desert, it is an angel who leads him to the cave where he settles as an *hēsychastēs* and achieves sanctity.[56] An angel again is sent by God to St John Chrysostom while the latter was still a monk, to announce to him God's plans that he should leave the monastery and preach God's word to the people. We read that in his early days St John Chrysostom had refrained from undertaking any of the 'petty offices' and concentrated, rather, on leading a pious life and on studying, because he was destined to become a vessel of God.[57] St Symeōn went to the temple 'not moved by his own self (*ouk autokinētos*) but by the Holy Ghost which filled him'.[58] It is an attitude which recalls the events surrounding Christ's birth, when the wise men, as Neophytos reminds us, set out not according to their own decision but rather 'moved by God' (*theokinētos*).[59]

Signs of God

Another hagiographical theme encountered in Neophytos' writings is that of a divine 'sign' (*sēmeion*) or intervention, through which God reveals a man's holiness and/or manifests that that man is divinely protected.[60]

Examples of the first case (revelation of holiness by means of a sign of God) are found in many of Neophytos' Saints' stories: when St Theosebios dies, his shepherd dog reveals to the people the cave where the Saint's body lay, 'not acting on its own, but carrying out a miracle of God to glorify his servant'.[61] St John Chrysostom's first conviction into exile, masterminded

---

[55] *Cod. Paris. Gr. 1189*, fol. 82β (*Panegyric 11*).
[56] *Cod. Paris. Gr. 1189*, fols. 174β–175β (*Panegyric 23*). On *hēsychia* see Part 2, Introduction, note 1.
[57] *Panegyric 20*, 18.11–16, 9.38–10.3.
[58] *Cod. Lesb. Leim. 2*, fol. 289β (*Homily 4*).
[59] *Cod. Lesb. Leim. 2*, fol. 267β (*Homily 2*).
[60] For parallel examples from eleventh- to thirteenth-century Byzantine Saints' *Lives* see *Life of St Symeōn the New Theologian*, 8–10; 28–30, para. 19; 32–4, para. 23 (the last two are described as 'Signs of God' (*theosēmeia*); *Life of St Meletios the Younger*, 47; *Life of St Leontios of Jerusalem*, 392, 394; *Life* of Nikēphoros Blemmydēs, 4–5, para. 5; 25–6, para. 47, para. 48.1–6; 35–6, para. 71; 16–17, paras. 28, 29; 33–4, paras. 65, 66; *Life of St Meletios the Confessor*, 611.
[61] *Panegyric 12*, 192.31–2.

by the evil empress Eudoxia, is accompanied by an earthquake and the appearance of a red-hot cloud over Constantinople; while on the Saint's second exit from the City as an exile God expressses His wrath by means of a great fire and a storm.[62] One evening, while St Alypios was on his column, the cross which he had attached to it shook, and the column was flooded by a divine light, witnessed 'not only by five eyes [*sic!*] or ten, but by many people'.[63] Similarly, on the transportation of St Stephen's relics to Constantinople, the donkeys dragging the cart on which his body lay stopped and spoke, revealing that the Saint should be buried at that precise spot.[64] Divine choice of the place of burial is also revealed in St Gennadios' story, where the Saint's body, carried to be buried, suddenly becomes so heavy that it cannot be moved any further. Prior to this, another sign had made people aware of the holiness of St Gennadios, when the priest who was dispatched to bury the unknown stranger who was found dead on the mountains was prevented from reaching the place by the miraculous appearance of a river. The river only disappeared when the bishop himself came and prayed, having realised that this was a sign of God, indicating the holiness of the dead man.[65] God intervenes in another *Life* to lead a man to sanctity, when St John the Almsgiver's unwilling marriage and parenthood come to an abrupt end since God, 'desiring to raise him to be a spiritual father of many, cut down by death the woman and children', and thus relieved St John of the married layman's daily duties and responsibilities.[66] Finally, at the burial of St Athanasia 'God revealed many signs' and 'thus all glorified God for having given victory' to St Athanasia.[67]

In Neophytos' narratives divine intervention often takes the form of protection of the holy man by God. Among the Saints who found a hagiographer in Neophytos, St Mamas is particularly protected in this way. When his parents die in prison, Mamas is saved by Matrōna, a woman whom an angel directed to take the baby and raise him. An angel, again, later saves St Mamas from the bottom of the sea, where he was thrown by his torturers to drown; and later still, an angel provides St Mamas with food for forty days while he is imprisoned.[68] Other Saints who are miraculously saved include St Hilariōn, whose *hēsychia* was disturbed by two robbers who came to harm him during the night: God veiled their sight so that they could not see St Hilariōn even though they were standing next to him.[69] In a similar way St Diomēdēs, chased by 500 Arabs, is saved when God's voice from above

---

[62] *Panegyric 20*, 12.21–5, 14.15–22.   [63] *Panegyric 22*, 192.32–193.3.

[64] *Cod. Paris. Gr. 1189*, fols. 219α–β (*Panegyric 28*).

[65] *Panegyric 30*, 226.33–227.10, 225.16–226.2.   [66] *Panegyric 29*, 149.10–16.

[67] *Cod. Paris. Gr. 1189*, fol. 84α (*Panegyric 11*).

[68] *Panegyric 2*, 134.11–16, 134.16–38 and 136.1–4.

[69] *Panegyric 13*, 139.20–35. On *hēsychia* see Part 2, Introduction, note 1.

directs him to make the sign of the cross towards his pursuers, upon which they all fall ill.[70] St Sabas, too, was once chased by five Arabs, who gave up the pursuit when the earth opened and swallowed one of them.[71]

Miracles

In hagiographical narratives miracles cannot always be clearly distinguished from divine signs of the kind just mentioned, through which God reveals the holiness of a man, sometimes by manifesting that he is divinely protected. The early Saint performed his miracles in the desert and then interrupted his solitude and moved back into the world. Then, miracles poured forth with great frequency and diversity. The first of these miracles often functioned as a sign, revealing to the world the man's holy status.[72] In *Lives* from the ninth to the eleventh century, Saints seem to perform fewer miracles of curing, resurrection or subsistence, while on the other hand foreseeing the future is a theme which appears more frequently than before.[73] In the twelfth and thirteenth century the scarcity of resurrectory or subsistence miracles becomes striking; while curative miracles are few but do persist.[74] Broadly speaking, there appears to be a shift in both the nature and the objective of the miracle; from the early position of the holy man apparently performing the miracle himself, to a situation whereby God performs miracles about the person of the holy man in a manifestation of divine protection of the holy man or in a manifestation of the latter's sanctity.[75] The subject of God's grace appears to have been by and large moved from man to the holy man; the obvious performer of the miracle to have shifted from holy man to God.

Most of Neophytos' Saints are recorded as having performed miracles while alive, with the exceptions of Sts Theosebios, Stephen, Gennadios, John the Baptist and Marina. Of these, again, the relics at least of Theosebios, Stephen and Gennadios become a source of miracles after their death.

---

[70] *Panegyric 17*, 214.1–12.
[71] *Cod. Paris. Gr. 1189*, fols. 174α–175β (*Panegyric 23*).　　[72] Patlagean (1968: 116).
[73] Patlagean (1981b: 95). For post-ninth-century examples of foresight see *Life* of St Meletios the Younger, 49–69, 11–39. Especially common is foresight by the holy man of his own death. See, e.g., *Life* of St Symeōn the New Theologian, 178–80, para. 125; *Enkōmion* of Athanasios for St Christodoulos of Patmos, para. 26, and see also Branouse (1966: 61); *Life* of St Meletios the Confessor, 622.
[74] E.g., *Life* of St Symeōn the New Theologian, 166, paras. 118–78, 124; 206, paras. 141–228, 152 (both before and after his death); *Life* of St Cyril Phileōtēs, 136, chs. 30, 32 (while alive); *Life* of St Christodoulos of Patmos, para. 15; *Enkōmion* of Athanasios for St Christodoulos of Patmos, paras. 25, 30–2; *Enkōmion* of Theodosios for St Christodoulos of Patmos, paras. 11–42; and see also Branouse (1966: 53, 61–2, 71–5) (miracles include subsistence miracles); *Life* of St Meletios the Younger, 49–69, 11–39; *Life* of St Leontios of Jerusalem, 399–403, 421ff.; *Life* of St Meletios the Confessor, 618, 623–4.
[75] See, e.g., Munitiz (1981: 166–7), referring to Blemmydēs.

But what is important is that for Neophytos the performance of miracles is not a prerequisite for sanctity but a mere proof of it. The Recluse is once more following a long hagiographical tradition, whereby, in the words of Peter Brown, 'the miracle condenses and validates a situation built up by more discreet means'.[76] The proof, again, is of use only to those who may need it to be convinced of the holy man's status, so that – as Neophytos writes – 'his closeness to God can be seen through the miracles performed'.[77] Miracles are, for the Recluse, a manifestation of divine grace, bestowed on the holy man, performed and narrated 'as a confirmation of the grace of God bestowed to the Saints'.[78] It is, in other words, clear that in Neophytos' mind a man does not have to have performed miracles to be deemed holy. A Saint may live and die without having performed a single miracle. Obviously, his life as a Saint becomes more impressive if he has performed spectacular miracles; but if he has not (and by the twelfth century the trend in hagiography was that he would probably have not), this does not detract from his sanctity. Besides, there is always the hope that his relics will become the source of miracles posthumously performed.

The struggle

Essential in the portrait of a Saint is the element of struggle. The Saint lives in a hostile world, and his acquisition of sanctity goes hand in hand with his fight against the forces of evil, a fight in which he eventually triumphs. Such a struggle, always conceived of as essentially a struggle against Evil (the devil), assumes in Neophytos' writings three forms. It appears as completely internalised (a fight of the holy man against his own passions); as a resistance to tyrants and other rulers who are pagan or heretical; or as a direct, often physical, fight against the devil.

Man must first defeat his own passions, his own body, before he achieves sanctity. Even then the fight goes on, for the devil always tries to induce the holy man, through the latter's senses, to fall into sin and thus to be won over by the devil and be lost to God. One of the reasons the theme of flight from the world persisted throughout Byzantine hagiography was precisely because of the belief that man must divorce himself completely from human culture (symbolising the socialised, sensuous man) and return to total solitude and to nature in order to recover his spiritual lost self. The holy man assumes his power 'by going to live in the desert, in close identification with an animal kingdom that stood, in the imagination of his contemporaries, for the opposite pole of all human society'.[79] This opposition

---

[76] Brown (1971b: 87).   [77] *Panegyric 14*, 205.15–17.
[78] *Panegyric 14*, 205.11–12, *Panegyric 12*, 187.2–3, *Panegyric 11*, 179.9.
[79] Brown (1971b: 92).

between nature and culture (the first revisited, the second renounced by the holy man) is expressed in the rejection of human company, the rejection or near rejection of clothing, the rejection of anything that might care for or beautify the body, the rejection, above all, of even what might sustain the body: abstinence from food is an essential part of *ascesis*. Peter Brown draws attention to how closely abstinence from food is linked to the rejection of kin and village ties, especially in the peasant societies of the Middle and the Near East, where these have always been expressed by the gesture of eating.[80] Evelyne Patlagean draws attention to the distinction made by Lévi-Strauss between the opposites of uncultivated, uncooked food on the one hand and cooked food on the other, an opposition essentially between nature and culture. She links abstinence from food with abstinence from sex and sees both of them as part of the holy man's rejection of culture and withdrawal into nature. The Saint's diet is composed of uncooked, uncultivated food, meat (especially associated with urban life) never forming part of it, and is, further, reduced to the bare minimum needed to keep the body alive. The ultimate version of the model is encountered in the *Life* of St Symeōn the Younger, in which the holy man has ceased to receive any food at all.[81]

As we saw earlier, Neophytos depicted St Nicholas as abstaining from food since he was born, accepting milk only every Wednesday and Friday evening; and the ten-year-old St Sabas as practising abstinence from food as a means of self-control.[82] St Theosebios, we read, took care to eat only as much as was necessary to keep him alive, 'for he was not bodiless, so as to be able to go completely without food'. He used to give his food to passers-by or to the birds.[83] The owner of the vineyard where St Polychronios worked realised that his labourer was a holy man when he noticed that even during days of hard labour St Polychronios would only eat very little once every two or three days.[84] St Hilariōn ate only once a day, and very little: his diet was composed of pulses or some vegetables. He ate so little that he eventually became quite ill, but persisted in his abstinence, only compromising to take bread after a few years and, when he became sixty years old, some oil, too.[85]

Abstinence from food is, thus, one of the means of *ascesis*, the aim being

---

[80] *Ibid.* 91–2.
[81] Patlagean (1968: 113–15); Lévi-Strauss (1949: esp. Introduction; 1965). Eleventh- to thirteenth-century *Lives* continued to emphasise the holy man's fasting habits, performed as part of his *ascesis*. See, e.g., *Life* of St Symeōn the New Theologian, 34, para. 25; 38, para. 28; *Life* of Cyril Phileōtēs, ch. 41, paras. 1–5; *Life* of Christodoulos of Patmos, especially para. 8, and see Branouse (1966: 51); *Life* of St Meletios the Younger, 6–7; *Life* of St Leontios of Jerusalem, 382–3; *Life* of St Meletios the Confessor, 614, 620.
[82] *Panegyric 24*, 393.28–394.6; *Cod. Paris, Gr. 1189*, fol. 174β (*Panegyric 23*).
[83] *Panegyric 12*, 183.25–184.3.
[84] *Panegyric 10*, 176.7–14.   [85] *Panegyric 13*, 139.6–12.

to defeat the body and every evil thing that may come from it. Sexual abstinence is, of course, also always practised by the Saint.[86] This is so much taken for granted by the Byzantine hagiographers that it is usually not even mentioned, except in particularly striking cases. Thus, Neophytos tells us that Andronikos and Athanasia became Saints because they fought human passion successfully, having transformed their husband-and-wife relationship into one of brother and sister.[87] The same goes for St Theosebios who, while married, remained a virgin and lived with his wife like brother and sister.[88]

Fighting against one's own passions is one of the ways in which the devil is fought. The struggle in this case is completely internalised. By contrast, the fight against evil may often mean that the holy man must fight against other people, people who have become instruments of the devil. Blemmydēs' auto-hagiography overflows with instances of such fighting against people who, incited by the devil, act to destroy him.[89] More usually, however, this fight takes the form of resistance to tyrants or rulers who are pagan or heretical. It is a resistance which may lead to the physical death of the Saint and at the same time, of course, to his acquisition of spiritual eternal life. The theme of martyrdom is am ongst the earliest encountered, and though it became much less freque itly used after the triumph of Christianity, it never ceased to be present in Byzantine hagiography. For instance, in the thirteenth century St Meletios the Confessor becomes such a martyr; while shortly after Neophytos' death Cyprus itself provided thirteen martyrs in the person of the thirteen Kantariōtissa monks who preferred to die rather than embrace Latin dogma.[90]

A number of Neophytos' Saints are martyrs: Mamas, Polychronios, Dēmētrios, Stephen, Marina, John the Baptist, John Chrysostom.[91] The distinction of whether the enemy is a pagan (as in the case of Sts Mamas,

---

[86] On Byzantine conceptions of sexuality, with specific reference to Neophytos, see Galatariotou (1989).

[87] *Panegyric 11*, 180.8–9.

[88] *Panegyric 12*, 185.14–18. Cf. *Life* of St Cyril Phileōtēs, ch. 6, para. 1. For other Neophytic examples of celibate matrimony see Galatariotou (1989: 132).

[89] *Life* of Nikēphoros Blemmydēs, 8–16, paras. 13–26; 27, para. 49.8–15; 29, para. 54; 29–30, para. 56; 31–2, paras. 59, 60, 61; 35–6, para. 71; 12, para. 19; 76, para. 68.1–2.

[90] St Meletios died over the *filioque* dispute; the Cypriot monks over the *azyma* dispute. See respectively, *Life* of St Meletios the Confessor, 617–22; *Martyrion Kypriōn* (also in Sathas, II, 20–39). St Hilariōn of Moglena also fought against heretics (Manicheans, Paulicians, Bogomils) and came very near to being stoned by them: *Life* of St Hilariōn of Moglena, and Turdeanu (1947: 83). Note that Blemmydēs, too, in presenting his fights against opponents is very careful to establish his firm Orthodox, anti-Latin, anti-Armenian and generally anti-heretical position: *Life* of Nikēphoros Blemmydēs, 57–63, paras. 25–40; 67–73, paras. 50–60; 73–5, paras. 61–6; 76–9, paras. 66–74.

[91] St John Chrysostom met a 'natural' death, but, as his *Life* makes abundantly clear, one which was caused largely by his deliberate maltreatment by his enemies.

Dēmētrios, Stephen, Marina, John the Baptist) or a Christian heretic (Sts Polychronios, Chrysostom) is made, but casually: the matter is polarised to the point where every non-Orthodox is a potential enemy. Whether he is a pagan, a heretic or a babarian is for Neophytos a point of finer definition and one which is somewhat irrelevant. St Polychronios is arrested, tortured and executed by the 'God-fighting and impious emperors' who, according to Neophytos, ruled after the death of Constantine the Great and who fought against the Orthodox.[92] St John Chrysostom is beleaguered by the heretical empress Eudoxia;[93] while St Gennadios is praised for having been a 'supporter of the Orthodox' during the reign of 'Anastasios the heretic'.[94] A number of Saints are addressed in phrases similar to that of 'the leader of the correct dogmas' (for St John the Almsgiver),[95] while others are depicted as actively propagating the Orthodox faith. St Dēmētrios is arrested and martyred because of his many conversions of pagans to Christianity.[96] St Arkadios is praised for upholding the Orthodox faith and for fighting against those 'of evil faith'.[97] St Nicholas takes part in an anti-pagan campaign launched during the reign of Constantine the Great, razing to the ground pagan temples. He also wages war against the heretics, taking part in the Oecumenical Synod against the Arians.[98] St Sabas, too, is invited by patriarchs to take part in the disputes concerning the heresies of Origen and Nonnos. He twice travels to Constantinople for this matter: Neophytos assures us that the emperors Anastasios and Justinian were both enlightened by St Sabas to move against the heretics.[99]

The fight for the Orthodox and against the non-Orthodox is, of course, essentially conceived of as a fight for Good and against Evil. Nowhere is this fight more dramatically illustrated than in the depictions of direct, often physical, fighting between the holy man and the devil. In Neophytos' writings such instances appear in his stories of Sts Hilariōn, Arkadios, Alypios, Sabas and Nicholas. The fight against demons was a theme already well established by early hagiography. In her study of this hagiography Evelyne Patlagean distinguishes three 'models' in its structure: the demonic, the ascetic and the moral model. She cites the demonic model as the one most deeply rooted in the unconscious, all three models representing three levels of the relationship of man and the world – a relationship always seen in terms of an attack which the holy man fights off through the power of sanctity. Referring to the demonic model, she describes how through demonic aggression are defined all the possible negative relations between

[92] *Panegyric 10*, 176.25–177.10.   [93] *Panegyric 20*, 11.35–14.6, 15.7–9, 16.7–19.
[94] *Panegyric 30*, 221.10, 222.11–20.   [95] *Panegyric 29*, 158.8.
[96] *Panegyric 15*, 49.20–9.   [97] *Panegyric 14*, 201.29–202.10.
[98] *Panegyric 24*, 403.3–29.   [99] *Cod. Paris. Gr. 1189*, fols. 176β–177α (*Panegyric 23*).

man and the world.[100] It is not surprising to find a theme of such all-embracing, fundamental symbolic significance persisting throughout Byzantine hagiography. Indeed, the symbolic significance of the depictions of the struggle between holy man and the devil was not one of which the Byzantines were consciously aware. For them, the demons were not abstract representations and symbols of evil, but rather real and tangible beings, who carried out attacks which were not only moral and mental but also physical. In the early *Lives* we find demons pushing St Sabas into the Dead Sea.[101] St Symeōn the Stylite is attacked by demons in the form of fantastic birds, while later he has to fight off a hand which pulls him down into the darkness.[102] After the ninth century, Saints' *Lives* continue to refer to physical attacks by demons against the holy man. Such examples are provided, for instance, by the eleventh-century *Lives* of St Symeōn the New Theologian and of St Cyril Phileōtēs, and the twelfth-century *Life* of St Leontios of Jerusalem.[103] Amongst Neophytos' Saints, St Alypios is also physically attacked by demons, who at one point resort to throwing stones at him, hitting him on the shoulder.[104]

Neophytos' story of St Alypios is well worth closer study because of the many layers of significance which it contains. Neophytos writes that when St Alypios decided to become an *hēsychastēs*, he chose to settle near a village which was 'full of Greek tombs and a much loved home of a multitude of demons'. A pagan statue of a beastly God (half bull, half lion) stood on a column, in the midst of the tombs. St Alypios demolished the statue and took up residence himself on the column. The battle which followed between the demons and St Alypios is described as one without cease, he fighting to throw them out of the village, they fighting to oust him and to regain their authority over the place. The battle is, further, described in physical terms, St Alypios being portrayed as 'armed with the armoury of God and the sword of the Holy Ghost'. When a stone, cast by the demons, hits St Alypios, he become furious: he tells the demons that they were really doing him a favour to stone him to death, for he would then gain eternal life, like St Stephen; and to prove his point, he demolishes the small wooden cage which he had constructed at the top of the column, so as to remain without any physical protection at all. This is the point at which the demons despair, concede defeat, and leave.[105]

[100] Patlagean (1968: 112–17).
[101] *Life* of St Sabas, 106.20–107.5; and see Patlagean (1968: 115).
[102] *Life* of St Symeōn the Stylite, para. 39; Patlagean (1968: 115).
[103] *Life* of St Symeōn the New Theologian, 12–14; 20–2, para. 13; 22–6, paras. 14–16; 154–6, para. 122; *Life* of St Leontios of Jerusalem, 399–402; *Life* of St Cyril Phileōtēs, chs. 53–4.
[104] *Panegyric 22*, 190.34–191.7.
[105] *Panegyric 22*, 190.5–191.15. Cf. the twelfth-century story of St Christodoulos of Patmos, who crashes a statue of Artemis in Patmos and sets up his monastery in its place: *Life* of St Christodoulos of Patmos, para. 14; see also Branouse (1966: 52 and note 2).

The whole story of St Alypios is built around a series of structural and symbolic oppositions: on the one hand, the tombs (death), demons, paganism, presided over by a bestial, irrational (*alogos*) god; on the other, St Alypios, demolishing the *alogos* god, taking its place as a new authority, offering the eternal life of Christianity as opposed to the death of paganism. The story can easily be seen as one depicting a power struggle. In this respect, St Alypios' story echoes the early days of Christianity, when it still had to fight to establish its authority over that of paganism. Further, it denotes the Christian belief in the victory of the spiritual over the bestial, the rational (*logikon*) over the irrational (*alogon*). It is worth pointing out, in this respect, that it is by argument, persuasion, force of words, that St Alypios achieves his final victory: the demons leave defeated after his furious words to them. The victory is thus not simply the victory of one man against demons, but that of the Orthodox faith against paganism, of the *logikon* against the *alogon*, of the intellectual and the spiritual against the bestial. It is the outcome of a power struggle between competing authorities that Alypios' story depicts, and the triumph of Christianity in this battle is seen as a victory of life over death.

This is the essence of every single fight between the holy man and the devil. It obviously assumes different forms depending on the context in which it is set. For example, an old variation of the theme is that of exorcism, which goes back to the days of early hagiography, very substantially diminishing after the ninth century. Peter Brown finds that the performance of exorcism of evil by the holy man is built 'on the theme of violence and authority. By exorcism, the holy man asserts the authority of his god over the demonic in the possessed . . . It is a dramatic articulation of the idea of the power of the holy man.'[106] A number of Neophytos' Saints are depicted performing exorcisms, often in scenes of great violence. In some of the exorcisms performed by St Hilariōn of men possessed by demons, the holy man violently attacks the afflicted person until the demon leaves his body.[107] St Sabas also exorcises an unclean spirit from the body of a young woman.[108] Through exorcism, the holy man forcefully ousts a demon from a person or even a beast (St Hilariōn exorcises a demon from a camel[109]); but quite often, exorcism also takes the form of ousting demons from a place: St Alypios, for instance, exorcises a whole village; St Sabas too, like St Alypios – though less dramatically – ousts a host of demons from a mountain near his *lavra*.[110] The *Life* of St Nicholas is particularly rich in such examples. In one instance, a demon had resided in a huge cypress tree, killing any person who

---

[106] Brown (1971b: 88–9).   [107] *Panegyric 13*, 141.7–24.
[108] *Cod. Paris. Gr. 1189*, fol. 177α (*Panegyric 23*).   [109] *Panegyric 13*, 142.22–3.
[110] *Cod. Paris. Gr 1189*, fol. 177β (*Panegyric 23*).

tried to cut the tree down. St Nicholas, called to exorcise the spirit, cuts the tree with his own hands and throws the demon out. Before leaving, the demon engages in a conversation with St Nicholas, lamenting his defeat, being rebuked by the Saint and warned by him never to dare take up residence anywhere near Lycia again. In another instance St Nicholas exorcises a demon who had resided in a water source.[111]

Apart from straightforward exorcisms the holy man also performs curative miracles, often of illness induced by the devil: so, in Neophytos' writings, do St Hilariōn and St Nicholas.[112] The holy man also has the power to dissolve works of the devil, such as magic spells (St Hilariōn), causing shipwrecks (St Nicholas), turning unaware persons against goodness or against the Saint himself (St John the Almsgiver, St Nicholas).[113] Often, the holy man will go out of his way to meet the devil in order to fight him: St Alypios chooses the place for his *ascesis* precisely because demons live there; St Nicholas razes a temple to the ground because he knows it to be full of demons; when St Hilariōn reaches Cyprus he deliberately chooses to stay near a pagan temple 'full of demons'.[114] The mere sight of a Saint is enough to set demons fleeing: at the transportation of St Stephen's relics at Constantinople, Neophytos writes, angels sung while demons shrieked: 'alas! we are being whipped when Stephen passes by'.[115]

The battle of the holy man against the devil is, thus, both a perpetual one (continued throughout the Saint's life and even posthumously) and one in which the holy man is victorious – hence, after all, his holiness. St Mamas is thus characterised by Neophytos as the healer of 'demonic wounds'; St Alypios as a 'victor over the demons'; St Sabas as a fighter 'against passions and demons', a 'mighty victor over visible and invisible enemies'; St Nicholas as a 'destroyer of demons'.[116] The battle is one of life and death. When St Peter and St Paul set out to spread the Gospel, Neophytos writes, it is in order to oust the devil from earth that they do so: the Recluse likens the devil to a crow which devours human flesh.[117] Ultimately, Christ's triumph is described as one 'over Hadēs and death; over the devil and his company'[118]. Clearly, the last four are identical, and the holy man does nothing other than continue Christ's work.

111 *Panegyric 24*, 396.18–398.4.
112 Respectively, *Panegyric 13*, 140.32–141.19, 142.4–21, 142.27–143.8, 145.11–12, *Panegyric 24*, 414.10–25.
113 Respectively, *Panegyric 13*, 141.25–142.3, 142.27–143.8; *Panegyric 24*, 400.34–401.6, 401.26–402.5; *Panegyric 29*, 153.2–30, *Panegyric 24*, 399.17–400.5.
114 *Panegyric 24*, 403.3–22; *Panegyric 13*, 145.11–19.
115 *Cod. Paris. Gr. 1189*, fol. 219α (*Panegyric 28*).
116 Respectively, *Panegyric 2*, 133.3–4; *Panegyric 22*, 194.5–6; *Cod. Paris. Gr. 1189*, fol. 179β (*Panegyric 23*); *Panegyric 24*, 392.8, 392.19, 393.5–6.
117 *Cod. Lesb. Leim. 2*, fol. 316β (*Homily 7*).
118 *Cod. Lesb. Leim. 2*, fol. 310β (*Homily 6*).

Conclusions

By now, the basic structure of Neophytos' Saints' stories has emerged. The basic structure of Neophytos' conception of sanctity has also emerged with it, for it is composed of the same themes which we have seen him utilise in his depictions of holy men and women. What in Neophytos' mind constituted the structurally essential thematic components of sanctity can be summarised in the following brief list.

An initial act of withdrawal from the world (*anachōrēsis*), sometimes objected to by the family or, if the holy man is already in a monastery, by the abbot. This may be followed by a subsequent flight, from fame, when the latter disturbs the holy man's *hēsychia*. A passage into sanctity, which is sometimes clearly defined but more frequently gradual and unspecified in time. This is seen both as a result of the holy man's ascetic life (which includes abstinence from food and sex); but also, very frequently, as a result of the activation of God's plans. The last element is at times so emphatically present as to amount to a depiction of predestination. The manifestation of miracles is not very frequent and it is clearly understood to be a proof of, but not a prerequisite for, sanctity. More important are divine signs, showing protection of the holy man by God, or simply revealing the Saint's holy status to the world. Finally, a continuous fight against the devil, in which the holy man eventually triumphs.

As comparison of Neophytos' hagiography with other Byzantine and early Christian examples of the *genre* clearly shows, what the Recluse personally understood to be the essential components of sanctity would also be readily recognised as such by the members of his society. This is so because Neophytos' conception of sanctity was built out of elements which formed part of a larger body of written and oral hagiographical traditions – traditions which belonged to the common cultural heritage of the society of which the Recluse was a member.[119]

[119] For a discussion of the literary and wider cultural context of Neophytos' hagiographical narratives see earlier, ch. 2.

5   The self-proclaimed holy man

Introduction

Two factors concerning sanctification in Byzantium in the twelfth and early thirteenth centuries are particularly striking, and suggest that for one who wished to be a Saint these were not the most propitious of times. First, there is a relative absence of hagiography. H.-G. Beck has rightly characterised the period of the Komnēnian dynasty (1081–1185) as 'hagiographically a disappointment';[1] and the same is true of the rest of the twelfth and, even more so, of the early thirteenth century. The Byzantine Saint only reappears on the scene with any frequency with the reign of Michael VIII Palaiologos (1259–82), and then within quite a different context.[2] Second, the relative absence of hagiography co-exists uneasily with a number of extremely negative contemporary accounts concerning men who claimed to be Saints. In the letters of John Tzetzēs, the commentaries of Theodore Balsamōn, the rhetorical works of Eustathios of Thessalonikē or the *History* of Nikētas Chōniatēs, the men who posed as holy men in the great cities of Byzantium are treated almost invariably with contempt. They are portrayed as superfluous at best, as greedy and fraudulent at worst.[3]

We must, of course, treat such evidence with caution. Concerning the negative accounts, it must be remembered that they refer to the presence of fraudulent aspiring holy men as an urban phenomenon; and that they were all written by highly placed intellectuals. Paul Magdalino has shrewdly detected the presence of snobbery and xenophobia in these accounts; and he

---

[1] Beck (1959: 271).   [2] Macrides (1981).
[3] Respectively, Tzetzēs, 25–7 (no. 14), 75–7 (no. 55), 79–84 (no. 57), 150–2 (no. 104); Balsamōn commenting on canons 42 and 60 of the Council in Trullo: *MPG*, 137, cols. 665, 716; Eustathios, *Opuscula*, 'De simulatione', 88–98, esp. 94ff.; and also 'Ad stylitam quendam Thessalonicensem', 182–96; Chōniatēs, *Historia*, 383.86–.6, 448.15–450.57, 558.27–40. See Magdalino (1981; also 1987: 37); Kazhdan and Wharton Epstein (1985: 92–5).

has suggested that the popularity of the twelfth-century holy men – especially with the aristocracy – made them suspect to the emperor and to the intellectuals, who thus had a vested interest in downgrading them.[4] Further, it may well be that the condemnation of those who fraudulently posed as holy sprang at least partly out of a sense of deep reverence for those deemed to be truly holy; that it was profound respect for the Saints that gave birth to the contempt and anger directed against the urban 'holy' *poseurs*, whose presence threatened to compromise the very idea of sanctity. If this feeling informs the texts, for instance, of Eustathios of Thessalonikē or of Theodore Balsamōn, then such contemporary accounts might be taken to represent not an attack against the idea of contemporary sanctity, but an attempt to defend it. Nevertheless, the presence of these accounts at the very least implies that claims of sanctity were viewed with a critical eye by a sector of the population; and Neophytos' own evidence suggests that this critical eye also operated beyond the urban world of Constantinople and Thessalonikē.[5]

The lack of hagiography is evidentially less ambivalent: there seems to be no good reason for not treating the absence of Saints' *Lives* as indicative of an absence of Saints. Particularly so, since hagiography, the most important *genre* of Byzantine popular literature, largly failed to materialise in what was otherwise one of the most flourishing periods of Byzantine literature;[6] and one noted for its interest in popular and popularising literature. It seems, therefore, reasonable to conclude that, compared with other periods, the twelfth and early thirteenth centuries produced fewer men who were ac-knowledged by their contemporaries as holy; or at the very least that fewer cults of those recognised as holy survived their subjects' deaths.

The question before us is: how did Neophytos, who lived in precisely this period, manage to achieve the status of a Saint and to become the focus of a cult still alive to this day? Part of the answer lies in Neophytos' conception of sanctity and of himself as a partaker of it. The Recluse's conception of sanctity has been reconstructed through the investigation of the structure of his own Saints' stories. I now propose to examine how Neophytos came to believe himself to be a Saint, and how he proceeded with the very delicate business of propagating his belief in his own sanctity.

---

[4] Magdalino (1981). See also Kazhdan (1984: 50); Morris (1984: 114).
[5] See later, e.g. pp. 163–7.
[6] Magdalino (1987: 37). Seel also Kazhdan and Franklin (1984: 50).

The writings

Neophytos, the chosen one

In his own Saints' stories Neophytos had often described the passage into sanctity within a context of predestination, depicting the Saints as following a path set out by God; or as being directed by God, at a crucial time in their lives, towards sanctity. On a number of occasions, Neophytos implies that this also formed part of his own experience of life. When, as a young monk, he witnessed the sudden deaths of fellow monks in the monastery of Koutsovendēs, he writes that he was shaken by the sudden realisation of the transitory nature of human life. His reaction was to beg his abbot to allow him to become a hermit on the nearby mountain 'in order to live on it with as much fortitude as divine providence may extend to me'.[7] Many years later, writing to his brother John about the adventures surrounding the building of the Recluse's new cell (the upper *enkleistra*), he asks John to come and visit this cell 'so that you too, like many others, will glorify God in Trinity',[8] as though it was God's decision that that cell should be built. In his directions to his monks concerning his burial Neophytos asks them to build up the entrance to his tomb and then cover the wall with a painting of 'whatever God brings to your mind',[9] apparently believing that God would extend his caring for Neophytos down to this last detail. But these are mere hints, and, taken on their own, could be read as simple expressions of piety. So, too, could statements of Neophytos' to the effect that he was aided by God on specific occasions during his life, such as when, 'with God's most excellent goodwill and aid', he ran away from home to the monastery; or that nobody knew of his thoughts to do so, except for 'God, who bestowed them on me'.[10]

All such statements, however, read quite differently when placed within the context of other, more numerous passages, in which the idea that Neophytos' own life followed a pattern set out by God is no longer implied but quite clearly stated. Neophytos writes, for example, in his *Typikon* that God stopped him from getting involved in the worries and burdens of the married layman's life (a clear parallel to which is found in the Recluse's *Life* of St John the Almsgiver). Further, he writes that God acquainted him with the sudden changes of life and the turns of fortune almost from birth (*ek*

---

[7] *Cod. Athen. 522*, fols. 384α–385α.   [8] *Letter 1*, 152.31–.32.
[9] *Typikon*, 103.5–.8.   [10] *Ibid.*, respectively 75.4–5; 74.32–3.

prōtēs balbidos).[11] We have already encountered in Neophytos' writings both the phraseology and the idea of such predestination since infancy: in his narratives concerning Saints such as Polychronios, Sabas and Nicholas.

Referring to his illiteracy, his subsequent acquisition of literacy and his becoming a hermit, Neophytos states that he only became 'what God had wished to make of me'.[12] The Recluse describes how, seven years after his entry to the monastery of Koutsovendēs, he wandered in the Palestinian deserts hoping to find a hermit and live with him, but failed to do so. He then had a vision, through which God's plan was revealed to him: he would achieve sanctity in another place and not in Palestine. He thus returned to Cyprus, thinking, he tells us, that perhaps God's desire that he should be a hermit could be fulfilled on the mountain of Koutsovendēs.[13] Neophytos' abbot, however, did not allow him to become a hermit. (The objection of the abbot, as much as the earlier objection of Neophytos' family to his plans are, as we have seen earlier, part of a well-established hagiographical *topos* which Neophytos himself had also used in his hagiography.)[14] This objection, Neophytos informs us, was only 'because God, who foresees everything, did not wish this to happen'.[15] He thus left Koutsovendēs and arrived at Paphos, hoping to go by ship to Mount Latros.[16] Imprisoned and robbed at Paphos, he was forced, in the absence of fare money, to remain in Cyprus. Neophytos stresses that he tells this story only in order to show how 'God extended to me this gift of this precipice and this smallest of caves', a place 'which before, I did not know at all'.[17] In his tract entitled *Sign of God*, the Recluse also presents his settlement in the *enkleistra* as part of a divine plan: he thanks 'God, who created me, and took me away from the dizziness, the

[11] *Typikon*, 74.8–9; *Panegyric 29*, 149.10–16.   [12] *Panegyric 20*, 9.17–18.
[13] *Typikon*, 76.1–.15.
[14] The theme of a difficulty presented to, and then overcome by, the holy man is also encountered frequently in post-ninth-century hagiography: e.g., St Symeōn the New Theologian's spiritual father stopped him from becoming a monk because of his tender age (St Symeōn was fourteen years old). Neophytos' abbot objected to his becoming a hermit for the same reason. St Meletios the Confessor's abbot objected to his plans of leaving the monastery until a vision directed him to let St Meletios go. See *Life* of Symeōn the New Theologian, 6, 10; *Life* of St Meletios the Confessor, 614; and see earlier, ch. 4, pp. 78–9, for illustrations of this theme of opposition presented by the Saint's family. Traditionally, individual monks were only exceptionally allowed to leave the *koinobion* and live as hermits, supported by the monastery: the right to live as a hermit was regarded as a particularly coveted accolade, won only after the monk had proved through years of *ascesis* his ability to live the solitary life. The Council in Trullo laid down as a bare minimum requirement three years' life in a *koinobion* and, of course, the abbot's consent. See Mansi XI, 964; and Rodley (1985: 238).
[15] *Typikon*, 76.16–17.
[16] The monastic centre of Latmos on the south-western coast of Anatolia was famous at least from the mid-ninth century. The first to settle there were probably refugee monks fleeing the Arab advance in the seventh century. The Mount had both *koinobia* and hermitages. See Wiegand (1913, III, i, 178—80); Rodley (1985: 238).
[17] *Typikon*, 76.16–31.

impurity, the terrible slavery and sea storm [of a layman's life], and anchored me, as if in some haven, in this precipice and in this *enkleistra*; and having turned it from an obscure place to a known one', God gave it to Neophytos – who, he assures us, in turn delivered it back to God's hands.[18] Likewise, the Recluse writes in his *Typikon* that he 'received' the *enkleistra* from God: 'For He extended it to me, deserted, and He again, embellished it as he wished'.[19] Neophytos tells us that some time after his settlement in his cell he heard a 'honey-dripping and strange and unusual voice', which reminded him not to forget what the vision in the desert had promised him.[20] Neophytos' ascent to his upper cell in 1197 is even more strongly imbued with God's intervention: 'It was, I believe, the decision of God first, and then of myself, to move higher up on the precipice, to ascend, with God's help'.[21] Having named his upper cell 'New Sion', Neophytos characterised it as 'the complete creation of God's providence'.[22]

Neophytos' belief that throughout his life he was guided by God, and that his life formed part of a divine plan, was a belief which grew gradually in him. As years went by, he came to believe in his preordainment. A fascinating example of how Neophytos' subjective interpretation – through the form of memory – of exactly the same facts changed through the years is provided by a comparison of three passages from his writings. In all three, Neophytos refers to his initial *anachōrēsis*: his flight from home in 1152 and his entry into the monastery of St John Chrysostom at Koutsovendēs.

The first passage comes from Neophytos' *Interpretation of the Commandments*. Neophytos explains that he was not given over by his parents 'to even a single day's learning of the alphabet'; and 'witnesses to my words', he continues, 'are not only my home town, but also the monastery of Chrysostom at Koutsovendēs, which received me, I having left my parental home'.[23]

The work from which this passage derives dates from 1176. The dry, matter of fact account of Neophytos' departure from home and entry into the monastery of Koutsovendēs assumes quite a different form when we next meet it, in 1197. By then, Neophytos had already been in the *enkleistra* since 1160, and had by now established fame as a recluse, a writer of Panegyrics, a man of authority, probably – already – a holy man.[24] Here is how he now remembers his departure: 'for, when some divine enlightenment from above urged me to leave the vanity of the worldly life and to direct my humble feet to the straight path and to the road of peace, of the only life; I secretly escaped parents and seven siblings, male and female, and

[18] *Sign of God*, 148.35–149.8.   [19] *Typikon*, 73.25–6.   [20] *Ibid.*, 77.19–22.
[21] *Sign of God*, 139.12–14.   [22] *Typikon*, 90.16–17.
[23] *Cod. Coisl. Gr. 287*, fols. 180β–181α.   [24] See later, Part 3, esp. ch. 7.

arrived at a holy monastery'.[25] In this account, twenty-one years on, what was before described as 'parental home' is now made emotionally more powerful by Neophytos' reference to his family of parents and seven brothers and sisters, so that the contrast between what Neophytos left behind him and the monastic life which he embraced becomes sharpened. Further, and more importantly, the divine makes a dramatic appearance. We read that Neophytos received some form of divine enlightenment, after which he secretly left home and directed himself to Koutsovendēs.

By 1214 when, in old age, Neophytos revised his *Typikon*, we encounter a third version of his departure from home and his entry into monasticism. The differences now are a marked emphasis on divine presence, not merely enlightening or pointing the way, but actually directing Neophytos 'from birth, almost' into monasticism. No longer contained in brief accounts, in what he evidently believed to be his last chance to put his life down in writing Neophytos uses thirteen folios in his *Typikon* to describe his life from birth and up to his entry and first years in the monastery of Kout-sovendēs. How does the eighty-year-old recluse now remember those far-away years? He now writes that God 'not only prevented me from becoming bound under the shackle and yoke of knavish life, but He further acquainted me almost from birth with its difficulty and with perceiving its sudden changes'.[26] We now read that while still a young lad in the village of Lefkara Neophytos had profound thoughts about the snares and vanity of worldly life, about death and the need for salvation. 'But these thoughts and ponderings were not of my youth and boorishness, but the work of certain divine grace and providence – this I artlessly assert in writing and in speech, and *God is my witness, I am telling the truth, I am not lying.*'[27] He had thoughts, he tells us, of leaving the world, and, had it been possible, he would have followed many a beggar who came knocking at his father's door, since he considered the beggar's life to be the better one. 'But no-one knew of these thoughts of mine, except God, Who bestowed them on me.' When his unsuspecting parents arranged a marriage for him, Neophytos, 'with God's most excellent goodwill and aid',[28] fled from home. There is no point, he says, in lingering on the havoc that was wreaked by parents, neighbours and relatives, who combed the island for two months until they found the runaway and brought him back to the village. Nor, Neophytos writes, is there any need to dwell on how it took him another two months of arguing his case until he finally succeeded in breaking the marriage contracts; 'but this I shall briefly say, that as the Lord wanted, so it happened'.[29]

[25] *Hexaēmeros*, 168.26–30.

[26] *Typikon*, 74.7–10.   [27] *Ibid.*, 74.18–22.   [28] *Ibid.*, 74.23–75.7.

[29] *Ibid.*, 75.7–12. The full passage is as follows: 'It seems to me right to state summarily, for the benefit of those who might wish to know, something of my life, and to thus urge the souls

This is a far more dramatic account than the previous one of 1197. Now God appears not simply to have enlightened Neophytos when he was eighteen, but to have guided him almost from the cradle. Not only are Neophytos' actions carried out by the will and help of God, but his very thoughts are no longer his own, but God's. Again, the difficulty of the severance of the bonds of lay kinship are here emphasised more than ever, since they now involve not the 'paternal home' of the 1176 account, nor the parents and seven brothers and sisters of that of 1197, but relatives, neighbours and acquaintances, plus a betrothed girl and – by implication – her own parents, relatives and acquaintances. Further, other dramatic elements have been added: the forceful return home, the fight and no longer unopposed flight, and the eventual success of Neophytos in overcoming the difficulties and earning the right to be a monk.

The changes from the first to the second and then to the third account witness the growth of Neophytos' belief in the involvement of the divine in his life. In the first account the divine is absent, and Neophytos invokes as his

of some God-loving people towards glorifying God; Who not only prevented me from becoming bound under the shackle and yoke of knavish life, but He further acquainted me almost from birth with its difficulty and with perceiving its sudden changes. For, one man lamented for the sudden occurrence of misfortune; another cried for the untimely death of his child; yet another, having fathered many children, was oppressed by poverty; another, while being rich and illustrious, suddenly fell upon penury, or death came to denude him of every happiness, and his good life was suddenly turned to a difficult one, laments and violent sobbing now filling the but recently happy household. Another, from honour and dignity fell into dishonour; another was greatly oppressed because of the ruthlessness of unsympathetic taxmen; and yet another lamented for a misfortune that unexpectedly hit him. Seeing all this, I kept thinking that the same will happen to me if I become entangled in worldly life, and that it would be impossible to escape such difficulties. For even if one manages to escape them, still death will come, and – as I hear – another world awaits us – so what benefit will he have derived in the end? But these thoughts and ponderings were not of my youth and boorishness, but the work of certain divine grace and providence – this I artlessly assert in writing and in speech, and *God is my witness, I am telling the truth, I am not lying.* I kept thinking and telling myself that even if I am lost in this world God will see me in the future world, and I shall be found again. And in what I am now saying *I am telling the truth,* in God: that whenever a poor man, a vagabond dressed in rags, came to my paternal house begging for bread, I considered his life to be enviable and blessed, and had this been possible, I would have instantly followed him. But no-one knew of these thoughts of mine except God who bestowed them on me. Thus it was that my parents hurried to get me married, I being then their eighteen-year-old son. Seven months earlier they had made the usual marriage contracts and the engagement, and while they rushed about preparing for the wedding, I rushed about trying to think of ways of fleeing. Then, with God's most excellent goodwill and aid, I left my paternal home secretly and fled to the holy monastery of St Chrysostom on the mountain of Koutsovendēs, considering that the steps of those who would try to track me down would not reach that place. There is no need to speak of the efforts of my parents and neighbours and acquaintances, ans of their searches in all districts of the island; nor do I wish to narrate at great length how, having found me after two months, they dragged me back; and what struggles and battles and persuasion I employed to cancel those marriage contracts; but this I shall briefly say, that as the Lord wanted, so it happened' (*Typikon*, 74.5–75.12 Italicised passages: 1 Tim., 2:7; Phil., 1:8).

witnesses the communities of his village and of the monastery at Kout-sovendēs; in the second, Neophytos appears as a subject of God's grace, enlightened by it; in the third, the divine no longer functions outside Neophytos, but produces his very thoughts: the Recluse's witness is now God. Neophytos has, in the last account, come to partake in divinity. In 1176, the Recluse wrote of a man who left his home and joined a monastery; in 1197, he wrote of a very pious man, one particularly loved by God; in 1214 he wrote, unmistakably, the story of a holy man (indeed, of one born holy) who partakes in God's grace and providence. Since the third account is contained in Neophytos' last will and testament (his *Typikon*), it is clear that it was by this account that he wished to be remembered. And in this account he had invested his life's story with a theme which we have seen him use in his Saints' *Lives*: that of a passage into sanctity as a result of divine plan and predestination.

The Saint in flight

The theme of flight also appears in Neophytos' writings in relation to himself. The Recluse describes his flight from the world as not simply a decision to leave human culture, but also as a decision to escape the bonds of marriage. This is a position which combines elements found in his *Lives* of Sts Hilariōn, John Chrysostom, Alypios and Sabas (a simple decision to leave the world), but also in those of St Nicholas and Sts Andronikos and Athanasia (whose *anachōrēsis* also involves directly a 'divorce' from marriage and parenthood). Neophytos' account of his withdrawal from the world includes two flights from it: he first left home and marriage; he later left the monastery to embrace *hēsychia*. We have already encountered the circumstances of these flights. The theme of the Saint desiring to embrace the life of *hēsychia*, yet not being able to do so immediately because of some obstacle which he eventually overcomes, is one with which Neophytos was familiar. He took care to familiarise his reader with it too by introducing it in his own Saints' *Lives*. In his *Life* of St Alypios, the Saint's plans of fleeing a clergyman's life in order to embrace the solitary life are at first frustrated by his bishop; though the Saint eventually succeeds in overcoming this obstacle.[30] In a parallel even closer to Neophytos' own life's story the Recluse describes how St Sabas, after an eight-year stay in a monastery (we note here Neophytos' seven-year stay), desired to leave it but was not permitted to do so by his abbot. The abbot subsequently relented, after a vision of St Sabas in the desert.[31]

The specific flight from the church or monastery to the Holy Land is

[30] *Panegyric 22*, 189.6–15, 189.30–9, 190.5–34.
[31] *Cod. Paris, Gr. 1189*, fols. 174β–175α (*Panegyric 23*); and see note 14 above.

again a theme which Neophytos commonly refers to in his Saints' *Lives*: Sts Gennadios, Nicholas, Sabas, Andronikos and Athanasia all go on a pilgrimage to the Holy Land.[32] Neophytos writes that St Alypios wanted to do the same, but was apprehended on his way and brought back by his bishop. Yet it is with St Alypios' story, at this point, that Neophytos' has much in common. Neophytos writes that St Alypios, having failed to carry out his planned pilgrimage to the Holy Land, was sad. He then saw a vision: an angel visited him in his dream and told him not to be sad, because the Holy Land is in reality everywhere, wherever a man who loves God fulfils God's wishes. Hearing this, St Alypios took to action, looking around for a place to be an *hēsychastēs*, until he found one at the foot of a mountain.[33] The pattern is the following: pilgrimage to the Holy Land, containing an expectation of hesychastic life → failure of the expectation to materialise → sadness → vision, leading to → action, leading to → success. Writing his own life's story, Neophytos follows this pattern exactly: he leaves for the Holy Land expecting to attach himself to an *hēsychastēs*, there → he fails, despite a six-month search → he is sad → he has a vision which tells him it is in another place that God desires him to be an *hēsychastēs* → he is thereby activated to return to Cyprus in the hope of becoming an *hēsychastēs* on the mountain of Koutsovendēs → he eventually succeeds in becoming an *hēsychastēs* in the mountains near Paphos.[34] (Another story providing a parallel to Neophytos' at this point is that of St Sabas, who, like St Alypios and Neophytos, also finds his way to a place of *hēsychia* after a vision.)[35]

But Neophytos' Saints do not only move away from the world in their quest for *hēsychia*. We have seen how another flight which Neophytos' Saints often perform is the flight from fame, a theme which appears in the Recluse's *Lives* of St Alypios and St Hilariōn. It also appears in the information which Neophytos gives us concerning his own life, in his tract *Sign of God*. In this work Neophytos describes his decision to leave his cell and move in to a new cell which he would construct higher up the cliff, and his adventures in so doing. Certain similarities between Neophytos' story and those of St Hilariōn and St Alypios are indeed striking. To begin with, the reason for the decision of the holy man to move from one place to another is stated to be that of flight from the fame which the holy man's sanctity has

---

[32] Respectively, *Panegyric 30*, 224.21–4; *Panegyric 24*, 401.12–25; *Cod Paris. Gr. 1189*, fols. 174β–175α (*Panegyric 23*); *Cod. Paris. Gr. 1189*, fols. 81β–82α (*Panegyric 11*). A frequently encountered theme in hagiography. For post-ninth-century examples see the *Life* of St Christodoulos of Patmos, para. 6, and see also Branouse (1966: 51); *Life* of St Meletios the Younger, 6,46; *Life* of St Leontios of Jerusalem, 388–9; *Life* of St Meletios the Confessor, 611.

[33] *Panegyric 22*, 190.1–11.   [34] *Typikon*, 76.1–33.

[35] *Cod. Paris. Gr. 1189*, fols. 174β–175α (*Panegyric 23*). For parallels from twelfth- and thirteenth-century Saints' *Lives* see, e.g., *Life* of St Leontios of Jerusalem, 394; *Life* of St Meletios the Confessor, 609.

produced. It is a move aimed at regaining the *hēsychia* which the crowds, drawn by the holy man's fame, destroyed. St Alypios decides to move, Neophytos tells us, 'because the fame of his works, attracting a multitude of people [*plēthos laou*] to him, interrupted the *hēsychia* of the righteous man, and the fighter, not bearing the disturbance [*ochlēsis*] of people, wanted' to leave his cell.[36] St Hilariōn, we are told, 'disturbed [*ochloumenos*] by the crowd [*plēthos*] coming to him, was vexed and annoyed'.[37] In the same *Life* we read: 'As for [St] Antony, he moved deeper into the desert because of the disturbance [*ochlēsis*] of those coming to him and depriving him of the serenity of *hēsychia*.'[38] Similarly, Neophytos writes of himself that he wanted to move elsewhere because of 'much gathering of people [*laou*] . . . unceasingly disturbing me [*enochlousēs me*]'. He decided to move into a small hole, higher up the cliff, 'unreachable to many, and there to remain as I desire to, escaping the great and untimely disturbance [*ochlēsis*] of the many, and so as not to be deprived of the friend *anachōrēsis*, and of *hēsychia*'.[39] Neophytos has thus borrowed from his own Saints' stories not only the motivation for moving, but also the very words to describe it: St Alypios, St Hilariōn and St Antony are all stated to have moved away from the *ochlēsis* of the *laos* or *plēthos*; so is Neophytos. The Saints move away to regain *hēsychia*; so does Neophytos.

St Hilariōn and St Antony moved deeper into the desert. St Alypios, however, moved up in an 'ascent on the column'.[40] Neophytos is imitating St Alypios when he states that he wished to 'go higher up on the precipice', 'ascend with God's help'.[41] It is quite possible that Neophytos saw himself as belonging to the tradition of that distinguished group of monks, the stylites.[42] Neophytos is indeed described as a stylite in the fifteenth-century Cypriot *Chronicle* of Machairas;[43] and even though it is preferable to remember Neophytos as he described himself (i.e. as a Recluse, an *enkleistos*), it is true that his life was not very different from that of the stylites. Perhaps Neophytos' special devotion to St Alypios was not motivated – as H. Delehaye seems to suggest[44] – exclusively by Neophytos' desire to commemorate his mother, who had died on the feast-day of St Alypios, but also by an admiration for the stylite's life.

That Neophytos may have believed himself to be a stylite is not surprising. A stylite in the strict sense of the word was a man who literally lived on a column (*stylos*), emulating the example of the first known stylite, St Symeōn, in fourth-century Syria.[45] Latter-day 'stylites', however, did not

---

36 *Panegyric 22*, 190.28–31.   37 *Panegyric 13*, 143.9–10.
38 *Ibid.*, 138.27–139.2.   39 *Sign of God*, 139.11–18.
40 *Panegyric 22*, 190.30–1.   41 *Sign of God*, 139.14.
42 See Delehaye (1923: esp. cxxxix ff.).
43 Machairas, I, 38, para. 38. See also Delehaye (1923: cxxxviii).
44 Delehaye (1923: lxxxi–lxxxii).
45 For early stylites see Delehaye (1923: esp. cxvii–cxliii).

necessarily live on a column. Of the solitaries in the Middle Byzantine period who lived in cells on the top of Cappadocia's cones at least two (Nikētas, the hermit of Güllü Dere, and Symeōn of Zelve) were called 'stylites'.[46] The same applies to the fourteenth-century hermit Athanasios of Meteōra.[47] In the early tenth century St Paul of Latros retreated for twelve years on what the monk Athanasios indicated to him to be a column 'not made by the hand of man' (*acheiropoiētos*). This was, in fact, nothing other than a steep, elevated rock, at the top of which there was a natural cave. And when St Cyril Phileōtēs saw a vision of a column in a pine forest near Derkos in Thrace (*c*. 11051–6), he constructed a cell there, evidently somehow equating the two in his mind.[48] H. Delehaye points out that St Paul of Latros believed himself to be a stylite, and that the same applied to Neophytos. The same scholar also notices that neither Saint actually called himself a 'stylite', and he suggests that perhaps the title was reserved for those who lived on columns 'made by the hand of man'. Indeed, Neophytos' lifestyle strikingly resembles that of a stylite in its anchoritic solitude, in its immobility, in its complete dependence on external help for food.[49]

Further, it appears from a series of civil-law references to stylites and recluses that both formed a special category in civil law (which granted them special privileges) and generally in society, which considered them an elite corps amongst monks, one composed of 'immobile' ascetics.[50] The prestige attached to the stylites and recluses might be one of the reasons why Neophytos so consistently defined himself as not just a monk but also 'an *enkleistos*' in almost all his writings. Thus, even though Neophytos may well have considered himself to be a stylite too, this might have become somewhat irrelevant, since by being a recluse he had already entered the most prestigious 'class' a monk could belong to. It is, nevertheless, interesting to note that Neophytos did think of himself as a stylite, too: the similarities between his life and that of St Alypios are, as we have seen, striking.

'Incidental' parallels

Apart from the themes of *anachōrēsis* (with its subsequent further flights) and of a life predestined by God to be holy, Neophytos' life shares a number of other features with his Saints' *Lives*. These concern various 'incidental' details, each of which, taken on its own, could easily be dismissed

[46] Wiegand (1913: 233–4); Schiemenz (1969: 254–5); generally Rodley (1985: 239).
[47] Nicol (1975: 94, 95); Rodley (1985: 239).
[48] *Life* of St Paul of Latros, 42–3, c. 13 (note that, like Neophytos, St Paul of Latros also directed a monastery from his cave/*stylos*); *Life* of St Cyril Phileōtēs, 106–9, ch. 22. See, generally, Morris (1985: 212–13).
[49] Delehaye (1923: cxlviii ff.).   [50] *Ibid.*, cxxxix ff. and esp. cxli.

as coincidental. Taken within the context of an accumulation of such details, however, they cease to be coincidental and become, rather, witnesses to Neophytos' frequent and liberal grafting of details from his own Saints' *Lives* onto his own. I list the most important of them immediately below.

Neophytos' six-month wandering in the desert of Palestine is paralleled by his description of the wanderings of St Hilariōn and St Sabas.[51] St Sabas' wanderings end when he is led by a vision (an angel) to his place of *hēsychia*: this is a 'cave difficult of access' in a ravine. Around this cave a *lavra* developed. The similarity with Neophytos' story is clear: Neophytos' wanderings in the desert also come to an end after a vision; and, as we saw, he describes that he was 'led' by God to his place of *hēsychia*. This is a cave which was 'difficult to find' and was situated in a ravine. This cave became later the centre of a *lavra*.[52]

The fact that Neophytos lived in a cave is emphasised by its numerous parallels in his Saints' stories. Apart from St Sabas, to whom we have just referred, other Saints of whom Neophytos wrote as connected with caves include St John Chrysostom, who spent three years in a cave of *hēsychia*.[53] St Alypios also stayed in the 'narrowest cell' for two years before his ascent on a column.[54] When St Gennadios, after a pilgrimage to the Holy Land, came to Cyprus, he rushed to the Paphian mountain where Hilariōn the Great had lived his 'hesychastic and ascetic' life – obviously, in a cave.[55] St Theosebios pretended throughout his life to be going out of the village for sheep grazing whereas, in fact, he spent his time in a cave in a mountain, praying and fasting.[56] He died in that same cave and was buried there, having indicated this desire of his in an appearance in his father's dream.[57] St Arkadios too 'hid in mountains and caves and the holes of the earth', occupying himself with fasting, vigils and prayers. He continued to do so even after he had become a bishop.[58] In his second *Panegyric* for the Holy Cross Neophytos describes the Cross as 'the pride of the cross-bearing life of the monks, and the support of the holy men in the mountains and in the caves and in the holes of the earth'.[59] Neophytos evidently liked this conventional literary figure, linking caves with holiness: he repeats it almost word by word in his *Panegyric* for St Sabas.[60]

---

[51] Respectively, *Typikon*, 76.3–10; *Panegyric 13*, 138.18–27, 139.3–8; *Cod. Paris. Gr. 1189*, fols. 174β–175β (*Panegyric 23*).
[52] *Typikon*, 77.6, 76.10–12, 78.4–13, 89.27.
[53] *Panegyric 20*, 10.11–16.   [54] *Panegyric 22*, 190.26–8.
[55] *Panegyric 30*, 224.24–8.   [56] *Panegyric 12*, 191.20–5.
[57] *Ibid.*, 192.13–24, 193.4–19.   [58] *Panegyric 14*, 205.5–10.
[59] *Cod. Paris. Gr. 1189*, fol. 52α (*Panegyric 8*).
[60] *Cod. Paris. Gr. 1189*, fol. 179β (*Panegyric 23*).

Less frequent similarities between Neophytos' life and those of his Saints should also not be lightly dismissed as coincidental. Nor should we disregard the evocative power of certain words or phrases on the Byzantine reader or listener. For example, as was mentioned earlier, Neophytos called his upper *enkleistra* 'New Sion'.[61] Apart from the wealth of evocations which such a name would produce in the mind of any Christian (and which Neophytos encouraged by his own references to the 'Sion of the Church' in his writings[62]), it is worth pointing out that Neophytos writes that St Nicholas' foundation was, also, called 'New Sion'.[63]

In another instance, Neophytos tells us that St Hilariōn was sixty-three years old when he moved from his monastery in search of *hēsychia*.[64] Neophytos was born in 1134. The *Sign of God* gives us the date when he moved to his upper cell: the year was 1197, and just like St Hilariōn, Neophytos was precisely sixty-three years old. Neophytos' *Life* of St Hilariōn provides another parallel with his own. The Recluse appointed as his successor *enkleistos* and abbot of the Enkleistra his own nephew, Ēsaias. The choice is placed in a different context, removing it from that of narrow nepotism, when it becomes obvious through other Neophytic Saints' stories that it was accepted practice for a holy man to single out one of his disciples. Such, Neophytos lets us know, was, for example, the case with St Hilariōn, who was loved 'more than the others' by 'Hēsychios, as his pure disciple'.[65]

Another example of similarity between Neophytos' life and those of his Saints, and indeed of Christ, is provided by the Recluse's extraordinary directions concerning his own burial. Neophytos writes that his body should be dressed for burial with the garments which he himself had made, and be placed in 'a coffin made of pine and cedar and cypress'.[66] Juxtaposed with a number of other passages by Neophytos, the choice of these three woods is explained by its references by Neophytos to Christ's cross. In his second *Panegyric* for the Cross Neophytos makes no less than five references to the Holy Cross as being composed of these three woods. Authorities such as Isaiah and the *Psalms* are quoted to support this, and so is the symbolism of the Trinity (through the three-wood composition of the Cross). Further, in describing his coffin, Neophytos places the names of the three woods which he had used in exactly the same order of succession as appears in his description of the woods of which Christ's Cross consisted.[67] The connection

---

[61] E.g., *Typikon*, 90.16; *Hexaēmeros*, 169.21.
[62] E.g., *Sign of God*, 155.15–16; *Panegyric 24*, 394.3, 394.25; *Cod. Paris. Gr. 1189*, fols. 210α–β (*Panegyric 27*).
[63] *Panegyric 24*, 398.8–9, 402.4.   [64] *Panegyric 13*, 143.9.
[65] *Ibid.*, 143.16.   [66] *Typikon*, 102.28–9.
[67] *Cod. Paris. Gr. 1189*, fols. 40β, 41α, 48α, 52α (*Panegyric 8*).

in Neophytos' mind between his coffin and Christ's Cross is obvious. Further, Neophytos gave directions to his monks that the entrance to the tomb should be built up and remain always closed. Neophytos refers to this as a *katakleisis* ('total enclosure') after death.[68] In a linguistically very close manner Neophytos tells us elsewhere that St Diomēdēs' tomb is *'kekleismenos* [totally closed] and is never opened'.[69]

Yet another example shows how even apparently trivial details from Neophytos' life have their parallels – reported by Neophytos – in other Saints' *Lives*. He refers, for example, to trouble breaking out in the monastery of the Enkleistra when, allowing the number of monks to be raised, Neophytos found out that four of them disobeyed him.[70] This recalls St Sabas' experience as described by Neophytos, when, after the Saint's *lavra* had grown with a multitude of followers, some of them proved troublesome: they 'disobeyed the father' and caused him to be sad.[71]

Finally, another description of Neophytos' closely paralleled by one found in one of his Saints' *Lives* is that concerning buildings around the holy man which are not made by the hand of man but by that of God. In his *Typikon* Neophytos writes that it is not wrong to describe the buildings built around the *enkleistra* as 'built by God' (*theodomēta*), 'since there was no intention on my part to build'.[72] Further, Neophytos describes in *Sign of God* how, while working for the structures of his upper *enkleistra*, he unearthed a stone inscribed with the signs K + X (the last being the initial 'Ch' in Greek). He decided that these symbols stood for *Kyriou Stavros* ('the Lord's Cross') and *Kyriou Cheir* ('the Lord's Hand'), and considered this to be a divine sign. Subsequently, he found another stone inscribed with a 'I' and 'Π', which he deciphered as the initials of John the Baptist (*Iōannis Prodromos*).[73] In a situation which is identical in substance (though not in its factual details) St Sabas is described by Neophytos as having found near his hesychastic cave an underground cave in the form of a church and some other structures which had not been made by the hand of man (*acheiropoiētous*).[74]

Neophytos did not simply confine himself to parallels between his life and those of his Saints. On occasions, he appears to be presenting himself as standing on a equal footing with the Saint he is writing about. So that, for example, he invokes St Sabas to cast a continuous protecting eye over both

---

[68] *Typikon*, 102.21–103.9.
[69] *Panegyric 17*, 216.35–217.1.   [70] *Typikon*, 79.15–30, 98.18–28.
[71] *Cod. Paris. Gr. 1189*, fols. 176α–β (*Panegyric 23*).
[72] *Typikon*, 89.25–6.   [73] *Letter 1*, 152.15–30.
[74] *Cod. Paris. Gr. 1189*, fol. 176α (*Panegyric 23*).

'your own *lavra* and my Enkleistra'.[75] On another occasion, he explains a theological point by reference to his own life. Neophytos writes that some people wonder 'very unthoughtfully' how it could be possible for God to create the waters first and then raise out of them the earth. Neophytos is very impatient with such thoughts ('such thinking is superfluous and silly', he objects); but before he dismisses the point he explains God's action in creating the waters by reference to God's action with regard to Neophytos: 'How indeed is one who has been called upon to be anchored to a place for ever, then moved to another place?'[76] In the same way, he explains, did God also create the waters and then earth. The reference is clearly to the Recluse himself: the *Hexaēmeros*, which contains this passage, was written in the same year that Neophytos wrote *Sign of God* (1197), when he moved from his first cell to the upper *enkleistra*.

Signs of God and protective miracles

Neophytos felt that he was personally and specially protected by God, just as we have seen him describe some Saints as having been. An early hint of this belief is found in his description of an earthquake which took place 'at the beginning' of his enclosure. He describes a series of seven tremors during one night. These were strong enough to demolish fourteen churches in the district of Paphos, including the great church of the Virgin Limeniōtissa in the castle of Paphos. According to Neophytos, by the morning 'everything was buried and broken'. So much so that, Neophytos tells us, 'many thought that I must have been killed that night, because of the crumbled nature of the precipice and of the cave of the *enkleistra*'. By contrast, however, those who came to see him in the morning, 'seeing that not even the stones which I had put in the shape of a dome around the entrance to the cave had fallen, they glorified God and asked to know the cause of the earthquake'.[77]

Several points claim our attention: one is the contrast which Neophytos makes between the devastation around him and his own building's unscathed escape. The implication that this was a result of divine protection is clearly present. Another point is how Neophytos' anxious visitors appears to share this feeling. Their reaction is twofold. First, they glorify God, specifically for having saved Neophytos. The implication is that only God could have saved him, and that therefore Neophytos' and his cave's preservation can only be explained by reference to divine intervention, revealing protection of this

---

[75] *Cod. Paris. Gr. 1189*, fol. 180α (*Panegyric 23*).
[76] *Hexaēmeros*, 166.23–167.5.   [77] *Panegyric 16*, 211.10–23.

sole man. Their second reaction is to ask Neophytos to explain to them what caused the earthquake. This represents a very important step in the locals' appreciation of Neophytos. To the Byzantines, earthquakes were amongst what they considered to be *sēmeia*, 'signs' from God, which only extremely pious or holy persons were considered capable of deciphering.

A *sēmeion*, as it appears in Neophytos' writings (and reflecting commonly held Byzantine beliefs) is a 'sign' from God, signifying something. Expressing time-honoured Byzantine beliefs, Neophytos characterises an eclipse of the sun as a 'sign' announcing the start of a period of famine, war, earthquakes and death;[78] and considers another eclipse to be also a 'sign' inaugurating a two-year period of famine and sadness.[79] A 'sign' could thus be made by God to announce the coming of disasters, and it was usually understood to have been caused by God's wrath against the sinning people.

But not all 'signs' were ominous: through a 'sign' God could also express approval of human conduct, or His choice of a particular person. Neophytos describes, for example, how Joseph was chosen to be affianced to the Virgin Mary by means of such a 'sign'. In the particular case, this took the form of a pigeon that sat on Joseph's rod.[80] On other occasions Neophytos uses the word in a more vague sense, such as when he writes that the 'signs' of the Son of Man will appear in the sky on the day of Judgment; or that among the 'signs' announcing the coming of the Day of Judgment will be a darkening of the sky and the moon and the fall of stars.[81] (Indeed, it is on the basis of the appearance of 'signs' such as the ones just described that the Byzantines often predicted the impending end of the world.)[82] Neophytos tells us that it is through a 'sign' that God will announce the day of Judgment; through 'signs' that Christ's birth was announced to the world;

---

[78] *Cod. Athen. 522*, fols. 78α–β. Eclipses were considered to be bad omens throughout Byzantine history. They are found in the sources as signs announcing the death of an emperor, the fall of cities, illness and serious danger, wars, God's displeasure with a particular person. For beliefs and practices concerning thunder, lightning, eclipses of the sun and the moon, blood-red rain, comets, falling stars, earthquakes, see Koukoules (1948–55, I, 2: 218–25). On 'signs of God' specifically within an eleventh- to thirteenth-century context see Ahrweiler (1976: esp. 12–14). In fourteenth-century Trebizond a sun eclipse was taken to signify God's wrath against a particular person, since following it people rose against their emperor, gathered together outside the citadel and hurled stones at him: see Bryer (1986). Moon eclipses were also considered to be bad omens, signifying the imminent occurrence of the fall of an emperor, the failure of a rebellion, the death of an illustrious person or raids of enemies. See Koukoules, above.

[79] *Cod. Athen. 522*, fols. 78β–79α.

[80] *Panegyric 21*, 536 [112].15–35.

[81] Respectively, *Cod. Athen. 522*, fol. 396α (also *Cod. Lesb. Leim. 2, Homily 3*, 150.375–6); *Cod. Coisl. Gr. 287*, fols. 137α–β.

[82] Ahrweiler (1976: 12–14).

through 'signs' that He then revealed himself as the Father of Man.[83] In all the above examples Neophytos uses the word *sēmeion*.[84]

Christ's life is described by Neophytos as filled with 'signs', often referred to as 'signs of God' (*theosēmeia*). When Neophytos uses the word *sēmeion* in reference to Christ, he often does so to indicate ways in which Christ's divinity was manifested: the miracles which he performed (such as the resurrection of Lazaros or the turning of water into wine) are included in the 'signs' manifesting Christ's divinity.[85] On other occasions, Neophytos makes a distinction between miracles and signs, such as when he writes that Christ 'filled Judea with myriads of miracles and signs of God [*theosēmeias*]'.[86] Very frequently, only a general, non-specific reference is given to the word: so that we read that Christ manifested 'signs' or 'signs of God' (*theosēmeias*);[87] that the Holy Ghost revealed Christ's divinity by means of a 'sign of God' (*theosēmeion*), or that Christ's burial was 'accompanied by signs of God [*theosēmos*]'.[88]

Occasionally, Neophytos uses the term in reference to holy men and women, indicating either a revelation of God – by means of a 'sign' – or the holy person's sanctity; or indicating the sanctity of the holy person as this is manifested through the residence of the Holy Ghost inside them and their subsequent acquisition of power to perform 'signs'. An example of the first case is provided by Neophytos' remark that God performed many 'signs' at the burial of St Athanasia, thus revealing her sanctity.[89] Examples from the second category include Neophytos' reference to the Fathers, who, 'strengthened by divine power performed many "signs"'; to the Saints, who 'were armed with the power of "signs of God"'; or to St Sabas, who built 'walls of "signs of God"' in the desert.[90]

Those of Neophytos' own experiences which he characterises as 'signs of God' belong to the first category described. It was in accordance with the belief that God could reveal the holiness of a person by a 'sign' that

---

[83] *Cod. Lesb. Leim. 2*, fols. 260α, 265α, 265β (*Homily 2*); *Cod. Paris. Gr. 1189*, fol. 44α (*Panegyric 8*).

[84] The *sēmeion* always expressed something unnatural and abnormal, hence the frequent use of the word together with the word *terata* (σημεία καὶ τέρατα): e.g. *Cod. Athen. 522*, fol. 396α; *Cod. Paris. Gr. 1317*, fols. 214α–β; *Cod. Lesb. Leim. 2*, fol. 270α (*Homily 2*); also *Cod. Lesb. Leim. 2* (*Homily 3*), 150.375–6. See Koukoules (1948–55, 1, 2: 218–26).

[85] Respectively, *Cod. Athen. 522*, fol. 391α; *Cod. Paris. Gr. 1317*, fol. 206α (also *Cod. Lesb. Leim. 2*, *Homily 9*, 270.113–14).

[86] *Cod. Coisl. Gr. 287*, fol. 141β.

[87] E.g., *Cod. Paris. Gr. 1317*, fol. 99α; *Cod. Lesb. Leim. 2*, fols. 296α (*Homily 4*), 323β, 324α (*Homily 8*); *Cod. Coisl. Gr. 287*, fols. 91β, 177β; also *Cod. Athen. 522*, fol. 391α.

[88] Respectively, *Cod. Paris. Gr. 1317*, fols. 214α–β; *Cod. Lesb. Leim. 2*, fol. 320α (*Homily 8*).

[89] *Cod. Paris. Gr. 1189*, fol. 84α (*Panegyric 11*).

[90] Respectively, *Cod. Paris. Gr. 1317*, fols. 11β, 20α; *Cod Paris. Gr. 1189*, fol. 179β (*Panegyric 23*).

Neophytos' most clear and sustained statement as to his own holiness is made. This comes in his tract *Sign of God*. Written in 1197, it tells the story of his decision to move higher up the precipice; his work in excavating the new cell; and his fall from the cliff during it, on 24 January. The unearthing of inscribed slabs during his excavations for his upper cell, he calls a 'sign' (*sēmeion*); his survival from the fall, a 'sign of God' (*theosēmeia*).[91] Indeed, the very fact that Neophytos entitles his work *Sign of God* (*Theosēmeia*) is sufficient to indicate how, by 1197, he had come to regard himself as a holy man, and therefore as the subject of divine manifestations.

In the *Sign of God* Neophytos expressly attributes his saving from the fall to divine help and protection (*theia epikouria*).[92] The Recluse writes that while he was held down by a stone which had fallen on him, 'the stone was seen to be pushed backwards, and abandoning its downward and natural direction', it started moving upwards, until it only pressed against Neophytos' right hand and the hem of his robe – 'so that I would not fall down'. He describes this as a 'miracle'.[93] Further, Neophytos describes how even though his right hand was under the stone, it was not hurt. This, he characterises as a 'supernatural and strange . . . sight' – in other words, another miracle.[94] Neophytos' elevated esteem of himself is also expressed in another passage, where he describes how his little finger and the back of his palm were hurt, and 'drops of blood' fell; 'and yet I neither saw nor felt anything concerning this wound'.[95] He places this within a heroic, Biblical context: just like those in the Chaldean furnace were not burned by the flames, he writes, 'thus, in a similar way, divine grace acted, in that case as in the present one, in a strange and supernatural way. For even though there stands an immeasurable amount of time between then and now, and there is much difference [between the two cases], yet divine grace exists always timeless and unaltered.'[96]

Convinced that his experience amounted to a divine sign (a conviction shared by others, such as his brother John[97]) Neophytos wrote and – in private[98] – spoke of it as such. But further, the Recluse composed a special service (*akolouthia*) for this 'sign' of God.[99] He prescribed that the monks

---

[91] *Letter 1*, 152.18, 150.7–8.
[92] *Ibid.*, 137 (title).   [93] *Ibid.*, 142.35–143.2.   [94] *Ibid.*, 143.15–17.
[95] *Ibid.*, 143.17–21.   [96] *Ibid.*, 143.21–34.   [97] *Letter 1*, 150.7–9.
[98] Neophytos was aware of the potentially ridiculous element in the story (that this 'divine sign' came, in fact, while he was excavating for a privy) and warned his monks to keep the story secret for precisely this reason: *Sign of God*, 141.24–142.3, 145.6–11. In this detail Neophytos' story bears an uncanny resemblance to one of Blemmydes' stories: he, too, had considered it a miracle when he survived the fall on him of the overhang of his house's privy: *Life* of Nikēphoros Blemmydēs, 33–4, paras. 65–6.
[99] *Sign of God*, 153.1–154.25.

should perform this liturgy 'inside and outside' his cell every year, while the Recluse was still alive, on the anniversary and in commemoration of the events of 24 January; and he states that he offers the liturgy as 'a gift' to God 'concerning the miracle performed by You for Your servant', Neophytos.[100] In one of the poems he composed for the liturgy Neophytos defines this 'miracle' as 'how [God] saved [Neophytos] from the inaccessible precipice and bitter death and the corruption of sudden death'.[101] In the last poem, which is meant to be read inside the Recluse's cell, Neophytos writes:

Your servant cried out, how can we glorify the all-doing and divine and philanthropic nature of the ever-existing Trinity? For after the many and great gifts that You gave me, You further even gave me extraordinary deliverance from precipice and death; and I survived the fall of three stones by calling the one of the Trinity, and the power of the fall was invisibly held back. And having found while digging letters on stone slabs not written by the hand of man, and of the same number as the Trinity, I understood that this was a sign from God.[102]

There can be no doubt that Neophytos believed that on 24 January 1197 he witnessed a miracle, whereby God altered the course of a falling rock so as to save his life. That, also, he believed this miracle to be a sign from God, coming after God had already embellished Neophytos' life with many gifts. We have seen that when a 'sign' (*sēmeion*) or 'sign of God' (*theosēmeion*) appears in Neophytos' writings in connection with men (and not simply with God or Christ) it appears always in connection with holy men. We have also seen how, in these cases, the sign comes either from God through the holy man; or directly from God, revealing the holy man's sanctity. The miracle, in the case which Neophytos describes in *Sign of God*, is attributed to God. The sign can thus only be construed as a sign from God revealing God's protection of Neophytos and the latter's holy status. Thus Neophytos took an extraordinary step and one which, as far as I know, is unparalleled in Byzantine history. For when, in 1197, Neophytos wrote a liturgy for *Theosēmeia*, he effectively wrote a liturgy for himself.

The importance of this fact in a self-sanctificatory process cannot be overestimated. It is clear that a local base of people believing that a man was holy was sufficient to create a cult; but further steps had to be taken to ensure the survival and spread of this cult. In early Christian times, and for many centuries afterwards, there was no procedure for official canonisation of Saints by the Church. Men and women deemed to be holy were honoured after their deaths by the local population. The cults which survived the passage of time were those about which a hagiographical tradition developed, accompanied by the creation of an icon – the painted image of the

---

[100] *Ibid.*, 153.3–4.   [101] *Ibid.*, 155.25–6.   [102] *Ibid.*, 155.30–156.6.

Saint. The hagiographical tradition essentially consisted of the recording of the name of the Saint in a commemorative register of Saints (such as a *Mēnologion*, a *Synaxarion* or a *Martyrologion*) in the monastery or church with which he or she was associated; together with the registering of a day for the Saint's commemoration. This was usually fixed on the Saint's day of death, and it became the Saint's feast-day. The Saint thus acquired 'official' status. His or her fame might subsequently be further enhanced by other developments: venerators might produce further hagiographical works concerning the Saint; if the cult spread and persisted long enough the Saint's name might also be registered in the patriarchal calendar.

In the eyes of the Orthodox Church, popular veneration leading to the registering of a Saint's name and feast-day in an ecclesiastical calendar constitutes an 'acknowledgment' of the Saint's status (*anagnōrisis*), to be distinguished from the procedure of official canonisation by the Church (*anakēryxis*).[103] The latter was a much more formal practice, and it first appeared in Byzantium in the thirteenth century. It had an intensely bureaucratic flavour, as it consisted of canonisation by synodical decision, based on the detailed evidence of miracles. In this aspect it greatly resembled the canonisation procedure which the western Church had evolved and practised since the late tenth century; and it was indeed probably a by-product of the contact between east and crusading west.[104]

Such important changes in ecclesiastical procedure could not, of course, have happened over night. A number of factors must have indicated that the introduction of a different type of canonisation might develop long before it actually did. It has been suggested, for example, that the reason for Nikēphoros Blemmydēs' writing of his self-canonising autobiographies was precisely his realisation that changes in the process of canonisation were afoot in the Orthodox Church; and that he thus resolved to put in writing all the evidence required for a synodical decision of canonisation.[105]

Even if Neophytos had not smelt changes in the air, he certainly knew

---

[103] The procedure for the canonisation of a holy man in Byzantium has not yet been comprehensively studied. For relevant discussions see Talbot (1983: 21–7); Patlagean (1981b: 103–4); Macrides (1981: 83–6); Beck (1959: 274); *Dictionnaire de spritualité*, ii, s.v. 'canonisation', 77–85; Ringrose (1979: 135, note 12); Papadopoulos (1934); Alibizatos (1941–8: esp. 21 ff.); Constantine, metropolitan of Serres (1956).

[104] See: *Dictionnaire de spiritualité*, ii, s.v. 'canonisation', 77–85. Papal canonisations first took place in 973: Talbot (1983: 22). On western canonisation see generally Delooz (1969: 24–32; 1983). On thirteenth-century western canonisation see Goodich (1975). The change of the Orthodox Church's attitude towards canonisation in late Byzantium has not yet been given the attention it deserves. For the earliest recorded canonisations by the Orthodox Church, in the late thirteenth century, see especially Macrides (1981: 83–6); Talbot (1983: 22–30); also Munitiz (1981: 168). For general references see also Beck (1959: 274); Alibizatos (1941–8: esp. 37–41).

[105] Munitiz (1981: 168).

that a Saint needed an icon, a feast-day and the registration of his name in an ecclesiastical calendar, if his cult was to achieve an 'official' basis which would safeguard it against the passage of time. It seems that the Recluse did not wish to leave his canonisation to chance or to any future venerator's initiative; and, indeed, it now appears that he had not totally miscalculated the situation:[106] for, unlike so many other monastic Saints, Neophytos found no hagiographer amongst any of his immediate disciples or successors; his name was never recorded in the *Synaxarion* of the Great Church of Constantinople; and to this day there exists no official *Synaxarion* of the Saints of the Autocephalous Church of Cyprus.[107] Their cults' 'official' recognition is still achieved through evidence of the existence of a popular cult, a feast-day and the inscription of the Saint's name in the liturgy.

Neophytos could not, of course, posthumously fix his own feast-day on the day of his death, but through the *Sign of God* he presented his monks with 24 January as an alternative feast-day.[108] The same work soothed other self-sanctificatory headaches: through the *Sign of God* Neophytos placed his name on the monastery's calendar, since his monks had to commemorate the events of 24 January annually; he made sure that on that day he would not simply be commemorated in the way that the dead commonly are in the Orthodox Church, but as part of a whole liturgy which he provided and whose tone was intensely self-sanctificatory; he clearly encouraged the creation or furtherance of a cult about his person while he was still alive, by prescribing that the annual celebration of God's 'sign' was to be put into effect immediately; and, in case such was needed, he also provided the evidential proof for his sanctity – the miracles. Thus, in 1197 Neophytos took, in effect, all the steps that he could possibly take to 'canonise' himself on an 'official' basis.

---

[106] Neophytos' cult was never abandoned, as is evident from the continuous existence of his monastery. His tomb was known throughout the Latin period of Cyprus, and is referred to by Etienne Lusignan. The tomb was subsequently forgotten, and was discovered with the relics of the Saint in 1750 (according to Tsiknopoulos and Merakles) or 1757 (according to Hackett): Tsiknopoulos (1976: 36); Merakles (1976: 130–1); Hackett (1901: 352). In 1778 archimandrite Kyprianos wrote and published two *akolouthiai* for St Neophytos, one to celebrate the discovery of his relics (on 28 September) and one to commemorate his death (on 12 April). For the *akolouthia* for 12 April Kyprianos seems to have used an earlier text, written by an unknown at an unknown point in time: Merakles (1976: 130). For a translation of the *akolouthia* see Cobham (1908: 227–30).

[107] A descriptive list of the island's Saints was compiled by archbishop Makarios III (1968).

[108] We do not know whether 24 January was regarded as the feast-day of St Neophytos uninterruptedly over the centuries. It is certainly a feast-day now, whose *akolouthia* draws from the *Sign of God* and the *Typikon* to celebrate amongst other things the Recluse's 1197 escape from death: Tsiknopoulos (1976: 15–31, esp. 19, 21, 25). But it is noted that in 1856 the feast-day commemorating the Saint's death (12 April) was transferred to 24 January because it occasionally coincided with Lent, thus interfering with a full celebration: Merakles (1976: 132).

Words of God and other mysteries

Neophytos performed no miracles. This would not have undermined his belief in his own sanctity: for one thing, the Recluse referred to a number of Saints as posthumous miracle-workers, and he may well have expected that he too would perform miracles after his death;[109] for another, the performance of miracles was for him a mere manifestation of, and not a prerequisite for, sanctity; and furthermore, Neophytos believed that he had become instead the subject of God's miracles, intended to protect him and to reveal his holy status to the world – as described by him in the *Sign of God*.

In his *Typikon* Neophytos also hints at other personal experiences of divine manifestations. The heading of the fourth chapter of this document informs us that it concerns 'some mystical experiences'. This refers to the vision which Neophytos had in the desert of Palestine, whereby he was ordered to go to 'another place' and be an *hēsychastēs* there.[110] The heading of chapter 5 of the *Typikon* also promises to speak of 'some mystical experiences' and Neophytos writes of two of these. The first is an experience which he had at least five years after his settlement in the *enkleistra*: he heard a strange voice telling him to remember his preordained mission and his vision in the desert. Some years later, in a vision or dream (the distinction is unclear in the text), Neophytos saw himself going up the mountain of Olympos, opposite his home-town of Lefkara, in order to venerate the Holy Cross. He then heard a voice saying to him 'After fifty days'; and, twice, 'After sixty days.' Neophytos no doubt took this to be a prophecy of some sort, but he confessed when writing his *Typikon* in 1214 that he remained perplexed as to its meaning to that day.[111] Neophytos claims to have had also other mystical experiences but, professing humility, he tells us that he will refrain from speaking about them, lest the reader might think that Neophytos is boasting.[112]

The instances in which the Recluse refers to visions, voices and miracles such as the *Sign of God* describes are limited to those already discussed, and are confined in time to his late, post-1197 years. But Neophytos had another way in which he almost incessantly propagated his belief in his own sanctity over the years, a way in which humility played a major role.

Expressions of humility are ubiquitous in Neophytos' writings. For example, writing about the Dormition of the Virgin (some time after 1191)

---

[109] And indeed miracles did occur at the tomb of St Neophytos after his death. The earliest references to them are found in the fifteenth-century Machairas and subsequently in Etienne Lusignan and Neophytos Rodinos: Machairas, I, 38.4–7; Lusignan, *Description*, 59; Rodinos, 28. See generally Merakles (1976: 130–1).

[110] *Typikon*, 75.13–14; also, 76.10–12.

[111] *Ibid.*, 77.1–2; 77.19–22, 77.25–78.1.   [112] *Ibid.*, 77.23–4.

Neophytos says that he who would dare to write about such a subject should have a 'truly divine voice capable of reaching the ends of the world, and such invisible eyes as to be able to look up to Heaven ... and an angelic voice, capable of glorifying superhumanly Your greatness'. By contrast, he says, 'I possess all the opposites.'[113] Other examples over the years include references to his 'humble self' (in 1197);[114] at around 1200 he describes himself as 'wretched', 'ignorant', and repeats again more emphatically: 'I am ignorant, just a hermit';[115] in 1204 he calls himself, yet again, 'ignorant', 'completely unlearned'[116] and 'uncultured';[117] at around 1214, 'unworthy'.[118]

Appearing to believe himself to be worthless of speaking or writing about divine matters, Neophytos constantly invokes the help of the Holy Ghost and begs to become enlightened by it: 'With burning tears I begged divine providence not to let my mind wander beyond the true meaning of the God-inspired Scriptures, but rather to be enlightened by the Holy Ghost ... [God], do not let my mind wander, or move outside the true aim of these writings, but enlighten my humble self ... with the ... Holy Ghost.'[119] This is a characteristic passage of Neophytos', written in 1197. Similar invocations filled his folios, both before this date and subsequently, stretching out to his last writings of around 1214.[120]

The apparent humility with which Neophytos presents himself (as ignorant and unworthy of speaking of divine matters) and the invocations to the divine for help must not be taken at face value. First, because they form part of a literary convention and a well-known *topos*, found in a multitude of Byzantine Saints' *Lives, enkōmia, Panegyrics*, as we saw earlier; and it is equally following established literary conventions that Neophytos' protestations of humility and worthlessness, as well as his apologies for writing, are followed by his actual writing about precisely the matters of which he declared himself ignorant and unworthy.[121] Second, because professed humility could be used as a defence by Neophytos against any accusations that he had become hubristic. Third, because Neophytos pushed and twisted literary conventions and rhetorical clichés until they gave

---

[113] *Cod. Lesb. Leim. 2, Homily 9*, 264.5–19.   [114] *Hexaēmeros*, 179.5–7.
[115] *Panegyric 25*, 8.8–12; 9.12–14.   [116] *Panegyric 9*, 87.14–19.
[117] *Panegyric 9*, 100.31–6.
[118] *Cod. Paris. Gr. 1317*, fol. 211α. Similar statements are also found in works of unknown date, e.g. *Cod. Lesb. Leim. 2*, fol. 319β (*Homily 8*); *Cod. Paris. Gr. 1189*, fol. 9α (*Panegyric 3*).
[119] *Hexaēmeros*, 169.37–170.3, 179.5–7.
[120] *Cod. Paris. Gr. 1317*, fols. 87β–88α; *Cod. Paris. Gr. 1317*, fol. 88α (concerning which see also the 1176 work in *Cod. Coisl. Gr. 287*, fols. 84β–85α); *Panegyric 9*, 87.5, 100.31–6, 112.9–10 (of 1204).
[121] See also pp. 24–5, 122–6.

expression to his self-sanctificatory ideas. Ironically enough, the Recluse used protestations of humility to propagate his belief in his own sanctity. The general idea in such cases is that Neophytos is so 'unlearned', so 'ignorant' and so 'worthless' that the act of writing about divine matters is only possible because he has become a vehicle of God: the words are not his, but God's.

Through reading even the most basic religious books, Neophytos was well acquainted with the Judaeo-Christian idea that God speaks and acts through certain chosen holy people. Such were the prophets, in whom God's wisdom resided so that the prophet became 'filled with the Holy Ghost', 'filled with God' (*entheos, enpneusmenos*). The prophets thus spoke even when they were quite unwilling to do so, for it was the Holy Ghost that spoke through them: instances found, for example, in Jeremiah, Ezekiel or the *Apocalypse*.[122] There is no doubt that Neophytos was deeply impressed by this idea. I have noted no less than twenty-nine passages in which the Recluse uses the formula 'God [/Christ/the Holy Ghost] said through the prophet [/apostle/holy man, etc.] . . .'; without counting the numerous passages where this idea is referred to by implication.[123]

Neophytos took good care to familiarise his reader too with this formula. He explains to his reader that the Holy Ghost is one and eternal, and that this is how men as separated through time as Isaiah and Peter were still filled with the same Holy Ghost when they spoke of divine matters. We read that the

---

122 Jeremiah, 20:9; Ezekiel, 2:9–3:11; Apocalypse, 10:8–10.
123 E.g., *Cod. Lesb. Leim. 2*, fols. 267α, 267β (*Homily 2*), 292α, 293α, 293β (*Homily 4*). For references to God see, e.g., *Cod. Athen. 522*, fols. 66α, 80β, 88β, 379β, 389α, 390β–391α; *Cod. Paris. Gr. 1317*, fols. 83α, 184β; *Cod. Lesb. Leim. 2*, fol. 271β (*Homily 2*); *Cod. Coisl. Gr. 287*, fols. 137α, 163α; *Cod. Paris. Gr. 1189*, fols. 26α (*Panegyric 6*), 41α, 43β, 44α (*Panegyric 8*), 210β (*Panegyric 27*); also, *Hexaēmeros*, 173.3; *Cod. Lesb. Leim. 2*, *Homily 3*, 148.282–3, 150.367–8. For reference to Christ see, e.g., *Cod. Paris. Gr. 1189*, fols. 34α, 34β (*Panegyric 7*). For references to the Apostles see, e.g., *Cod. Paris. Gr. 1317*, fol. 58α; *Cod. Paris. Gr. 1189*, fols. 210α, 214α, 216β (*Panegyric 27*); also *Cod. Athen. 522*, fol. 421β; *Cod. Lesb. Leim. 2*, *Homily 1*, 210.27–8; *Panegyric 21*, 535[111].43–536[112].2. In respect of the subject through whom God speaks see, for references to 'the prophet', e.g. *Cod. Athen. 522*, fol. 66α; *Cod. Lesb. Leim. 2*, fol. 271β (*Homily 2*); *Cod. Paris. Gr. 1189*, fols. 34β (*Panegyric 7*), 210α, 214α, 216β (*Panegyric 27*); for references to prophets, apostles and teachers see, e.g., *Cod. Athen. 522*, fol. 80β; *Cod. Paris. Gr. 1189*, fol. 216β (*Panegyric 27*); for references to 'the mystics of the Orthodox creed' see, e.g., *Cod. Paris. Gr. 1317*, fol. 58α; for references to 'the Scriptures' see e.g., *Cod. Paris. Gr. 1189*, fol. 43β (*Panegyric 8*). Frequently the subject through whom God speaks is specified principally as: Isaiah: see, e.g., *Cod. Athen. 522*, fol. 389α; *Cod. Paris. Gr. 1317*, fols. 83α, 184β; *Cod. Lesb. Leim. 2*, *Homily 1*, 210.27–8; *Cod. Coisl. Gr. 287*, fol. 163α; *Cod. Paris. Gr. 1189*, fols. 26α (*Panegyric 6*), 34α (*Panegyric 7*), 41α (*Panegyric 8*), 210β (*Panegyric 27*); and David: see, e.g., *Cod. Athen. 522*, fol. 88β; *Cod. Lesb. Leim. 2*, *Homily 3*, 148.282–3; *Cod. Coisl. Gr. 287*, fol. 163α; *Cod. Paris. Gr. 1189*, fol. 44α (*Panegyric 8*); *Panegyric 21*, 535[111].43–4. Also mentioned are Solomon: see, e.g., *Cod. Athen. 522*, fol. 421β, p. 48; Moses: see, e.g., *Cod. Athen. 522*, fol. 389α; Ezekiel, Elizah and Elisha: see, e.g., *Cod. Athen. 522*, fols. 390β–391α; Jeremiah: see, e.g., *Hexaēmeros*, 173.3; Joel: see, e.g., *Cod. Lesb. Leim. 2*, *Homily 3*, 150.367–8; Malachi: see, e.g., *Cod. Coisl. Gr. 287*, fol. 137α.

prophets, the apostles 'and every God-bearing teacher', all are in complete agreement, all speak with the same voice, merely using different words, since it is, in fact, through being enlightened by the Holy Ghost that they speak.[124] So much so that they no longer speak their own thoughts. It is the Holy Ghost who speaks, through them. As Neophytos says, 'these are not human thoughts, but sayings of the Holy Ghost through prophets and apostles'.[125] Or, as he describes St John saying about his *Apocalypse*, 'it is not I but God who speaks these words to you'.[126]

The Recluse also tells us that a few, selected people were given a gift from God. Such a gift, Neophytos writes in his *Catecheseis*, could be the gift of the ability of understanding or of speaking well, of singing psalms or of reading, or writing, of carrying out spiritual work or even simply of being clever with one's hands.[127] Neophytos believed that God fills certain chosen people with His spirit and thus orders them – even against their own inclinations – to become his spokesmen, the intermediaries between the human and the divine.[128] Neophytos came to consider himself to be such a chosen person, whom God had blessed with a number of such gifts (certainly those of understanding, speaking, reading and carrying out spiritual work);[129] and he believed that his particular functions were discharged through his activities as a writer and preacher of God's words. He tells his audience that he teaches them so that they, too, might be filled with the Holy Ghost.[130] He sees his writings and spoken words as a medium of catharsis for those who read or hear them. Thus, the result of people having heard a *Catechesis* by Neophytos would be that they have been purified 'because of the *logos* which I have told you'. Thus, they will have moved, he assures them, a step closer to God.[131]

It is impossible to pinpoint exactly when Neophytos' wish to be filled with the Holy Ghost, to be *entheos*, became, in his own mind, a reality. It appears that by the time he started writing, in the 1170s, he already believed that he was God's mouthpiece. What changed through the years was the frequency and the confidence with which he stated this belief: in his early writings he was on some occasions quite open about the matter, but on other occasions coy; whereas in later years he states consistently and uncompromisingly that

[124] *Cod. Athen. 522*, fol. 400α.   [125] *Cod. Athen. 522*, fols. 399α–β.

[126] *Panegyric 9*, 92.146–7. Alternatively, reference is made to mysteries being revealed by the Holy Ghost to the subject holy man, who then speaks out what has been revealed to him: 'and the mystery was not revealed by man, but through one to whom the Holy Ghost revealed it' (*Cod. Athen. 522*, fols. 392β, 34α–β).

[127] *Cod. Paris. Gr. 1317*, fols. 74β–75α.

[128] *Cod. Athen. 522*, fol. 390α.

[129] It was a view of himself which was shared by others, e.g. his brother John: see *Cod. Paris. Gr. 1317*, fol. 6β, p. 268.8–19.

[130] *Cod. Paris. Gr. 1317*, fol. 192α.   [131] *Ibid.*, fol. 194β.

God speaks through him. For example, writing about Christ's commandments in 1176 he confines himself to saying: 'I shall speak about these
matters, not just with my own words, but from Biblical laws we shall
present the meaning of these sayings, with God's help.'[132] In the same year
he also writes, a touch more boldly, that those who may find his writings
'precious' should not glorify him, for he is only 'the harp and its strings'; but
they should glorify God, 'the craftsman' – implying that it is He who
inspired Neophytos to write.[133]

In these early years of Neophytos' activities as a writer he often expresses
no more than a hope that he will be inspired by God. In 1179, for example,
he writes: 'if the Grace of the Holy Ghost extends to me the spiritual
knowledge [*gnōsis*] and the words [*logos*] I shall dare an *Interpretation*'.[134]
Although the implication is that the Holy Ghost did oblige (or else
Neophytos would not have written the work), it is, nevertheless, important
that this is simply a conditional statement.[135] Such expressions of hope,
rather than certainty, are repeatedly recorded throughout Neophytos' writings. For instance, in another work he writes how, when the feast-day of the
Annunciation approached, he was tormented because he had no written
work to read out so as to glorify the Virgin. He had, he says, neither old
writings nor the wealth of knowledge or the enlightened mind which was
needed to write something new himself. In the end, 'I thought of crying out
with an archangel's voice to the Virgin Mary "Hail!"', hoping that Her grace
would enlighten my hegemonic mind and provide me with the words [*logos*]
upon the opening of my mouth, so as to glorify Her.'[136] On the other hand,
sometimes the feeling expressed is not so much one of hope as one of
expectation. Thus, for example, Neophytos begins his *Interpretation of the
Song of Songs* (of 1179) saying that he will write it 'as best I can and as the
grace of the true bridegroom will extend to me the knowledge and the words
[*logos*]'.[137] And the following bold statement appears at the beginning of his
Book of Fifty Chapters, where he sternly warns his brother, to whom the
work is addressed:

And you brother, heed these as words of God, and not as words of mine. For I am not
saying [to you] pretentious and empty words, but only such as the grace of the Holy

---

132 *Cod. Coisl. Gr. 287*, fol. 118β.
133 *Cod. Coisl. Gr. 287*, fol. 180β.
134 *Cod. Athen. 522*, fol. 413β.
135 See, e.g., *Panegyric 4*, 531[107].11–15.
136 *Cod. Lesb. Leim. 2, Homily 5*, 238.25–240.40. Neophytos' expectation that upon opening
his mouth the Holy Ghost would come and fill it with divine words is repeated by him
elsewhere: e.g. *Cod. Paris. Gr. 1317*, fol. 7β; also *Letter 3*, 215; *Cod. Coisl. Gr. 287*, fol.
143α; also *Cod. Leab. Leim. 2, Homily 9*, 268.82–7.
137 *Cod. Athen. 522*, fol. 421β, p. 48

Ghost brings forth [in me] for Its glory and for your benefit and perhaps for the benefit of some others. Such words, truly, we, enlightened, shall write.[138]

By 1197, in the *Hexaēmeros*, Neophytos is confident enough repeatedly to compare himself to Moses: he states, for example, that he will speak of the third day of Creation 'just as the grace of the divine Ghost reveals and enlightens the mind, that same Holy Ghost that enlightened the mind of the Great Moses'. In the same work he states that he will write his eleventh *Homily* 'as the Holy Ghost extends Its grace'.[139] By *c.* 1200 he demonstrates that he has mastered the art of the self-sanctificatory statement through the use of humility: 'The grace of the Holy Ghost wishes to say a few things through my wretchedness, about this matter', he writes.[140] And again, in another passage: 'And I, the ignorant, thought that such arguments were supposedly irrelevant . . . But the grace of the Holy Ghost revealed to me that they are not irrelevant but on the contrary that there is great importance in the arguments concerning such matters.' And later, in the same work: 'And all these words of mine are not artful creations, for I am ignorant, just a hermit; but I was strengthened to write about this present matter from what the grace of the Holy Ghost revealed to me.'[141] The 'present matter' was a theological one, of which Neophytos was indeed ignorant. It seems that the more aware he was of his real ignorance (and not ignorance feigned for reasons of humility), the more he emphasised his divine enlightenment.

Towards the end of his life, Neophytos' monks, listening to his *Catecheseis* (*c.* 1214) would hear him say, characteristically: 'the words that I say to you . . . are words that are spoken from divine grace through me to you';[142] or, 'this, my beloved brothers, the Great Basil through me said to you today'.[143] His *Catecheseis* are written 'as grace above . . . extended the words to me': they are written *theosdotōs*, given, that is, by God, 'the giver of *logos*'.[144] He would end one of his *Catecheseis* by informing his audience that 'next Sunday we shall speak again, through divine grace'; or that 'all these – concerning lust – I

---

138 *Ibid.*, fol. 12α, p. 44. See also *Cod. Lesb. Leim. 2*, fol. 319β (*Homily 8*).
139 *Hexaēmeros*, 166.7–10, 205.22–5. See also *Panegyric 4*, 529[105].6–9.
140 *Panegyric 25*, 7.1–2.
141 *Ibid.*, 8.8–12, 9.12–14. Other examples of Neophytos' self-sanctificatory use of humility: in his Panegyric for archangel Michael the Recluse writes that God obviously extended this Panegyric to him since no human mind can of its own write an *enkōmion* about angels and archangels. Thus, Neophytos reasons, God gave this Panegyric to him so that he could glorify Michael: *Cod. Paris. Gr. 1189*, fol. 12α (*Panegyric 3*). In his *Homily* on the Pentecost Neophytos says that he postponed writing it because of fear and awareness of his limitations, since he knew that 'a superhuman mind was needed' for this task. However, he says, he later gave in to the wishes of the Holy Ghost which 'urged me to speak about it': *Cod. Paris. Gr. 1317*, fol. 213β; see also *Cod. Paris. Gr. 1317*, fol. 211α.
142 *Cod. Paris. Gr. 1317*, fol. 93α, p. 327.38–40 (*Catechesis 19, Book 1*).
143 *Cod. Paris. Gr. 1317*, fol. 25α.
144 Respectively, *Cod. Paris. Gr. 1317*, fol. 109β, p. 298.41–2 (*Catechesis 23, Book 1*); *Cod. Paris. Gr. 1317*, fol. 112α, p. 302.48, p. 302.50 (*Catechesis 24, Book 1*).

said today, through divine grace. And next Saturday, God extending the words to me, I shall speak [again]'.[145]

Neophytos used the combination of humility and divine enlightenment not only to illustrate his belief that he was a Saint, but also to defend himself from those who accused him of arrogance and sin because he dared to write about divine matters. As we shall see in Part 3, Neophytos became the subject of such attacks, specifically referring to his literary activities, and especially in his early years of writing.[146] In defending himself, the Recluse clearly stated his belief that he was divinely inspired. In 1176, answering such an accusation, Neophytos admits that his hand has indeed written several books, but claims that it was not really he who wrote them: 'not I, but as the grace of the Holy Ghost gave me' the words. Just as myriads of books were written by Fathers who came after the apostles, 'the same mind, with God's help, is contained also in the books written by me'. This apology appears in the *Panegyric* for St Diomēdēs, which Neophytos ends by saying that he wrote 'as the grace of the holy Diomēdēs came upon us'. For added support, Neophytos writes of a dream which he had, and which he interprets as the Saint having appeared to him beckoning him to write his *Panegyric*.[147]

Again, addressing his brother John in the *Interpretation of Christ's Commandments* (of 1176), Neophytos writes: 'You had begged me to write; and if God had not wished me to obey your request, I would not have recognised the strength in your request.' He calls as his witness the fact that, having started writing, he was stopped 'by an attack of the devil'. He took up writing again, he says, only after John begged him to do so. Then, thinking that perhaps it was God who urged John to order Neophytos to write, 'as to a divine order, we obeyed'. The Recluse therefore wrote 'nothing out of my human mind' but as 'the divine and inexpressible glory . . . extended Its grace to me'.[148]

In this way Neophytos presented his writing as something which he did not so much want as was obliged to do.[149] In this mood he writes to John in his *Catecheseis* (c. 1214):

---

[145] *Cod. Paris. Gr. 1317*, fols. 148αβ, 165α–β. See also *Cod. Paris. Gr. 1189*, fol. 147α (*Panegyric 19*); *Panegyric 26*, 456.41–3; *Cod. Paris. Gr. 1189*, fols. 207β, 208α, 210α, 216β (*Panegyric 27*).

[146] See later, pp. 163–7.

[147] *Panegyric 17*, 218.4–6, 218.11–20, 218.26–219.21.

[148] *Cod. Coisl. 287*, fol. 193α; *Cod. Coisl. Gr. 287*, fol. 23β.

[149] In another example Neophytos' answer when he was criticised for daring to pronounce on divine matters was that it was men, made of earth and living on it, who had spoken of God: the difference between them and other men was that they were filled with the Holy Ghost – a gift which, Neophytos says, God does not give to angels but to men, thus honouring the human race: *Cod. Lesb. Leim. 2*, *Homily 5*, 238.4–19.

Because I was not motivated to write these by myself, but only fulfilling your command and in obedience to God and through persuasion I wrote and sent these to you, I know that I have committed no sin. Rather, I would not be sinning if I said that these are not my thoughts, but that having written down the words of the Holy Ghost I send them to you. For, you see, God's spirit, in the times of Balaam, too, through inexpressible providence speaks even through the unworthy. For this reason, sir my brother, as words of God then, do not cease from reading them out to the brothers whose abbot you are.[150]

Thus, Neophytos turned another ecclesiastical literary convention (the apology for writing) into yet another statement that he had become God's mouthpiece.[151]

A striking example of how this kind of self-promotion under guise of humility was actually effective comes from the early years of Neophytos' career as a writer. The Recluse ends his *Book of Fifty Chapters* by addressing his brother John, informing him that he has now fulfilled his brother's request to write this book, 'with the grace and help of God'. If John finds the book precious, he should glorify God 'from whom stems every spiritual knowledge and good giving, and every perfect gift is sent'. Should John find the book a superfluous piece of work, then he should blame Neophytos' ignorance.[152] A note at the bottom of folio 412β of the manuscript records the response of one reader (probably John): 'This book, father, is indeed precious, through divine grace, for me as well as for everyone. The Holy Ghost, father, having resided in you, brought forth a source of words of life.'[153] (It is worth pointing out here that after Neophytos' death his manuscripts were regarded as venerable as his icons or his physical remains: a marginal note which appears in folio 56 of the *Cod. Coislin* 245 states that the manuscript was preserved in the Enkleistra 'as a relic'.[154])

It was based on his belief that he had become *entheos* that Neophytos ventured into interpretations of the Scriptures – a bold step and one, as we shall see, for which he was condemned by a number of his contemporary Cypriots. Again, there is a difference between the way he interpreted Scriptures in his early years, and later. Two examples are sufficient to illustrate this. In 1179, in his *Interpretation of the Song of Songs* he tells us that he will first write the text of the *Song of Songs*; 'Then, if the grace of the Holy Ghost gives me the spiritual knowledge [*gnōsis*] and the words [*logos*], I shall dare an interpretation.'[155] It is an idea which Neophytos repeats at the

[150] *Cod. Paris. Gr. 1317*, fol. 211α.   [151] See ch. 2, p. 24.

[152] *Cod. Athen. 522*, fol. 412α, p. 44.

[153] *Cod. Athen. 522*, fol. 412β, Dyovouniotes (1937: 43).

[154] *Cod. Coislin. 245*, fol. 56. This is one of the manuscripts owned by Neophytos. See Darrouzès (1950: 171); Sophronios of Leontopolis (1934: 229–31); Devreese (1945: 225).

[155] *Cod. Athen. 522*, fol. 413β, p. 47.

beginning of his *Interpretation*. He subsequently proceeds to transcribe the text as he found it, and then ventures into an interpretation which is hardly distinguished by its originality. By contrast, in his *Interpretation of the Apocalypse*, after 1204, Neophytos is very confident, very bold – and probably very blasphemous. He uses 'humility' to ask Christ to forgive him for any tampering with the text. Christ is begged to forgive Neophytos, 'the ignorant and completely untaught', and not to consider it a crime if he leaves out some passages and changes others, or if he interprets parts of the text. He will be doing so, he says, not out of arrogance, but as a 'zealot of the words of Your Holy Ghost, I shall act as It will enlighten my mind's eye'.[156] He writes that his aim is to divide the text into fourteen parts (*hypotheseis*), as he believed it should be divided, 'and which I shall recognise with God's help'. Later, he asks Christ to forgive the alterations which he has made in the text, pleading innocence, since he is only writing just as the Holy Ghost enlightens him.[157]

It is an apology much needed, for, by contrast to his treatment of the *Song of Songs*, Neophytos does not simply transcribe the text of the *Apocalypse*. Instead, he leaves out entire passages from it, divides what he considers is the true text arbitrarily, and interprets it equally arbitrarily.[158] He records his opinion of the full text of the *Apocalypse*: he found it full of 'confusion and impropriety'. In an extraordinary manifestation of arrogance, he admits that he cannot tell whether the text's confused and improper passages were written like this from the beginning (i.e. by St John) or whether they are the result of subsequent copying. The reason he gives as to why he cannot tell whether the text was like that 'from the beginning', does nothing to redeem Neophytos' opinion of St John as a writer: the Recluse cannot tell simply because 'these words are heavenly and strange, and it is not fit for us to listen with undue curiosity to what has been revealed by God and angels from Heaven'.[159] He somewhat redresses his criticism of St John later. After his *Interpretation* he writes an *apologia* addressed to those who doubt that the *Apocalypse* was written by St John the Theologian because of its 'many and base words'. Neophytos states that he believes the text to have been written by 'the Theologos' because of its 'highest form of theory'. As for the 'many and base words', which Neophytos evidently agrees exist, he attributes them to St John's response to the baseness of the audience he was addressing.[160]

An illustration of Neophytos' belief in the divine nature of his activities as a writer, and of how the unconscious part of his mind also pursued this self-image, appears in his *Hexaēmeros* (1197). In his third *Homily* there

---

[156] *Panegyric 9*, 87.14–19.   [157] *Ibid.*, 87.2–5, 87.14–19.
[158] For a striking example of one such arbitrary interpretation by Neophytos see Galatariotou (1984–5: 70–1).
[159] *Panegyric 9*, 111.1–8 (*epilogos*).   [160] *Ibid.*, 112.2–5 (*apologos*).

Neophytos tells us that he had read St John Chrysostom's *Hexaēmeros* and wanted to find St Basil's work too. For thirty-seven years he was unable to do so. After his move to the upper *enkleistra* in 1197, when he found he had more *hēsychia* and more time on his hands, Neophytos again searched for St Basil's *Hexaēmeros* in the monasteries of the districts of Paphos and Arsinoe, only to be depressed by the fruitless outcome of his search. During the days of Lent, 'my mind started thinking about the theory of the *Hexaēmeros*, and soon indeed its words came to my mouth; and after a few days my mind urged me to dare also writing'.[161] Neophytos is clearly referring to inspiration from above. Following this, he describes how his mind started daring him to write about the *Hexaēmeros*; 'Yet I thought I would be attempting the impossible and that this is a trick played on me by my mind.' Just to satisfy his urge, Neophytos says, he picked up a piece of paper, thinking that his mind would leave him in peace if he wrote five or six lines. Once he started, however, he found that the words flowed interminably, and so he wrote on 'until with God's help the first *Homily* was completed'. Following this, he was overtaken by a desire to write a second *Homily*, and begged God to enlighten him so that he would not say anything beyond the true meaning of the Bible, but that he would rather be 'enlightened' in the same way that Moses was.[162]

Neophytos' anxiety, hesitation and self-image as a God-filled writer on a par with Moses, St Basil, St John Chrysostom or 'the Theologian', all came together in a dream which he had that very night. He dreamt that he had taken an old, 'written on' book and that he started writing on its unwritten pages about the *Hexaēmeros*. While he was writing, someone brought a handsome, big book and placed it by Neophytos' side. The same person also brought a church candle-holder with a lighted candle in it and placed it next to the book. When Neophytos saw this book he thought that this was the book of the Theologos, and that he would read it as soon as he could spare the time. Then, he woke up.[163]

Placed within the context of Neophytos' thoughts before he went to sleep, at least one level of the dream's significance lends itself to an interpretation. It seems reasonable to surmise that the old, 'written on' book represents St Basil's *Hexaēmeros*, for which Neophytos had searched for so many years and in whose absence he had just started writing his own *Hexaēmeros*. Neophytos' writing his own *Interpretation* of the *Hexaēmeros* in the unwritten pages of that same book, relates to Neophytos' self-image, according to which his writings are no less significant than St Basil's. The same belief surfaces again in his reaction towards the book of 'the Theologian': he would read that, he

---

[161] *Hexaēmeros*, 168.26–169.27.
[162] *Ibid.*, 169.27–170.3.   [163] *Ibid.*, 170.3–14.

thought, when he found the time, that is to say, some time after he had finished writing his own book. Evidently, Neophytos considered this activity of his as important as – if not more important than – reading 'the Theologian's' work. The lighted candle could easily lend itself to the interpretation of symbolising enlightenment. The fact that it is placed in a church candle-holder provides the specific context of this enlightenment.

It would be both wrong and pointless to claim that this is the only possible interpretation of Neophytos' dream. It is, however, one which fits exactly Neophytos' beliefs about his value as an ecclesiastical writer, as well as his anxieties concerning his daring (within the context of his society) activities as a writer. It can be understood as a wish-fulfilling and anxiety-solving dream, seen by Neophytos precisely because he wanted to see it. The dream provides Neophytos with the reassurance or proof that he should write on, since it provides him with proof that he is enlightened and equal to great ecclesiastical writers. Evidence in support of such an interpretation of Neophytos' dream comes from the Recluse himself: he tells us that after this dream he woke up convinced that his writing was something 'holy' and not the outcome of a 'trick' of the devil.[164] From then on, Neophytos' *Hexaēmeros* is filled with claims that it is 'a God-given' scripture, its writer imbued by the same Holy Ghost as Moses was. Planning originally to write six *Homilies*, Neophytos, subjected to the grace of the Holy Ghost, ends up writing sixteen more.[165]

The struggle against the devil

Let us now finally focus on another theme present in a Saint's *Life*: the fight against the devil. In this respect, Neophytos' life is no exception amongst Saints' *Lives*. Neophytos feels that he inhabits a hostile universe, where demonic power is ever-present and ever-ready to attack. Expression of this feeling is given in such passages as contain his repeated invocations to God to protect the monastery of the Enkleistra from 'visible and invisible enemies' – the latter being, of course, demons.[166]

Neophytos' ascetic way of life itself represented a fight against the devil in the sense of one of the categories we have seen represented in his Saints' stories: that is to say, in the internalised sense of fighting against passion. In this Neophytos considered himself triumphant, since he had conquered sexual passion and gluttony. He stressed his own ascetic way of life, and in particular his seclusion, by calling himself an *enkleistos* in almost all his

[164] *Ibid.*, 170.11–12.
[165] *Ibid.*, respectively, 175.6–7; and 166.6–10, 179.1–7, 205.22–5, 187.10–17.
[166] *Typikon*, 74.1–3; *Sign of God*, 140.9–10, 146.34–5.

writing. He also recorded his abstinence from food, an element which, as we have seen, is repeatedly present in his own Saints' *Lives*.[167] As we shall see later, Neophytos also felt that he was fighting against men who moved against him, inspired by the devil.[168] The Recluse also looked upon his role as a spiritual father and writer of divine words as another aspect of his struggle against the devil. In one of his *Catecheseis* (and possibly referring to the persecution of the Orthodox Church of Cyprus by the Latins[169]) he writes that since the spiritual exhortations ceased, the works of evil multiplied; since the divine words became fewer, Satan's evil grew; since the God-sent preaching stopped, the enemy devil caused the fall of many. He urges his brother John to continue preaching and speaking out God's words (through reading out Neophytos' writings) so that the devil will be defeated.[170]

Further, Neophytos felt that he had personally become the subject of demonic attacks. Some of these were directed specifically against his activities as a writer: Neophytos explained that a demonic attack had caused him to stop writing a *Homily*, until God enlightened him to take it up again.[171] But the most serious case of physical attack by demons against Neophytos is reported by him in the *Sign of God*. The simple incident of his fall from the cliff Neophytos transfers to the cosmic plane of a battle between Good and Evil. His descriptive opening of *Sign of God* summarises his view of the incident thus: 'Recording of the strangely enacted divine protection towards him [i.e. Neophytos]. And the deliverance from untimely death from rock and precipice, which the all-cunning demon plotted against him, but which the all-charitable God dissolved, He who has the power over life and death.'[172] The fall of the rock on Neophytos is described as the work of a 'mid-day demon'.[173] The whole incident is seen as a 'demonic fall', 'snares of hunting demons' having staged and prepared 'snares of death'.[174] It was because of Neophytos' efforts to achieve a closer link with God that 'the adversary, feeling attacked, tried by machinations to destroy my efforts'.[175] While he dug, Neophytos prayed to God 'that I should not fail in my present aim, so that the cunning and evil-thinking demon shall not be triumphant'; and that he would not 'be seen to be the victim of the enemies'.[176] When Neophytos fell and hung in the precipice 'without having any hope of salvation', he believed that 'seeing me in this terrible position and

[167] *Ibid.*, 86.32–87.9.
[168] Regarding Neophytos' 'visible enemies' see later, pp. 163–7.
[169] See ch. 10.   [170] *Cod. Paris. Gr. 1317*, fols. 7β–8α.
[171] *Cod. Coisl. Gr. 287*, fol. 193α.   [172] *Sign of God*, 137, title.
[173] *Ibid.*, 141.2–3, 141.7, 142.16–17.   [174] *Ibid.*, 147.20, 141.5–6, 142.18.
[175] *Ibid.*, 155.1–4.   [176] *Letter 1*, 151.11–12; *Sign of God*, 140.10.

misfortune, the invisible hunters rejoiced greatly'.[177] The fear, frustration and anger which Neophytos felt after his rescue is again externalised by him in terms of a cosmic battle: 'And I wanted to take that hammer and with my own hand to smash that rock, for the glory of God and the shame of the demon.'[178] Neophytos thanks, amongst other divine powers, the angel of God for having protected him against 'the tyranny of demons and many dangers and Satan's mania'.[179]

As we saw earlier, Neophytos described his saving as a miracle, an intervention of God protecting his specially loved servant, and revealing the latter's holiness. Neophytos thanks God for this and invokes Him to 'surround us with Your holy angels' so that 'the workers of darkness . . . will be ousted, . . . shamed . . ., having achieved nothing'.[180] Neophytos' fight against the devil thus ends as it always does in Saints' *Lives*: with the triumph of the holy man and the defeat of the devil.

The paintings

Neophytos' belief in his own sanctity was imprinted not only in his writings but also on his physical surroundings: the caves of the Enkleistra. In his *Typikon* Neophytos writes that in the twenty-fourth year of his enclosure 'the Enkleistra was painted throughout'.[181] This refers to the cycle of paintings which were executed in 1183. Another cycle, quite distinct in style and execution, dates from *c.* 1200.[182] The paintings which concern us here are amongst those adorning the walls of three caves, one of which served as the church of the monastery, and the other as its sanctuary, while the third was the cell and tomb-chamber of Neophytos, his own *enkleistra*. The three caves are adjoining: the sanctuary is in the middle, being separated from the church by a screen decorated with icons (an *iconostasis*) and from the cell by a door.[183]

The caves and their paintings have been studied by a number of scholars, including Cyril Mango and Ernest Hawkins (who also restored them) and more recently by Robin Cormack.[184] They are, however, well worth further consideration, placed side by side with the Recluse's writings, for the two are inseparably interrelated. They represent two different but interlocked expressions of steps taken within one and the same process, that of the

---

[177] *Ibid.*, 143.2–6.   [178] *Ibid.*, 144.35–8.   [179] *Ibid.*, 147.30–3.
[180] *Ibid.*, 149.28–32.   [181] *Typikon*, 78.9–13.
[182] Mango and Hawkins (1966: esp. 204).
[183] For a detailed description of the caves and their painted decoration see Mango and Hawkins (1966: esp. 140–60, 162–72).
[184] Mango and Hawkins (1966); Cormack (1985: ch. 6). Cormack makes a much needed and successful attempt to place the Recluse and the paintings within their wider cultural context. See also Wharton (1988: 53–90, esp. 87–90).

5 Cell, north wall. Painting of the *Deēsis*.

Recluse's self-sanctification.[185] Thus, in discussing Neophytos' paintings in the Enkleistra we shall also have the opportunity to refer to the complexity of motivation behind Neophytos' self-sanctificatory statements – whether painted or written.

I refer to the paintings of the Enkleistra as though they were painted by Neophytos himself. This, as far as we know, is not, strictly speaking, true. We do not know the name of the artist who executed the *c*. 1200 paintings; but we know that the painter Theodore Apseudēs executed the 1183 paintings: in an inscription in the cell he left us one of the earliest known 'signatures' of a

---

[185] I thus disagree with Robin Cormack's view that it was above all through the paintings of the Enkleistra that Neophytos expressed his belief in his own sanctity, and that this belief was 'inexpressible and impermissible in verbal terms': Cormack (1985: ch. 6, *passim*, esp. 250–1).

Greek medieval artist.[186] But the actual identities of the painters are somewhat irrelevant, since in one crucial sense the creator of these paintings was the Recluse himself. For if the artist is the person who conceives of the subject-matter, then decides on its pictorial arrangement and finally materially produces it by applying colours on a surface; then certainly Neophytos must be credited with at least the first two stages of this creative process. It is clear from the rest of the Enkleistra's painted decoration that Theodore Apseudēs and the *c.* 1200 artist were ordinary, conventional Byzantine painters. They would have executed paintings of such extraordinary content and subject-matter as the ones discussed below only if they were directed to do so in very specific terms indeed. And the only person who would have given them such directions is the Recluse himself. Therefore, even though Neophytos did not, in fact, paint the pictures, he did, in effect, create them.

Neophytos had his portrait painted at least twice, and possibly three times on the walls of the Enkleistra. In the monumental *Deēsis* in the cell, to the conventional representation of Christ enthroned and flanked by the Virgin

6 Cell, north wall. Detail of the *Deēsis*, showing Neophytos and inscription.

186 Mango and Hawkins (1966: 182–3).

7 *Bēma*. Painting of Neophytos between the archangels Michael and Gabriel.

Mary and John the Baptist was added another figure: that of Neophytos, kneeling at Christ's feet. An inscription on a scroll next to Neophytos' figure, containing a prayer of the Recluse, identifies him. Neophytos is represented with grey–brown hair, wearing a tonsure at the crown of his head, a drooping moustache entirely covering his mouth, a long beard, arched eyebrows and large, brown eyes.[187] It is certainly a lifelike portrait, and we find it again among the paintings of the sanctuary, also painted by Theodore Apseudēs in 1183. This time Neophytos appears not in the lower part of the wall but at the very top of the ceiling, facing a scene of the *Ascension* and escorted by archangel Michael and Gabriel.[188] Neophytos, a commanding figure of 0.99m height, is depicted standing between the two Archangels, who hold him by the shoulders. The initials 'N' and 'E' appear on Neophytos' left and right side, identifying him as Neophytos the *Enkleistos*. The sallow face bears the same characteristics as that of Neophytos' in the *Deēsis* scene. Finally, amongst the paintings of the church, of *c*. 1200, a portrait of a monk appears to represent the founder of the monastery, that is to say, Neophytos. This

---

[187] See plates 5 and 6. Also, Mango and Hawkins (1966: 181).
[188] See plates 7 and 8. On the paintings of the sanctuary see Mango and Hawkins (1966: 162–72); on their dating, see *ibid.* (193–8).

8 *Bēma*. Neophytos with wings: detail of the painting of Neophytos between the archangels Michael and Gabriel (see plate 7).

portrait shares the same facial characteristics as the other two portraits of Neophytos' in the cell and in the sanctuary: a dark complexion, straight nose, a full white beard and a drooping moustache, deep-set large brown eyes, flowing hair, a tonsure on the crown of the head.[189]

Through these self-portraits on the walls of the Enkleistra Neophytos in fact made sure that future venerators would be provided with his icon.[190] (Indeed, to this day representations of Neophytos on icons are always based on Enkleistra portraits.) The icon was an essential ingredient of Orthodox

9 *Naos*. Portrait of Neophytos.

[189] See plate 9. For the paintings of the church see Mango and Hawkins (1966: 140–60); for their dating, see *ibid*. (198–202). For the portrait of Neophytos see *ibid*. (159, 201).

[190] I am using the word 'icon' not exclusively in its acquired sense (of representation of a religious image on a wooden panel) but in its original, wider meaning of 'representation' or 'image'.

Byzantine religious life in general, and in the establishment and growth of a cult in particular.[191] The cult of icons was certainly of central importance to the Orthodox Cypriots. The *Synodikon* of Cyprus, dated to 1170, contains four passages which are not found in any other known *Synodikon*. These concern the doctrine of images, and in strong language provide a defence for the 'legitimacy' and veneration of icons, reminiscent much more of the bitter days of Iconoclasm than of the unchallenged twelfth-century veneration of the icons.[192] It is worth bearing in mind that Cyprus, due to its divorce from Byzantium during the Iconoclastic controversy and due also to the Autocephalous status of her Church, was not forced to and did not subscribe to Iconoclastic policies. Indeed, the 'Seventh Oecumenical Council' of 754 at Constantinople, which condemned the veneration of icons, anathematised George, the archbishop of Kōnstantia in Cyprus, as an iconophile, together with the Patriarch of Constantinople, Germanos, and John of Damascus. In the Seventh Oecumenical Council of 787, which ordered the restoration of images, no less than six bishops from Cyprus were present, and the Cypriot archbishop Constantine distinguished himself in the fourth session by narrating miracles connected with icons in the Cypriot towns of Kōnstantia and Kition and at Gabala in Syria.[193] During Iconoclasm the island became the refuge of many an iconophile monk, and the veneration of icons was never shadowed by any doubt.[194] It is probably this background, together with a pride felt by the Cypriot Church for its eventually vindicated undaunted belief in icons, that the *Synodikon* of Cyprus expressed in the twelfth century. A particularly strong cult of icons in Cyprus could also possibly be connected

---

[191] Essential for the establishment of the cult were a hagiographical tradition and the visual image: see the discussion earlier, pp. 113–15; and Talbot (1983: 27). For a general analysis of the rise of icons in sixth-century Byzantium see Brown (1973); Cameron (1979); for their importance in the twelfth century see generally Kazhdan and Wharton Epstein (1985: 96–7).

[192] Cappuyns (1935: esp. 490–3 and 502).

[193] On the Autocephalous status of the Church of Cyprus see ch. 3, pp. 45–6; on Cyprus and Iconoclasm see Hackett (1901: 51–3). On Iconoclasm see generally Herrin (1987: 307 ff.), and on the Oecumenical Councils of 754 and 787 *ibid* (368–70, 417–24); Cormack (1985: ch. 3).

[194] E.g., according to the *Life* of St Stephen the Younger, the only safe refuge for the iconophile during the Iconoclastic period was found only in lands where the emperor's jurisdiction could not be effectively enforced: the northern shores of the Black Sea, the southern shores of Asia Minor, Italy and Cyprus: *Life* of St Stephen the Younger, 1160. See generally Mango (1977: 4); Herrin (1987: 382). The geography of the regions mentioned in this context in the *Life* of St Stephen the Younger has been disputed: Ahrweiler (1977). Note that even though Cyprus remained strongly iconophile, the recent discovery of ninth-century aniconic decoration in the church of St Paraskevē at Yeroskipou might indicate that the island was not totally devoid of supporters of Iconoclasm. For St Paraskevē see Stylianou and Stylianou (1985: 384–5). The decoration was discovered on the eastern dome of the church. The church of St Solomonē, at Koma tou Yialou, also contains aniconic decoration from this period: Athanasios Papageorgiou (personal communication).

with recent suggestions that in the thirteenth century the island was a very important centre of production of icons.[195]

Neophytos remains unparalleled as an example of a Byzantine holy man who, in effect, posed for his own icon. In the Byzantine sources, we rarely meet cases of Saints whose icons were painted during their lifetime, and when we do these tell quite different stories from Neophytos'. In the fifth century St Daniel the Stylite was furious with the disciple who had St Daniel's likeness painted in a church. He angrily removed the icon so as 'not to receive the glory of men'.[196] In the seventh century St Plotinos also expressed a similar dislike with the paintings of 'live saints' – a dislike linked, no doubt, with humility.[197] A more positive reaction was manifested by St Theodore of Sykeōn in the early seventh century. He was faced with a painting of himself, secretly executed by a painter who had been set to this task by the monks of a monastery which St Theodore was visiting. St Theodore agreed to bless the icon and, after an initial complaint that the painter had stolen his likeness, he forgave him. It is, however, worth pointing out that according to the Saint's *Life* the monks commissioned the work secretly from St Theodore, because they feared that he would not consent to his portrait being painted.[198]

Portraiture painted during the lifetime of the subject became the standard way for holy men to be venerated both during and after their lifetime. But this was an honour procured by the public, not one which the holy man himself performed.[199] Byzantine history has not, to my knowledge, provided us with an example of a monk (and even more strikingly a recluse) who had his own icon painted in his own cells – except for Neophytos.

The image of the Saint certainly played a very important role in the cult which he inspired. This was a fact which Neophytos knew well: he himself narrates the story of a monk who travelled from Cyprus all the way to Constantinople to commission the painting of an icon of St Diomēdēs.[200] As the *Life* of St Symeōn the New Theologian explains, the icon was considered to be a proof of sanctity: 'for the icon is the triumph and revelation and painting for remembrance, on the one hand, of those victorious and distinguished, and on the other hand, for the shame of those defeated by and subjugated to evil'.[201] (This eleventh-century *Life* provides a striking illustration of the significance of icons and of the passion which, long after the

---

[195] Mouriki (1985–6).

[196] *Life* of St Daniel, 13.15–26. See also Herrin (1982); Dawes and Baynes (1948: 13–14).

[197] Breckenridge (1974: 107–8); Herrin (1982).

[198] *Life* of St Theodore of Sykeōn, ch. 139. See also Cormack (1985: ch. 1, esp. 39); Herrin (1982: 65; 1987: 308–9).

[199] Herrin (1982: esp. 65–6). Note also that in the Early Byzantine period some patriarchs displayed their images and those of Church leaders such as (in the late sixth century) bishop Abraham of Luxor: Herrin (1987: 308–9).

[200] *Panegyric 17*, 215.123–216.14.

[201] *Life* of St Symeōn the New Theologian, 126.21–3.

10 The natural 'dome' of the *Naos* with the *Ascension* at its apex. The shaft
can be seen in approximately the middle of the *Ascension* (see also plate 11).

Iconoclastic period, icon depictions could still arouse: St Symeōn was
accused of venerating his spiritual father as though he was a Saint, the
accusation focusing above all on the fact that St Symeōn had his spiritual
father depicted in icons. Despite his defence of his action to the Synod, the
patriarch ordered the icons to be removed and destroyed, while St Symeōn
himself was led to exile.[202])

There can be no doubt as to the presence of the self-sanctificatory factor in
the execution of Neophytos' portraits in the Enkleistra. But perhaps the most
extraordinary feature of the Enkleistra in terms of Neophytos' process of
self-sanctification is not one of its paintings but a peculiar and highly
theatrical structural device, in the form of a simple shaft. After Neophytos'
move to the upper cell in 1197, a hole was opened on the roof of the church,
connecting the church with a small sanctuary of Neophytos' which was
situated directly above it. One of the reasons for the opening of the shaft was
to allow Neophytos to listen to the service in the church below without having
to climb down from his new cell. The shaft is at the apex of what can be
described as the natural 'dome' of the church, and which was covered by a
painting of *The Ascension*. According to Mango and Hawkins' reconstruction, the image of Christ, in a mandorla upheld by four angels, was by

202 *Ibid.*, 110, para. 81–132.23, esp. 120.19 ff.

11 *Naos*. Detail of *Ascension* and the shaft.

necessity projected into the shaft in order to be accommodated in the restricted space.[203]

This shaft, however, was also the main passage of communication between Neophytos and the rest of the world. The effect of opening it at the precise spot in which it was opened was that whenever Neophytos' face appeared through the shaft, it appeared next to the face of Christ in Triumph, surrounded by a mandorla of flying angels. It is an arrangement which Mango and Hawkins found 'most extraordinary' and even 'verging on the blasphemous'; while Cormack observed that this amounted to the creation of a living icon.[204] From that hole also tumbled down Neophytos' teachings to his monks or to the people gathered for the celebration of a feast-day. They would be standing in the church, itself a dimly lit cave filled with wonderful and mysterious colours and with the smell of incense, surrounded by the paintings of Saints and scenes from the life of Christ, topped with *The Ascension* – next to which Neophytos' face would be seen, and his voice would be heard, descending from a picture which represented Heaven and Christ in Glory. Neophytos' identification with the divine could hardly have been

[203] See plates 10 and 11; and Mango and Hawkins (1966: 141, 200–1 and fig. 19).
[204] *Ibid.*, 129, 141–2; Cormack (1985: 248–9, figs. 82, 87).

more emphatically and pictorially depicted. He must, indeed, have appeared to his audience, in visual and auditory terms, to have already entered the Lord's Kingdom.

That Neophytos believed his own places of abode to be holy even before he died is clear from what he says about them in his *Typikon*. There he claims that his *enkleistra* was God's gift to Neophytos and that its buildings were built by God.[205] Also, in making arrangements so that his tomb would be part of his first cell he made sure that his relics (an important ingredient in a cult[206]) would remain intact and in the specific context of a place which he had already immersed in holiness. This is one of the reasons behind Neophytos' great concern (once more unparalleled amongst Byzantine holy men) about his death and the procedure for his burial.[207] Besides, there can be but little doubt that Neophytos expected his relics to become a source of miracles – as, indeed, they did become.[208]

It appears, therefore, that in every way that Neophytos possibly could he imbued the buildings of the Enkleistra with all that was required successfully to turn them into the focal point of a cult. The creation of specific structural elements in the Enkleistra and of some of its paintings formed part of the process of Neophytos' self-sanctification. On occasion, the Recluse used artistic conventions in ways similar to the ways in which he used literary convention – to mask but at the same time to promote the idea of his own sanctity: he transformed the conventional portrait of the founder or donor into an icon; a simple shaft was turned into a frame for another – living – icon, and so on. As Mango and Hawkins observed, in the Enkleistra Neophytos built a monument to himself.[209] In so doing, he provided also a striking example of the interconvertibility of material and symbolic capital.

This was certainly the effect of Neophytos' actions. It would be wrong, however, to assume that the only way in which either the writings of the Recluse or the paintings of the Enkleistra can be interpreted is exclusively on the basis of a calculated and consciously pursued programme of self-sanctification on Neophytos' part. Though Neophytos' belief in his own sanctity is not in question, the presence and the extent of conscious deliberation in his self-sanctificatory actions is. The question of the psychological

---

[205] *Typikon*, 73.24–6; 89.25–9; 103.17–24.
[206] On the importance of relics for the growth of a cult see Macrides (1981: esp. 84).
[207] *Typikon*, 102.6–103.16. Nikēphoros of Medikiōn also had prescribed the place of his burial, but in a manner incomparably simpler to Neophytos': *Life* of St Nikēphoros of Medikiōn, 424, 18.27–8 and 424, 19.1.
[208] See above, note 109.
[209] Mango and Hawkins (1966: 129).

dynamics which motivated Neophytos' actions is important enough to merit consideration. And because such discussions can easily become, for the lack of palpable evidence, pointless exercises in speculation, I shall consider only those interpretations for which support can be adduced from Neophytos' own writings and paintings.

Apart from the consciously deliberate pursuit of self-sanctification, Neophytos' actions may have also addressed at least two other psychodynamic factors. Both of these would have existed on an unconscious level, the first a personal and the second a collective one.

On the personal level, part at least of the process of Neophytos' self-sanctification may have existed within the context of repeated actions of wish-fulfilment: his wish to be a Saint was fulfilled through his own self-sanctificatory expressions. Having acquired concrete expression through writing or painting, these expressions turned the Recluse's wish into a personal 'reality', which in turn justified and fed further his growing 'realisation' that he was a Saint. According to this interpretation, Neophytos literally 'realised' his wish to be a Saint: that is to say, he turned his wish into reality by allowing himself to believe in the truth of his own expressions of self-sanctification – which were, in fact, no more than expressions of wish-fulfilment. The fact that other people also believed that Neophytos was a Saint would have helped – if help was needed – to add support to his own belief in his sanctity.

Faced especially with the painting of *Neophytos between the Archangels*, Sigmund Freud's thoughts concerning the psychodynamics of art come to mind.[210] Freud believed the artist to be in rudiments an introvert, oppressed by powerfully excessive instinctual needs, who desires to win honour, power, fame and love, but lacks the means for achieving these satisfactions.

Consequently, like any other unsatisfied man, he turns away from reality and transfers all his interests, and his libido too, to the wishful constructions of his life of phantasy . . . An artist . . . finds a path back to reality in this matter . . . and he knows, moreover, how to link so large a yield of pleasure to this representation of his unconscious phantasy that, for the time being at least, repressions are outweighted and lifted by it. If he is able to accomplish all this, he makes it possible for other people . . . to derive consolation and alleviation from their own sources of pleasure in their unconscious which have become inaccessible to them; he earns their gratitude and admiration and he has thus achieved *through* his phantasy what originally he had achieved only *in* his phantasy: honour, power and . . . love.[211]

---

210 See plate 7.
211 Freud (1916–17, XVI: 375–7). Freud appears to use 'love' here in an unnecessarily restricted sense ('love of women'), but it is clear from the general context of this passage and of his entire works that by 'love' he meant something much wider than the obvious manifestations of heterosexual conquest of women by men.

Freud's interpretation of the creation of a work of art as wish-fulfilment should not, of course, be generalised to all instances of artistic creation; but it certainly applies in a number of such instances, and we are here faced with one of them. The painting of *Neophytos between the Archangels* supports Freud's interpretation, and indeed it does so in more ways than one: in the general and obvious sense of the Recluse depicting himself amongst archangels, but also in a number of details. Details such as, for example, the way the angels' wings have been painted in this depiction. Departing from the usual Byzantine artistic convention, to which other paintings of the Enkleistra adhere, both the archangel Michael (who stands on Neophytos' right) and Gabriel (who stands on Neophytos' left) have their left wing painted in anything but a mirror image of their respective right wing. The wings which are away from Neophytos (Michael's right and Gabriel's left wing) follow an almost straight, almost vertical line. The wings which are close to Neophytos, however, protrude in a much wider angle from their shoulders, disappear behind Neophytos' shoulders and reappear lower down, behind his buttocks, forming an imaginary 'X' behind the Recluse.[212] This has an almost *trompe l'œil* effect: it requires little imagination for the onlooker who, naturally, focuses his or her eyes on Neophytos to see the Recluse as possessing wings! The image of *Neophytos with Wings* is not one which would necessarily be consciously perceived as such, but one which would, through the power of association and evocation, be very likely to be unconsciously so perceived and registered. Nor, on an equal footing, was it necessarily created with conscious deliberation.

Another important detail in the same picture is provided by the presence of an iambic distych of Neophytos' which the Recluse had inscribed above the head of his painted image. The short poem goes as follows:

> Τὸ σχῆμα τοῦτο δυὰς ἡγιασμέ[νη]
> εἰς ἔργον ἐλθε[ῖ]ν ἱκετεύω σὺν πόθ[ῳ]

Its exact meaning is not clear. One scholar understood it to be: 'O holy twain, I fervently pray that this image should come true'; and therefore to

---

[212] See plate 8; also, plate 7. Compare the wings of the angels in *The Ascension* and *The Annunciation* in the Sanctuary, all of whom follow nearly straight lines, and where each wing appears to be almost the mirror image of the other in each pair. See Mango and Hawkins (1966: figs. 61–3, 72, 73). For other examples from Cyprus see Stylianou and Stylianou (1985: esp. figs. 85, 87, 88, 92 (Panagia tou Arakou, Lagoudera), 283 (Christ Antiphonitēs, Kalogrea)) for the twelfth century; and for examples ranging from the sixth to the sixteenth century see *ibid.* (figs. 17 (sixth century), 65–6, 299 (fourteenth century), 116, 197, 205, 247 (fifteenth century), 34, 165, 168 (sixteenth century)). Pairs of wings in which each wing follows a completely different direction are also found, and they clearly appear to belong to another conventional way of representing angels' wings, and one which is again very different from their representation in *Neophytos between the Archangels*. See *ibid.* (figs. 86 (Panagia tou Arakou, Lagoudera) and 255 (Holy Apostles, Perachōrio)) for twelfth-century examples; also *ibid.* (115, 146 (fifteenth century), 156 (sixteenth century)).

express Neophytos' wish to appear thus on the Day of Judgment.[213] Another scholar's reading is to the effect that Neophytos wishes 'to be indeed enrolled amongst the angels by virtue of my [monastic] habit'.[214] Another suggestion is that, in keeping with the spirit of his times, Neophytos intended the poem to have both meanings: a pun, with double meaning – a familiar preoccupation of the Byzantines of the time.[215] I would tend to agree with this last view; but the important thing is that all readings agree between themselves on one point, that is in the expression, precisely, of wishful thinking on the part of Neophytos.[216]

A final example is provided by the back wall of Neophytos' tomb-chamber, where a niche is occupied by the painting of an enthroned *Virgin and Child*. The Virgin holds a scroll, inscribed: 'Grant, O my Son, remission to him that lies here' (that is to say, Neophytos). Christ's answer, which is now unfortunately invisible, read: 'I grant it, moved as I am by thy prayers.'[217] Supplicatory inscriptions and prayers for salvation are common amongst founders and donors, and Cyprus itself provides a number of such examples.[218] In all these inscriptions, however, the donor, the founder or – less commonly – the painter prays to God or to an intermediary for intercession, or asks the visitors to pray for him. Neophytos is unique in depicting the Virgin Mary herself as already interceding in his favour, and Christ as already fulfilling the request.[219] Just as he did in the depiction of himself between the archangels, Neophytos expresses here too his wishful thinking which, having been externalised in the form of painting, provides what Freud described as the path from phantasy back to reality.

All this is not to claim that the paintings and inscriptions discussed above should be explained as nothing other than expressions of wish-fulfilment on Neophytos' part. It is, rather, simply to point out another possible layer of significance, different from that of conscious pursuit of self-sanctification in

---

[213] Tsiknopoullos (1955d: 115; 1965: 30). Translation by Mango and Hawkins (1966: 166).

[214] Mango and Hawkins (1966: 166).

[215] My thanks to Valerie Nunn for this suggestion. The poems of Ptōcho-Prodromos present a good example of the Byzantine capacity for pun and intentional multiplicity of meaning: see Alexiou (1986); and below, pp. 193–4, 196–7.

[216] See also the comments in Cormack (1985: 242).

[217] See plates 12 and 13. Also Mango and Hawkins (1966: 184); Indianos and Thomson (1940: 190). Translation by Mango and Hawkins (1966: 184).

[218] For twelfth-century examples from Cyprus see Mango and Hawkins (1964); Stylianou and Stylianou (1985: 159, fig. 85 (Panagia tou Arakou, Lagoudera)); and see also Stylianou and Stylianou (1985: 324, fig. 192) (thirteenth century); 425, fig. 256 (fourteenth century); 331–2, fig. 196; 90, fig. 40; 246, fig. 139; 331–2 (a painter's request) (fifteenth century)).

[219] A more oblique pictorial statement to the same effect is found in the *Deēsis*. See plates 5 and 6. This inscription appears to be closer to the conventional supplicatory inscription, but see the perceptive comments of Cormack (1985: 233).

12 Cell, north wall: the tomb chamber.

that on this layer (of wish-fulfilment) Neophytos primarily addresses none other than himself. Neophytos' propaganda concerning his own sanctity may thus be seen as having the unconscious function of convincing Neophytos (whose phantasy, having been turned into 'reality' through acquiring concrete presence as a painted or written work, he can now believe in with greater ease), as much as convincing everybody else.

There is another point to be made concerning pictorial representations and human thoughts and feelings, this time on a collective level. It concerns the original, primary function of art, as it appeared in the very first pictorial manifestations of the interconvertibility of material and symbolic capital: in the painted representations created at the dawn of human civilisation. Such are, for example, the Stone Age murals in the Trois Frères cave, with their famous representations of animals and a man (a priest?) in an animal mask. The function of art in this case is to give man mastery over nature, power in the world which he inhabits. By painting the prey, man believed that he acquired power over it. By the process of 'making alike', he transubstantiated both the depicted object and his relationship to it. The parallels from almost every culture that we know of are unlimited and ever-present. Magic, then, was the primary function of art, as Ernst Fischer pointed out years ago.[220]

[220] Fischer (1963: 13–14, 29–38, 156–65).

Resemblance has a magical function, and Byzantium in particular, with its Iconoclastic crises, reminds us just how enormous the implications of pictorial representation – especially within a religious context – can be. For if art's primary function was magic, it is also a function which has never been eroded and which is particularly, if unconsciously, strongly present in religious art.

Even though he would, of course, give it a different name, Neophytos, for one, seems to have been in no doubt as to the magical function of art. He wrote, addressing his monks:

And I make this known to you, brothers, that this, my older and first *enkleistra* possesses a measure of a holy place, because of the holy and pure icons which have been

13 Cell. Detail of the tomb chamber, showing the niche with the Virgin and Child between two bishops, and inscription.

painted in it. That is why some people who rushed once and twice to sit in it found that they were unable to do so; and I do believe that to this day no one can sit in it.

Neophytos warns that it is 'unholy and wretched' and self-destructive for any person to mistake this cave and to attempt 'to sit in it as it were a simple, ordinary cell'.[221] The *enkleistra* was thus mysteriously, magically transformed from a simple cell to a holy place, because its walls were painted with portraits of Saints and scenes from the life of Christ.

It is worth pointing out in this respect that the material from which an object is created, and its physical surroundings, cannot be divorced from it, and that caves are possessed of a particularly potentially rich and mysterious symbolic content.[222] It is not by sheer coincidence, therefore, that a particular inscription was painted in Neophytos' cell, on the eastern part of its ceiling. Partly destroyed now, the inscription originally consisted of eight lines at least. The letters that remain mention the monastery of St John Chrysostom at Koutsovendēs (in which Neophytos spent the first seven years of his monastic career); a castle (presumably the castle of Paphos in which Neophytos was wrongfully imprisoned for a day and a night); and *hēsychia*.[223] Clearly, this inscription (of 1183) described in short Neophytos' monastic career. This was also a description which Neophytos took great care to expand in detail in his *Typikon* and in other, earlier writings of his.[224] Yet there was good reason for duplicating the same information: for painted on a wall, between icons of Saints and Christ, the inscription took on some of the same magical power of the images next to it. Inscribed on such a wall, it ceased to be a description of a man's life; it became instead a description of a Saint's *Life*.

The difficulty which faces us when trying to distinguish between Neophytos' conscious and unconscious motivations is due partly to the fact that Neophytos at times deliberately hid the former, as a defence against those who would accuse him of posing as a Saint. For example, in none of his portraits does he appear with a halo. Is this because he did not consciously dare identify himself with the divine so uncompromisingly? Or is it because this would indeed be a blunt, direct statement which would certainly have caused Neophytos' enemies to accuse him of blasphemy and hubris?[225] We shall never know. The fact, however, that his portrait appears not only in the conventional humble, small size and posture of the donor or founder, at

---

[221] *Typikon*, 103.17–24.
[222] See, e.g., Fischer (1963: 156–65).
[223] Mango and Hawkins (1966: 174, fig. 84).
[224] E.g., *Typikon*, 73.8–78.13; *Cod. Coisl. Gr. 387*, fols 180β–181α; *Hexaēmeros*, 168.26–30.
[225] See ch. 6, pp. 163–7.

Christ's feet,[226] but also between archangels, large, imposing: this in itself does not make a direct statement of sanctity, but one which is indirect and yet inescapable because of the power of association and evocation which such a representation under such circumstances had. Because of this the portrait ceased to be a simple portrait and it became instead an icon – halo or no halo.

We have seen how in his manuscripts Neophytos avoided the direct statement of his belief in his own holiness, but used instead hint and evocation. Never irrevocably committing himself, he was therefore always ready to produce a different interpretation concerning his motivations for writing.[227] The same applies to the paintings and the structures of the Enkleistra. Neophytos would thus probably claim that the poem in the representation of himself between the archangels reflects nothing other than the fervent desire which any pious Christian has: namely to be saved on the Day of Judgment; or simply to be found pure in the hour of his death. In support of the latter, Neophytos could invoke local custom and popular belief, the existence of which is recorded by him in his writings. In his *Book of Panegyrics* he writes that 'at the time of death, angels and demons gather', and if the good deeds of the dying man outweigh his evil ones, then the angels take his soul away. But 'if, because of his many evil deeds, the demons are closer to him than the angels are, who can speak of the tragedy and devastation which ensues?', as the demons take the soul away.[228] Neophytos could state that all that he meant the picture to depict was simply the first of these two scenes: an illustration of popular belief. He could claim equally that the shaft in the middle of *The Ascension* in the church was opened there purely accidentally; and that the archangels' wings were painted the way they were equally accidentally.

It is fruitless to search for the exact extent of the Recluse's true intentions: it will escape us, probably because it escaped him too. One fact is certain: that, consciously or unconsciously, Neophytos used convention and the power of evocation possessed by culturally accepted symbolic representation ultimately to relay the message of his own sanctity. The process worked in a way which was different from the way it worked in his writings. Because, even though all representation is symbolic, yet the evocative power of the painted representation is different, and it is perceived in a generally greater number of commonly understood ways. This is so no less because the conventional religious image is, in terms of the society in which it was created,

---

[226] A convention followed in the *Deēsis*: see plate 5; and the comments in note 219, above. For other examples from Cyprus see Stylianou and Stylianou (1985: figs. 57 (twelfth century), 192 (thirteenth century), 31, 40, 71, 140, 196, 206, 256, 258 (fourteenth to sixteenth century)).

[227] See earlier, pp. 97–128 and below, pp. 164–7, 241.

[228] *Cod. Paris. Gr. 1189*, fols. 152α–β (*Panegyric 19*).

universal. Art in general addresses a collective system of belief, one which can transcend class distinctions and momentarily create a collective which appears to be 'universally human'.[229] This, if anything, applies with particular force to religious art.

Furthermore, in Neophytos' society the painted image created a reality which ignored the huge division between the literate and the illiterate.[230] As St John of Damascus had said in the eighth century, 'an icon [serves] the illiterate in the same way in which a book [serves] those who can understand letters';[231] and as patriarch Phōtios wrote, referring to the mosaic representation of the Virgin and Christ in the apse of St Sophia, 'the comprehension that comes about through sight is shown in very fact to be far superior to the learning that penetrates through the ears'.[232] Neophytos had filled his manuscripts with hints concerning his sanctity; but for the vast majority of the people in his society who could not or would not read, and for those who would never hear Neophytos' works read out, the cave paintings provided the solution to this problem in Neophytos' process of self-sanctification. They were immediately accessible to all; and within the confines of that society totally 'universal'. Put simply: not everyone could read manuscripts, but everyone could 'read' pictures. And the message they would be getting would be exactly the same as the readers or listeners of the Recluse's writings would be receiving: that Neophytos was a Saint.

Conclusions

Subtly, sporadically and over a period of many years, Neophytos filled his own life's story with wonders and divine manifestations. He gave to the reader of, or listener to, his writings all the components which were necessary to construct a picture of Neophytos as a Saint. His own conception of what constituted sanctity was one undoubtedly shared by the society from which he purported to have withdrawn, and it was also a conception which through his own hagiographical writings Neophytos reaffirmed, validated and perpetuated.

The information which through his writings Neophytos gave his audience concerning himself fitted that conception neatly, the same themes which structured his Saints' stories forming, according to Neophytos, part of his own life's experience: the theme of *anachōrēsis*, opposed by the family; that of

---

[229] The observation is Bertolt Brecht's, quoted in Fischer (1963: 10–11). Brecht was referring to art in general, but his comments are particularly applicable to religious art.

[230] For a discussion of literacy and education in Neophytos' society see ch. 6.

[231] John of Damascus, I, 93, para. 17.5–7.

[232] Homilies of Phōtios, 294, translated by C. Mango.

flight from the monastery, opposed by the abbot; the further flight, from fame; the theme of a life following a pattern predestined and led by God; the manifestation of divine signs, protecting the holy man and revealing his holy status; the ascetic life (including abstinence from food); the belief that the holy man has been enlightened by God, who works through him; the incessant struggle against the devil which assumes the proportions of an archetypal, cosmic fight between Good and Evil, life and death. All this, Neophytos shared with his Saints, and it all appears in the many snippets of information of a personal nature with which he sprinkled his writings. He further gave his future venerators a centre for his cult, a feast-day, a liturgy. Last but not least, he gave them his icon. The Recluse was a complicated man and his motivations, conscious or unconscious, can be debated endlessly. But there can be no doubt that through his actions he set in motion a long, complicated and at times ingeniously subtle process of self-sanctification.

The dossier on Neophytos' self-sanctification closes here. I hope that there remains no doubt that Neophytos believed in his own sanctity and that he did all he could to convince his public of it. Yet the question of how Neophytos became a Saint, which faced us at the outset of our investigation, has been but partly answered. True, Neophytos modelled his life's story in a way which fitted perfectly his own and his society's understanding of what a Saint's *Life* was; and the very fact that he was a recluse already placed him amongst an elite of monks. But the fact that a recluse believes himself to be a Saint, and proceeds to propagate this belief, is clearly not in itself sufficient (especially in the absence of even a single miracle performed by him) for a cult to be born even before he dies and to flourish thereafter. After all, Neophytos was not the only monk, hermit or *enkleistos* living in Cyprus at the time.[233]

The question remains: why Neophytos and not someone else? Why indeed should a Saint appear at all in the province of Cyprus at the close of the twelfth and the beginning of the thirteenth century? The trails of historical evidence lead us to a different route of investigation – and to Part 3 of this book.

---

[233] See Makarios III (1968: 4–5).

Part 3

The social context of sanctity

In the following pages I shall be pursuing various trails of investigation with one single objective in mind: as full an appreciation as possible of the relationship between Neophytos and the Orthodox society of Cyprus, a relationship which assumed its final expression in Neophytos' sanctification. The fields of enquiry which will be explored in this connection are many and varied: they range from education to Neophytos' audience; from politics (secular and ecclesiastical) to Neophytos' patrons; from political and religious ideology to Neophytos' commentary on social conditions. If, during the course of this investigation, the single aim of reconstructing Neophytos' process of sanctification is sometimes lost from sight, seemingly drowned under the sea of evidence, I must ask the reader to bear with the text until the fourth, and final, part of the book. There, I have tried to make explicit the connections between these different and apparently unconnected aspects of life and culture, and Neophytos' sanctification.

6   Education

It is obviously impossible to reconstitute exactly what Neophytos read in his cell. It is clear, however, from his own works that his literary culture did not extend far beyond the narrow confines of texts of routine patristic, ascetic and hagiographical content (even though it was not absolutely confined to them); and the surviving manuscripts from the Recluse's library corroborate this evidence.[1] Despite the limitations of his library, Neophytos gave great emphasis to his reading, and especially to his activities as a writer. In his scattered references to matters concerning education he is brief but revealing on such questions as the availability of books and education in Cyprus.

Neophytos refers to his own initial complete lack of education on four separate occasions. In his *Panegyric* for St John Chrysostom he says that when, at the age of eighteen, he arrived at the monastery of Koutsovendēs he did not even know what 'a' or 'b' was.[2] He was, in other words, an illiterate, what the Byzantines called *analphabētos*.[3] Neophytos' second reference to his illiteracy appears in his *Interpretation of the Commandments*, of 1176, where he writes:

And those of you who happened to have been trained in the cyclical education [*enkylios paideia*], do not think that we ever saw even a trace of it, and do not proceed to object to our simple and unadorned way of speaking. For I used to live a layman's life originally, and not only was I unfortunate in not receiving the outer [*exō*] and only true education, but I was not given over by my parents even to a single day's learning of the alphabet.[4]

Lack of education (*apaideusia*) was considered a misfortune by the Byzantines, and Neophytos' complaint against his parents for not having educated him is not the only one we find in Byzantine sources: Joseph Bryennios

---

[1] As was noted earlier, Neophytos recorded once that he consulted a chronicle (probably Theophanēs), and twice Eusebius' *Ecclesiastical History* and, through it, Josephus. For this, and for the Recluse's library, see ch. 2, pp. 21–3, and note 9.

[2] *Panegyric 20*, 9.13–17.

[3] See Koukoules (1948–55, I,1: 37–8).

[4] *Cod. Coisl. Gr. 287*, fols. 180β–181α.

complains of the same thing.[5] By his complaint Neophytos may be pointing to a practice whereby parents themselves taught their children the rudimentary letters, just as St Gregory the Theologian recommended that fathers should and as a number of Saints' *Lives* assert that parents did.[6] Alternatively, Neophytos may mean that he had not been sent by his parents to an elementary-school master. This teacher of rudimentary letters is a character frequently encountered on the Byzantine scene, who would often have a second job as a notary (*taboularios*) or letter writer.[7] Neophytos is clearly referring here to an absolutely rudimentary education, the mere learning of the alphabet. Elementary schools in which children were taught how to read and write were, according to Robert Browning, not confined to the capital. He believes that village schools were widespread, even though they probably taught little more than functional literacy. In this village school a teacher (*grammatistēs*) would teach the child letters, syllables and words. The provincial town would then usually provide a grammarian (*grammatikos*) who would teach the child to read with respect to form and content.[8]

The reference by Neophytos to the *exō paideia* points to the Byzantines' distinction between the *exōthen* or *thyrathen* ('outside') learning, which was secular, based on ancient Greek literature and philosophy; and the *esōthen* or *kath' hēmas* (the 'inside' or 'our') education, which was ecclesiastical, based on the Holy Books.[9] These two co-existed and up to a point coincided with two other descriptions, that of the 'holy letters' (*hiera grammata*) and 'cyclical education' (*enkyklios paideia*). The first represented the primary

---

[5] Bryennios, I, 109.

[6] Gregory, 381. A *Life* of Mary written around the time of Iconoclasm presents Mary learning the letters from her father: Epiphanios, 192; and see Beck (1959: 513). The two sisters of St Stephen the Younger (whose *Life* was written in 806) were taught the letters by their mother: *Life* of St Stephen the Younger, 1076. St Hilariōn (+845) was also instructed by his parents: *ASS* June, I, 746–8. See generally Moffat (1977: esp. 88, 90).

[7] Browning (1975). For a thirteenth-century poem written by a *taboularios* in Cyprus see Banescu (1913). For examples from Saints' *Lives* (limited to the Iconoclastic period) of children being handed over by parents to a teacher for elementary education, see Moffat (1977: 88–9). Saints' *Lives* of the eleventh to thirteenth century almost always stress the Saint's education, tracing its beginnings to childhood when the Saint was given over by his parents to a teacher. See *Life* of St Symeōn the New Theologian, 2–4; *Life* of St Cyril Phileōtēs, ch. 1; *Life* of St Christodoulos of Patmos, para. 4, and see Branouse (1966: 51) (he was given over to a *grammatistēs*); *Life* of St Meletios the Younger, 2–3, 42 (a slow learner, he became a brilliant student after he hid under the altar during the liturgy in order to receive God's blessing); *Life* of Nikēphoros Blemmydēs, 4, para. 3; *Life* of St Meletios the Confessor, 609 (he was given over to a *grammatistēs*).

[8] Browning (1964: 5; see also 1975: 4–5; 1978: esp. 46–8). Moffat also concludes that during the Iconoclastic period, too, elementary education was available in Byzantine city and province, that it was not unusual, and that therefore many people must have been literate. See Moffat (1977: 88).

[9] Constantinides (1982: 16); Nicol (1969: 24–5); Koukoules (1948–55, I,l: 66–7, 105).

cycle of elementary education which was begun at about the age of six or seven and consisted of reading, writing and spelling based mainly on religious texts. The second, the 'cyclical education' to which Neophytos refers above, was the next cycle of education. It lasted five or six years, was based on secular texts and aimed at giving a general learning of poetry, rhetoric, mathematics and especially grammar.[10] Confirming Browning's thesis, it does appear that the *enkyklios paideia* could be found easily in the main provincial towns of Byzantium in the twelfth and thirteenth centuries.[11]

It is instructive to look at eleventh- to thirteenth-century Saints' *Lives* in this context. St Symeōn the New Theologian was given over by his parents to basic schooling (*propaideia*) and then to the *thyrathen paideia* before he finally went to Constantinople for further studies. St Cyril Phileōtēs received religious education. St Christodoulos of Patmos was given over by his parents to a *grammatistēs*. St Meletios the Younger was given over to the *paideian* or *hiera grammata* and to the *thyrathen philosophian*. St Meletios' *Life* by Nikolaos of Methōnē provides an illustration of how education could be considered as a divine gift and even as a divine 'sign': St Meletios was a slow learner, until he hid under the altar during a church service so as to receive God's blessing; following which he became a brilliant student. Nikēphoros Blemmydēs, undoubtedly one of the most highly educated Byzantines of his times, began his education as a child, studied the Scriptures, received 'university' education at Nicaea, and continued studying throughout his life. Finally, St Meletios the Confessor was given over by his parents to a *grammatistēs* and studied the *hiera grammata*.[12] The wide variety of the levels and kind of education received is obvious, but so is also the consistency with which parents appear to have cared for their children's education, making Neophytos' complaint against his parents all the more poignant.

Neophytos' expressed high regard for not just the elementary, religious cycle of education, but also for the secondary, secular cycle of learning finds him in agreement with the Great Basil, who also approved of it; but it is worth noting that it seems to run contrary to monastic attitudes closer to

---

[10] On the *hiera grammata* see Constantinides (1982: 1, 7); Koukoules (1948–55, I,l: 35–105); Buckler (1948: 202–3); Lemerle (1971: 99–100); Moffat (1977: 88–92); on the *enkyklios paideia* see Constantinides (1982: 1, 7); Koukoules (1948–55, I,l: 105–37); Buckler (1948: 204–6); Lemerle (1971: 100–1); Moffat (1977: 88–91).

[11] Constantinides (1982: 7); Angold (1974: 178).

[12] *Life* of St Symeōn the New Theologian, 2–4; and see also 30, para. 20; 40, para. 36; 180, para. 130; *Life* of St Cyril Phileōtēs, ch. 1; *Life* of St Christodoulos of Patmos, para. 4, and see Branouse (1966: 51); *Life* of St Meletios the Younger, 2–3, 42; *Life* of Nikēphoros Blemmydēs, 4–8, paras. 3–12.4; *Life* of St Meletios the Confessor, 609. Note that the Byzantine 'university' was a system of high schools rather than a university in the modern sense of the word: see Kazhdan and Wharton Epstein (1985: 129–30).

Neophytos' own time.[13] At the end of the tenth century St Symeōn the New Theologian expressed himself forcefully against secular education, and his words were echoed in the fourteenth century by Gregory Palamas.[14] Significantly, St Symeōn the New Theologian's *Life*, which describes him as having been given over by his parents to *propaideia*, followed later by the *thyrathen paideia*, is highly critical of the latter. The Saint, it states, was wise enough to have absorbed only the grammar from it.[15] On the other hand, it is true that not a single lay author is found amongst Neophytos' books. This appears to have been characteristic of the situation in Cyprus in general, to judge from surviving manuscripts: the far from negligible number of eleventh- to thirteenth-century Cypriot manuscripts surviving today is equally confined mainly to either basic Church books (*Gospels, Metaphrastes*) or the works of Church Fathers (with St John Chrysostom by far the best represented).[16]

Neophytos' third reference to his complete illiteracy before he entered the monastery at Koutsovendēs appears in his *Hexaēmeros* of 1197.[17] In 1214 he again recorded that his parents had not given him even a single day's learning, so that he was completely illiterate at the age of eighteen.[18] It was because of this illiteracy that he was assigned to tend the vineyards of the monastery at Koutsovendēs since, as he wrote, 'I could be of no other use at all.'[19] This last statement is of some importance, as it reflects the monastic use of allocating the hard, menial tasks to the illiterate monks.[20] Neophytos' status in the monastery changed, indeed, as soon as he learned how to read and write. He did so during his five years' work in the vineyards, even

---

[13] St Basil, esp. 43–4.   [14] Nicol (1969: 28).

[15] *Life* of St Symeōn the New Theologian, 2–4. Meyendorff (1975: 72–3) links the monastic opposition to 'secular philosophy' to the recurrent remarks by hagiographers that Saints, especially monks, stopped their education to enter monasticism.

[16] Only occasionally do we find a manuscript from this period containing Canons of Councils, Canonical letters and so on (e.g. the *Cod. Coisl. 209*); *Lives* of Saints, sayings of the Fathers or ascetic narrations (e.g. *Cod. Paris. 913; Cod. S. Sabas. 66; Cod. S. Sabas. 234; Cod. S. Sabas. 259; Paris. Cod. 1179 [Colbert 7]; Cod. Sinai. 789*); or, more interesting still, reports of such current events as the *Praktika* of the council of 1170 at Constantinople on the issue of 'My Father is Greater than I' (*John*, 14:28) together with the 1166 Council at Constantinople and the 1167 Council at Ephesos. Such is the *Cod. Vatopediou 280* (of the end of the twelfth century), which also mentions the participation of the Cypriot archbishop John in the Council of 1170. The manuscripts were almost invariably owned by a monastery or, less often, a church, a bishop or a priest. They sometimes bear a note recording that they were given by an individual to a monastery or church. See ch. 2, note 5. On the *Cod. Vatopediou 280* see Sakkos (1967). See generally Darrouzès (1950, 1957); Browning (1989).

[17] *Hexaēmeros*, 168.33–169.8.

[18] 'Because I was not given over by my parents to even one day's study of letters, I was ignorant of even the first letters of the alphabet' (*Typikon*, 75.21–3).

[19] *Ibid.*, 75.23–6; also in *Hexaēmeros*, 169.4–5; *Cod. Coisl. Gr. 287*, fol. 181α.

[20] For the division of monks and nuns into 'church' and 'labouring' ones, as reflected in monastic *typika*, see respectively Galatariotou (1987a: 99–101; 1988: 271–4).

though he is evasive as to how exactly he did learn his letters. His statement in the *Interpretation of Christ's Commandments* to the effect that he prefers not to say how he acquired his learning lest it be taken for boasting, suggests that he was self-taught.[21] At any rate, as soon as he became literate he learned the Psalter by heart, as a result of which the abbot raised his position to that of a 'church' (as opposed to a 'labouring') monk: Neophytos became a sub-sacristan for the next two years.[22]

Neophytos repeatedly refers to his limited education, calling himself on a number of occasions 'unlearned' (*amathē*), in comparison to those who were 'given the gift of theology',[23] to those who 'can in art and in word and in deed and in theory write homilies of benefice', and to such as 'happened to be taught in the *enkyklios paideia*' and who may therefore find Neophytos' writings 'simple' and 'unadorned'.[24] As we saw in Part 2, through these expressions Neophytos certainly reproduced conventional literary expressions of humility, as well as twisted them to propagate his own sanctity;[25] but his attitude also reflects the prevailing twelfth-century Byzantine attitude towards the written language. The time when a Byzantine writer could safely claim, as Leontios of Neapolis had done in the seventh century, that he wrote in an unadorned and 'low' style deliberately so that all, even the illiterate, could understand him, had come to an end by the ninth century.[26] In the period between the tenth century and Neophytos' lifetime there is ample evidence to the effect that the 'unadorned' style was rejected as linguistically and stylistically unsatisfactory. A sharp distinction was made between how people spoke and how they wrote. Classicising Attic, rhetorical convolutions, every kind of word-play and literary reference imaginable was employed. This is obvious to any reader of Symeōn Metaphrastēs, Michael or Nikētas Chōniatēs, Eustathios of Thessalonikē, Anna

---

[21] 'And in what manner and how I learned the very few letters I know, I do not wish to tell, lest it be taken that I am saying so for the sake of vainglory' (*Cod. Coisl. Gr. 287*, fol. 181α). For references to Neophytos' work in the vineyards see *Cod. Coisl. Gr. 287*, fol. 181α; *Hexaēmeros*, 168.33–169.7; *Typikon*, 75.25–6.

[22] *Typikon*, 75.25–9; *Hexaēmeros*, 169.7–8. Cf. the example of St Iōannikios who, illiterate until the age of forty-two, spent two years learning the first thirty *Psalms* and three more years the remainder of the Psalter: Ševčenko (1979–80: 721). Repeated references in secular and ecclesiastical sources show that the Psalter was usually the first book which would be read by children. They were taught syllables and reading from it. See Koukoules (1948–55, I,l: 55–6; Browning (1978a: 53).

[23] *Cod. Lesb Leim. 2, Homily 5*, 238.6–7; *Panegyric 25*, 8.8; *Cod. Coisl. Gr. 287*, fols. 40β–41α.

[24] *Cod. Coisl. Gr. 287*, fols. 40β–41α, 180β–181α. By 'theory' Neophytos probably meant theology: see Kazhdan and Wharton Epstein (1985: 123).

[25] See ch. 5, pp. 116–26; and earlier, p. 24.

[26] Leontios' *Life* of St John the Almsgiver, 344.61–72. Leontios wrote the preface of the *Life* in 'high' style but used simple language for the rest of the narrative. This was a device commonly employed by hagiographers. Exceptional is Cyril of Skythopolis, who used the one and same – simple – style throughout his writings: Festugière (1974: 15).

Komnēna, Michael Psellos, to give but few examples. It is true that in the twelfth century a change is discernible, in the use and acceptance of 'popularising' (though not necessarily 'popular') language in poetry; but such use and acceptance remained comparatively limited: the climate of the times in its attitude towards the written word was exemplified instead by the order of patriarch Nicholas Mouzalōn (1147–51) for the destruction of a *Life* of St Paraskevē the Younger because it was written 'in a vulgar dialect, by some peasant'.[27]

Whenever a learned writer wrote in simple language, he took the trouble to explain precisely why he was doing so: usually because he was 'writing down' (to use Robert Browning's expression) to an audience less educated than himself. The closest example we have of another Byzantine apologising in a manner similar to Neophytos' for his 'low' style is that of Philip the Monk, author of the *Dioptra* (a devotional work written some time between 1095 and 1097). He, rather like Neophytos, states that he is 'inexperienced with letters' and begs his reader not to condemn or deride him because of his simple style of writing. He asks the reader to pay attention instead to the meaning of his words, which were addressed to all the people, including those who were, like him, uneducated and not rhetoricians or teachers.[28]

It is not surprising that Neophytos' education remained limited despite his evident thirst for it. Such evidence as he gives concerning the availability of books in Cyprus during his lifetime points to a real scarcity. In his *Hexaēmeros* Neophytos describes how after his seclusion he came across the *Hexaēmeros* of St John Chrysostom. His desire to get hold of St Basil's *Hexaēmeros* remained unsatisfied for thirty-seven years. As we saw earlier, when Neophytos found himself in greater *hēsychia* in his upper cell in 1197, he started searching once more for St Basil's book, but his search in the monasteries of two districts (those of Paphos and Arsinoē) proved fruitless.[29] Yet St Basil's *Hexaēmeros* was a very common book in Byzantine times.[30] Similarly, Neophytos records that he 'just came across' St John's *Apocalypse*, which he had only heard of before. Neophytos' *Interpretation* of it contains a reference to the 1204 fall of Constantinople. In other words, Neophytos had to reach his seventieth year of age before he came across a

---

[27] See Browning (1978b); and for Mouzalōn see Beck (1959: 640). The only twelfth-century examples of 'popularising' language, apparently close to the vernacular, are the four poems usually attributed to Theodore Prodromos, the didactic poem whose author is called Spaneas, and Michael Glykas' jail verses. See Browning (1978b); Kazhdan and Wharton Epstein (1985: 83–6).

[28] Examples of 'writing down' to a less educated audience include Psellos' introductory works, Tzetzēs' and Manassēs' texts presumed to be for the ladies of the imperial court. See Browning (1978b: 122–3; 1964: 13ff., esp. 15). On Philip the Monk, see Philip the Monk, *Dioptra*, esp. 12–13, 224, 228–9; Jeffreys (1974: 162–3).

[29] *Hexaēmeros*, 169.7–27.

[30] Over 100 manuscripts of this work are known. See Mango and Hawkins (1966: 127).

book which was also common in Byzantium.[31] Writing a *Homily* for the Annunciation (of uncertain, but probably late, date) Neophytos complains that in the long years which he had spent in his cell he had never come across a book, old or new, of *Homilies* concerning the Virgin Mary, or a book containing *Homilies* on the important main feast-days.[32]

It is indeed this scarcity of books that Neophytos used as his main argument against those who accused him of daring to write about divine matters. He repeatedly and angrily claims: 'I do not have in the Enkleistra, privately, those holy books', referring to no rare theological textbook but to Christ's commandments.[33] And yet the year was 1176, Neophytos had been tonsured a priest, a *lavra* had developed around his cell since 1170, and he had been a protégé of the influential Paphian bishop Basil Kinnamos since 1166. The situation does not appear to have changed much when, very late in his life, Neophytos was writing a *Panegyric* for the Presentation of the Virgin. He writes that if no-one would lend him any of the books needed for the occasion, then he would do well to search the holy books 'in the houses of the truly rich', and to ask for such books (presumably to borrow them) in order to read them and celebrate the feast-day properly.[34] Neophytos' statement is clear in its implications: only the 'truly rich' kept books ('holy' or not[35]) in their houses – and even these must have been quite limited in numbers and content.

How many books Neophytos' own library had is a matter of debate. Tsiknopoulos estimated that the Recluse had at least a hundred books, excluding his own works.[36] By contrast, Mango and Hawkins came to the conclusion that the Enkleistra possessed a total of about fifty books by the end of the Frankish rule in Cyprus. This number excludes Neophytos' own works, and was obviously lower during Neophytos' own lifetime. Mango and Hawkins base their calculations cn the twenty-five manuscripts from

---

[31] *Panegyric* 9, 87.1–2.
[32] *Cod. Lesb. Leim.* 2, *Homily* 5, 238.20–5. For the date see the Appendix, p. 281.
[33] *Cod. Coisl. Gr.* 287, fol. 22β.
[34] *Cod. Lesb. Leim.* 2, *Homily 1*, 236.456–8. Borrowing books from neighbouring monasteries or lay households was not unusual in Byzantium. In the early ninth century Theophanēs recorded doing the same thing; while in the late thirteenth century Maximos Planoudēs complained that many books which had been borrowed from his school had not been returned. See Theophanēs, I, 4; Mango (1975a: esp. 35–7); Constantinides (1982: 70–1); Ševčenko (1979–80: 721).
[35] Eustathios Boilas comes to mind as an example of a rich person who had a library at home. Boilas' library did contain lay books: the myths of Aesop, the romance of Leukippē and a Dream Book lay side by side with his many religious books: Boilas, 24.141–25.166, esp. 25.160. The evidence of surviving manuscripts from Cyprus, however, suggests that lay books were rare on the island. See earlier, p. 23 and notes 1 and 16 above. For Boilas' will see Lemerle (1977: 38–63); Vryonis (1957).
[36] Tsiknopoulos (1954h: ηα' ff.). He estimates that the monastery held at least 150 books by the end of the Turkish occupation of Cyprus.

the Enkleistra which are still preserved in the Bibliothèque Nationale in Paris, plus a number of liturgical books which a monastery would reasonably be expected to have had.[37] Even though their conclusions cannot, obviously, be verified, the total figure they arrive at seems much more realistic than Tsiknopoulos', especially in the light of what little we know of Byzantine monastic libraries and of Neophytos' own comments on the scarcity of books in Cyprus.[38]

We have entered here a much-debated but still unresolved question amongst Byzantinists, concerning the price and availability of books and, more generally, the extent of availability of education in Byzantium. A number of scholars agree with Cyril Mango's conclusion that books in the Byzantine empire were 'very scarce' and 'fantastically expensive'.[39] However, other evidence suggests that book owning and literacy were not confined to a small, learned circle. Robert Browning suggests that both were widespread, and points out that the extent of Byzantine literacy remains an open question.[40]

Neophytos' evidence suggests that the situation in twelfth-century Cyprus (and – Constantinople apart – the rest of the Byzantine world?) was a combination of both views: that books were both very scarce and expensive; but also that functional literacy was widespread. On the last point the reader may recall Neophytos' complaint that his parents did not give him even primary education, a complaint surely implying that this was easily accessible even to the villagers of Lefkara. We also have a demotic poem from Cyprus, in whose forty-six verses one Constantine, a *taboularios*, addresses his student (son?) and explains to him that whatever punishments he suffered were imposed on him for his own good, in order to make him learn his letters well. The poem supports the picture of the presence and avail-

[37] Mango and Hawkins (1966: 128 and note 36).

[38] In the ninth century patriarch Phōtios complained of the absence of books in the monastery in which he was confined. In the thirteenth century the monastery of Megas Agros possessed thirty-five books, but it appears that it had a reputable library in the ninth century, when Theophanēs the Confessor wrote his *Chronicle* there. At the close of the thirteenth century Maximos Planoudēs lamented over the unkept and greatly neglected state of the book in the 'imperial library' of the 'imperial monastery' in which he lived. The good library which apparently existed in the hermitage school of Prodromos, where Nikēphoros Blemmydēs was also taught, appears to have formed an exception amongst Byzantine monastic libraries. See Mango (1975a: 42); Ševčenko (1979–80: 721); Mango and Ševčenko (1973; 266 and notes 152–3); Constantinides (1982: 70–1, 8).

[39] Mango (1975a: 43), referring to the eighth and ninth centuries. See also N. Wilson (1975); and for the thirteenth century, reaching the same conclusion, Constantinides (1982: 135–44). Note that the eleventh century *Cod. Paris. Gr. 625* (containing an *Hexaēmeros*) was purchased in Cyprus in 1136 for eight *hagiogeorgata*: *Cod. Paris. Gr. 625*, fol. 282β. See Darrouzès (1950: 178); Laurent (1951); Chatzipsaltes (1988: 347).

[40] Browning (1978a: esp. 42ff. and 53–4; 1989: esp. 121–2), the latter referring specifically to Cyprus, though in the Lusignan period.

ability of teachers of both cycles of education on the island.[41] Also pertinent are Neophytos' remarks concerning two Cypriot brother Saints, Arkadios and Theosebios. In his *Panegyrics* for them Neophytos praises their parents who took care that both their children would learn the 'holy letters', despite the fact that they were not wealthy.[42] The parents then kept St Theosebios at home, as their youngest son, but the elder son (and evidently by custom the more privileged), St Arkadios, was sent to Constantinople. Neophytos writes that he does not know whether St Arkadios was sent to Constantinople to further his education or for some other reason – plainly suggesting that further education in Constantinople was not something unheard of even for peasant Cypriots.[43] The example of the Cypriot who goes to the Byzantine metropolis to further his education is also encountered in the thirteenth century, in the person of George of Cyprus who left the island and went to Nicaea for this reason.[44]

Perhaps Neophytos should not have complained unduly about the lack of books and education in Cyprus. When he found himself in a position where he could do something for education (through his own monastery) he expressly prohibited the teaching of lay children in the Enkleistra.[45] To be fair to him, this reflected the general monastic attitude, followed also, for instance, by Neophytos' contemporary Cypriot abbot of the monastery of Machairas, Neilos.[46] Byzantine monastic schools did exist, but they were normally only for the training of novices.[47] As scholars have observed, the Orthodox monk had no utilitarian view of his calling and he was not called upon to be the educator of society.[48] Where education for novices was provided, it was usually strictly confined to the 'holy letters' (*hiera grammata*). Nikēphoros Blemmydēs had established a hermitage school for monks in Emathia in the mid-thirteenth century, which was organised and run according to the strict rules of his educational ideals and which included the teaching of secular learning. But this formed an exceptional situation, reflecting to a great extent Blemmydēs' own love of learning and his highly idiosyncratic personality.[49] Certainly, Neophytos would not have behaved like the abbot whom Eustathios of Thessalonikē castigated for having sold a beautiful calligraphic manuscript of Gregory of Nanzianzos because he could think of no use for it;[50] but on the other hand, it is clear that Neophytos was no Blemmydēs either.

---

[41] See Banescu (1913). This is one of the earliest demotic poems surviving from Cyprus, and it appears in a thirteenth-century manuscript. The situation it reflects can only have been either no different or better in twelfth-century Cyprus, in view of the depressing state of the Orthodox Cypriots under the Lusignans: see esp. chs. 9 and 10, below.
[42] *Panegyric 12*, 191.2–6; *Panegyric 14*, 199.17–30.
[43] *Panegyric 14*, 199.26–8.   [44] Constantinides (1982: 25–6).   [45] *Typikon*, 80.5–8.
[46] *Diataxis* of Neilos, 50.8–14.   [47] Browning (1964: 6).   [48] Nicol (1969: 27).
[49] Constantinides (1982: 23–5).   [50] Eustathios, *Opuscula*, 249.57–84; also 245.31–86.

Yet the Recluse had a great admiration for the educated. This is apparent in his comparisons between himself and those better educated (which we encountered earlier) but also in his highly approving remarks about the person who was knowledgeable enough to be called 'wise', 'learned', 'a philosopher'.[51] In his Saints' *Lives* Neophytos refers to their education with such frequency that it becomes, in common with other Byzantine hagiography, a *topos*, a component almost of sanctity. The fact that the education of the Saint is a hagiographical *topos* does not mean that such statements should be disregarded for, as other scholars have also pointed out, they cannot have represented something impossible or even out of the ordinary.[52]

In Neophytos' hagiographical writings St Mamas is described as being taught his letters by his stepmother. A quick learner, St Mamas came to grasp 'pious meanings' while still a child, and started preaching to other children about Christ.[53] St Polychronios' father is praised for having taught his son the holy letters, even though he was a simple peasant.[54] St John Chrysostom is described as having devoted himself to studying night and day, before he set out to preach to the world.[55] St Alypios is depicted having been taught the holy letters by the bishop of the town to whom his widowed mother had delivered him.[56] St Nicholas is also described as having been given a teacher by his parents and his archimandrite uncle when he reached school age – and indeed, one of his first miracles was performed while he was going to school, accompanied by his nanny.[57] Finally, we have already encountered Neophytos' remarks on the education of Sts Arkadios and Theosebios.

Even though the Recluse expressed his admiration for secular learning, it comes as no surprise to note that what he repeatedly stressed was the importance of reading religious writings.[58] He attributes the 'discovery' of letters and writing to Moses, who is presented as having been 'taught' them by God.[59] Neophytos himself goes to considerable lengths in his effort to back his own sayings with Scriptural authorities, by quoting or referring to Biblical authors.[60]

It was, no doubt, partly due to his pride in having acquired an education (though also partly due to the belief in his sanctity) that Neophytos came to

---

[51] *Cod. Paris. Gr. 1317*, fols. 176β, 166α.
[52] Browning (1978a: 48); Patlagean (1987: 564). Very similar views are expressed by Ševčenko with regard to another hagiographical *topos*: Ševčenko (1979–80: 723). On the high degree of literacy amongst Byzantine Saints see Browning (1978a: 42). On the importance of education in Saints' *Lives* see Morris (1981: 44–5); and earlier, p. 155.
[53] *Panegyric 2*, 134.21–4.   [54] *Panegyric 10*, 175.15–17.   [55] *Panegyric 20*, 10.1–3.
[56] *Panegyric 22*, 189.3–8.   [57] *Panegyric 24*, 394.7–19.
[58] E.g., *Cod. Paris. Gr. 1317*, fols. 186α, 207β; *Cod. Coisl. Gr. 287*, fols. 42β–43α, 65β–66α.
[59] *Cod. Coisl. Gr. 287*, fol. 196β.   [60] See ch. 2, pp. 23–4.

manifest distinct traits of intellectual snobbery. His advice to all his successor *enkleistoi* and abbots of the Enkleistra is not to talk to many people, 'and especially to stupid ones'.[61] It is also probably with reference to the same reasons that Neophytos' attitude towards those with whom he disagreed can be explained. This attitude is one of impatience, anger, dismissiveness and intolerance in the extreme.

On occasions involving theological matters, perhaps Neophytos' angry and dismissive attitude could be explained on the grounds of defending the Orthodox faith. Perhaps, therefore, we can put down to this factor his characterisations of such dissenters on one occasion as 'very thoughtless' of 'superfluous and unthinking thought';[62] as, on another occasion, 'speaking boldly and thoughtlessly', 'more wooden than the wood itself', 'ridiculous', 'weird', 'unbecoming' and 'blasphemous'.[63] Yet on occasions where the dispute does not involve any question of compromise of the Orthodox faith Neophytos again appears to be absolute in his own beliefs and dismissive towards any other. One such instance occurs in a passage where Neophytos discusses no great theological point, but what substance Noah used to seal his Ark after it was built.[64] Revealingly, Neophytos' greatest vehemence and intolerance is directed not against those whom he might have seen as threatening the Orthodox faith, but against those whom he saw as threatening himself. In a passage to which we shall have occasion to return, Neophytos answers those who accused him of overreaching himself in writing about divine matters. He describes his accusers as 'some jugglers and stupid and moaning people', who 'spoke not knowing what they were saying'.[65]

But who were Neophytos' accusers, the people whom he elsewhere refers to as his 'visible enemies'? There is ample evidence, provided by Neophytos himself, that certainly in his early years of seclusion he was neither unquestioningly accepted by all as a holy man, nor as revered by all those who did accept him as a holy man (or at least as an abbot) as his subsequent fame of sanctity might suggest. What is particularly interesting in the context of the present discussion is that Neophytos complained of people's behaviour towards him on two counts, both of which were related to one result of his education: his activities as a writer. The Recluse complained that some people did not pay attention to his writings, which were read out to them; while some others did pay attention to his writings, but only in order to criticise him.

In his *Catecheseis* Neophytos writes that he is hopeful that his efforts of writing and preaching have not gone to waste, since he speaks to listeners

[61] *Typikon*, 86.6.   [62] *Hexaēmeros*, 166.23, 167.4.
[63] *Ibid.*, 184.15–32, 187.21.   [64] *Ibid.*, 210.15–20.   [65] *Panegyric 17*, 218.7–11.

who are eager to hear his good words.[66] However, in the very same work, he repeatedly gives evidence to the contrary. He complains that he went to the greatest of troubles to write the *Catecheseis*, for no reason other than the benefit of the monks' souls. By contrast, his monks are reluctant to listen to him: they feel this to be a heavy duty, because of the early morning hour, because of having to stand, because of having to listen.[67] At the end of another passage Neophytos says that he will end his *Catecheseis* there: he wants it to be short, he says, so that some of the monks will not get tired and absent-mindedly start thinking of other things instead of listening to his words.[68] Elsewhere, talking about sloth (*akēdia*), Neophytos writes that it is not absent from monasteries. On the contrary, he says, it attacks monks while they are singing the Psalms, while praying, keeping vigils or standing; making them lazy, tired and sleepy, causing them to yawn and to neglect their duties.[69] The same awareness that his audience might be falling asleep while he is talking to them is also clearly expressed in his *Panegyric* for the Birth of the Virgin Mary and in his second *Panegyric* for the Holy Cross.[70] In both he states that he will end his *Panegyric* soon, so that his audience will not be bored and feel sleepy. In another passage, in his *Typikon*, Neophytos complains that the monks, lazy and sleepy, make up various excuses in order to avoid going to church and performing their duties (which included listening to Neophytos' preachings). He rebukes them for not responding to the church bell as eagerly as they do to that of the refectory.[71] Neophytos' entire experience of how carefully the monks listened to his words is summed up in his advice to his brother John. Towards the end of his second book of *Catecheseis* he urges John to persist in preaching the monks of Koutsovendēs through reading out the *Catecheseis*, 'even if nobody pays any attention, nobody listens or derives any benefit'.[72]

It is obvious from the above passages that Neophytos' audience did not always behave towards him with the respect expected to be demonstrated towards a holy man. They rather behaved with the same lack of enthusiasm which the monks would have demonstrated towards any abbot whose sermons they found overlong and boring. But if Neophytos felt hurt and angered by his monks' response to him, he felt outraged at the response of some of the people outside the Enkleistra's walls. Some of Neophytos' early

---

[66] *Cod. Paris. Gr. 1317*, fols. 13α–β.
[67] *Cod. Paris. Gr. 1317*, fols. 95α–β; pp. 327.42–328.4 (*Catechesis* 19, Book 1).
[68] 'And we shall now curtail the speech and end it, for we do not want such speeches to turn to volumes or be long; so that some of you will not – becoming absentminded because of the tiring effects of standing – allow their mind to wonder away to other matters' (*Cod. Paris. Gr. 1317*, fol. 160β).
[69] *Cod. Paris. Gr. 1317*, fols. 135α–133β (*sic*).
[70] Respectively, *Panegyric 4*, 531[107].15–24; *Cod. Paris. Gr. 1189*, fol. 56α (*Panegyric 8*).
[71] *Typikon*, 94.23–30.   [72] *Cod. Paris. Gr. 1317*, fols. 211α–β.

writings reveal that some people thought that he was not a holy man but, on the contrary, an arrogant, even blasphemous and – perhaps worse still – ridiculous person.

Significantly, as I indicated earlier, all these attitudes were expressed in respect of Neophytos' activities as a writer. They are first recorded by Neophytos in 1176. In his *Interpretation of the Commandments* Neophytos writes that many people come and ask him to write a *Homily* for them, but that he is not sure as to their motivation: 'Whether they truly ask this for their benefit, or whether they do so in order to tease me, I do not know.' Neophytos says that he is not writing this to taunt those people who honestly want his writings; but his remarks following this statement show that he remained unconvinced: 'Indeed, I greatly respect their love for learning, but I just marvel how these gentlemen ask me, the ignorant, to write, instead of asking those who can, in art and in word and deed and theory, write.'[73]

More seriously, however, Neophytos was not just teased but criticised for his writings. In the same work in which the above passage is found, he also writes that there were people who condemned him for writing about divine matters. The Recluse should have not been surprised by such condemnations, for they were very much in the spirit of the times. In eleventh- and twelfth-century Byzantium there was an attitude against critical opinion on a number of issues, but especially in theological matters. The events of the trial of John Italos in 1082 (when he was nearly lynched by the crowd) show that this was a widely held attitude and not one exclusive to the intellectual elite. The long series of show trials for heresy which followed that of Italos amply demonstrated the results to be expected from speculations and pronouncements on dogma.[74]

Neophytos does, therefore, appear to have been treading on dangerous ground when he wrote about the divine – and especially when he wrote interpretations. He felt that he had to defend himself against his accusers:

I consider it only fair to present an *apologia* for those who wonder how I dare write of such matters, and who condemn me for this. Some say that 'the Church received so many scriptures and writings and interpretations, that she not only has sufficient for her needs and for her congregation's, but even overflows in preachings. Which is why in our own times many wise men do not attempt such undertaking. Even though they are capable, through knowledge and the art of letters, to embellish their writings, yet they keep silent for the said reason, that is to say that the Church overflows in Godly writings.'

---

[73] *Cod. Coisl. Gr. 287*, fols. 40β–41α.
[74] About twenty-five trials for 'intellectual' heresy are recorded in the Komnēnian period, apart from those for 'popular' heresies such as Bogomilism. See Browning (1975: esp. 12ff.); Kazhdan and Wharton Epstein (1985: 158–63). See also the outline of careers of teachers in Browning (1962, 1963). Concerning specifically John Italos' trial see Clucas (1981).

The dig at Neophytos for his limited education, but also, more seriously, the implication that Neophytos is overreaching himself in arrogance and even hubris is clearly present in the accusation. Neophytos does not say who exactly his accusers were, but he strongly hints that they were to be found in ecclesiastical and monastic circles, as well as amongst the lay aristocracy: 'And to such words, brother or father or despot or lord, and generally whoever you may be who speaks thus, I say . . .'[75] Neophytos' answer, which follows this passage, is that of a very angry man indeed, who distorts his true feelings in his effort to justify his actions:

Know that I write these for myself, and not for anyone else. I do not want anyone to have my writings, nor will I lament if no-one ever touches them. 'What then', they say, 'are you yourself not satisfied with the mystical writings of the Fathers?' Yes, I am satisfied, but I do not have in the *enkleistra* their holy books. 'And how do you know then what's in them?', they ask. I did not say that I never saw or heard of their contents, but that I do not have in the *enkleistra*, privately, those holy books of theirs. And I therefore decided to gather the holy commandments of God, our Lord and Father Jesus Christ, in a small box; having judged that it is better to have these scriptures in writing, even if my keeping them will cause me to be condemned, rather than, in order to avoid condemnation, to deprive my memory of their marvellous presence . . . Having decided, as I said above, to collect the commandments of the holy Gospel, I did not at all want to dare an *Interpretation*, for fear that instead of interpreting I might do a disservice to the text . . . Having started writing about the first commandment (I mean the one concerning saving repentence), and having found such a treasure in the text of 'Repent, for the kingdom of heaven is at hand', I began, insolently, to interpret the text. Then, I stopped writing (for reasons which I explain in that text) and absolutely gave up the attempt. Then again, having been begged by my own brother to write the rest, as to a command of God, we succumbed to his request.

Neophytos ends his defence in an angry mood: 'I think I have said enough for an *apologia*. And to him who will not be satisfied with what I said, I say that he will never be satisfied, no matter how many words I use.'[76]

The same criticism of Neophytos provoked a similar response from him, expressed in his *Panegyric* for St Diomēdēs, a work of the same year as the work above – early in his writing career. There, Neophytos characterises his accusers as 'jugglers', 'moaning' and 'stupid' persons, who 'spoke not knowing what they were saying'. He points to the multitude of books which were written after the Gospels, and says that many 'wise' and 'prudent' men admire his writings. Significantly, he stresses that he never moved outside Orthodox dogma in his writings, thus indicating, perhaps, that it was a charge of heresy which Neophytos feared the criticism against him might culminate in.[77] The Recluse also states that he wrote the *Panegyric* for St

[75] *Cod. Coisl. Gr. 287*, fols. 16α–17α.   [76] *Coisl. Gr. 287*, fols. 22α–24β.
[77] Like those brought against a number of highly placed churchmen and intellectuals in the eleventh and twelfth century. See note 74 above.

Diomēdēs succumbing to a priest's request, so as not to sadden the priest and the Saint:[78] his strategy of defence was thus the same as he had followed in the *Interpretation of the Commandments*, where he also claimed that he only wrote because his brother pressed him to. Again, on this occasion, just as on the previous one, Neophytos includes in his defence statements as to his enlightenment from God, while his obvious identification with the crucified Christ in the description of his accusers as men who 'do not know what they are saying' would not have been missed by any reader or listener.

We do not know whether the accusations against Neophytos were voiced only in his early years as a writer, when his fame as a holy man had not yet been consolidated. It appears more likely that this was the case, although he remained defensive about his writings to the end of his life. In his very late *Homily* for the Presentation of the Virgin he asks his listeners not to think that he is saying anything which is outside the scope of that *Homily*.[79] In another *Panegyric*, which appears to be also of late date, we find yet another *apologia*. Only part of the accusation survives, and it is again contained in one question: 'and how then dare you attempt speaking of matters which are above you?'. Because the beginning of the passage is lost, we do not know whether it refers to a contemporary accusation or to one voiced in past years; or indeed whether Neophytos is answering an imaginary accusation in the process of his pursuit of self-sanctification: for Neophytos' answer is composed of a now much more confident statement of his divine inspiration; and, again, of an argument based on the lack of books in Cyprus, and his concomitant need to compose something himself in order to celebrate the feast-days properly.[80]

These accusations in Neophytos' early years as a writer were also themselves an indication of another fact: that already by 1176 Neophytos had achieved sufficient fame as a writer to be talked about, criticised and condemned by some; but also, no doubt, to be admired, respected and revered by others. Who comprised the latter, who, in other words, comprised Neophytos' 'public', is a matter of crucial importance in the understanding of his rise to sanctity.

---

[78] *Panegyric 17*, 217.33–218.29.   [79] *Cod. Lesb. Leim. 2, Homily 1*, 232.399–234.401.
[80] *Cod. Lesb. Leim. 2, Homily 5*, 238.4–240.40.

7   Neophytos' public

Like any hermit would, Neophytos became known to the local people almost as soon as he settled in his *enkleistra* in 1159. An early reference to people knowing about him comes in his *Panegyric* concerning earthquakes. It refers to the very early days of his seclusion – around, therefore, the year 1160. It is apparent from this passage (which we encountered earlier) that he was known to the local people; that he had begun to be recognised by them as a man specially protected by God; and as an authority on divine matters: he was evidently considered capable of answering questions concerning the causes of an earthquake.[1] Neophytos' career seems at this point to have taken the course followed by many a Byzantine hermit, who was treated by the locals as a highly respected and maybe even holy man, perhaps with a cult briefly flourishing after his death and vanishing into obscurity shortly afterwards. Cyprus itself provides a number of examples of such anonymous and long-forgotten Saints.[2]

The crucial turning point in Neophytos' career as a holy man came with the appointment of Basil Kinnamos to the see of Paphos. About Basil Kinnamos we know little. Concerning his links with Cyprus, our basic information tells us that he was appointed bishop of Paphos in 1166, and that he was still there in 1190.[3] His successor, bishop Bakchos, is first attested in 1194.[4] Almost everything else concerning Basil's subsequent life and death remains a matter of speculation: he may have died shortly after 1190, as one scholar assumes,[5] or (as the same scholar suggests elsewhere) perhaps he was still alive in 1192, when Pisan and Genoese pirates attacked a ship bound for Constantinople, near Rhodes: the hostages taken included an – unnamed – bishop of Paphos.[6] Again, a seal of one Basil Kinnamos, dated to the eleventh or the twelfth century, may or may not have belonged

---

[1] See earlier, pp. 109–10.   [2] See Makarios III (1968: 3).
[3] *Typikon*, 78.2–4. See Laurent (1949b).   [4] *Ibid.*; also Mango (1976a: 9).
[5] Mango and Hawkins (1966: 124, note 13).
[6] See Mango (1976a: 9; Micklosich and Müller (1860–90, III: 38); Dölger (1924–65: no. 1612 (Nov. 1192)).

to our bishop.[7] It is possible that he was a member of the family which was prominent from the eleventh to the fourteenth century, and therefore a relative of John Kinnamos, the historian and close associate of emperor Manuel I Komnēnos (1143–80);[8] although here we must be cautious: the assumption that Byzantine persons bearing the same surname must have belonged to the same blood family is not necessarily a safe one.[9]

Our information regarding Basil Kinnamos does, however, allow us to draw at least a few inferences with certainty. One of these is that during the evidently long period in which he was bishop of Paphos, Basil became Neophytos' first and most effective patron. When, in old age, the Recluse wrote his revised *Typikon* for the monastery of the Enkleistra, he remembered the beginnings of his association with Basil in 1166 with evident fondness and gratitude:

During those years the see of Paphos was vacant, and in the seventh year of my sojourn in the *enkleistra* it was wedded to that blessed man, Basil Kinnamos. Led by God, he showed great kindness and faith in my humble self: he did not cease, for four whole years, to urge me – now he himself coming to me, now advising me through his high officials – until he placed me under the yoke of priesthood, and convinced me to take one disciple, to live with me, having provided – by means of a *sigillion* – also the necessary grant. And it was since that time, then, that the structures of the *enkleistra* begun to be widened and embellished, and the whole length of the precipice was hewn out for the construction of cells.[10]

Thus, with the recognition of Neophytos by a member of the ecclesiastical elite came also Neophytos' 'socialisation': he was turned, in 1170, into an abbot as well as a recluse, his cell became the centre of a *lavra* rather than the solitary cave of a hermit. Evidence of the subsequent spread of Neophytos'

[7] The seal is in the Dumbarton Oaks collection in Washington, and has been published by Laurent (1932: no. 605). See also Mango and Hawkins (1966: 205 and fig. 123).

[8] On the family of the Kinnamoi see Allatius (1664: 149f.); and the Preface in Kinnamos, xxiii–xxvi; (in the fourteenth century) Kantakouzēnos, II, 223.21–2, 549.17, 584.2–3, 599.17–19. See generally Mango and Hawkins (1966: 205). The name would be familiar to readers of *Digenēs Akritēs*, 86.1640, 168.122–200.630 *passim*; and see Galatariotou (1987b: esp. 44–51). There is an interesting possible link between Basil Kinnamos and John Kinnamos, even though it is too speculative to lead to any firm conclusions regarding the relationship between the two: it is reasonably assumed that it was Basil Kinnamos who informed Neophytos of the 'My Father is Greater than I' controversy, which prompted Neophytos to write about it: see Jugie (1949: 1–7). The bishop is not known to have played any part in the controversy, but the historian John Kinnamos did get actively involved in it after Manuel Komnēnos' death. Basil would have been kept informed of the developments through his ecclesiastical contacts anyway, but is it not possible that it was John Kinnamos who informed Basil of the details of the controversy, before the latter, in his turn, informed Neophytos?

[9] An assumption made, e.g. repeatedly by Mango and Hawkins (1966: 205) (concerning the Kinnamoi); Mango (1976a: 9 and note 28) (concerning the Kinnamoi and other families in Cyprus).

[10] *Typikon*, 78.2–13.

fame, no longer just in the immediate vicinity but all over Cyprus, and not just amongst the peasants but amongst the provincial aristocracy too, can be gathered from careful reading of his writings.

By 1176 Neophytos was sufficiently well known outside the monastic world as a writer of *Panegyrics* for the priest of a church of St Diomēdēs to have travelled for 'many days' and then to have waited another day and night outside Neophytos' cell in order to get a *Panegyric* from him.[11] As his fame grew, people from different walks of life would visit Neophytos and talk to him about what was happening in the world outside the Enkleistra. Their subjects ranged from a layman's talk about the rise of crime, to politics, to monks' and priests' talk about religious matters.[12] Neophytos' rising fame attracted to the Enkleistra visitors from abroad, monks from Palestine (in 1187) and from Antioch, and travellers from Attaleia.[13]

In 1214 Neophytos referred to the multitude of people who came to visit the Enkleistra because of its fame,[14] a fact which already by 1197 had spoiled the Recluse's *hēsychia* and caused him to move to his upper cell.[15] Some time between 1198 and 1209, at a time when the see of Paphos was again vacant, Neophytos wrote a circular letter. He addressed it to all the people of the district of Paphos, secular and ecclesiastical, and castigated them for breaking the fasting rules of Lent.[16] This letter reflects two attitudes: on the one hand, Neophytos' own view of himself as a holy man and guide of the people, a natural leader in this case, in which the Paphians were left without one; on the other hand, it also reflects a response which Neophytos must have been receiving from the people. They must have given him sufficient proof that he was accepted as a leader – and perhaps as a holy man – or else Neophytos would not have the confidence to address such a vast audience in the first place. Again, Neophytos' *apologias* were clearly aimed at an audience wider than the small circle of the monks of the Enkleistra.

But even though popular support is essential for the creation of a cult, there can be no doubt that Neophytos treasured, above all, his connections with the aristocracy. He would certainly not have been satisfied only with the respect and reverence shown to him by the peasants. For, parallel to his intellectual snobbery, Neophytos was no stranger to class snobbery either. Peasants were, to Neophytos' mind, persons of lower worth. In a telling aside in one of his writings Neophytos refers to the supreme insult which

---

[11] *Panegyric 17*, 216.19–21, pp. 217.24–218.3.
[12] Respectively, e.g. *Cod. Coisl. Gr. 287*, fol. 187β; *Letter 4*, esp. 10.15–16; *Panegyric 25*, 8.28–9.5.
[13] Respectively, *Panegyric 5*, 162.11–163.1, 163.6–7; *Panegyric 16*, 211.34–212.1; *Panegyric 11*, 180.21–2.
[14] *Typikon*, 80.23–4.   [15] *Sign of God*, 139.9–18.   [16] *Letter 5*.

one could use against the son of a king, and this is to call him 'a peasant and a bastard'.[17] The charge of illegitimacy bore for Neophytos and his society an extremely heavy burden: the very word 'bastard' (*nothos*) was one of the worst derogatory terms with which one could be attacked; and on a personal level Neophytos reflects this social attitude when, for instance, in another passage he equates ultimate shame and total decadence with the accusation of illegitimate birth.[18] The charge of being a peasant was apparently equally abhorrent to Neophytos.

He was, of course, not alone, even within the walls of his monastry, in looking down on those who did not belong to the rich and the influential. In a long passage he refers to his monks' quarrelling amongst themselves and their habit of calling each other names. In his advice to them to stop this practice the Recluse recorded the epithets which his monks used to abuse each other. It was considered an insult to call one 'mad', 'a fool', but also 'poor', 'a peasant', 'dressed in rags'. Neophytos reminds his monks that all men are children of God and therefore equal.[19] It was a reminder which he himself certainly did not keep. For the Recluse, class was tied up with relative worth. People who were members of the ruling class were not only deemed to be worthy, but were expected to behave in a way manifesting a higher moral state than that of their lesser fellow citizens. Thus, in a passage utterly condemning homosexuality, Neophytos recorded with horror that when, following an earthquake in Constantinople, emperor Leo ordered the arrest of all found partaking in homosexual activities, many such men were discovered 'not just amongst the run of the mill characters, but even amongst the most leading and illustrious men'. Clearly, a higher moral standing was expected of the powerful, to mark their distinction from the mass of the commoners (the *tychontes*).[20]

In another passage, in his *Typikon*, Neophytos advises his successor *enkleistos* that he must not allow 'whosoever wishes freely to ascend in the upper *enkleistra*'. Instead, he should only admit 'a few'.[21] This distinction against 'the many', who should not have free access to the Recluse's cell, was clearly practised by Neophytos. In the *Sign of God* he gives as his reason for moving to the upper cell its 'inaccessibility to the many', so that he

---

[17] *Cod. Lesb. Leim. 2, Homily 3*, 149.339–40.
[18] See Koukoules (1948–55, III: 301); for Neophytos, see *Psalms*, p. 28, Ps. KA. For a social anthropological description and analysis of the phenomenon of shame attached to the child born out of wedlock, as well as to its mother, see Campbell (1964: 187), with reference to twentieth-century Sarakatsan beliefs.
[19] *Ptōchos, agroikos, rakas, salos, moros*: *Cod. Coisl. Gr. 287*, fols. 63α–β.
[20] *Panegyric 16*, 209.29–31. Neophytos was hardly exceptional, even amongst other Saints of the period, in being a snob: see Magdalino (1984). For aspects of Byzantine conceptions of sexuality, with specific reference to Neophytos' thought-world, see Galatariotou (1989).
[21] *Typikon*, 87.16–19.

would 'escape the disturbance of the many'.[22] Only a selected few, then, had access to Neophytos' cell, especially after his removal to the upper *enkleistra*. Such few would certainly have included Neophytos' brother John, to whom Neophytos wrote, saying that he expected him to come and visit his new cell.[23] No doubt, too, persons considered by Neophytos as particularly pious or bearing interesting information (such as the travellers from Palestine, in 1187, or from Antioch and Attaleia) would be admitted. But, above all, it was members of the ruling elites – secular and ecclesiastical – who had free access to Neophytos' cell.

Neophytos stresses his connections with the bishops. His emphasis of his links with the ecclesiastical elite is exemplified by the ratification of his *Typikon* not just by one but by two successive bishops – a unique phenomenon amongst surviving Byzantine monastic *Typika*.[24] As we saw earlier, Neophytos recorded that bishop Basil's generosity towards him had already been expressed in material terms in 1170, when Kinnamos provided the grant for the upkeep of Neophytos' first disciple.[25] This in itself creates the impression of a very personal relationship between the bishop and the Recluse: evidence from this period suggests that Basil provides a rare (if, indeed, not the only surviving) example of active patronage of a holy man by a highly placed member of the Church.[26] It is possible that the expenses of the 1183 paintings of the Enkleistra, executed by Theodore Apseudēs, were also paid by Kinnamos.[27]

If the payment for the paintings did not come out of the purse of the bishop of Paphos, then it must have come out of that of one or more laymen. Neophytos recorded that, following Basil's grant, various 'illustrious men' readily provided the retainer required for the upkeep of the subsequent greater number of monks in the Enkleistra.[28] There is nothing surprising in

---

[22] *Sign of God*, 139.14–16. The same attitude is reflected also in the provisions of the *Typikon* concerning the number of monks: the Recluse again prefers few rather than many, because experience had taught him that 'many' only cause trouble. It was an attitude which Neophytos carried with him to the grave: his tomb, he instructs his monks, must remain built up and hidden 'so that many of the strangers would not know that there is a grave inside'. The few, the non-strangers, would know (*Typikon*, 79.15–30; 103.5–10).

[23] *Letter 1*, 152.31. Whether John was welcome because he was Neophytos' brother or because he was an abbot, it is impossible to say. The most likely answer is a combination of both, since both correspond to character traits of Neophytos' – the first reflecting his nepotism (on which see Galatariotou 1987a: 111), the second his snobbery.

[24] *Typikon*, 91.20–92.14. See Galatariotou (1987a).

[25] *Typikon*, 78.8.

[26] See Galatariotou (forthcoming a).

[27] Mango and Hawkins (1966: 205–6) suggest so, further suggesting that it was Basil who, through his links with Constantinople, brought Theodore Apseudēs from there to execute the paintings. There is, however, no clear evidence that Apseudēs, or indeed any of the artists working in Cyprus in the twelfth century, was brought from Constantinople. See Cormack (1984: 163–5).

[28] *Typikon*, 79.16–22.

this: patronage of monasteries by laymen was a common and significant phenomenon throughout the empire from the eleventh century onwards;[29] and it was partly encouraged by the contemporary institution of the *charistikē*.[30] As was noted in Part 1, the phenomenon of the increasingly frequent foundation, endowment and decoration of monasteries and churches in Cyprus during the late eleventh and the twelfth century was also closely connected with the expansion of lay patronage.[31]

We know of some of these laymen who were patrons of churches and monasteries in Cyprus during this period, and their names are, indeed, connected with the most important of such foundations on the island. The *magistros* Epiphanios Paschalēs patronised the foundation and decoration of the monastery of the Virgin of Alypou, some time before 1091.[32] The foundation of the monastery of the Virgin of Kykko is traditionally linked with aristocratic and imperial patronage: Manuel Boutoumitēs, who had played such an important role in the suppression of the 1092 revolt of Rapsomatēs, endowed it with three villages; emperor Alexios I Komnēnos with funds and an icon of the Virgin attributed to St Luke.[33] Eumathios Philokalēs, the first *doux* of Cyprus after the 1092 revolt of Rapsomatēs, patronised the building and the paintings of the chapel of the Holy Trinity in the monastery of St John Chrysostom at Koutsovendēs.[34] In 1106 the

[29] See Morris (1984). In Cappadocia, lay patrons patronised the decoration of at least three chapels of hermitages; the church of St Barbara, on the site of the hermitage of St Luke of Phōkis, was built by the *stratēgos* Krinitēs Arotras out of gratitude for advice which he received from the hermit: Rodley (1985: 239–40). Lay patronage has been linked with the development of *lavriote* monasticism in the tenth and eleventh centuries: Morris (1985). On monasticism and the aristocracy in the same centuries see also Patlagean (1981b: 100–1). Most sought-after was, of course, imperial patronage: see below, e.g. pp. 215–17, 219–20.

[30] The institution of the *charistikē* was established by the tenth century. The beneficiary of the *charistikē* (the *charistikarios*) would undertake to supervise and administer a monastery, his obligation being to support financially the monks and the buildings. In return he would receive the usufruct of the gift by appropriating the remaining revenues of the monastery. On the *charistikē* and its consequences see Ahrweiler (1967); Charanis (1948); Janin (1964: 9–15); Morris (1984: 126–8); Konidares (1984: 182–7); Galatariotou (1987a: 87–8, 101–6, 113–16).

[31] For a list of monasteries and churches founded and/or decorated in Cyprus during this period, and for a discussion of patronage on the island, see earlier, ch. 3, pp. 57–9.

[32] Darrouzès (1957: 141).

[33] According to Anna Komnēna, Boutoumitēs returned to Constantinople as soon as order had been restored in Cyprus; and it is clear that he was only occasionally on the island after 1092: *Alexiad*, II, 164.20–2. It is not, however, implausible that he may have stayed on in Cyprus a little longer than Anna suggests – until, for instance, the arrival of Eumathios Philokalēs. According to tradition the monastery of Kykko was founded by the monk Ēsaias; he received aristocratic and imperial patronage after he miraculously cured Boutoumitēs and the daughter of Alexios I Komnēnos of an illness. See Hackett (1901: 331–45); Hill (1948–52, I: 302–3); Machairas (1932, I: 36–8, para. 37). Alexios I Komnēnos commissioned a major – and now lost – work at the monastery: see Cormack (1984: 164).

[34] The monastery was founded by one abbot George in 1090. See Mango and Hawkins (1964: 334ff.); and for legends connected with its foundation Hackett (1901: 356–8).

magistros Nikēphoros Ischyrios patronised the foundation and decoration of the monastery of the Virgin of Assinou.[35] The monastery of Machairas obtained privileges and money from three Byzantine emperors: Manuel I Komnēnos gave it grants of money, the mountain on which it was situated, and a *stavropēgion* (which made it independent from the local bishop); Isaac II Angelos (1185–95) gave it money and one of the most important orchards in Lefkōsia; Alexios III Angelos (1195–1205) extended further privileges and also gave it twenty-four serfs.[36] As is evident from the above account, the patrons active in Cyprus included not only the emperor and men posted from Constantinople to serve on the island for limited periods of time (such as Manuel Boutoumitēs or Eumathios Philokalēs), but also members of the local ruling class, such as Epiphanios Paschalēs and Nikēphoros Ischyrios.

Neophytos' monastery thus formed no exception in being patronised by members of the local ruling class. Indeed, it is the rich laymen among Neophytos' admirers who must have kept the monastery going until the Latin occupation. Neophytos' statement that he never provided for the morrow, nor had acquired any property until 1191, and yet God provided the Enkleistra with all necessities, must surely be taken as an indication of active patronage from one or more sources.[37] Another indication that the rich supported the Enkleistra financially is provided by the fact that Neophytos felt the need to acquire some property for the monastery only after 1191. He said that this was so because of the hard times in which the Enkleistra, like the rest of Orthodox Cyprus, fell after the Latin occupation.[38] This despite the fact that the Latins had left all the Orthodox monasteries in Cyprus in peace, at least until 1214 – as Neophytos himself

---

[35] The paintings of Assinou are stylistically very close to those of St John Chrysostom and it has been suggested that they were executed by a pupil of the painter of Koutsovendēs: Winfield (1972).

[36] The monastery was founded when Neophytos, a hermit refugee from Palestine, settled on mount Aoos, south-west of the village of Lythrodonta, and was joined by the monk Ignatios. After his death Ignatios was joined by Prokopios. In 1172 they were joined by the monk Neilos, who had also come from Palestine, and who subsequently succeeded Ignatios as the monastery's abbot. Neilos was a particularly enterprising abbot and a brilliant organiser. In the *Typikon* of Neilos the extensive and detailed instructions and descriptions regarding its economic and administrative organisation leave no doubt that the monastery was one of the largest and most efficiently organised agricultural units on the island. See *Diataxis* of Neilos, 37.18–50.3; also Mango (1980: 121–2); Galatariotou (1987a: 130–1); generally Hill (1948–52, I: 310–11); Hackett (1901: 345–8). Other monasteries founded during this period include that of the Virgin Chrysorrogiatissa, on Mount Rhoia (founded in 1152 by the monk Ignatios according to tradition recorded on one of the monastery's icons); the monastery of Mamas in the village of Morphou (traditionally also dated to the Komnēnian era); the monastery of the Virgin Trooditissa, on Mount Troodos (traditionally founded *c.* 1200). See Hackett (1901: 354–6).

[37] *Typikon*, 80.17–19, 81.1–4.   [38] *Ibid.*, 80.20–8.

admits in his *Typikon*.[39] The reason for which the Enkleistra experienced hardship for the first time after 1191 was simply because, as Neophytos recorded elsewhere, the ruling class of Cyprus 'with great haste sailed away in secret to foreign lands and to the Queen of Cities';[40] while the vast majority of those who remained were reduced to poverty. Suddenly, after 1191, Cyprus lost its local aristocracy, and Neophytos lost his patrons.[41]

Yet even though the Enkleistra suffered financial hardship after 1191, Neophytos may, nevertheless, have somewhat understated his case concerning the Enkleistra's financial resources after this date. It is clear, for a start, that other patrons at least partially replaced those who left; for, after all, not all the members of the local ruling class became refugees after 1191.[42] These patrons were wealthy enough to patronise the expensive, gilded decorations of the Enkleistra, executed in *c*. 1200.[43] Again, Neophytos tells us in his *Typikon* in 1214 that the monastery's hardship led his monks to urge him to allow the Enkleistra to acquire some property, 'and I thus succumbed to their wishes, that is to say to acquire a small plot of arable land, a vineyard and a few head of cattle'.[44] Notes contained in an early thirteenth-century manuscript are more forthcoming concerning the landed properties of the Enkleistra, and they document the expansion of the monastery's properties after 1191 – after, that is, Neophytos judged it necessary to compromise his rule against acquisition of property by his monastery. The notes are contained in the *Cod. Paris. 301 (Colbert 614)*, and have been partly published by Darrouzès.[45] The manuscript was copied in 1203–4 by George of Rhodes for the church of St Epiphanios, 'that is to say, of the Enkleistra'. A note further clarifies that this refers to a church of St Epiphanios 'of Koubouklion [τῶν Κουβουκλίων] which is now a *metochion* of the holy Enkleistra'; which Enkleistra has also a sanctuary, 'the so-called Great Dēmētrios of Nikoklia [τῆς Νικοκλίας] and St Andronikos of Mantrōn [τῶν Μαντρῶν]'. As if to add confirmation to clear evidence that St Epiphanios was a *metochion* of the Enkleistra, the copyist made marginal corrections in copying his model *Evangelion*, containing the usual feast-days of the Church of Constantinople. These corrections are additions indicating local preferences for Saints who enjoyed particularly popular cults in Cyprus – Saints such as those Neophytos had been writing *Panegyrics* for (e.g. Sts Andronikos and Athanasia for 9 October instead of St John the

---

[39] Ibid., 95.30–96.3.   [40] *Letter 4*, 11.3–4.
[41] Bishop Basil Kinnamos also probably left Cyprus in 1192. See Mango (1976a: 9). Basil's successor, Bakchos, is first attested in 1194. See Laurent (1949b).
[42] Mango (1976a: 9).
[43] Mango and Hawkins (1966: 206).   [44] *Typikon*, 80.27–8.
[45] Darrouzès (1950: 172–3). See also Omont (1896, II: pl. LI).

Apostle; St John the Almsgiver for 12 November rather than St Neilos; St Marina for 17 July). It therefore appears from the note referred to above that the Enkleistra had at least three *metochia* by 1203–4.

Darrouzès did not identify the localities mentioned in these notes, writing that he expected a Cypriot to take the trouble of identifying them. Νικοκλία must surely refer to the same village which today appears on official maps of Cyprus as Νικοκλεία. The village τῶν Μαντρῶν can with confidence be identified as today's village of Μανδριά (especially since in spoken Cypriot the village is always referred to as τά Μαντριά, rather than τα Μανδριά, and is thus very close to the τῶν Μαντρῶν of the manuscript). Mandria and Nikokleia are very close to each other, and between them lies the place which is today known as Κούκλια: this is the manuscript's site of των Κουβουκλίων. The site is well known as Κουβούκλια from medieval sources: Machairas cites it as one of the villages pillaged by the Saracens in 1426; the French knew it as 'La Covocle'; and the – very common – dropping of the intervocalic 'β' subsequently produced Κούκλια.[46] The three locations are very close to each other, and they are situated south-east of, and not very far from, the Enkleistra (Kouklia being about 11 kilometres east of the new town of Paphos).[47]

We do not know the precise extent of these *metochia*, but there is no reason for believing that Neophytos' rather vague testimony in his *Typikon* is unrelated to them: one of the sites could indeed have been the 'small plot of arable land', the other that of the 'vineyard' and the third the home of the 'few head of cattle' he referred to. In such case, these possessions would not have made the monastery of the Enkleistra a wealthy one, but one which was self-sufficient. This corroborates Neophytos' own testimony, as to the reasons for which he permitted the acquisition of these properties. It also provides support for the view that the wealthiest patrons fled after 1191 (thus forcing Neophytos to take measures to safeguard the material survival of his monastery); as well as for the view that nevertheless a few patrons did continue to be able to support the Enkleistra through, for example, donations of land – for there would have been no other way in which the Enkleistra could have acquired these properties. In the last case, it is not necessary to search for very wealthy patrons; only for some Orthodox inhabitants who would have been sufficiently well off to own a 'small plot of arable land', and who would not necessarily have belonged to the group of the 'illustrious' men who had patronised the monastery in the pre-1191 years.

---

[46] *Machairas*, I, 632.8–9, II, 216 para. 652; Menardos (1907: 376).
[47] It must be noted here that the dating of these notes has been disputed: Egglezakes (1979–80: 80–1) dates them to the fifteenth century.

Even as late as 1214, however, Neophytos did not relinquish his links with whatever was left of the local 'illustrious' men, and it is to them that the *Typikon* draws our attention again. It was no doubt one of them that Neophytos appointed as warden (*epitropos*) of his monastery through his *Typikon* of 1214.[48] The fact that the Recluse calls him a 'benefactor' indicates that he was already a financial provider of the Enkleistra.[49] Was this warden the same person to whom Neophytos addressed his most famous writing, his letter concerning the misfortunes of Cyprus? The answer can at this stage be only speculative, but the certain fact is that Neophytos knew intimately a person such as the addressee of that letter. He was a man of great wealth, who left Cyprus 'together with all his people' (presumably his retainers and/or a contingent of troops that owed allegiance to him) and who had been received by emperor Alexios III Angelos (1195–1203) in Nicaea and honoured by him with the title of *sebastos*.[50] It seems quite possible that this powerful person would be the same man whom Neophytos chose to be the warden of his monastery and to act as a mediator between the monks and the emperor in case of a petition by the monks.[51] Note, finally, that Neophytos must have known some at least of the 'truly rich' from whom he used to borrow books.[52]

What was the precise relationship between Neophytos and such representatives of the ruling class as the *sebastos* to whom the Recluse wrote? There can be little doubt that some, if not all, of the 'illustrious' men of Neophytos' acquaintance were his spiritual sons. Neophytos' eagerness to be a spiritual father is manifested in his spiritual adoption of his own blood brother, John, whom he addresses as his 'spiritual child'.[53] It is also manifested in his circular letter concerning those who did not observe the rules of fasting in the district of Paphos. In this letter Neophytos clearly plays the role of the scourging spiritual father for both laymen and clergy.[54] Evidence that the Recluse acted as the spiritual father of the rich and powerful comes from his letter concerning the misfortunes of Cyprus. The emigré to whom Neophytos addressed the letter is expressly stated to be 'our spiritual son'.[55] It has already been observed by scholars that the political role which the holy man came to play in Byzantium was based on his relation of spiritual kinship with the high and mighty of his society. In yet another example of the interconvertibility of material and symbolic capital, the acceptance of the Saint by a large body of people showed itself in concrete form in

---

[48] *Typikon*, 78.14–79.2.   [49] *Ibid.*, 78.20.
[50] *Letter 4*, 10.12–16; and see Mango (1976a: 9).
[51] *Typikon*, 78.21–79.2.   [52] *Cod. Lesb. Leim. 2, Homily 1*, 236.456–60.
[53] Τέκνον πνευματικόν: *Cod. Coisl. Gr. 287*, fol. 42β.
[54] *Letter 5*.   [55] *Letter 4*, 10.12.

increased patronage of the foundations set up by the holy men concerned, and in their rising reputations as spiritual guides.[56] The same people, then, who financed Neophytos' paintings, his expanding numbers of monks, his books and his writing materials, would very probably have also been his spiritual sons, just as the *sebastos* was.

Post-ninth-century hagiography frequently stresses the connection of the holy man with the powerful of his society, a connection based usually on the holy man's role of spiritual father.[57] This became a hagiographical *topos* but, as in the case of other hagiographical *topoi*, this does not necessarily compromise the credibility of the incidents described in Saints' *Lives* from the period.[58] What these *Lives* describe in this respect is very revealing. According to them, St Cyril Phileōtēs received visits from Anna Dalassena, Constantine Choirosphaktēs, Eumathios Philokalēs, Michael *protostratēr* (brother of the empress), George Palaiologos (brother-in-law of the empress) and ultimately from the emperor himself and all his family. Later the emperor visited St Cyril again to ask for his advice concerning an expedition which he planned against the Turks. Significantly, a number of these distinguished visitors (the emperor included) combined their visits with donations of money.[59] St Christodoulos of Patmos repeatedly met Alexios I Komnēnos and negotiated at length Alexios' proposal that he should take charge of the monasteries in Thessaly. Eventually St Christodoulos succeeded in convincing Alexios to grant him the island of Patmos. Alexios also granted to the new monastery an annual subsidy.[60] St Meletios the Younger also received a retainer from the same emperor.[61] St Leontios of Jerusalem held conversations with Manuel I Komnēnos, whose offers for various archiepiscopal sees (including that of Cyprus) he rejected until he was offered the Patriarchate of Jerusalem.[62] St Hilariōn of Moglena was depicted as guiding Manuel back to the correct path of the Orthodox faith as opposed to that of various dualist heretics (Manicheans, Bogomils, Paul-

---

[56] See Morris (1981: 46ff.), referring to the eleventh century. For the link between spiritual ties and patronage see Morris (1984: 115ff.; 1985: 226–31).

[57] Pre-ninth-century examples are also found: in the seventh century St Theodore of Sykeōn was wined and dined by three successive emperors. In the eighth century St George of Amastris had a very close relationship with Constantine VI, Eirene and especially Nikēphoros I. In the ninth century St Nikēphoros of Medikiōn (+813) was also a friend of unspecified emperors. Later in the same century St Eustratios travelled to Constantinople to secure imperial help for his monastery of Agauros, near Prusa. See Ševčenko (1979–1980: 722–3, 719–20 and note 12).

[58] See, e.g., the comments of Ševčenko (1979–80: 723); Patlagean (1987: 564).

[59] *Life* of St Cyril Phileōtēs, chs. 16–17; chs. 34–6; ch. 46, paras. 1–16; ch. 47, paras. 1–14; ch. 48, paras. 1–3; ch. 51, paras. 1–3.

[60] Alexios became the monastery's ἐτήσιος σιτοδότης: *Life* of St Christodoulos of Patmos, para. 13, and see also Branouse (1966: 52).

[61] *Life* of St Meletios the Younger, 49.

[62] *Life* of St Leontios of Jerusalem, 412–14.

icians).[63] St Meletios the Confessor's fame also reached the emperor;[64] while John Batatzēs and his son were recorded by the would-be Saint Nikēphoros Blemmydēs as being great admirers of his.[65] Amongst the eleventh- to thirteenth-century *Lives* perhaps the most striking illustration of the authority which a spiritual father could muster comes from the *Life* of St Symeōn the New Theologian, written by the Saint's own spiritual son, Nikētas Stēthatos. The spiritual father is described as being infinitely more important than the natural parent; and St Symeōn so admired his own spiritual father (also named Symeōn) that after his death he venerated him as a Saint – a belief to which he persisted despite his trial by the Synod for it and his subsequent condemnation to exile.[66]

The exact relationship between spiritual father and child remains an area still awaiting comprehensive study.[67] But there is no doubt that the spiritual father stood in a position of great authority and power *vis-à-vis* his spiritual child. The latter fully trusted the guide of his conscience with his innermost secrets, and followed his advice. It has been suggested that the spiritual child's dependency on the spiritual father stemmed from the conviction of the first that he received help from the spiritual father in two ways: by modelling himself on the example of the spiritual father's daily life; and through a 'disclosure of thoughts': the spiritual child's confession of his sinful acts and thoughts to the spiritual father – a confession which the father invariably followed by a prescription of the penances necessary to alleviate the sin and by advice concerning the future conduct of the child.[68]

The fact that the holy man had entered into relations of spiritual kinship with members of the ruling class of his society was a sure indication that he had achieved the greatest possible social acknowledgment of having reached the pinnacle of his profession. This happened to Neophytos, despite the fact that he appears to have stood at a disadvantage to other spiritual fathers: the post-ninth-century spiritual fathers referred to above were revered for 'a

[63] *Life* of St Hilariōn of Moglena, and Turdeanu (1947: 83).
[64] *Life* of St Meletios the Confessor, 615.
[65] *Life* of Nikēphoros Blemmydēs, 36–44, paras. 73–89. On the *Life*'s auto-hagiographical nature see earlier, p. 71.
[66] *Life* of St Symeōn the New Theologian, 110, para. 81–132.23. See also: *Life* of St Cyril Phileōtēs, ch. 19, paras. 1–3. And Patlagean (1987: 612–13).
[67] See Morris (1976: 16 and note 53; 1981: 46 and note 15; 1984: 115ff.; 1985). See also Patlagean (1981b: 96 and note 56; 1987: 609–13). For a study concentrating on one such example see Turner (1985). There exists one general study, but it is not a historical one, and at any rate it concentrates on the desert Fathers: Hauscherr (1955). On tenth- and eleventh-century spiritual kinshsip see Turner (1985); and Morris (1978: ch. 1, parts V and VI; 1981: 46ff.; 1985: 226–31). See also Patlagean (1981b: 96–7), referring to the period of the ninth to the eleventh century; also Patlagean (1987: 609–13).
[68] Ware (1982: esp. 36–43).

sanctity associated with the qualities of curing, prophecy and asceticism'.[69] Of these, Neophytos could only claim the last.

Our evidence thus shows that Neophytos was linked with the ruling secular and ecclesiastical elites in Cyprus. But a cult needs a broader base than this. Neophytos the holy man needs a public which must be wider than the local aristocrats or the monks of his own monastery. He needs, in fact, a mass public if his cult is to be born and sustained. Yet at the same time he had expressly set the aim of only coming into contact with a selected 'few'. Let us examine, then, how Neophytos managed to get in touch with 'the many'. The key to this lies in the answer to the question of whom Neophytos wrote for. To whom, in other words, was Neophytos addressing his writings, and who did he expect to read or hear them?

A number of Neophytos' surviving writings are addressed to specific persons, often expressly stating that they were written at that person's request. By far the most frequent bearer of such requests appears to have been Neophytos' brother John. Glimpses of John's own monastic career in the monastery of St John Chrysostom at Koutsovendēs are traced through Neophytos' writings, from a reference to his already high position as the bursar (*oikonomos*) of the monastery in 1176, to another reference to his recent investiture as abbot some time before 1214.[70] Through the years Neophytos wrote repeatedly for John. Both the *Interpretation of the Commandments* of 1176 and the *Book of Fifty Chapters* of 1179 contain addresses to John throughout the text.[71] In 1197 Neophytos wrote to John about his 'sign of God'.[72] A biographical note dated to after 1206 also mentions John, while the books of *Catecheseis* were also written for him, around 1214.[73]

Of the remaining writings some are clearly addressed to specific persons. The most famous writing of Neophytos (his letter concerning the misfortunes of Cyprus) is addressed to an aristocratic spiritual son of his, as we have seen. Another letter is addressed to one Euthymios, monk and priest of the monastery of St John Chrysostom; while a speech concerning obedience is addressed to Neophytos' monks.[74] Sometimes it appears from the text

[69] Morris (1981: 46 and note 16).
[70] Respectively, *Cod. Coisl. Gr. 287*, fol. 181α; *Cod. Paris. Gr. 1317*, fols. 6α–β, p. 268.1–7 (Prologue, *Catecheseis*, Book 1).
[71] Respectively, e.g. *Cod. Coisl. Gr. 287*, fols. 105β, 181α, 183α, 186β, 193α, 193β, 194α; *Cod. Athen. 522*, fols. 11α (p. 43), 11β (p. 44), 12α (p. 44), 14α, 28β, 34α, 36α, 44α, 90α, 397β, 412α (p. 44).
[72] *Letter 1*, 150.7–152.39.
[73] Respectively, *Bibliographical Note*, 126.4–5; *Cod. Paris. Gr. 1317*, e.g. fols. 6α–β, p. 268.1–7 (Prologue, *Catecheseis*, Book 1), fols. 7α–β, 8α, 30β, 112α (p. 302.46–56) (*Catechesis 24*, Book 1), 210β, 211α.
[74] Respectively, *Letter 4*, 10; *Letter 3, Cod. Coisl. Gr. 287*, fol. 202β, p. 215; *Homily* in *Cod. Coisl. 287*. fol. 198α.

that Neophytos is addressing someone in particular, because of the use of the second-person singular (for example, in the *Homily* for the Presentation of the Virgin, or in that for the Holy Lights[75]); but whether Neophytos is writing for a specific person or whether he is simply using the singular form of address as a device for reaching out to every single reader or listener, it is impossible to tell. Again, a letter survives vaguely addressed 'to an abbot', while on another occasion, as we saw earlier, Neophytos wrote a circular letter addressed to all the inhabitants of the district of Paphos.[76]

We know that a number of Neophytos' writings were specifically requested. John had specifically asked Neophytos to write the *Interpretation of the Commandments*, the *Book of Fifty Chapters* and the *Catecheseis*;[77] and it is obviously also in the form of fulfilling a promise or answering a question put to him that Neophytos wrote the letters to his spiritual son, to the unspecified abbot and to Euthymios.[78] We can also be certain that at least some of Neophytos' *Panegyrics* were written on request (though we do not know whether they were commissioned in exchange for money). Such is apparently the case with the *Panegyric* for archangel Michael, in which a number of passages make it clear that it was intended to be read out in a church which formed the centre of a local cult of the archangel, and to its congregation.[79] The title of Neophytos' *Panegyric* for the consecration of the Church of the Resurrection includes the information that the same work was also meant to be read out on the occasion of the consecration of 'any' church, thus pointing at an extremely flexible use for this work.[80] A confirmation that Neophytos was writing *Panegyrics* to be read out in places other than his own monastery or (through John) the monastery of Koutsovendēs, appears in the Recluse's *Panegyric* for St Diomēdēs. Neophytos records there that in 1176 the priest of a church of the Saint had travelled to the Enkleistra especially in order to place a request with Neophytos to write a *Panegyric*.[81] This, together with other *Panegyrics* which seem to be addressed to someone, were evidently requested. Neophytos' statement that 'many' ask him to write for them, seems to have been perfectly well founded.[82] It is also

---

[75] Respectively, *Cod. Lesb. Leim. 2, Homily 1*, 236.452–3, *Homily 3*, 141.74–5, p. 141.80–1.
[76] Respectively, *Letter 2, Cod. Coisl. Gr. 287*, fol. 201β, p. 215; *Letter 5*, 63–4.
[77] Respectively, e.g. *Cod. Coisl. Gr. 287*, fols. 42α, 142β, 193α–β; *Cod. Athen. 522*, fol. 412α; *Cod. Paris. Gr. 1317*, fols. 7α–β, 112α (p. 302.46–56) (*Catechesis 24, Book 1*), 210β.
[78] Respectively, *Letter 4*, 10.16–17; *Letter 2*; *Letter 3*.
[79] *Cod. Paris. Gr. 1189*, fols. 7β, 10β–11α, 12α (*Panegyric 3*). If the church referred to survives today, it may well be that of the archangel Michael at Katō Lefkara: of the (six, according to Stylianou and Stylianou) surviving medieval churches of Cyprus dedicated to the archangel this is the only one which appears to date at least from the twelfth century, containing paintings which are closely connected to other late twelfth-century paintings in Cyprus; and its location – at Neophytos' birthplace – makes it an attractive candidate: surely the locals would have been particularly proud of their village's most famous man. On the church see Stylianou and Stylianou (1985: 447–50).
[80] *Cod. Paris. Gr. 1189*, fol. 24β (*Panegyric 6*).
[81] *Panegyric 17*, 217.33–218.3, p. 218.25–6.
[82] *Cod. Coisl. Gr. 287*, fol. 40β.

important to note that this statement was made as early as 1176. It is impossible to tell whether by that time Neophytos, tonsured priest and turned abbot in 1170, had acquired the fame of a holy man. What is certain is that he had achieved widespread fame (and, as we saw earlier, notoriety) as a writer.

Neophytos may not have expected that his writings would be widely read, but he could and did expect that they would be widely heard. Even his letter to his spiritual son is obviously meant for public perusal (there would be no other reason for Neophytos to narrate events of which the *sebastos* had himself first-hand experience); while the letter to Euthymios is character-ised in its heading as a *logos*.[83] The only occasion on which Neophytos appears to have intended a writing of his to remain a private matter between himself and the addressee concerns the first ten folios of his *Book of Catecheseis*. He addresses John and expressly states that he writes these opening lines for John's eyes only, a fact which Neophytos expected to surprise John: 'And these now I, sir my brother, write to you, and do not consider it strange that I write them for you alone.'[84] On all other occasions Neophytos expects his writings to have a wider audience. Obviously, the most immediate public of Neophytos' was that of his own monks. All the *Panegyrics*, *Catecheseis* and *Homilies* of Neophytos' were read out to them on the particular day for which each was written. Another obvious audience was, through John, that of the monastic community of Koutsovendēs'. Addresses to monks, whether those of the Enkleistra or of Koutsovendēs, are found throughout the *Book of Fifty Chapters*, the *Hexaēmeros*, the *Catecheseis*, the *Typikon*, the *Interpretation of the Commandments*.[85]

But Neophytos was read and heard beyond the narrow confines of these monasteries and the limited number of their monks. For instance, the *Panegyric* for which the priest of the church of St Diomēdēs had travelled to the Enkleistra, was obviously intended to be read out in his church, to a lay congregation, on the feast-day of the Saint. On that day the greatest possible number of venerators of the Saint would gather; but further, many more people would be attracted by the *panegyris* of the Saint which long before Neophytos' time had acquired a strong commercial character expressed in the customary fair which was held during it.[86] The same can be said with

---

[83] *Letter 4*; *Letter 3*. Letters were generally considered by the Byzantines to contain public rather than private statements. See Patlagean (1987: 562–3, 579–618); Mullett (1981: esp. 77, 78).

[84] *Cod. Paris. Gr. 1317*, fol. 10α.

[85] Respectively, e.g.: *Cod. Athen. 522*, fol. 12α, p. 44; *Hexaēmeros*, 175.25–6; *Cod. Paris. Gr. 1317*, fols. 10α, 22α, 26α, 28α, 35β, 39β, 43β, 44α, 46β, 50α, 52α, 57β, 63β, 64α, 65β, 67α, 70β, 71α, 75β, 79β, 80α, 84α, 85β, 98α, 104α, 112β, 115β, 117α, 120β, 122α, 122β, 123α, 135α, 138α, 146β, 149α, 151β, 155α, 157β, 162β, 165β, 168β, 172β, 179α, 182α, 185α, 188α, 191β, 194β, 205α, 208α; *Typikon*, 80.28, 81.1, 84.1–33, 94.5, 95.31, 96.25, 97.12, 100.12, 103.25–31; *Cod. Coisl. Gr. 287*, fols. 85α, 171α.

[86] On the Byzantine *panegyris* see Vryonis (1981).

certainty about the *Panegyric* for archangel Michael, where specific reference is repeatedly made to a church devoted to the archangel, the centre, apparently, of a local cult, boasting miracles and holy water.[87] Again, a maximum number of people could be safely expected to gather on the day of the archangel's *panegyris*. The *Panegyric* concerning the consecration of a church could be read out on any such occasion: yet again, such an occasion would attract a great number of people.

Evidence from other *Panegyrics* also suggests an audience much wider than that of monks. In the *Homily* for the *Hypapantē*, the use of addresses of 'lovers of feast-days' (*phileortoi*) and 'lovers of Christ' (*philochristoi*), rather than 'brothers', 'monks' and the like, again suggests a lay public listening to it.[88] In other *Panegyrics* no specific reference is made to any particular church outside the Enkleistra, but reference is made to an audience which included not only monks but also laymen. In his *Panegyric* for the Holy Cross Neophytos refers to the crowd of people (*laos*) which had gathered and taken part in the vigil and the liturgy celebrating the feast-day of the Holy Cross. The *Panegyric* makes specific reference to the Enkleistra, and thus it is obvious that Neophytos is referring to a gathering of lay people to celebrate the feast-day in the monastery.[89] A similar reference is made to the *Panegyric* for St Sabas, where Neophytos invokes the Saint to look after the Enkleistra and all the writers, readers, listeners, singers of the Psalms, commemorators 'and all the gathering of the people [*laos*]' on the occasion of the Saint's *panegyris*.[90]

A reference to writers, readers, listeners and commemorators is also made in the *Panegyric* for St Theosebios.[91] There, Neophytos addresses 'the gathering' and, revealingly, monks but also 'men' as well as 'women'.[92] If not only men but also women were meant to listen to Neophytos' words, as he urges them to, then the *Panegyric* must have obviously been read outside the Enkleistra, since the monastery was an area strictly prohibited to women.[93] The reference to an audience of monks, too, indicates what was probably true of all Neophytos' *Panegyrics* and *Homilies*: that they were meant to be read both inside the Enkleistra (with perhaps the words irrelevant to the Enkleistra being removed) and outside it.

It also appears that the *Panegyrics* were not the only writings of Neophytos which were read out to an audience wider than that of monks. His *apologias*, obviously meant to be heard as widely as possible, were not only contained in *Panegyrics* and *Homilies* (i.e. those for St Diomēdēs, the Annunciation and the Presentation of the Virgin) but also in his *Interpretation of the Commandments*, a work specifically addressed to John and

[87] *Cod. Paris. Gr. 1189*, fols. 7β, 10β–11α, 12α (*Panegyric 3*). See also note 79, above.
[88] *Cod. Lesb. Leim. 2*, fol. 285β (*Homily 4*).   [89] *Cod. Paris. Gr. 1189*, fol. 38α (*Panegyric 7*).
[90] *Cod. Paris. Gr. 1189*, fol. 180α (*Panegyric 23*).   [91] *Panegyric 12*, 197.10–11.
[92] *Ibid.*, 182.27, 187.37–188.1, respectively.   [93] *Typikon*, 89.3–14.

containing references only to an audience of monks. It is thus certain that Neophytos' *Homilies* and *Panegyrics* were read out, as Neophytos' own works, to a public which – through choice of feast-days of the most popular Saints in Cyprus – would be the widest possible one; and it is, further, possible that even works which Neophytos specifically addressed to monks were still read outside monasteries, in the form perhaps of sermons.

Undoubtedly the most striking indication of Neophytos' intention to reach out to the widest possible public is expressed in his circular letter, apparently motivated by his concern that people failed to follow the fasting rules during Lent. As we saw earlier, this was written at a time when the see of Paphos was vacant; Neophytos assumed the authority of the absent bishop, castigating both the laity and the priests of the district of Paphos and placing all who broke the fasting rules under *anathema*. In this instance, the intended public is obviously and expressly the entire population of the district.[94]

Having established that Neophytos had a public composed of much more than the small circle of his monastic community and that of Koutsovendēs, or that of the aristocratic elite connected with him, let us now examine what exactly this lay audience of people flocking to a Saint's feast-day *panegyris* heard. What, in other words, was Neophytos telling this public which he never saw?

[94] *Letter 5*, 63–4.

8   Social commentary

Already in the earliest of his surviving writings Neophytos emerges as a recorder and commentator of the society of which he was, despite his seclusion, very much a part. His writings reveal a man deeply concerned with the fortunes – and especially the misfortunes – of the mass of the Cypriots who did not belong to the ruling class. For even though, as we saw, Neophytos took pride in, and cultivated, his links with the lay and ecclesiastical elites on the island, yet he also never forgot his own peasant background. For instance, his references to his vineyard tending (an art which he learned in his village, and which he was also assigned to practise for five years while a novice in the monastery of Koutsovendēs) are repeated and proud, showing that he cherished at least some aspects of his peasant upbringing.[1] Again, it was this background that made him keenly aware of the harsh realities of peasant life, and which partly accounts for his deeply felt and life-long sympathy for the peasants.[2]

Neophytos' writings of the pre-1191 period to which I shall be mainly referring immediately below are the *Interpretation of the Commandments* of 1176 and the *Book of Fifty Chapters* of 1179. In both these works the Recluse's concern for the peasants is expressed in various ways, one of which assumes the form of very long and concerned references to droughts. Writing in 1176, Neophytos refers to a drought during the previous year, the resulting lack of growth and the consequent sadness and poverty which befell the peasants. According to Neophytos the drought was caused by God's rightful wrath at the sinning people.[3] In the year Neophytos was

---

[1] Neophytos writes, addressing his monks: 'As you yourselves know, I am a most expert vineyard tender, and this I say not just so as to praise myself' (*Cod. Paris. Gr. 1317*, fol. 41α (*Catechesis* 6, Book 1)). For tending the vineyards at Koutsovendēs see *Typikon*, 75.23–7; also *Cod. Coisl. Gr. 287*, fols. 180β–181α.

[2] See below, and see, e.g., the precise reference to his native village: *Typikon*, 77.26. See also Mango and Hawkins (1966: 123).

[3] 'And now everybody lives in sadness and in poverty and in great hardship . . . ; and the hardship of our lives is caused by our perverse and careless way of life, and the trespassing of the holy and saving commandments' (*Cod. Coisl. Gr. 287*, fols. 102α–β).

writing rain, 'very frequent and peaceful', fell again.[4] It came, Neophytos tells us, 'late in the season', which, in terms of Cyprus' meteorological conditions, indicates late winter or spring in 1176. Unfortunately for the Cypriots, what Neophytos saw as a manifestation of God's philanthropy was not be repeated soon enough. Writing in 1179, Neophytos again refers to a year of drought and poverty. He was sufficiently concerned to make this the subject of one of his chapters in the *Book of Fifty Chapters*.[5] People's sins are again blamed for the lack of rain: 'The rain will not come', Neophytos writes, 'Our land has confiscated and hidden the fruit and the produce which she once gave us.' He sadly describes how people sow, but the results are meagre; how the trees in the valleys and on the mountains bear inedible fruit; 'And we see', he says in another passage, 'the sky turned to iron, the earth turned to copper, and a whole winter has gone by without rain.'[6]

To make things worse, the poverty and hardship which would at any rate have been caused by a year of drought was much aggravated by the situation of the three previous years. The first of these was a year of famine (the same one that Neophytos had recorded in his 1176 work), followed by a rainy year. But, as Neophytos says, 'before we had our fill of bread, two continuous years of famine came'. When the Recluse was writing in 1179, the Cypriots were experiencing the second of these years.[7] Neophytos paints in the darkest of colours the picture of poverty to which the Cypriots were reduced. In 1176 he had described the year as one of sadness, poverty and great hardship, in which even bread, the basic staple food, became scarce.[8] By 1179, that year is described as 'unlivable' and 'difficult', another year full of sadness and hardship, of extreme poverty and lack of bread and of every other food necessary to keep body and soul together.[9] This three-year disastrous drought and famine was also recorded by Neilos in his *Typikon* for the monastery of Machairas. Neilos, who was sent to Cilicia to beg for food for the upkeep of the monks who lived with him, also recorded that massive numbers of people starved to death.[10] The misery of the Cypriots was made even deeper by a plague which broke out in 1174, five years before Neophytos wrote the *Book of Fifty*

[4] *Ibid.*, fol. 188β.   [5] *Cod. Athen. 522*, fol. 9β, p. 42; 77β–78α.
[6] *Ibid.*, fols. 74β–75α, 77β.
[7] 'For the whole winter has gone by without rain and lo, poverty and sadness and hardship oppresses and kills the human race, because of the lack of bread and of overwhelming poverty. And, worse of all, in the previous year we had a terrible famine; and barely one year went by when, before we had our fill of bread, another famine came our way for not just one but two consecutive years' (*Cod. Athen. 522*, fols. 77β–78α).
[8] *Cod. Coisl. Gr. 287*, fols. 187α and 102α–β (and see note 3 above).
[9] *Cod. Athen. 522*, fols. 79β; 9β (p. 42); 77β–78α (and see note 7, above).
[10] *Diataxis* of Neilos, 13.8–10; 14.13–14.

Chapters.[11] The inhabitants' gloom was further darkened by a series of earthquakes and eclipses: one total eclipse of the sun and another partial one in 1178 are recorded by Neophytos.[12]

One of the results of this succession of disasters was the depopulation of the island.[13] Writing in 1176, Neophytos makes no mention of such an occurrence, but by 1179 he writes that 'our country is left nearly uninhabited', 'barely one third of the people' still living on it.[14] This, he observed, was partly the result of emigration of unhappy Cypriots to foreign lands; partly the result of death because of famine which left entire villages completely depopulated, killing people of all ages, and their livestock; and partly the result of the plague, whose great numbers of victims were unceremoniously buried wrapped in wicker rather than the usual burial clothes, because of the deteriorated state of their bodies, caused by the illness.[15]

As if all these misfortunes were not enough, the Cypriots found themselves raided by outsiders. Neophytos presents a Biblical list of the gruesome effects of such a raid: 'deserted land; burning towns; the coming of a foreign people; the snatching away of all food and produce by a foreign people; destruction of the earth and desertion and devastation, from a foreign, as it is said, barbaric people's raid; and we have been forsaken according to the rightful judgment of God'.[16] Neophytos writes this quoting Isaiah, and comments that exactly the same fate befell the Cypriots in the form of 'barbarians' raids'.[17] He refers to a particularly disastrous raid in a place which he names as 'so called Cholestrio' and which he places between

---

[11] 'I speak of death, meaning not the usual kind of death – for all men, being mortal, die; but I mean rather the death that visited us from God, because of God's rightful wrath and vengeance, the death we witnessed five years ago occurring through the plague; which plague caused many bodies to burst open, so that those who buried them in graves could not do so in the usual way, but had to envelope their burst bodies in wicker, in order to be able to commit them to burial. And we also witnessed death caused by famine, three years ago; which famine cut down pitilessly and terribly people of all ages' (*Cod. Athen. 522*, fols. 79β–80α, also 66β).

[12] *Ibid.*, fols. 67α, 78α (earthquakes); fols. 78β–79α (eclipses).

[13] On estimates of the population of Cyprus see ch. 3, p. 60.

[14] 'And our country is left almost uninhabited; and some of the people sailed away to foreign lands, while others were consumed by death, caused by famine . . . And this sign signified the plague and death that followed. It was a great plague, and death was unceasing, so that great numbers of not only people but also of beasts and birds perished . . . And since then and until now famine and earthquakes and destruction and civil wars and successive waves of sadness have not ceased upon this land; and barely one third of the people is left, and many villages, bereft of human habitation because of the famine, the death and the loss of property, now stand deserted' (*Cod. Athen. 522*, fols. 67α, 78β).

[15] *Ibid.*, respectively fols. 67α (see note 14, above); 78β (see note 14, above), 79β–80α (see note 11, above).

[16] *Ibid.*, fols. 63α–β.   [17] *Ibid.*, fols. 65β, 66β.

the towns of Lefkōsia and Kerynia and near the village of Dikōmo. He narrates that 'a few years ago' 'barbarians' annihilated the forces of Cyprus, took prisoner the governor of the island and a bishop together with many others and raided the country, returning to their land 'with our fruit and our food'. 'They left our land and our country', Neophytos concludes, 'deserted.'[18]

A note in the margin of one of the folios containing this passage gives a clue as to which one of the many raids which Cyprus suffered Neophytos is referring to. The marginal note reads: 'Τὸν ᾿Αντιοχείας πρίγκηπα λέγ...'[19] This reference to a 'prince of Antioch' brings to mind two of the recorded raids against Cyprus which were led by men whose formal titles linked them with Antioch, and whom we have already encountered earlier, in Part 1: the first was the 1155/6 raid of Renaud de Châtillon; the second, the 1161 raid of Raymond III of Antioch. Renaud de Châtillon was the husband of the princess of Antioch and it is much more probable that it is to him, rather than to Raymond of Antioch, Count of Tripolis, that the marginal note refers as 'the prince of Antioch'. Further, it was Renaud de Châtillon's raid which appears to have been by far the most devastating of the two, and descriptions of it by other contemporary commentators confer the same feeling of horror that informs Neophytos' description. The place called 'Cholestrio' to which Neophytos refers remains an unidentified place, but this is not the case with Dikōmo: it is a village situated in northern Cyprus, half-way between Lefkōsia and Kerynia and quite near the monastery of Koutsovendēs, where Neophytos was, at the time of the 1155/6 raid, a monk. This (as well as the attested brutality of the invaders) would account for the deep impression which this raid evidently left on Neophytos: he remembers it vividly and describes it in a very lively manner many years later, while he leaves other raids unmentioned. And it is indeed northern Cyprus which must have suffered the full brunt of Renaud de Châtillon's attack: since he came from the southern shores of Anatolia, it is reasonable to suppose that he landed on and departed from the island's northern shores.[20]

The outcome of a period marked by droughts and famine, plague, earthquakes and eclipses, raids, death and depopulation, was dramatically reflected in the social behaviour of the people. Of this there was – as would be expected under the circumstances – a marked deterioration, which Neophytos recorded. In 1176, after a year of drought and famine, the

---

[18] *Ibid.*, fols. 75α–β, p. 45.1–9.
[19] *Ibid.*, fol. 75α. The first three words clearly refer to 'the prince of Antioch'; the end of the fourth word is missing, and the most reasonable assumption is to read it as λέγ[ει]: 'he says', i.e. 'he means', 'he refers to'.
[20] See ch. 3, pp. 51–2, for these and other raids.

Recluse angrily complains that instead of repenting in the face of God's wrath 'we were rather turned to the worse'. He records an increase in the rate of murder, theft and greed: a visitor tells Neophytos that on his way to a place he came across the dismembered and decapitated remains of a man, his murderers having aimed at making their victim unrecognisable; another man tells the Recluse of robbery on the highways; a third, that his house had been burgled of all his possessions; a fourth, that thieves stole what little he had of bread, bringing him and his family to the brink of starvation. Neophytos writes that such stories of thefts and robberies in the towns and on the country roads were daily told him.[21]

The rise of theft and robbery and the fall of social moral constraints would be an unsurprising result of extreme poverty and hunger, even though Neophytos only saw it as a further fall into sin by people who were already being punished for their sins. The situation could not have improved by 1179, when more suffering had accumulated. Now, Neophytos speaks of people whom famine had turned into 'wild beasts'.[22]

But despite Neophytos' rebukes of the people for their sins, his severest castigations are reserved for the rulers rather than the ruled. For apart from the suffering caused by plague, drought, famine, earthquakes, eclipses and enemy raids (all attributed by Neophytos to God's wrath), the Recluse also records the people's sufferings at the hands of those who composed their ruling class. Neophytos was acutely aware of the social stratification in Cyprus, especially in its more polarised expression. 'The rulers' (*archontes*) whether judges, administrators, highly positioned churchmen or simply the rich, are all sharply differentiated by Neophytos from 'the ruled' (*archomenoi*), and are roundly condemned as composing a brutal, oppressive, corrupt and cruel ruling class.[23]

Already in 1176 Neophytos is bold and direct in his criticism of the ruling class: 'Beware and tremble', he warns; 'even if you are a Church leader, and even if you are a king, and even if you are a governor or some other ruler of the people.' He warns them to be careful not to soil their name or cause people to criticise them for being thieves, devious men and persons forsaken by God. 'No king', Neophytos thunders, 'who is impious is ever deemed to

[21] *Cod. Coisl. Gr. 287*, fols. 187α, 187β–188α.
[22] *Cod. Athen. 522*, fol. 79β.
[23] *Archontes* was a term generally used by the Byzantines of the period to refer to the powerful in social, political or economic terms. See Angold (1984c); Ahrweiler (1976: esp. 7–12). It is interesting to note the continuing use in modern rural Cyprus of the term *archontes*, as distinct from the *plousioi* ('the rich'). The first term carries connotations of leadership, largess, nobility of manner, fairness. It tends to apply to those elder men who are seen by the villagers as being wise enough to be asked questions on important issues – from local history to morality. See Loizos (1981: 25); Peristiany (1965: 177–8; 1968: 83).

be a king, but rather a tyrant. No Church leader who is in the grip of madness and folly is truly a Church leader, but only one falsely named thus.' The point of being made a ruler, he continues, is not to behave towards the ruled like wolves do with sheep, nor in order to grab their possessions.[24]

At another point in the same work Neophytos castigates the rich, accusing them of corruption and unfair gain. Daily, he writes, we see the rich oppressing the poor:

Not only do they give no food and no drink to those in need, but they even grab the food and drink from the pauper's mouth; not only do they not offer hospitality to those who need it and do not clothe the naked, but they even, sadly, deprive such people of their homes and undress them of their ragged clothing. Not only do they not visit those who are ill or in prison, but in fact they cause those who are healthy to become bedridden, by beating them cruelly; and those who live out of the prison they lock in it.

Neophytos then castigates those who amass riches through grasping, greed and slander.[25] (Three years later he was to characterise the rich as 'wild beasts' and 'rapacious wolves'.)[26] There is no mistaking the passion with which Neophytos makes these exclamations or of his personal involvement with the people for whom he speaks up.

In another passage Neophytos focuses more particularly on the administrative officials, hinting at grievances caused by heavy taxation. The memory of the heavy taxes under Byzantine rule remained with Neophytos to the end of his life: in 1214, in his *Typikon*, he recalls men who suffered under the great burden of the ravenous, unsympathetic taxmen, as one of the examples of suffering which he saw around him as a youth before he left Lefkara.[27] The burden of heavy taxation was further aggravated, according to Neophytos, by corruption. Indeed, one of the reasons for which Neophytos declined, until 1191, to allow the acquisition of property by his monastery was that he did not want to place the Enkleistra under the 'men of the fisc'.[28]

These people, Neophytos claims in 1176, are not satisfied even with taking one-third or one-fifth part of one's property, but they further greedily grab and steal the property of people. In a particularly angry passage, using the very direct and personal form of address of 'you' (*sy*), Neophytos points an accusing finger at one such corrupt official, exclaiming:

'You overflow in unfairness, stealing and being greedy. And from what you stole, you may even distribute small obols, or commission a pricey icon, or build a church

[24] *Cod. Coisl. Gr. 287*, fols. 147α–148α.
[25] *Ibid.*, fols. 130α–132α; see also *Cod. Athen. 522*, fols. 403β–404α.
[26] *Cod. Athen. 522*, fols. 403β–404α.
[27] *Typikon*, 74.5–17, esp. 74.15–16.   [28] *Ibid.*, 80.10–19, esp. 80.16–17.

for such and such a Saint, and you fancy that you have achieved something great. Yet the holy icon that you embellished with the fruit of your greed you have soiled rather than embellished, since you dressed it up with what you greedily grabbed. The Saint who you thought you embellished will say to you: 'Why do you sin by thinking that I am like you? The offerings of thieves and of the greedy are abhorrent to the Lord, because they are unlawfully made. You must honour God with the fruits of your own fair labour . . . As for me, living as I do in the Kingdom of Heaven, I have no need for your offerings. But those whom in your greed you treated unfairly, are now much oppressed by great poverty and lack even the basics of life, that is to say food, drink, clothes and blankets. You must therefore do good to those whom you have wronged.'[29]

Neophytos focused also on another group of the ruling class: the judges. Again using the direct and personal form of 'you' (*sy*), he accuses a judge of corruption:

You, man, a sinner and overflowing with millions of sins, judge the innocent; and you, the guilty one, condemn them. Yet on many occasions you pronounced innocent the sinner because you were bribed, and you pronounced him, the guilty one, to be not guilty; while depriving the fair one of fairness you condemned him as guilty.[30]

Thus, Neophytos says, 'we see many judging and condemning unfairly, behaving with insatiable greed and pitilessly condemning not only the guilty but also, very frequently, the innocent'. And yet, the Recluse complains, they are left completely unquestioned and unchecked about their doings: not only 'they are not themselves judged', but further 'their evil deeds cause them to flourish and to live in power and glory and wealth'.[31] 'You', Neophytos says, addressing the judge, 'sit on a throne and judge and condemn the ruled with arrogance, pretending to be above them in body and soul . . . You preside pretending to be fair – you who are filled with evil – and you pitilessly condemn the ruled as guilty.' In a statement striking in its forceful egalitarianism, Neophytos calls the people the judges' brothers and says: 'You are a brother of these ruled people even if you have a higher position than they do and even if you preside over them; and do not let the human glory of presiding delude you into believing that you are somebody truly great.'[32]

Neophytos' indictment of the ruling elite, whether represented by *doux*, administrative official, priest, judge or rich man, was in 1176 as absolute as

---

[29] *Cod. Coisl. Gr. 287*, fols. 62α–β. The person accused was not named by Neophytos. It appears that the Recluse was not referring to a specific individual, but that he used the singular address as a rhetorical devise, to sharpen his attack on the whole group of persons represented through this fictional man.

[30] *Ibid.*, fols. 120α–β. The commentary in note 29, above, applies also in this case.

[31] *Ibid.*, fols. 121α–β; also 126β–127α; 121α–β.   [32] *Ibid.*, fols. 146α–β.

it was cutting. Sadly, Neophytos was describing a situation which was not new in Cyprus.[33] In the eleventh century Kekaumenos mentioned Cyprus as one of the islands suffering in the hands of corrupt imperial navy officials who, under the pretext of protecting the coasts and the islands, levied all sorts of produce and other possessions from their inhabitants.[34] In the beginning of the twelfth century (in 1110 or 1111) Nicholas Mouzalōn resigned the archiepiscopal see of Cyprus and later wrote an apologetic poem explaining the reasons for his abdication.[35] In it he describes the conditions the Cypriots lived under in the darkest of colours. The suffering of the Cypriots and the causes of this suffering are given by Mouzalōn in terms which show that nothing had changed for the better since the beginning of the century. There is no doubt that it was in Mouzalōn's self-justificatory interests to present a wholly negative picture of the internal conditions in Cyprus, but the gist and several details of his evidence are, in fact, corroborated by Neophytos' own.

Like Neophytos, Mouzalōn describes the Cypriot peasants as living in the misery of extreme poverty, having no clothes, food or shelter, but feeding themselves with 'the food of the Prodromos' and living in caves. Their land, he says, yields all kinds of fruit but their rulers take away all the labours of the peasants and ask for even more. The taxes are unbearably high, the administrative officials thoroughly corrupt. Because of the system of the *allēlengyon*, Mouzalōn says, the peasants had no escape: if the officials did not receive what they asked of one man, another suffered in his place.[36]

---

[33] Note that in the ninth century patriarch Phōtios also reprimanded the governor of Cyprus for oppressing the people: *Letters of Photios*, 527, no. 213.

[34] Kekaumenos, *Strategikon*, 292.28–294.6 (Litavrin ed.), *Logos Nouthetētikos*, 102.6–19.

[35] Nicholas Mouzalōn arrived in Cyprus in 1107, after a sea voyage of ten days: Mouzalōn, 119. Doanidou dates the poem to 1110, Mango and Hawkins to 1111. See Doanidou (1934: 142); Mango and Hawkins (1964: 339). On Mouzalōn see also Dölger (1935); Hill (1948–52, I: 303–4).

[36] Mouzalōn, 136.885–137.912. The term *allēleggyon* is a notoriously confusing one. References to *allēleggyon* such as Mouzalōn's are curious in view of Skylitzēs' unequivocal statement that Rōmanos III Argyros (1028–34) abolished it completely: ἐξέκοψε δε καὶ τέλειον ἀπερρίζωσε τὸ ἀλληλέγγυον: Kedrēnos-Skylitzēs, II, 486.7. Ostrogorsky equally unequivocally writes that 'the old system of extra payment, which had been a basic element in Byzantine taxation, first as the *epibolē* and then as the *allēlengyon*, disappeared for good' (Ostrogorsky 1968: 322). P. Lemerle, however, distinguishes between the term τὸ ἀλληλέγγυον and ἀλληλεγγύως (-γγυα): the first refers to Basil II's measure whereby the 'powerful' were obliged to pay the taxes of the 'poor' who had defaulted or disappeared; and which Skylitzēs and Zōnaras called τὸ ἀλληλέγγυον. By contrast, ἀλληλεγγύως (-γγυα) refers to the ancient principle of joint fiscal liability of the commune, whereby because its members are jointly responsible they must provide the tax of the members of the commune who have defaulted or disappeared. See Lemerle (1979: 62, 75, 78–80). Mouzalōn is clearly referring to the latter of the two in his poem.

Again, Neophytos' wholesale castigation of taxman and tax-collector, civil, ecclesiastical and judicial dignitaries, echoes Mouzalōn's comments. Addressing a bishop Mouzalōn writes that he condemns the innocent and justifies the unjust.[37] The leaders of the Church, writes Mouzalōn, are so corrupt that the people do not dare to go to them for judgment since they know what lies in wait for them.[38] Of the five cases of corruption to which Mouzalōn refers, three involved bishops, the fourth a monk and the fifth an abbot.[39] Like Neophytos, Mouzalōn also mentions bribery. On one occasion, a deposed abbot returned to his post by force of arms, having first bribed the chief tax officer (*archiphorologos*) and the governor (*dioikētēs*).[40]

The conspiratorial co-operation between all the members of the ruling class in serving each other's interests and suppressing the people, which Neophytos hints at, also formed part of Mouzalōn's bitter experience of Cyprus. He mentions a bishop who worked for the tax officials, delivering judgments against his flock and upholding as innocent the greedy taxmen. When Mouzalōn urged him to repent, the bishop went straight to the governor and Mouzalōn found himself threatened by the authorities.[41] Whenever Mouzalōn punished a corrupt and disobedient bishop, monk or abbot, they bribed and used their contacts with the local ruler, completely ignoring ecclesiastical rules and privileges. When Mouzalōn sent his men to bring back to the monastery a monk who had left it to become a soldier in the tax-collector's service and to marry, the archbishop's men were beaten up. When Mouzalōn went to the governor to complain, the latter told him to leave the man alone. Bishops and abbots were reinstated by civil authorities, by force and with complete disregard to the higher ecclesiastical authorites.[42]

Another point of similarity between Mouzalōn's description and that of Neophytos concerns the rich sinner who commissions churches and icons to ease his guilty conscience. As has already been observed by scholars, Mouzalōn refers by a pun to the *doux* of Cyprus at the time, Eumathios Philokalēs, and to another high functionary who was apparently called

---

[37] Mouzalōn, 121.336–40.   [38] *Ibid.*, 130.662–5.   [39] *Ibid.*, 119.306–128.627
[40] *Ibid.*, 128.596–129.627. The two titles may well have been held by one and the same person. On the very extensive powers of a *doux* after the second half of the eleventh century, and his tendency to appropriate functions which were normally part of the civil administration, see Ahrweiler (1960a: esp. 52–78). Herrin also points out that by the twelfth century the governor had come to control all aspects of taxation, the judiciary, the local economy and provincial defence. It was within his effective power to raise or lower the rate of tax levies, to exercise his right to personal services and transportation, and to ignore ecclesiastical privileges: Herrin (1975: 267).
[41] Mouzalōn, 120.306–122.377.
[42] *Ibid.*, 122.378–125.483; 126.521–129.627.

Eusebios.[43] Now, Eumathios Philokalēs is also described as a pitiless and cruel governor in other sources, for example in the *Life* of St Cyril Phileōtēs.[44] Yet it is Eumathios who, while governor of Cyprus, financed the building and paintings of the church of the monastery of St John Chrysostom in Koutsovendēs. And indeed, Eumathios' connection with the monastery may also explain the rather odd toponymic of 'Koutsovendēs'. If, as Menardos has already suggested, κουτσοβέντης is a corruption of κουτσαφέντης, meaning 'the lame master';[45] and if the *Life* of St Cyril Phileōtēs is correct in depicting Eumathios Philokalēs as lame in both legs; then we have this 'lame master' of the monastery in the person of the *doux* Eumathios Philokalēs, undoubtedly the most powerful patron of the monastery. A dedicatory inscription bearing his name was uncovered in 1962 by Cyril Mango and Ernest Hawkins, who suggest that Eumathios built the church in public expiation of his behaviour in Cyprus which had caused Mouzalōn's abdication.[46] The full facts of the case would certainly have been known to Neophytos, through his close connection with the monastery of Koutsovendēs. Obviously, even if Neophytos himself is not referring to Eumathios, it is reasonable to suppose that other high officials behaved in a very like manner.

The picture of bribery, corruption, injustice and oppression of the people by the tax-collectors and the entire ruling class (lay and ecclesiastical) is by no means one which was confined to Cyprus. It appears, in fact, with regularity in reports from eleventh- and especially twelfth-century Byzantine provinces. For example, Michael Chōniatēs, metropolitan of Athens (1182–1205), was an eloquent recorder of a very similar, depressing state of

---

[43] *Ibid.*, respectively, 112.41 (ὁ μεν τις ἐστὶν εὐμαθὴς εἰς κακίαν) and 113.48 (ὁ δ' εὐσεβής φεῦ! τὸν Σατὰν σεβὼν μόνον). See Hill (1948–52, I: 299–300, 304); also Mango and Hawkins (1964: 339).

[44] When Eumathios went to St Cyril for a cure (according to the *Life* he was lame in both legs) St Cyril called him a 'lone wolf, who hast no fear or respect for the shepherd and his dogs, and mercilessly rendest the flock assunder'. See Mango and Hawkins (1964: 339; from which this translation is taken); Laurent (1932: 332); Gedeon (1899: 310). By contrast Anna Komnēna describes Eumathios Philokalēs as a man of remarkable qualities: *Alexiad*, III, 142.15–143.3; also II, 164.10–22. The career of Eumathios Philokalēs is well attested in Byzantine sources. He had been a *stratēgos* of Crete before he became *stratopedarchēs* of Cyprus. See Marinatos (1930). Note, however, that the attribution by Marinatos of a Cretan inscription to Eumathios Philokalēs has been refuted: Laurent (1931a: 801ff.); Zakyntinos (1941: 265f.); and Mango and Hawkins (1964: 337) (supporting the refutation). It is certain that Philokalēs became a *stratopedarchēs* of Cyprus after the 1092 revolt of Rapsomatēs. Between 1092 and 1118 he was twice *doux* of Cyprus, from after 1092 to *c*. 1103 and from *c*. 1110 until before 1118. By 1118 he was serving as grand *doux* and *praitor* of Hellas and Peloponnessos. See Mango and Hawkins (1964: 335–9); Hill (1948–52, I: 299–300); Guilland (1951: 224f.); Schlumberger (1884a: 189–90); Laurent (1931b: 332–3; 1962: 55ff.); Doanidou (1934: 142–3); Herrin (1975: chart, note 6); Bon (1952: 197–9, no. 48).

[45] Menardos (1907: 399).

[46] Mango and Hawkins (1964: 339).

provincial affairs in the province of Hellas and Peloponēssos; while a century earlier Theophylact of Ochrid had sent similar reports regarding the taxmen operating in Bulgaria.[47] With specific reference to Cyprus, attention has been drawn to the fact that, instead of a total annual tax yield of about 15,000 gold pieces, Cyprus is recorded as having yielded by the end of the twelfth century somewhat over 50,000 *hyperpyra*, an 'eloquent testimony', as Mango put it, 'to the success of the Byzantine tax collectors'.[48]

Neophytos' outraged view of the rulers of Cyprus in 1176 was not improved by 1179, when he wrote his *Book of Fifty Chapters*. There, referring to Isaiah (and clarifying that this also applies to Cyprus) the Recluse reminds his audience that God called the rulers and the people of the sinning Jews 'archons of Sodom and Gomorrah', since both the rulers and the ruled had immersed themselves in sin. In his comments following this, however, Neophytos concentrates again on the rulers rather than the ruled. They are accused, once more, of injustice, theft, greed, unlawful judging; of upholding the wrongdoer because of bribery, of condemning the righteous, of murdering and sinning. 'Hence', Neophytos concludes, 'you are called the archons of Sodom and the people of Gomorrah'.[49] Now, a number of high officials could easily fit one or more of Neophytos' descriptions above (and it is quite possible that more than one office was held by a particular person[50]), but the judiciary can easily be singled out.[51] As for the 'people of Gomorrah', these can only be the Cypriots who were prepared to bribe officials: thus, almost by definition, the rich. When, in the next few lines, Neophytos speaks of gatherings amongst such dignitaries resulting in plots, conspiracies and murders, and points out that such people are 'unlawfully performing evil instead of performing divine feasts', there can be no doubt that Neophytos is including members of the clergy amongst the corrupt ruling class.[52] Neophytos, echoing the idea of an implicit conspiracy amongst the members of the ruling class which he had already hinted at in 1176,[53] states that God will not accept the prayers offered by people whose

[47] On the abuses perpetrated against the population by the administrative officials, the judges and the rich, see Herrin (1975); Brand (1968: 1–13, 31–2; 61–6); also Ahrweiler (1976: 7–12); Charanis (1951: esp. part I); on Theophylact, see Obolensky (1988: 53–4, 78).

[48] Mango (1976a: 10). Nor was it just the Byzantine tax collectors who were so 'efficient'. According to Arnold of Lubeck, Cyprus yielded somewhat over 50,000 *hyperpyra* in the late twelfth century, a figure which agrees with that given by the continuators of William of Tyre for the early thirteenth century (30,000 *bisanti*). See Hendy (1985: 173, 598–9), who urges caution despite the apparent agreement between the sources: the figure does not make much sense when compared to revenues from other places, though of course it is possible that we have the correct figure for Cyprus and incorrect figures for elsewhere. See also ch. 3, pp. 52–4.

[49] *Cod. Athen. 522*, fols. 64α–β.

[50] See the conclusions of Ahrweiler and Herrin in note 40 above.

[51] Neophytos could be referring to lay or ecclesiastical judges. Bishops also acted as judges. See Mouzalōn's comments, earlier.

[52] *Cod. Athen. 522*, fol. 65α.   [53] *Cod. Coisl. Gr. 287*, fols. 121α–β.

hands are stained by thefts, who are grasping, greedy and, further, compromised by beatings and murders.[54] Again, the judiciary, the administrators, the rich and very probably the clergy are the obvious targets of Neophytos' attack – just as they were three years earlier, when he had included kings, the rich and priests amongst those who should repent.[55]

Neophytos' castigation of the political rulers of Cyprus, hinted at before, culminates in his reference to the people of Cyprus who, broken by misery, having ceased to be human and have been turned into beasts, ruled by even more beastly rulers. Death, Neophytos says, came to the sinning Cypriots in three forms: through plague, through famine and through what the Recluse calls 'that infamous "plague" and death, the one caused by the deeds of Kamytzēs'. This was a form of death which Neophytos says that he did not himself witness, but whose 'wretched and horrible and unnatural' nature was described by eye-witnesses.[56]

The name of Constantine Kamytzēs appears on our list of governors of Cyprus.[57] In common with many other Byzantine governors of the island, Constantine Kamytzēs appears to have belonged to a prominent family, if – in his case – one of comparatively recent eminence.[58] There seems to be no reason why Neophytos' Kamytzēs (evidently a person of immense power on

[54] *Cod. Athen. 522*, fols. 67β–68α.   [55] *Cod. Coisl. Gr. 287*, fols. 147α–148α.
[56] *Cod. Athen. 522*, fols. 79β–80α.
[57] For a list of governors see earlier, ch. 3, pp. 46–7.
[58] Hendy draws attention to the absence of their name from the territorial description in the 1198 treaty between Byzantium and Venice, as opposed to its appearance in the *Partitio Romaniae* of 1204. He suggests, therefore, that the Kamytsai were not magnates of long standing but rather a family of relatively newly acquired wealth, beneficiaries of the great hand-out of state lands that seems to have taken place under Alexios III Angelos (1195–1203). By that time they had certainly acquired close links with the imperial family: Manuel Kamytzēs was a near relation to Euphrosynē Doukaina, wife of Alexios III; and he staged an unsuccessful revolt against that same emperor. See Hendy (1985: 106, 134); Brande (1968: 119–20, 133); on Manuel Kamytzēs, local toparch or *archōn* of Macedonia and Thessaly before 1204, see also Nicol (1980). The family does not appear to have suffered much as a consequence. We find it amongst the aristocratic families that dominated the empire in the thirteenth century: Charanis (1951: part I, esp. 104). Other information, however, might indicate that the Kamytsai were of a longer standing than Hendy suggests: Gautier has suggested that the family was founded by a Turk who had defected to emperor Alexios I Komnēnos: Gautier (1971: 259); Mouzalōn's poem, written in 1110 or 1111 may refer to one Kamytzēs as, possibly, governor of Cyprus (see immediately below); as we just saw, Neophytos also refers to a Kamytzēs as a person of great power on the island, almost certainly a governor (he does not indicate a date: our *terminus ante quem* is 1179, date of Neophytos' *Book of Fifty Chapters*); in c. 1149 Theodore Prodromos wrote a poem on the death of a *pansebastos sebastos* Constantine Kamytzēs (*Theodoros Prodromos, Historische Gedichte*, 497–500, LXIV). I would suggest, therefore, that it is more likely that the Kamytzai were originally beneficiaries of Alexios I Komnēnos' (1081–1118) hand-outs of state land. Nothing precludes the possibility that they received further grants of land under Alexios III Angelos, and indeed perhaps much larger ones – hence their inclusion in the 1204 but not in the 1198 document.

the island, with authority to pass death sentences) should not be identified with the *doux* Constantine Kamytzēs, or perhaps with another member of the same family holding this post on the island. If this is so, then perhaps we meet the same man again in Mouzalōn's poem.

Mouzalōn describes a corrupt bishop, whom the archbishop condemned. The bishop's reaction was to appeal to the *archōn* of Cyprus, who re-established him to the priesthood.[59] This man is described by Mouzalōn as a 'most sacrilegious *archōn* of demons', who brought the deposed bishop back to Church in flagrant violation of ecclesiastical rule and privilege, 'κἂν δοκῇ καὶ καμμύειν'.[60] In the light of Mouzalōn's references by way of a pun to Eumathios Philokalēs and to another official, Eusebios, it is highly likely that the line quoted contains a pun for one Kamytzēs – either the *doux* we already know (Constantine Kamytzēs) or another member of the same family.[61] The family may well have, indeed, derived its name from the nick-name *kammytsēs* (meaning 'one who blinks his eyes').[62] It is impossible to ascertain exactly what office this man held during Mouzalōn's brief stay in Cyprus (1107–10/11) because of the vague way in which the poem refers to him. We can only say that he was governor of Cyprus between around 1107 to 1111. Certainly, when Neophytos refers to the wicked 'deeds of Kamytzēs' in 1179, he does so within the context of referring to something which he had not witnessed, and which occurred in the past, though he gives no clue as to how distant that past was.[63] As for the 'wretched, horrible and unnatural' way of people's death at Kamytzēs' instigation, Mouzalōn's poem, again, provides either an answer or a parallel case. He describes the tortures to which the Cypriots were subjected in the course of the extortion of taxes from them. These included hanging men up, their hands and feet tied, with dogs hung up next to them and pricked on to tear the hanged men's flesh. Many, Mouzalōn laments, died of this torture.[64]

After such descriptions, it is not surprising to find Neophytos referring to rebellions on the island. The Recluse hints twice at internal disorder in Cyprus, in his *Book of Fifty Chapters*. On the first occasion he refers to 'upheavals' (*akatastasiai*) as part of a list of misfortunes which afflicted the

[59] Mouzalōn, 122.378–124.444, esp. 122.389–123.422.
[60] *Ibid.*, 123.430–4; quote from 123.434.
[61] For Mouzalōn's similar references by way of pun to Eumathios Philokalēs and to Eusebios see earlier, and note 43 above.
[62] On *kammytsēs* as a nick-name see Koukoules (1948–55, VI: 479).
[63] Neophytos' sense of chronological sequence was not always precise; e.g. referring to the raid led either by Raymond of Antioch, Count of Tripolis (in 1161), or – more likely – by Renaud de Châtillon (in 1155/6). Neophytos says that it took place 'a few years ago' when in fact he was writing eighteen or – more possibly – twenty-three or twenty-four years later. See earlier, pp. 187–8.
[64] Mouzalōn, 137.903–12.

Cypriots; and perhaps it is intentionally that this word follows that of 'prisons' in Neophytos' text.[65] This reference is quite vague; but on another occasion Neophytos makes an unmistakable (though, unfortunately, brief and uncommented on) reference to nothing less than civil war: 'And from then and up to this day, famines and earthquakes and deaths and civil wars (*emphylioi polemoi*) and successive misfortunes, have not ceased upon this land.'[66]

Mouzalōn had, indeed, wished for arms in his frustration with the corruption and misgovernment of the island at the beginning of the twelfth century.[67] This same way of government, and in particular the economic suppression of the people, can easily be linked with the two revolts which we know occurred in Cyprus in the eleventh century: the 1042 (or 1043) revolt of Theophilos Erōtikos and the 1092 revolt of Rapsomatēs.[68] It would be a mistake to see these separatist revolts as exclusively representing attempts of ambitious governors to establish their own independent state in Cyprus (like Isaac Komnēnos succeeded in doing in 1184). There can be little doubt that even though this was true of both eleventh-century rebellions, deep grievances of the people were also associated with them. Theophilos Erōtikos had been on the island for too short a time (only two or three years) to have gained much personal support for any cause. Yet he cleverly and quickly won the Cypriots over by accusing the *protospatharios* Theophylaktos, who held the office of judge and chief tax-collector (*dikastēs kai praktōr tōn dēmosiōn phorōn*) of extortion. Irrespective of whether the charge against Theophylaktos was a fair one or not, the fact remains that the Cypriots would not have responded to it so readily had they not been already exasperated by heavy taxation. Some fifty years later the much more serious revolt of Rapsomatēs is linked even more clearly with grievances of the people. A reference to the rebellion in the *Muses* of Alexios I Komnēnos (supposedly written by the emperor, and certainly written at the end of his reign) clearly suggests that the uprising was a popular one: it refers collectively to 'the Cypriots avoiding the rule of law', rather than to their governor's exclusively own rebellion.[69] Further, we know from Anna Komnēna that Alexios felt that tax extortions lay behind the Cypriots' initial support of Rapsomatēs' rebellion, as is illustrated by the measures which the em-

---

[65] *Cod. Athen. 522*, fol. 26β. Note that in Neophytos' *Catecheiseis* 'prisons' are definitely placed within the context of unfair imprisonment of the poor by the rich: *Cod. Paris. Gr. 1317*, fols. 133α–β.
[66] *Cod. Athen. 522*, fol. 78β (see note 14, above).
[67] Mouzalōn, 132.748f.
[68] For the relevant bibliography see ch. 3, notes 4 and 5.
[69] Alexios, *Mousai*, 357.295. This translation by R. H. Jordan *et al.*, from work in the seminar on the *Mousai* held at the Queen's University, Belfast, convened by R. H. Jordan and M. Mullett.

peror took in the aftermath of the suppression of the rebellion. In his effort to ensure the future safety of the island Alexios appointed a new judge and assessor of taxes (*kritēs kai exisōtēs*), a man by the name of Kalliparios who, Anna assures us, was distinguished by his sense of justice and of disregard for money (*aphilochrēmatia*).[70]

The 'civil wars' which Neophytos mentions in 1179 fit very well with the general twelfth-century picture which provincial Byzantium presents, when separatist revolts, products both of ambitious local rulers and of a deeply dissatisfied population, took place with increasing frequency and varying – but also increasing – degrees of success.[71] We cannot tell with absolute certainty whether the Cypriot 'civil wars' were, indeed, caused by the people's suppression by a cruel and corrupt ruling class, but Neophytos' evidence certainly suggests so. In this respect, there can be no doubt whose side Neophytos was on.

By contrast to his early writings, Neophytos becomes strangely silent about social conditions later on. The break came with Isaac Komnēnos' assumption of power in Cyprus. Only one dated writing of Neophytos' from the years of Isaac Komnēnos' rule (1184–91) survives, and this is the *Panegyric* concerning the fallen monk in Palestine, which contains no reference to internal conditions on the island. However, two later writings (of 1196) refer to Isaac's rule. In the *Panegyric* for the Holy Cross Neophytos refers briefly to Isaac's rule, to say that the country 'was greatly saddened' during it.[72] In his letter concerning the misfortunes of Cyprus Neophytos is much more forthcoming. There Isaac is described not simply as one who 'despoiled' the country, but who, more specifically, robbed the rich of their money ('thousands upon thousands') and daily 'hounded and oppressed its nobles'. Thus, Neophytos writes, 'all lived in distress, and sought how by any means they might protect themselves against him'.[73]

To the *Panegyric* concerning the fallen monk we should also add Neophytos' *Panegyric* against the Jews as another writing from the years of Isaac's

---

[70] *Alexiad*, II, 164.10–15. I agree with Chalandon that the revolt of Rapsomatēs was provoked by the fiscal extractions. This view has been somewhat lightly dismissed by Ahrweiler, on the basis of Karykēs's murder by the Cretans during the co-ordinated revolts of Rapsomatēs in Cyprus and Karykēs in Crete. Ahrweiler sees Karykēs' murder as proof that the Cretans remained loyal to the empire. But even if we accept this deduction for Crete, its generalisation to Cyprus seems unwarranted. See Chalandon (1900: 147–9); Ahrweiler (1961: 226 and note 3).

[71] See generally Angold (1984: 275–8); Brand (1968: 1–4, 10ff.; also 61ff.) (for measures of Andronikos I Komnēnos which were evidently aimed at alleviating some pressure from a peasantry suffering under heavy taxation and corrupt government); Herrin (1975: 255, 267, 269–70); Ahrweiler (1966a: 185–6, 199).

[72] *Cod. Paris. Gr. 1189*, fol. 37β, p. 48.17 (*Panegyric 7*).

[73] *Letter 4*, 11.4–7, 12.3–5.

rule. No overt reference is made to Isaac in this *Panegyric*, but there is a passage which appears to refer to his rule. Neophytos refers to 'highly placed and leading men', persons who previously 'overflowed in power, wealth and prowess', and who now were 'humiliated', treated like cattle, 'just very like what our island of Cyprus is suffering nowadays; and most of its powerful are now imprisoned, and in chains'. The passage is brief and, tellingly, Neophytos suddenly cuts the narrative short by saying: 'About which I wish to say no more – for this is no time for such talk.'[74] The few lines of information were, it seems, impetuously written.

Neophytos' snippets of information, both in their reference to a general misfortune suffered by all the people of the island and more specifically to the impoverishment, humiliation and imprisonment of members of its ruling class, agree with the information which Nikētas Chōniatēs also gives us concerning Isaac Komnēnos' rule of Cyprus. Specifically referring to Isaac's treatment of the rich on the island, Chōniatēs writes: 'He irresponsibly robbed once prosperous households of all their belongings, and those indigenous inhabitants who but yesterday and the day before were admired and rivalled Job in riches, he drove to beggary with famine and nakedness, as many, that is, whom the hot-tempered wretch did not cut down with the sword.'[75]

In the above passages, an important shift in the emphasis of Neophytos' comments before and after 1184 is noticeable. Faced with what Neophytos obviously – and rightly – considered to be a threat to Cyprus in respect of its links with Byzantium, he now paid only the most general attention to the condition of the mass of the people, and concentrated instead on the fate of its ruling class. There is no doubt that Neophytos contemplated with horror a divorce of Cyprus from the byzantine *oikoumenē* and regarded Isaac with particular dislike for his act of separating Cyprus from Constantinople.[76] Within this context, the previously castigated members of the ruling class are now seen to be the legitimate leaders (good or bad) of society and the incarnate proof of the existence of Cyprus within the Byzantine world. The destruction of this ruling class became, thus, equated with the destruction of Byzantine Cyprus. Threatened in such a way, the class conflicts and divisions between the Cypriots were suddenly diminished in importance, and Neophytos' polemic was directed from the inside (criticism of members of the society in which he lived) to the outside (criticism of the power – in this case, Isaac – which threatened the whole of that society).

It is a pattern which was to remain with Neophytos for the rest of his life,

---

[74] *Cod. Paris. Gr. 1189*, fol. 209α (*Panegyric* 27). And see the Appendix pp. 265–6, for Egglezakes' dating of the *Panegyric* to 1186.
[75] Chōniatēs, *Historia*, 291.48–52. Translated by Magoulias (1984: 161). See also ch. 3, pp. 42–3.
[76] For a discussion see below, chs. 9 and 10.

since the turbulent years of 1191 and 1192 spelt the irrevocable separation of Cyprus from Constantinople. When Neophytos talks of poverty under the Latins (from 1192 onwards) he no longer makes a distinction between rich and poor Cypriots. He only makes a distinction between the Orthodox Cypriots and the Latins. Already in 1196, after five years of Latin rule, Neophytos complains of poverty amongst the Cypriots, their enemies robbing them of the fruit of their labours.[77] For five years, he writes, 'the Franks' held the country in slavery and raided it; and, once again, Neophytos stops himself from commenting further: 'But I do not want to say much about these things.'[78] In his *Catecheseis* Neophytos complains of long years of deprivation,[79] a deprivation which in his *Typikon* he states to be a result of the Latin occupation: 'Our country having fallen to the Latins and all the people having been deprived of every necessity, it was obviously natural that we would also fall upon hard times.' Especially so, since, as Neophytos says, his monastery now had to support a greater number of monks and visitors.[80] Neophytos does not state whether either the monks or the visitors (or both) were attracted to the monastery because of their poverty. But even though he states that the number of visitors increased because of the rising fame of the monastery, he also clearly links this increase of visitors with an increase in the monastery's expenses, which indicates that, far from providing the monastery with an income through donations, such visitors were, instead, rather provided for by the monastery, which possibly offered them food.

Certainly, most of the rich and powerful Cypriots who had once supported the Enkleistra were now unable to do so, or at least were unable to be as generous as they had been previously. The Recluse records that those who could leave left, abandoning their 'big and great' houses, which now stood empty.[81] In his letter concerning the misfortunes of Cyprus Neophytos expands more: 'all her rich men', he states, 'have forgotten their wealth, their fine dwellings, families, servants, slaves, their many flocks, herds, swine, cattle of all kinds, grainbearing fields, fertile vineyards and variegated gardens, and with great care and secrecy have sailed away to foreign lands and to the Queen of Cities'. Of the rich who did not leave, 'who is fit to set forth the tragedy of their suffering? The searches, the public prisons, the exaction of money squeezed from them, thousands upon thousands.'[82]

For the mass of the Cypriots who stayed after 1191, living – Neophytos

---

[77] *Cod. Paris. Gr. 1189*, fol. 37α, p. 48.3–7 (*Panegyric 7*).
[78] *Ibid.* fol. 37β, p. 48.22 (*Panegyric 7*).
[79] *Cod. Paris. Gr. 1317*, fol. 83β, p. 57.5–9.
[80] *Typikon*, 80.20–4.
[81] *Cod. Paris. Gr. 1317*, fol. 83β, p. 57.7.
[82] *Letter 4*, 10.19–11.7, 12.3–5; translated in Cobham (1908: 10–11).

has no doubt about it – in the 'terrible slavery' and 'captivity' of the Latins, life does not seem to have been much better.[83] For even though there is no doubt that Neophytos is rhetorically exaggerating in generalising in such absolute terms the fate of *all* the Orthodox under the Latins,[84] yet equally there is no doubt that the economic and social status of the vast majority of the Orthodox who remained on the island was far worse under the Latins than it had ever been under Byzantine rule. Wilbrand of Oldenburg, who visited Cyprus in 1211, described the social situation on the island as one deeply divided between the Latins, who are described as the rulers, and all the others, 'Greeks and Armenians, who obey the Latins like villeins [*coloni*] and pay tribute like slaves [*servi*]'. He also noted the latters' extreme poverty and degenerate way of life. Thus, supporting Neophytos' account, Wilbrand of Oldenburg clearly testifies that the vast majority of the original population were reduced, by 1211, to the same pitiful position of total and humiliating subjection to alien domination.[85]

About three years later, in his *Catecheseis* (*c.* 1214), Neophytos refers to a Latin ruling class which was no different in its greed against the people than their Byzantine predecessors at their worst. If anything, its foreign, Latin character made it infinitely worse for the Orthodox. Love of money, writes the Recluse, alters the nature of both the rulers and the ruled: they are both turned to the worse, the first through their pressure on the ruled to give them money, the second through being oppressed to so do. Neophytos clearly states that the greed of the rulers and the oppression of the ruled led directly to many 'disorders' and 'upheavals'; it brought untimely death, harsh torments, imprisonments, laments and mournings, murders and betrayals.[86] In a passage of 1196 Neophytos had already connected the economic oppression of the people with troubles on the island. Love of money, he said, is the cause of wars; 'the fruit of our labours is taken away by our enemies'; the Franks 'raid' our country.[87] He refers to 'troubles' in Cyprus later, too: in a passage in his *Catecheseis* he talks of burning and darkness, of fires, laments and mourning; of courts and prisons; of people sentenced and of irredeemable sadness.[88]

Amongst the general picture of devastation, oppression and misery which Neophytos describes the Cypriots as living in, it is not surprising to find

---

[83] *Typikon*, 82.15, 95.29, 95.30; *Cod. Paris. Gr. 1189*, fol. 37α, p. 48.19 (*Panegyric 7*). On the classes of Cypriots living under the Latins see Hill (1972, II: 8–10), who notes that the landed gentry among them disappeared.

[84] Not all the Orthodox were reduced to poverty, nor did all the members of the Orthodox elite leave the island. See p. 175.

[85] Wilbrand of Oldenburg, 180; translated in Cobham (1908: 13). See Hill (1972, II: 7).

[86] *Cod. Paris. Gr. 1317*, fols. 133α–β.

[87] *Cod. Paris. Gr. 1189*, fol. 37α, p. 48.3–7, 37b, p. 48.19–20 (*Panegyric 7*).

[88] *Cod. Paris. Gr. 1317*, fol. 113β, 133α.

references to a depopulation of Cyprus. This, of course, cannot refer to the flight of its grandees.[89] Rather, Neophytos refers to a general decrease of the Cypriot population: 'We became few in number; and a foreign people has multiplied in our land', he wrote twice in 1196.[90] By about 1214, he claims that 'many houses and almost all the large villages' were left deserted and uninhabited.[91] It is possible that in the 1196 passages Neophytos was merely recording his dislike of the arrival of a multitude of foreign settlers in Cyprus following the establishment of the Latin kingdom, rather than an actual great reduction of the Cypriot population. But the 1214 reference, even allowing for exaggeration, does indicate a massive emigration of Cypriots. This was, indeed, something which also worried the first Latin king of Cyprus. During his brief reign (1192–4) Guy de Lusignan tried to repopulate the island. He made proclamations to neighbouring countries, inviting those Cypriots who had emigrated to return to Cyprus within a fixed period of time, promising the return of their houses and properties to them. Should they fail to return, their lands and houses would be handed over to newcomers. The measure bears witness not only to Guy's initial efforts to befriend the Cypriots, but also to a mass emigration which began during the years of Isaac's rule and which the bloody events of 1191 and 1192 did nothing other than accelerate. Guy's measure met with no response from the emigrés, and he invited new settlers. These flocked in from Palestine, Syria and Cilician Armenia to be granted fiefs by Guy, and it is no doubt to these 'foreign people' who 'multiplied' in Cyprus that Neophytos alluded in 1196.[92]

The writings of Neophytos which refer to social conditions after 1192 stand in sharp contrast to those before it. Neophytos' sympathy and compassion for the poor, the weak and the underprivileged remained with him to the end of his life, finding expression in a number of his post-1191 writings;[93] but now these expressions assumed a very general, very brief form: the Virgin Mary is addressed as the protectress of the orphans and the poor, as the joy of those in sadness; the Holy Cross is described as the protector of widows and orphans; St Hilariōn is seen thankfully as the free doctor of the maligned people; St John the Almsgiver as the supporter of the poor, the orphans, the widows.[94] All these are expressions of a general philanthropy

---

[89] *Ibid.*, fol. 83β, p. 57.7; *Letter 4*, 10.12–11.4.
[90] *Letter 4*, 12.19–20; *Cod. Paris. Gr. 1189*, fol. 37α, p. 48.6–7.
[91] *Cod. Paris. Gr. 1317*, fols. 83α–β, p. 57.3–9.
[92] See ch. 3, pp. 60ff.; Hackett (1901: 70–1); Hill (1972, II, 39–40).
[93] E.g., *Cod. Lesb. Leim. 2, Homily 9* (and possibly *Homily 5*); *Panegyrics 8, 13, 29*.
[94] *Cod. Lesb. Leim. 2, Homily 5*, 262.403–4, 262.411 (assuming that this is indeed a late *Homily*); *Cod. Paris. Gr. 1189*, fol. 52β (*Panegyric 8*); *Panegyric 13*, 138.5; *Panegyric 29*, 149.32–150.26, 158.16–19, 158.22–4, 158.33–8.

(as well, of course, as well-known *topoi*) and share little with Neophytos' pre-1191 statements concerning the poor. Again, even though he continued to speak up against the rich and against moral corruption (for example, in Constantinople[95]), Neophytos never resumed the cutting, direct polemic against social injustice in Cyprus.

Part of the reason would seem to be fear: as we saw Neophytos do in his references to Isaac, he repeatedly speaks of the Latins seemingly on impulse, and abruptly stops himself short of further comments.[96] The other reason why Neophytos wrote not simply less passionately but also far less frequently about social injustice after 1191, was that he was no longer interested so much in the suppression of the people by their ruling class. Rather, he became increasingly concerned with a new form of suppression: that of the Byzantine by the Latin, of the Orthodox by the Schismatic. It is to this more directly political field that Neophytos diverted his polemic after the inglorious end of Isaac's rule.

[95] *Panegyric 9*, 111.8–112.21; *Panegyric 13*, 146.35–147.3.
[96] *Typikon*, 82.15–16; *Cod. Paris. Gr. 1189*, fol. 37β, p. 48.22 (*Panegyric 7*).

9 Secular politics

The news of events of purely military or political significance which reached Neophytos' cell was not confined only to major events. He knew, for example, of Andronikos I Komnēnos' murder of his twelve-year-old co-emperor Alexios.[1] Neophytos' laconic reference to this event must have been the gist of one of many a story that reached his cell. As a general rule the Recluse avoided written references to events of strictly political or military significance. He spoke of such events only when they had profoundly shocked him. Four such events are recorded by Neophytos: the battle of Myriokephalon in 1176; the fall of Jerusalem in 1187; the fall of Cyprus (to Isaac in 1184, to Richard I of England in 1191 and subsequently to the Latins); and the fall of Constantinople to the Crusaders in 1204.

Neophytos discussed in writing a number of major military and political events which took place in Cyprus: such as the raid of Raymond of Tripolis or (more likely) of Renaud de Châtillon, Isaac Komnēnos' assumption of the rule of Cyprus, Richard the Lionheart's conquest of the island and its subsequent sale to the Lusignans. These might seem peculiar preoccupations for a recluse, though they are understandable as naturally concerning the native – *enkleistos* or not – of a country which underwent such traumatic events.[2] They are, however, more comprehensible when they are seen within a broader ideological context: that which insisted that Cyprus was part of Byzantium, and that Romania was God's chosen empire. It is within this context that we begin to understand Neophytos' great shock at

[1] *Letter 4*, 11.20–12.1. The fact that Neophytos knew of the brutal murder of Alexios two months after Andronikos' coronation in September 1183 indicates the horror with which this murder was seen by Byzantines: sufficient to carry the news to Neophytos' cell. It may also point to the active efforts of aristocratic Constantinopolitan refugees to spread the news, trying to gain support against Andronikos from east or west. It was an effort recorded by Eustathios of Thessalonikē. See generally Brand (1968: 26ff., 38ff.); Ostrogorsky (1968: 394–6).

[2] For the raid see *Cod. Athen. 522*, fols. 75α–β, p. 45. For Isaac see *Letter 4*, 11.16–12.3; *Cod. Paris. Gr. 1189*, fol. 37β, p. 48.16–24 (*Panegyric 7*); implicitly in *Cod. Paris. Gr. 1189*, fol. 209α (*Panegyric 27*). For Richard I of England see *Letter 4*, 11.8–15, 12.6–12. For the sale of Cyprus to the Lusignans see *ibid.*, 12.11–13; *Typikon*, 80.20–2, 95.29–31; also *Cod. Paris. Gr. 1189*, fol. 37β, p. 48.22.

three other events, none of which took place in Cyprus and none of which directly affected the island's predominantly peasant population in any way other than a purely emotional one.

The defeat of the Byzantine armies at Myriokephalon is the first of these. Writing three years later, Neophytos' deep emotion is hardly masked. What happened in Myriokephalon is 'truly worthy of tears', writes the same man who elsewhere stated that tears should not be shed even for the dead, but should be reserved only for penance and prayer.[3] 'A host of soldiers', Neophytos writes, 'a multitude of illustrious men and beloved sons of such illustrious men and many others, were – o divine tolerance – slaughtered.' He says that he can find no time to narrate the laments, the grief, the tears, the extent of the disaster.[4] Neophytos devotes no less than five folios to the battle at Myriokephalon. As we shall see shortly, the physical annihilation of Manuel I Komnēnos' army is actually the only aspect of the factual reality of the battle which the Recluse recorded correctly.[5]

Eleven years later, Neophytos was deeply upset to hear of Jerusalem's fall to Saladin. In 1196, nine years after the event, Neophytos writes that Jerusalem was 'held' (*kratētheisēs*) by 'the godless Saladin'. He then states the reason for which he was outraged: namely, that the tomb of Christ and the rest of the holy relics were given over 'to the Muslim dog'. 'At this great calamity every Godloving soul weeps.' The Crusaders, Neophytos continues, achieved nothing in Jerusalem 'for Providence was not well pleased to thrust out dogs, and to bring wolves in their room'.[6] In another passage, while writing a *Panegyric* for St Sabas, Neophytos suddenly breaks his narrative concerning the Saint to refer to the 'godless dogs who took' Jerusalem, and to lament because 'the holy of holies was given to the dogs'.[7]

Neophytos' most painful words concerning the loss of Jerusalem were written in 1187. For Neophytos, Jerusalem's fall was an event not just worthy of tears, like the defeat at Myriokephalon had been, but an event worthy of deep mourning: 'Who would not lament from the depths of his heart and soul at such disaster, upon seeing and hearing of such a turn of affairs – how the holy flock in that Holy Land was ousted, and the holy of

---

[3] *Cod. Athen. 522*, fol. 75β, p. 45.12.
[4] *Cod. Athen. 522*, fols. 75β–76α, p. 45.9–19.
[5] On the battle of Myriokephalon see Brand (1968: 16–18); Chalandon (1912: 460–6, 498–518); and Hendy (1985: 146–54), who relocates Myriokephalon at today's Barsak Dere Boğazi (some 200 kilometres to the south-east of its previously suggested approximate site): this has a number of important implications concerning the battle that took place. See also Ahrweiler (Glykatzi) (1960b) on Manuel's fortifications.
[6] *Letter 4*, 10.4–11; translated in Cobham (1908: 10).
[7] *Cod. Paris. Gr. 1189*, fols. 179β–180α (*Panegyric 23*).

holies was delivered to the dogs?'[8] Neophytos' grief, certainly shared by
Christians of east and west, was, of course, intimately linked to the Christian conception of Jerusalem as the holiest of cities.[9] As such, it was very
difficult for Neophytos to understand how 'He who guards it fell asleep',
and allowed the Muslims to take it. The Recluse admits his 'amazement',
'incomprehension' and complete inability to understand God's purpose in
this particular case. For the first and last time in Neophytos' writings we
find evidence of a shock so deep as to bring the Recluse to the brink of
questioning God's acts. It is only a momentary lapse: Neophytos quickly
reassures himself that some people, at least, must have sinned in Palestine,
and this must have caused God's wrath.[10]

But if Jerusalem was 'holy', the focal point of Neophytos' religious
ideology, Constantinople was the 'Queen City', the focal point of his
political ideology and more: Constantinople was considered to be both the
New Jerusalem and the New Rome, divinely protected, unassailable and
uniting absolute supremacy as the centre of the political and religious life of
the empire.[11] For Neophytos, as much as for other Byzantines, it was simply
inconceivable that the Queen City, the one protected by the Virgin Mary,
would fall into the hands of enemies. Yet this, the inconceivable for the
Byzantines, happened in 1204. The fall of Constantinople momentarily
shook to its foundations an entire system of beliefs concerning the Byzantine Empire, its Church, its emperor, its Queen City and its position in
God's plans. Neophytos referred to this elaborate ideological structure in
one single phrase, when he invoked St John the Almsgiver to mediate 'in
favour of our City and Church and most pious emperors who are fought by a
foreign people attempting to alter the eternal boundaries which the Lord
and ancient Fathers have drawn'.[12] For Neophytos, the Byzantine Empire

---

[8] *Panegyric 5*, 172.11–173.7.
[9] See e.g. *Cod. Athen. 522*, fol. 56β. On Jerusalem's siege and surrender to Saladin see
Runciman (1978, II: 462–8); Setton (1969–85, II: 45–7); and (on the western reaction to its
fall) *ibid.* (49, 89–91); Runciman (1978, III: 3ff.). Christians mourned the loss of Jerusalem
in east and west. King William II of Sicily dressed himself in sackcloth and went into retreat
for four days; pope Urban III reputedly died of grief: Runciman (1978, III: 4).
[10] *Panegyric 5*, 172.11–24.
[11] For Neophytos' references to the 'Queen City' see, e.g., *Letter 4*, 11.4; *Panegyric 9*, 111.10;
Panegyric 24, 404.5–6, 415.28; *Panegyric 29*, 156.24; *Panegyric 30*, 227.18–19; also, *Cod.
Paris. Gr. 1189*, fol. 175β (*Panegyric 23*). Constantinople also claimed monopoly on 'high'
culture from the eighth century onwards, following the losses to the Persian and Arab
conquerors of Alexandria, Beirut, Antioch, Jerusalem. See Alexander (1962); Ševčenko
(1979–80: 712–16); also Hendy (1989, III: 19). The westerners also regarded Constantinople as a particularly holy city, a feeling expressed by the chroniclers of the First Crusade.
This feeling had been dramatically reversed by the end of the twelfth century, by which time
Constantinople was no longer seen by the Latins as holy. See Runciman (1955: 103–4,
140–1).
[12] *Panegyric 29*, 159.25–30.

was created and guarded by God. To attempt to destroy it was not only a political but also a piacular crime. In his writings the Recluse echoed the horror expressed by other Byzantines: the feeling that a 'cosmic cataclysm', as Euthymios Tornikēs put it, had taken place.[13] It was a horror also felt by at least some western observers.[14]

There was, however, an important difference between Neophytos' reaction to the fall of Jerusalem and to that concerning the fall of Constantinople. In the first case he was deeply grieved, and was even frustrated with God. In the second case he was frustrated, bitter and angry with the Queen City herself. In his *Panegyric* for St Hilariōn Neophytos asks the Saint to mediate 'in favour of all the world and the people who, sinning, are rightly scourged'. She, Neophytos writes, who used to be the ruler and leader of all cities, and who was honoured with presiding over them, has now fallen to a foreign people. Constantinople's 'great suffering' is fully justified by the Recluse as an expression of 'rightful judgment of God for sinful acts'.[15]

That Constantinople fell because of her inhabitants' sins and God's rightful wrath, was a feeling widely shared by other Byzantines.[16] Up to a point this was to be expected: Byzantine authors commonly attributed disasters – including military defeats – to God's anger with the sinning people;[17] and, indeed, we have just seen Neophytos providing the same explanation for Jerusalem's fall. Yet in the case of Jerusalem Neophytos seems to be clinging to this explanation as a means of comprehending the incomprehensible, and of defending his own belief in God. By contrast, Constantinople's fall became almost a means which enabled Neophytos to express a bitterness born out of deep disappointment with Constantinople long before 1204. Neophytos' veneration of Constantinople was sincere; but the other side of that same coin was inscribed by an accumulated feeling of anti-Constantinopolitanism. It was a feeling which political and religious ideological constraints had not allowed Neophytos to express (or indeed perhaps even to admit to himself) earlier: he could and did, in the past, complain bitterly about Constantinople's representatives on the island; but

[13] Euthymios Tornikēs, 82.28–83.1.
[14] The horror felt for the fall and sack of Constantinople was recorded by Byzantines such as Nikētas Chōniatēs, Nikolaos Mesaritēs, Akropolitēs and others, but also by westerners such as pope Innocent III. Crusader chroniclers also refer to the fall and sack of the City. See Setton (1969–85, II: 153–85); Runciman (1978, III: 122–4). Bryer (1973: 87–8) points out that the fall of 1204 was only a culmination of an internal social, geographical and political disintegration. See also, Bryer (1981: 104–9); Nicol (1966: 286–7; 1967: 330).
[15] *Panegyric 13*, 146.37–147.1.
[16] For example, the first patriarch of the Nicaen empire, Michael Autoreianos: Michael Autoreianos, 118.37–48. The same belief is echoed in the speech of Michael VIII Palaiologos, upon receiving the news of the recovery of Constantinople, as recorded by Pachymerēs. See Angold (1975: 54, 68–9).
[17] Thus, e.g., Attaleiatēs explained the Byzantine defeat at Mantzikert: see Alexander (1962).

he could not bring himself to speak against Constantinople herself. After the City's fall, however, the Recluse could legitimise his wrath against the City through identifying with what he perceived to be God's own wrath against her. Now he felt that his worst and most hidden fears were proved right: Constantinople was *so* bad, that God had forsaken her. Neophytos' overwhelming feeling was that Constantinople deserved what she got, that she was being rightly punished for her inhabitants' sins, and that on this as on so many other occasions she had let down God and – inseparably linked to Him – the Byzantine *oikoumenē*.

The angriest, most bitterly anti-Constantinopolitan comments of Neophytos came in his *Interpretation* of the *Apocalypse*, written in the wake of the fall of the City and while he was still in deep shock because of it. In one passage he refers angrily to the foolish extravagance of the Constantinopolitans' way of life: 'What good did we see from the wealth and luxury and richness of the City? Within the time it takes to blink an eyelid, and with the speed of a river's torrent, all was finished, and we were delivered in the hands of our enemies.' He returns to the same point later, to expand it and, in terms of bitter disappointment, to identify Constantinople with the Whore City of the *Apocalypse*: 'Her whom we glorified as a great Queen, God perceived as a filthy whore . . . When the time of judgment came, her great wealth and luxury and power achieved nothing for her. For wherever the wretched shame of sin reigns, human glory and wealth count for nothing'. Neophytos castigates what he considered to be the foundations of hypocrisy and vainglory on which Constantinople's churches and monasteries stood: 'Indeed, she had many monasteries, and icons embellished with gold and silver, and sweet-sounding psalmodies and apparent propriety; but the cup of its nature was filled with the spittle of wretchedness and every kind of filth . . . ; and because of that, her great wealth did not suffice to deliver her from the rightful exasperation of God.'[18]

Anger with Constantinople because of what was perceived to be the extravagance and loose morals of her inhabitants was certainly not a feeling which Neophytos bore alone: it was also expressed – perhaps most tellingly – by Constantinopolitans themselves, such as Michael Chōniatēs and Tzetzēs. For the provincials, on the other hand, the Constantinopolitans' wealth and way of life formed only one of a long list of grievances which had accumulated against the Queen City by the end of the twelfth century. The City's once unassailable authority and prestige had by then been seriously undermined in provinces exhausted by heavy taxation, corrupt administration and Constantinople's inability – if not unwillingness – to protect them from raiders; while the well-documented snobbish attitude of the

---

[18] *Panegyric 9*, 108.97–9, 111.9–112.19.

Constantinopolitan elites towards the provincials (including the provincial aristocracy) could have done nothing other than exacerbate the latters' exasperation. It therefore comes as no surprise to read that when, in 1204, the Constantinopolitans took whatever of their possessions they could hastily grab and fled into exile, the Thracian peasants stood by and watched them, rejoicing at their fall; or that, as Nikētas Chōniatēs recorded further, 'they called our miserable poverty and nakedness, equality'. For by that time 'the love of many people had been turned to frozen ice', as the same historian concluded sadly.[19]

In Neophytos' *Interpretation* of the *Apocalypse*, even the respect for the emperor (a respect which in 1196 had caused the Recluse to state without any comment whatsoever that Andronikos I Komnēnos was a child murderer[20]) now vanishes: 'and the emperors who whored with her, standing, as they say, at a distance because of the smoke from her suffering, shout "alas!", and mourn and cry'.[21] Such low regard for the emperor is extraordinary for Neophytos, and the fact that it only appears on this one occasion in all his writings is indicative of the state of shock in which the fall of Constantinople threw him: just as the fall of Jerusalem had caused him momentarily to question God's wisdom and had thus tested his faith in God, so Constantinople's fall caused him momentarily to criticise the emperor and thus tested his faith in God's representative on earth.

For, this unique instance apart, Neophytos' beliefs and feelings concerning the Byzantine emperor represented nothing less than a full subscription to a Byzantine imperial ideology which insisted on the image of an emperor who feared God and was himself a representative (*ekprosōpos*) of God on earth, crowned by God and guarded by God; a father to his people; a larger-than-life fusion of civil and even religious authority into one person.[22] Such is, for example, the ideal emperor whom Anna Komnēna embodied in

---

[19] Chōniatēs, *Historia*, 593.70–594.78. On anti-Constantinopolitanism in the provinces see Ahrweiler (1976: 13–14, 18; 1975b: 25–9); Brand (1968: 5). See also Herrin (1975: 255, 269); Angold (1975: 49). At the top level of the social hierarchy, snobbery went both ways: the provincial aristocrats could be as mistrustful and derogatory about their Constantinopolitan counterparts (up to and, on occasion, including the emperor) as the latter were of them: *Digenēs Akritēs* and Kekaumenos bear testimony to this: see note 26, below. On Constantinopolitan snobbery particularly as regards Cyprus see below, pp. 221–4; and see generally Magdalino (1981: 56–9; 1984).

[20] *Letter 4*, 11.20–12.1.

[21] *Panegyric 9*, 112.19–21.

[22] Hunger condenses the Byzantine imperial ideal into four basic elements: (1) The power of the emperor comes from God, the emperor being an imitation of God on earth and a pious, God-loving man; (2) the emperor is concerned for his subjects; (3) he is the guardian of justice; (4) he is generous and philanthropic. Kazhdan points out that by the mid-eleventh century the portrait of the ideal emperor included two further elements: nobility and military prowess. See Hunger (1964: 49–154); Kazhdan and Franklin (1984: 23–86, 50–1); Kazhdan and Wharton Epstein (1985: 110–16).

her father and hero of the *Alexiad*; the awesome monarch of whom Kekaumenos wrote 'the emperor is not subject to the law, but is law'; the idealised
Manuel I Komnēnos of the histories of John Kinnamos and William of
Tyre, or of Euthathios of Thessalonikē's *Funeral Oration for Manuel*.[23] It
was an imperial image which in this period had grown out of the Komnēnian
revival and which Manuel I Komnēnos had taken deliberate measures to
carry a step further: Manuel turned the essentially aristocratic Komnēnian
system created by Alexios I Komnēnos more into a prosopolatric one,
focused exclusively on the person of the emperor rather than generally on
his clan.[24] It is certain that the limited but existing *Kaiserkritik* of Manuel
Komnēnos and other Byzantine emperors by Constantinopolitan authors,
such as Nikētas Chōniatēs, either did not find a receptive ear in Neophytos
or (much more likely) never reached him.[25] Nor does Neophytos share the
critical way in which the emperor was perceived by other provincial
authors: his references to the emperor are not characterised by the ambiv-
alence which permeates the portrayal of the *basileus* in *Digenēs Akritēs*; his
unswerving loyalty towards the emperor is not tinged with the calculated
self-interest which informed Kekaumenos' allegiance to his emperor.[26] For
Neophytos the Byzantine emperor was God on earth, very nearly as unquestionable in the exercise of his authority as God was. Hence Neophytos'
extreme reluctance to express any derogatory comment for any Byzantine
emperor.[27]

Hence, also Neophytos' great resentment of the ruler of Cyprus, Isaac
Komnēnos. The fact that Isaac had challenged the authority of no less
blood-stained an emperor than Andronikos I Komnēnos made no difference to the Recluse. Nor was Neophytos' hatred of Isaac mainly motivated

[23] *Alexiad, passim.*; Kekaumenos, *Strategikon*, 274.1–2, (Litavrin ed.), *Logos Nouthetētikos*,
93.1–2; Kinnamos, e.g. 274.23–278.5; Eustathios, *Opuscula*, 196–214, esp. 200. See Bryer
(1981: 97–9); Angold (1975: 52–5); Magdalino (1983: 326, 337–8); also Kazhdan and
Franklin (1984: 146, 182); Kazhdan and Wharton Epstein (1985: esp. 113, 115).

[24] See Magdalino (1981: 62–3). On Byzantine imperial ideology see generally Karagiannopoulos (1974: 10–17); Nicol (1967: 316); Alexander (1962: 355); Ahrweiler (1975a).

[25] See Magdalino (1983).

[26] *Digenēs Akritēs*, 132.971–134.1008, 136.1023–46, 138.1048–53, 138.1066–140.1082,
140.1087–9; Kekaumenos, *Strategikon*, e.g. 122.3–9, 122.22–124.14, 126.4–9, 152.23–
154.3, 156.28–158.10, 198.15–200.17, 248.13–250.13, 268.8–13, 298.15–302.33 (Litavrin
ed.); 3.14–20, 4.3–26, 5.14–18, 18.12–24, 20.19–30, 40.32–41.33, 64.15–65.10, 73.24–
74.3, 76.16–78.27 (Wassiliewsky and Jernstedt, eds.). Neophytos is much closer to the
author of *On Skirmish Warfare* in terms of unquestioning loyalty towards the emperor. See
generally Ševčenko (1979–80: 726–35); on *Digenēs Akritēs* see also Galatariotou (1987b: esp.
40–4).

[27] Hence also Neophytos' acceptance of Andronikos I Komnēnos as an emperor, despite his
murder of Manuel's son. Neophytos expressed rejection of a Byzantine emperor only with
regard to the emperor of Constantinople in 1204; and with a number of Byzantine emperors
condemned by Byzantine state and Church as heretical: those who, according to Neophytos,
fuelled heresies 'after the death of Constantine the Great', men like the 'iconoclast' Leo the
Isaurian, the 'heretical' Anastasios. See below, ch. 10.

by the latter's tyrannical way of governing the island.[28] Neophytos hated him above all because through his actions Isaac had disturbed deeply held beliefs about the Byzantine world order. He was the instigator of a separatist act; he had therefore disturbed what Blemmydēs had called 'the harmony' (*harmonia*) and Nikētas Chōniatēs 'the order' (*taxis*) of the world. Since any tendency against the emperor was conceived of as a threat to the very existence of man and the world, it follows that by declaring Cyprus independent of Byzantium Isaac had constituted a *kainotomia* (an abhorrent, to the Byzantines, break with tradition); he was guilty of vainglory (*doxomania*) and even of some kind of heresy.[29] In a world divided, in Neophytos' mind, between those who lived in the Byzantine *oikoumenē* and the other, lesser inhabitants of the earth, Isaac had divorced Cyprus from the *oikoumenē* and had allied it with the dark world of the pagans, the non-Christians and the barbarians (the *ethnē* and *barbaroi*). He had allied himself with the Norman king of Sicily, William II, whose sister he married; he had joined forces with the Sicilian 'pirate', Margarito, defeating the fleet of Isaac II Angelos and humiliating the Byzantine forces; he reputedly became a great friend of 'the godless Saladin', the conqueror of Jerusalem. Indeed, when Alexios III Angelos wrote to pope Innocent III in 1201 reclaiming Cyprus for Byzantium, the pope's answer was that the island had ceased to be part of the empire not when the Crusaders arrived in 1191, but when Isaac began his rule in 1184. In Neophytos' mind Isaac was not a true *basileus*. He was rather a tyrant (*tyrannos*). No matter how much power the latter held, 'the people dreamt of his deposition', as Manuel II Palaiologos wrote.[30]

Even though Neophytos' open references to Isaac are scarce (only twice does he mention him by name[31]), there can be no mistaking of his resentment of Isaac. There can be little doubt that Neophytos is pointing at Isaac when, in about 1214, he writes of vanity and envy. He first mentions the angels who fell because of vanity and envy and became demons; he then says that this passion is still rife, and that one need only look around to see how a king's or bishop's throne, that of an abbot or of any 'God-given glory', is envied. Often, Neophytos says, it is persons not worthy of them who want to have them, and many such persons are eventually removed from power, disgraced and humiliated.[32] Even though Neophytos calls Isaac a *basileus* in

---

[28] On Isaac Komnēnos' rule of Cyprus see also ch. 3, pp. 42–3 and 199–200.
[29] See Ahrweiler (1976: 3–4, 5, 8); Nicol (1967: 316–19).
[30] Manuel II Palaiologos, *Hypothēkai*, 373.
[31] In the *Panegyric* for the Cross and, more extensively, in the Letter concerning the misfortunes of Cyprus: *Cod. Paris. Gr. 1189*, fol. 37β, p. 48.17 (*Panegyric 7*); *Letter 4*, 11.4–7, 12.3–5.
[32] *Cod. Paris. Gr. 1317*, fols. 118α–β.

the letter concerning the misfortunes of Cyprus, he precedes this by writing that, having arrived in Cyprus, Isaac 'proclaimed himself a king' (*phēmizetai basileus*) and that since then he 'holds' (*kratei*) Cyprus – rather than 'rules' or 'reigns' (*archei*), which is reserved by Neophytos for legitimate rulers.[33] There would be no doubt in the mind of any of Neophytos' contemporary readers that he is referring to an arbitrary rule.

Neophytos' reference to Isaac in his *Panegyric* for the Holy Cross is very short and very revealing: 'For seven years this country was held rebelliously (*antartikōs*) by Isaac Komnēnos.'[34] It is the only occasion in the entire body of Neophytos' surviving writings that the word *antartēs* is used in respect of a human being. On all other occasions Neophytos uses this word to describe Satan. Satan is characterised as an *antartēs*, a rebel, in his relationship to God.[35] Undoubtedly, other terms used by Neophytos for Satan, such as 'dissenter' (*apostatēs*) and 'tyrant' (*tyrannos*), would in Neophytos' mind also be perfectly applicable to Isaac.[36] Neophytos' logic is clear: Isaac may hold the power of a king over Cyprus, but he is nothing other than a rebel towards the Byzantine emperor. Since that emperor is God on a human scale, it follows that Isaac is Satan on the same scale.

Amongst all Byzantine emperors, Neophytos recognises two as outstanding: Constantine, who is acknowledged as 'the Great' and as a defender of the Orthodox faith, after whose death the heretics found it easy to spread; and the 'most pious *basileus*' Manuel I Komnēnos.[37]

In the *Book of Fifty Chapters* Neophytos gives a fascinating example of Byzantine imperial ideology in practice. He devotes one of his chapters to 'our most pious *basileus*, sir Manuel Komnēnos', and he then fills five folios with a description of the battle of Myriokephalon.[38] We have already come across his expressions of grief over the defeat and slaughter of the Byzantine army. Almost the entire text, however, focuses, in fact, on a description of Manuel's behaviour at Myriokephalon. Now, according to other sources, Manuel's crushing defeat appears to have been caused by his bad judgment before the battle. During the battle itself, Manuel panicked

---

[33] *Letter 4*, 12.2–3, 12.7, 12.10. Neophytos uses the same word (*kratei*) to describe Saladin's rule in Palestine and Jerusalem: *Cod. Paris. Gr. 1189*, fols. 179β–180α (*Panegyric 23*).

[34] *Cod. Coisl. Gr. 1189*, fol. 37α, p. 48.16–17 (*Panegyric 7*).

[35] E.g., *Cod. Athen. 522*, fol. 17β; *Cod. Coisl. Gr. 287*, fol. 107β; *Cod. Paris. Gr. 1189*, fol. 54α (*Panegyric 8*).

[36] E.g., *Cod. Paris. Gr. 1189*, fol. 33β (*Panegyric 7*).

[37] For Constantine see *Panegyric 10*, 176.26–31; *Panegyric 24*, 404.7; *Cod. Paris. Gr. 1189*, fol. 219α (*Panegyric 28*). Note that Attaleiatēs also praises Constantine the Great for piety and military skill. See Kazhdan and Franklin (1984: 31–2). For Manuel see *Cod. Athen. 522*, fol. 9β, p. 42; *Letter 4*, 11.16.

[38] *Cod. Athen. 522*, fols. 9β (p. 42), 75β–77β (pp. 45.9–46.24).

totally. He made no attempt to save his men, and his own life as well as those of a small group of his followers were saved only through Kilidj Arslan's mercy.[39]

Neophytos' recording of the battle presents a picture quite antithetical to the one described above. In its gist, the information which Neophytos imparts almost certainly originated in the official (and heavily distorted, in terms of factual reality) version of events, which would have reached Cyprus and other provinces through imperial bulletins.[40] An official version exonerating the Byzantine emperor from blame would certainly have been what Neophytos had wished for, for he eagerly seizes and elaborates on such an interpretation. To begin with, he is careful to exonerate Manuel from any charge of mishandling the whole affair by throwing in such sidelines as 'suddenly and unexpectedly, an innumerable multitude of Muslims fell upon him'.[41] Neophytos presents Manuel as overcome with emotion upon witnessing the slaughter of his troops. 'Seeing the disaster that had befallen his people, Manuel did not bear to see them in such danger.' Armed with God's hope, continues the Recluse, he charged forth in the midst of the enemy. Manuel is described as an emperor (*autokratōr*) surrounded by wild beasts. 'The King of Heaven saw the King of earth and admired his bravery.' God knew that 'whenever the *basileus* is in danger, the whole of Byzantium and Christianity is in danger too'. And since it was impossible for Manuel to escape such a huge crowd of enemies, or to kill them all, God extended His helping hand, strengthening and protecting Manuel. Thus, Neophytos explains, the emperor succeeded in killing many enemies and then in escaping unharmed. 'Manuel went about the Turkish lines mighty and brave, proving his enemies weak. An extraordinary sight he was, one single God-crowned man, fighting against so many arms with his only two, supported by God.' He looked like Samson, Gideon, Goliath and David, surrounded from all sides by enemies, yet defeating all. 'Thus' Neophytos concludes, addressing his readers or listeners, 'those wise amongst you will understand how one can defeat a thousand, glory be to God.'

---

[39] See Brand (1968: 16–18); and note 5, above. Nikētas Chōniatēs paints a picture of Manuel in his last years as a superstitious and cowardly ruler. This picture contrasts, it is true, with that given by Eustathios of Thessalonikē. See Chōniatēs, *Historia*, 219.71–222.64; Eustathios, *Opuscula*, 196–214 (Funeral Oration for Manuel) esp. 212–13. See also Brand (1968: 23–30); Chalandon (1912: 606).

[40] It is known from other sources that there was an official version of the events in Myriokephalon: see Vasiliev (1929–30: esp. 236–40); Eustathios, *Orationes*, 1–3; on imperial bulletins dispatched to the provinces see Eustathios, *Orationes*, 77; Chōniatēs, *Historia*, 191.26–33; and MacCormick (1986: 190–6).

[41] *Cod. Athen.* 522, fol. 75β, p. 45.12–15. Note that in another passage, in the *Panegyric* for St Dēmētrios, and possibly referring to Myriokephalon, Neophytos states that the defeat 'recently' suffered by the Byzantines was not due to the generals' inefficiency, but to the people's sins (*Panegyric 15*, 54.198.201).

In this extraordinary passage, Manuel's defeat has been turned into Manuel's victory. Myriokephalon might have been, by Neophytos' own earlier admission, the scene of the slaughter of the Byzantine army, but through Neophytos' portrayal of Manuel it became the scene of a personal victory of the emperor. Neophytos embodies Manuel with every characteristic of that image projected by imperial ideology which we encountered earlier: he is a living father to his people, risking his own life because he cannot bear to see them being slaughtered. As a soldier, he is brave and strong.[42] In relation to God, it is obvious that the difference is only one of scale: God is the King of Heaven, Manuel that of earth. Because of Manuel's faith, piety and bravery, God makes him invincible. The Turks are dwarfed, and Manuel emerges as the victor, the mighty, fatherly, brave, provident, pious emperor, whose closeness (*parrēsia*) to God is indisputable. Compared to what actually happened at Myriokephalon, Neophytos' passage bears extraordinary witness to distortion of factual reality through ideology.

It is uncertain whether Neophytos' attitude would have been the same towards any Byzantine emperor, or whether he particularly 'revered' Manuel. It is possible that Manuel I Komnēnos was generally more respected by the Cypriots than other Byzantine emperors. We find his name recorded and remembered by the Cypriots far more frequently than that of any other emperor's. Significantly, Manuel's name is linked with the Cypriot Church and monasticism. When between 1156 and 1169 John, bishop of Amathus, was deposed by the archbishop and a Synod of the Cypriot Church, it was to Manuel that he appealed for redress. The latter referred the matter to patriarch Luke Chrysobergēs and the Oecumenical Synod, who pronounced the sentence invalid.[43] The story illustrates well the authority which even members of the Autocephalous Church of Cyprus felt Manuel commanded. Another hint concerning Manuel's power with respect to the Autocephalous Cypriot Church comes in the *Life* of St Leontios of Jerusalem: as we have seen, Manuel is depicted offering Leontios the archiepiscopal throne of Cyprus – evidently acting as though it was his to give.[44] As far as monasticism went, Manuel had provided the funds, land and a *stauropēgion* for the foundation of the important monastery of

---

[42] The inclusion of military prowess as part of the ideal Byzantine emperor's image appears in the mid-eleventh century, when we also first encounter coins of emperors in military dress. Kekaumenos includes *andreia* (courage) as one of the characteristics of the ideal emperor; and even though he is referring to spiritual rather than physical courage, other writers (such as Theophylact of Ochrid or Theodore Prodromos) also describe the emperor as an ideal warrior: Kazhdan and Franklin (1984: 38–40, 110–11); and see note 22, above.

[43] On this point, and as to whether the interference of the Oecumenical patriarch was an act of ecclesiastical intrusion, especially in view of the Autocephalus status of the Cypriot Church, see Hacket (1901: 54–5); Mitsides (1976: 13–14; 1973: 27–31); and generally ch. 3, pp. 45–6.

[44] *Life* of Leontios of Jerusalem, 412–14. See ch. 3, pp. 45–6.

Machairas; while the foundation of another important monastery (that of the Virgin of Chryssorhogiatissa) was also, according to tradition, founded during his reign, in 1152.[45] The nature of Machairas' foundation agrees with Chōniatēs' description of Manuel's motivations for founding the monastery of Kataskepē, in deliberate reaction to the type of foundation favoured by the Komnēnoi before him: it was neither a family mausoleum, nor was it in or near Constantinople.[46]

Apart from ecclesiastical matters, Manuel's name was also linked with secular Cypriot affairs: when Richard I of England conquered Cyprus, one of the steps which he took to befriend the inhabitants was to confirm to them by charter the laws and institutions which were granted them under Manuel.[47] Again, the trauma of the 1153 raid by Renaud de Châtillon (regarding which the Cypriots had sent a bitter complaint to Manuel) might have been somewhat alleviated in the Cypriots' minds by Renaud's total and humiliating begging of Manuel's forgiveness in 1159.[48] Perhaps it was also because the Cypriots were in awe of Manuel that they were so credulous of Isaac Komnēnos' forged letters of appointment as governor of the island: at least one contemporary (Benedict of Peterborough) states that Isaac was immediately accepted by the Cypriots because of his kin relationship to emperor Manuel.[49] Further, the monk whom the rebellious Cypriots proclaimed 'emperor of Cyprus' during their ill-starred revolt against the English in 1192, might have been chosen not so much because he was a relative of Isaac Komnēnos', but because he was, through Isaac, a relative of Manuel's.[50]

Whether Manuel did enjoy a particular 'cult' in Cyprus is a question which must remain, for the time being at least, an open one. But there can be no doubt as to Neophytos' feelings on the matter; and the whole question of Manuel's 'idealisation' by Neophytos (and possibly by most Cypriots) bring us to another aspect of Byzantine imperial ideology, this time expressed through Neophytos' conception of Cyprus as part of Byzantium. It is a very striking fact that Neophytos refers to the emperor and the empire after 1184 and indeed after 1191, as if Cyprus was still under Byzantine rule.

---

[45] For the monastery of Machairas see *Diataxis* of Neilos, 11.21–12.6. See also Menardos (1929); Hackett (1901: 346–7); Hill (1948–52, I: 310–11). The tradition concerning the foundation of the monastery of Chryssorhogiatissa is recorded on one of the monastery's icons. See Philippou (1935: 12ff.); Hill (1948–52, I: 310); Hackett (1901: 354–5).

[46] Chōniatēs, *Historia*, 206.71–208.15. On Manuel's ecclesiastical policy with regard to monasteries see Magdalino (1981: 62–3).

[47] Benedict of Peterborough, II, 168. See Hill (1948–52, I: 320).

[48] William of Tyre, I.2, 859–61. See Hill (1948–52, I: 306–8).

[49] Benedict of Peterborough, I, 255. Manuel was Isaac's great uncle. See Hill (1948–52, I: 312–13, esp. 313, note 1); Hackett (1901: 55–7, 59ff.).

[50] Benedict of Peterborough, II, 172; Roger of Hoveden, III, 114. See Hill (II: 34); Hackett (1901: 64–5).

In 1196 Neophytos refers to the emperors Manuel I Komnēnos, Andronikos I Komnēnos and Alexios III Angelos in his letter concerning the misfortunes of Cyprus.[51] There can be no doubt that the *basileis*, as whose protector the Cross is described in Neophytos' *Panegyric* for the Holy Cross (of the same year) are the Byzantine ones; or that 'our most faithful and most pious God-crowned *basileis*' who appear in a post-1191 passage, are the Byzantine emperors – still referred to by Neophytos as 'our' emperors.[52] In passages written after 1204 Neophytos continues to refer to Constantinople as the 'Queen City' (*basileuousa polis*) and to ask the Saint whose *Panegyric* he is writing to intervene in favour of the city and Church and 'most loyal emperors' who are fought by a foreign people.[53] In his *Catecheseis*, written at around 1214, Neophytos writes that God 'enlightened the soul's eyes of faith of our most faithful and God-crowned emperors and strengthened the rule of Truth most mightily'.

Neophytos' most surprising references to Byzantium are found in his *Typikon*. The Recluse entitles the seventh chapter of his *Typikon* as 'concerning the king (*rēgas*) of Cyprus' and the warden (*epitropos*) of the Enkleistra. The chapter contains a request to the warden to mediate if any of the monks is ever sent by the monastery to the *basileus* with a petition. This is followed by an '*hypomnēsis* to the *basileus*' – a model text to be used by the monks in the event of such request and visit. In the passage, the ruler to whom the *hypomnēsis* is addressed is described as 'king' (*basileus*), 'lord' (*despotas*) and 'emperor' (*autokratōr*), 'guarded by God' (*theophrouroumenos*); the monks are described as 'my disciples and your servants who are praying for you'; and Neophytos ends the passage by praying that Christ would 'strengthen and protect and make powerful for many years your reign'. Later, the Recluse advises his monks not to start building a new church, except if 'an emperor's hand' is extended to help them.[54]

Close examination of these passages and their surrounding circumstances leaves no doubt that Neophytos is referring to the Byzantine emperor in all of them, and not (as has been suggested[55]) to the Latin king of Cyprus. My conclusion is based on consideration of three factors. First, the epithets used to describe the ruler (especially *theophrouroumenos*, *despotas* and *autokratōr*) are only used by Neophytos, throughout his writings, in respect of the Byzantine emperor. Second, it is impossible that Neophytos would be referring to the actual king of Cyprus in 1214, the Latin Hugh I, since the Recluse is abusive towards the Latins in that very same *Typikon*, calling for instance the Latin rule 'a terrible slavery'.[56] Finally, it is highly unlikely,

---

[51] *Letter 4*, 10.15, 12.16, 12.21.
[52] Respectively, *Cod. Paris. Gr. 1189*, fol. 38α (*Panegyric 7*); *ibid.*, fols. 52α–β, 54α, 57α (*Panegyric 8*).
[53] E.g., *Panegyric 29*, 156.24, 159.25–30.   [54] *Typikon*, 78.14–79.2, 79.3–12, 90.20–7.
[55] Egglezakes (1979–80: 60).   [56] *Typikon*, 95.29–30; also 80.20–2.

too, that Neophytos would expect any king other than an Orthodox one to contribute towards the building of a church in Neophytos' monastery. Certainly the Latin king under whose reign the persecution of the Orthodox Church of Cyprus was hotly pursued could not conceivably have been expected (or indeed desired) by Neophytos to do so.

The fact is that in 1214, some thirty years after Isaac divorced Cyprus from Byzantium and twenty-three years after the establishment of Latin rule, Neophytos not only looks upon the emperor in Nicaea as the Cypriots' figurehead, but as the actual ruler of Cyprus. He takes for granted not only that requests could be made to him by Cypriots, but that he would also meet such requests, the execution of the request taking place in Cyprus. The monks and all Cypriots are, for Neophytos, still the servants of the Byzantine emperor. If one had only these Neophytic passages to go by, he or she would be forgiven for believing that Cyprus never ceased to be a province of Byzantium. One is indeed reminded of the words of G. Ostrogorsky, who wrote that 'no one could show more contempt for facts when they contradicted theory than the Byzantines. When facts and belief contradicted each other, beliefs prevailed.'[57] What Neophytos manifested in these 1214 statements was not just the distortion of factual reality through ideology, but the negation of factual reality through ideology and the adherence to that 'other', cultural, reality. He manifested the power which perceived reality can have, over and against factual reality itself.

At first sight, there appears to be a contradiction between such passionate defence of the idea of Cyprus as an integral part of Byzantium; and Neophytos' pre-1191 castigations of the island's rulers and his bitter anti-Constantinopolitan comments immediately after the fall of the City in 1204. Such a contradiction would have puzzled Nikētas Chōniatēs, who thought that by 1204 the provincials had experienced a complete change of heart towards Constantinople, their 'love' having been turned to 'frozen ice'. Valuable though it is, Chōniatēs' appreciation suffers from being two-dimensional. For in at least some Greek Orthodox provinces it was precisely the previous existence of 'love' for the Queen City that subsequently gave provincial anti-Constantinopolitanism its particularly bitter but also eventually multi-dimensional quality. If all the Orthodox provincials bore only the feelings of one who had been abused by a stranger, they would have simply hated Constantinople. Their feelings towards the City were much more complicated than that: they were not only hateful or uncaring ('frozen') feelings, but they were conflicting feelings precisely because the provincials had not only experienced and suffered abuse; they had also experienced, in Chōniatēs' word, 'love' – and had suffered utter disappointment from the one they loved.

[57] Ostrogorsky (1956: 5). See also Nicol (1967: 320).

You may, if you prefer, replace 'love' by 'a system of ideologies', one which had during the long years of Byzantine rule placed provincials like the Cypriots into a relationship of a young child to a parent: no matter how bad, that parent was still a parent, with all the mixture of love, resentment and ultimate dependency that that entailed. Or you may read, instead of the existence of 'love', the existence of 'a multitude of ties of material and symbolic significance', through which the Cypriots perceived themselves to be links in a seemingly unbroken chain that tied them to the Byzantine *oikoumenē* and its emperor, and through the latter ultimately to God. No matter how you phrase it, the end result was the same: momentarily rejecting the Queen City who had neglected and abused them, the Cypriots subsequently could not quite forget her and all she stood for, because their cultural existence was – symbolically as well as materially – inextricably bound up with hers. When she, as well as they, faced total catastrophe, they closed ranks.

After 1184, and especially after 1191, the issue for the Cypriots ceased to be one of class conflict or of daily grievances: the issue became one of identity. They were members of the Byzantine *oikoumenē*, and no matter how badly run that *oikoumenē* currently was, it was the ony one with whom they could identify. The fact that they also had to deal with a new regime which was in every way far worse than the one it replaced certainly aggravated their feeling of despair for being part of the Byzantine empire no more. Their 'love' for the empire, which had turned into bitterness born of disappointment, resurfaced with a power that swept aside the factual realities of the earlier unhappy state of affairs under Constantinople's rule.

Thus, in some provinces at least, 'love' for Constantinople survived – whether by being rekindled or resurrected – after the City's utter humiliation in 1204; and it was accompanied by the belief that God would restore the Byzantine *oikoumenē* to its former glory, for, after all, this was His *oikoumenē*, His kingdom on earth.

Neophytos was certainly not alone in his undoubted belief that one day soon God's punishment for the Byzantines' sins would run its course, and Cyprus would be restored fully in the order (*taxis*) of the Byzantine universe. That this was very much a Byzantine's turn of mind is manifested by the parallel firm belief of the Byzantines in Nicaea, that one day, their sins paid for by their suffering, they would return to Constantinople, regain, indeed, the *Imperium Romanum*, and order would be restored in the universe.[58] Concerning Cyprus, it must be remembered that the island's links with Constantinople always remained close, despite the sufferings of the population under Byzantine rule. I have already referred to Cyprus' 'special

[58] See Nicol (1967: 317–20); Angold (1975: 53–5, 59, 62–3, 68–9).

relationship' with Manuel I Komnēnos. His endowments for the monastery of Machairas were enhanced by further privileges granted it by Isaac II Angelos and Alexios III Angelos;[59] while Neophytos expected that the Enkleistra could also be the beneficiary of imperial grants.[60] Since Cyprus was no longer under Byzantine control during the reign of Alexios III Angelos, it has been suggested that his grants to the monastery of Machairas were issued to Cypriot refugees from that monastery in Constantinople, aimed at turning the monastery into a bulwark against foreign domination.[61] Certainly, Isaac II Angelos had tried to recover the island from Isaac Komnēnos by means of arms, while in 1201 Alexios III Angelos made another effort (diplomatic, coupled with threats of force of arms if diplomacy failed) to regain Cyprus from the Lusignans.[62]

It is difficult to say whether (as has been suggested) the revolts of the Cypriots against the English (in 1191) and against the Templars (on Good Saturday, 5 April 1192) were secretly fomented by the Byzantine Court.[63] Their unprepared and impetuous nature – hence, their quick suppression in blood – suggest rather that they were spontaneous and purely local affairs.[64] The same could be said of the raids of Kanakēs, a Cypriot who led a group of his compatriots to revolt against the Latins. (Escaping from Cyprus he took refuge in Karamania, from where, supported by another Cypriot, Isaac, the seigneur of Antiochetta, Kanakēs carried out raids against the Latins in Cyprus which culminated in the capture of the queen of Cyprus, Echive d'Ibelin, and her children.)[65] But certainly the imperial capital (Constantinople, Nicaea after 1204 and Constantinople again after 1261) was always a place of refuge for Cypriot emigrés. We have seen how Neophytos' spiritual son was received by emperor Alexios III Angelos and was honoured by him with the title of *sebastos*, a very high honour in the twelfth century.[66] In his *Typikon* and in a bibliographical note of about the same date Neophytos refers to monks from the monastery of St John

---

[59] *Diataxis* of Neilos, 16.18–17.6.   [60] *Typikon*, 90.20–7.

[61] Menardos (1929: 7).

[62] Chōniatēs, *Historia*, 369.74–370.12. See Hill (1972, II: 62–3; 1948–52, I: 314); Brand (1968: 172); Hackett (1901: 77–8).

[63] Hackett (1901: 77).

[64] For accounts of these revolts see Hill (1972, II: 34, 36–7); Hackett (1901: 64–6). Note that in the fifteenth century Machairas narrated that Guy de Lusignan was fearful of a rebellion by his Cypriot subjects, in which he believed (according to Machairas) that 'they will have the emperor of Constantinople to help them': Machairas, I, 20, para. 22.

[65] See Hackett (1901: 76–7); Hill (1972, II: 57).

[66] Ahrweiler (1966b); Mango and Hawkins (1964: 338). Note, however, that Nikētas Chōniatēs complained that during the reign of Alexios III Angelos this title was bought and sold at crossroads and markets, by bakers, linen sellers, Cumans and Syrians: Chōniatēs, *Historia*, 483.60–484.65. See also Brand (1968: 144).

Chrysostom who were now in Constantinople.[67] And we have already encountered the cases of Cypriots going to Constantinople (or Nicaea) for studies, or to commission an icon.[68]

All this despite the attitudes of the Constantinopolitans towards the empire's provincials.[69] They and the provincials undoubtedly shared a very substantial common cultural ground; but they were also inevitably separated by varying degrees of cultural difference. The Constantinopolitans did not regard this difference as denoting exactly that (i.e. a cultural difference), but as denoting inferiority on the part of the provincials. The latter were conceived of by the metropolitans as crude, unrefined, unsophisticated, uncultured. There was a relative – if oscillating and never clearly defined – scale in this metropolitan appreciation: the more pronounced the difference between themselves and a particular group of provincials, the more derogatory the Constantinopolitans' appreciation of those provincials became. They thus usually reserved, for instance, the description of 'barbarians' for the non-Greek, non-Orthodox provincials (a point to which we shall return in the next chapter);[70] but they did conceive of all non-Constantinopolitans (including the Greek Orthodox) as 'foreigners', in degrees which ranged from the nearly insignificant to the very pronounced.[71] Occasionally, the appreciation of the provincials as foreigners was accompanied by an implicit suspicion that even Greek Orthodox provincials were not really worthy of being considered true *Romaioi*.

With specific reference to Cyprus, scholars have noted Skylitzēs' reference to the Cypriots as the *ethnos tōn Kypriōn* – a description striking in its implications, since the term *ethnos* was normally applied to foreigners and even barbarians.[72] Again, more than one scholar has pointed out the young George of Cyprus' disappointment at being unable to meet Nikēphoros Blemmydēs because the Cypriot was considered too young, poor and, significantly, a foreigner (*xenos*).[73] And Hélène Ahrweiler has shown that the title of *sebastos* was often (though certainly not only) given to foreign

---

[67] *Typikon*, 102.4–5; *Bibliographical Note*, 126.3–7.

[68] See earlier, pp. 35, 161.

[69] By 'Constantinopolitans' I am by necessity referring, of course, only to those of the Queen City's inhabitants whose writings survive.

[70] See the discussion below, pp. 226ff.

[71] The notion that any person who did not inhabit one's own home town was a foreigner (*xenos*) was not exclusive to the Constantinopolitans, though the latter were particularly prone to using the term in a derogatory way: see Galatariotou (forthcoming b).

[72] Kedrēnos-Skylitzes, II: 549.16–550.5, esp. 549.21, 550.2. See also Mango (1976a: 10–11); Egglezakes (1979–80: 31); and see below, pp. 227–9.

[73] Lameere (1937: 181.15–23); Angold (1975: 66) (who refers to this incident as an example of xenophobia by the Byzantines at Nicaea); Constantinides (1982: 25–6) (who sees the incident rather as an example of 'Blemmydophobia' by the locals).

leaders, as well as to leaders of ethnic groups living in Byzantium.[74] The evidence is slim, but indicative.

However, Cyril Mango has greatly overstated the case concerning Cyprus, clearly implying that it was regarded with particular contempt by the Constantinopolitans. He cites as evidence some of Constantine Manassēs' comments on Cyprus, recorded in his *Hodoiporikon*; and interprets them as showing that Manassēs' opinion of Cyprus, which Mango assumes to be representative of a general Constantinopolitan attitude, was wholly unfavourable and characterised by nothing other than sneering contempt. This interpretation, which is threatening to become a *topos* in the secondary literature concerning the relationship between Constantinople and Cyprus, is based on a very biased reading of the *Hodoiporikon* and needs to be reconsidered.[75]

In the *Hodoiporikon* Constantine Manassēs recorded in verse his impressions of the long round journey which in 1161–2 took him and the *sebastos* John Kontostephanos on an imperial mission from Constantinople to Palestine. After a pilgrimage there, the *sebastos* and Manassēs parted company at Tyre. Having fallen ill Manassēs went to Cyprus, where he stayed for some time as a guest of the governor of the island, Alexios Doukas. After a short trip to Isauria Manassēs returned to Cyprus, where he was subsequently reunited with John Kontostephanos before returning finally to Constantinople.

I have argued elsewhere, on the basis of a comparative study of Byzantine travellers' accounts from this period and of an internal examination of Manassēs' poem, that, far from being wholly representative of general cultural attitudes, the *Hodoiporikon* is to a large extent a very personal account, and to that extent it is representative of individually rather than collectively held attitudes. This applies particularly to Manassēs' comments about Palestine and Cyprus.[76] Here, I shall confine myself only to a few points regarding the Constantinopolitan aristocrat's views on Cyprus.

[74] See Ahrweiler (1966b). See also Chōniatēs' comments concerning this title during the reign of Alexios III Angelos: note 66 above.

[75] Mango (1976a: 9–11). See also Angold (1984: 276–7); Egglezakes (1979–80: 31). Mango (1976a) also greatly overstates his case on a number of other points. To give but one example, he suggests that the Cypriot who encountered Manassēs in church 'may not even have understood the words addressed to him'. This clearly implies that the Cypriots and the Constantinopolitans either spoke different languages, or at least that to the Cypriots the Constantinopolitans' Greek was incomprehensible. Yet we know that the Cypriots understood and themselves used the more 'elevated' spoken and written Greek: our witnesses are all the surviving Cypriot inscriptions and literature from the period. The latter includes, of course, Neophytos' own writings, which were not only read but also read out to congregations of Greek Cypriots – who would certainly not have stood listening to panegyrics and sermons delivered in an incomprehensible language. See Mango (1976a: 10–11); followed by Angold (1984: 276–7). On a different point see earlier, pp. 63–6.

[76] Galatariotou (forthcoming b).

Towards the end of the poem Manassēs narrates what he considered to be an amusing and funny story. He describes how he nearly fainted when a Cypriot, 'more senseless than all the Cypriots', stood next to him in church, reeking of garlic and wine. Having asked the Cypriot twice to move away, and having had no response, Manassēs struck him in the face and thus got rid of him.[77] This episode Cyril Mango has treated as representative of a general Constantinopolitan attitude towards the Cypriots. Yet an indication that this is not so, and that this incident reflects Manassēs' own personal and generally unrepresentative bias, is contained in the text itself. For Manassēs ends his little story with a very telling line: 'and that was that, *although some would disapprove*'.[78] He knew, in other words, that he was not representative, and that at least some members of his Constantinopolitan aristocratic audience (to whom the poem was obviously addressed) would find his behaviour in Cyprus unacceptable or at least in very poor taste.

Again, it is true that, as Cyril Mango points out, Manassēs described Cyprus as a cultural desert, complained that it was 'bitterly evil-smelling', and likened it to a prison from which escape was difficult because the waters around it were infested with pirates.[79] But to point out only these passages is to do the text a disservice. For Manassēs also calls Cyprus 'famous' and 'the greatest of all islands'; he mentions three of its towns without any derogatory comment (his simple description of one of them – Tremithousia – as 'poor' hardly amounts to a grave insult); he testifies that Cyprus has a healthy climate, that it is the subject of hymns, that it has a ferile, rich-bearing soil.[80] Furthermore, Manassēs clearly indicates that he knew that his negative comments were not representative of a general attitude but entirely subjective to him – for he half-apologetically admits his personal bias and contrasts it to a more generally held, and positive, attitude towards Cyprus. He says, characteristically: 'And now I dwell in Cyprus, this subject of hymns, / this fertile soil, this rich-bearing land, / which is a sweet-smelling marshplant [*kypeiron*] *to others, but to me*, it is *Kypros*'.[81]

We must also, of course, see Manassēs' comments on Cyprus within the context of the whole poem. Considering what he says in the *Hodoiporikon* about other lands he visited, and especially considering his negative and even hubristic comments about Palestine (which was, after all the Holy Land in which he went as a pilgrim), Cyprus actually fares not too badly in

77 Manassēs, 344.89–345.130.
78 καὶ τοῦτο μὲν τοιοῦτο, κἄν μέμφοιτό τις: *ibid.*, 345.130 (my italics).
79 *Ibid.*, 336.53–347.186, especially 337.98–102 (lack of culture), 342.8 (evil-smelling), 346.153–347.186 (Cyprus likened to a prison).
80 *Ibid.*, 336.63–5 (famous, healthy climate), 337.84–5 (subject of hymns, fertile), 339.18 (greatest of all islands), 342.14–15 (Paphos, Kition, Tremithousia).
81 *Ibid.*, 337.84–6 (my italics).

his hands.[82] It is clear that his impressions of and feelings towards Cyprus as recorded in the *Hodoiporikon* were mixed rather than wholly negative; and that the internal evidence of the poem does not allow us to interpret the episode with the Cypriot in church as representative of the general attitude of the metropolitans especially towards the Cypriots: to do so is to fail to take into account the personal bias of the author which is not only clearly if implicitly in the text, but which the author himself explicitly admits.

In short, as far as the Constantinopolitans' estimation of Cyprus is concerned, neither the *Hodoiporikon* nor any other source provides evidence to suggest that Cyprus fared worse than other provinces. On the contrary, the patronage of its monasteries and churches by emperors and other members of the Constantinopolitan aristocracy, or the fact that Manassēs felt the need to clarify that his negative comments reflected personal bias and were at variance with those of others, could be construed as indicating that Cyprus may in fact have even fared somewhat better than other provinces in this respect. On the other hand, the Cypriots were provincials and as such, to the metropolitans' mind, inferior. There is in short no doubt that Constantinopolitan snobbery operated against the Cypriots; but at the very least it did so no more than it did against other Greek Orthodox provincials; and indeed there are hints that the very opposite might in fact have been the case.

At any rate, snobbery on the part of the Constantinopolitans did not stop the Cypriots from looking upon Constantinople (or Nicaea) for guidance, shelter and hope. In times of crisis, the Cypriot Church readily turned to Constantinople for guidance (we saw an example of this earlier), and the island's Church was probably the first actively to recognise Nicaea as the new centre of the Byzantine world. Barely one year after the establishment of the Patriarchate in Nicaea, Sabas, bishop of Paphos, travelled to Nicaea to obtain confirmation of the validity of the election of Ēsaias as archbishop of Cyprus. The next Cypriot archbishop, Neophytos (who is not to be confused with our Recluse), went to Nicaea to receive his investiture (*procheirēsis*) from emperor Theodore Laskarēs. The same archbishop later wrote to emperor John Batatzēs, assuring him that both he and his flock regarded John as their true lord. When the Latin persecution of the Cypriot Church began in earnest in 1221, the Cypriot archbishop and bishops fled to Nicaea. And while the Cypriot Church asked for spiritual guidance from Nicaea (at the same time sternly maintaining its Autocephalous status and rebuffing what it saw as attempts by patriarch Germanos II to ignore this

---

[82] *Ibid.*, 333.280–334.330, 335.1–24; and see also 343.36–40 for his comments on Isauria and the town of Sykē. See Galatariotou (forthcoming b). On the personal nature of Manassēs' comments on Palestine, see also Kazhdan and Wharton Epstein (1985: 153–4).

status), the feeling of the people was exemplified by the martyrdom of thirteen monks of the monastery of Kantariōtissa in 1231: they preferred torture and death rather than to betray their perception of themselves as Orthodox Byzantines.[83]

Placed within the wider context of the evidence above, Neophytos' own attitude of steadfastedly refusing to admit, accept or even acknowledge the factual reality of Latin rule in Cyprus becomes more comprehensible. It also leads us to the next area of our investigation, that of Church politics and religious ideology with reference to Neophytos and the society in which he lived.

---

[83] On the relations of the Church of Cyprus with the Nicaean empire see Angold (1972; 1975: 59–60); Chatzipsaltes (1951, 1964). On the succession of Cypriot archbishops see Laurent (1949a; esp. 35–6). On the investiture of Neophytos by Theodore Laskarēs see Lampros (1917: 43, no. 28, 11.5–7). On Archbishop Neophytos' letter to John Batatzēs see *ibid.* (42, nos. 28, 11.24–8, 43, 11.7–9). On archbishop Neophytos and other bishops seeking refuge in Nicaea in the 1240s see *ibid.* (39, no. 25, 11.12–17). For Germanos' letter to the Cypriots in 1223 urging them not to concede to Latin demands, and archbishop Neophytos' rebuff of this letter, see patriarch Germanos II, *Letters*; Lampros (1917: 41–3). On the martyred thirteen monks, see *Martyrion Kypriōn*. On an appeal of Germanos II to pope Gregory IX on behalf of the persecuted Cypriots in 1231/2, see Sathas (1872–94, II: 39–46). On the importance of the patriarch of Nicaea in fostering Nicaea as a national-Orthodox centre in lieu of Constantinople see Ahrweiler (1975b: 38–9).

10   Ecclesiastical politics

Neophytos' conception of Christianity took no vague, all-embracing form, but one strictly defined by the dogmas of the Orthodox Church and thereby sharply differentiated from any other dogmatic formulation of religious belief. The Recluse's position in religious matters was, above all, polemical and political.

Neophytos clearly states that the relationship between the Orthodox believers and the rest of humanity is one of the undoubted supremacy of the first: 'We, above every other religion and belief, are correct in our faith.'[1] In another passage he states equally categorically: 'Our faith is the pure and correct and all-holy one, and apart from it there is none other.'[2] For Neophytos it is therefore a crime to neglect salvation while having been born in the privileged position of being a member of the Orthodox Church.[3] It is for the Orthodox faith that Neophytos believes all the Saints struggled; and the Church of this faith is the 'one, holy, catholic and apostolic Church'.[4] The creed of this Church is defined not only by the Gospels but also, in more detail, by the Canons of the Councils of the Church: Neophytos makes extensive references to the Oecumenical Council of Nicaea I (of 325), to the Sixth Council and to that of Laodicaea.[5] The Orthodox Church is defined by the Recluse most frequently as 'the organisation [systēma] of the faithful'.[6]

Against this Church we find, in Neophytos' writings, the rest of the world. Kakodoxoi and kakopistoi (people 'of the wrong belief' and 'of the wrong faith') were accusations frequently hurled against the Latins by the

---

[1] Cod. Paris. Gr. 1317, fol. 12α.
[2] Ibid., fol. 82α.   [3] Ibid., fol. 114α.
[4] E.g., respectively, Panegyric 24, 406.8–10; Cod. Paris. Gr. 1189, fol. 28α (Panegyric 6).
[5] For references to the Gospels: Cod. Lesb. Leim. 2, Homily 5, 242.75–7; for references to the Oecumenical Councils: Cod. Paris. Gr. 1317, fols. 81β–81α; Cod. Paris. Gr. 1189, fol. 46α (Panegyric 8); Letter 5, 63.
[6] Cod. Coisl. Gr. 287, fol. 91α; Cod. Lesb. Leim. 2, fol. 285β (Homily 4), Homily 5, 242.76, 242.87, Homily 9, 266.40; Cod. Paris. Gr. 1189, fols. 38α (Panegyric 7), 39α, 56α (Panegyric 8).

Orthodox, to differentiate them from the 'infidels'.[7] As far as Neophytos was concerned, those who did not subscribe to the Orthodox creed fell into two categories: the complete infidels, those who are characterised by 'utter lack of faith'; and those who believed in Christ but lapsed into heresy, described as 'those who through thinking wrongly fell into a myriad heresies'.[8] The Recluse considered any further elaboration useless, and he was not exceptional for so thinking. Even though the Byzantines distinguished sharply between 'us' and 'them', they never developed a consistent view of who 'they' were. For instance, Theognōstos (the near-contemporary of Neophytos and compiler of a *Thesaurus*) makes a distinction different from the Recluse's. He divides the human race into three groups: the Christians (including the heretics, since even they believed in Christ); the Jews, Ishmailites and Hagarenes (who remained in darkness, the first because they did not accept the light of divine grace, the other two because they were led to darkness by Mohammud's teachings); and the Cumans (who are totally godless, live like senseless beasts and are 'most inhuman').[9] Reading different sources, Evelyne Patlagean concludes that the Byzantines' classification of humanity involved four categories: the savages (godless and close to being savage beasts); the non-Christian barbarians; the Christian barbarians; and the 'dualist' heretics (Paulicians and Bogomils).[10] Curiously enough, the inconsistency is of no great significance. Living in a polarised universe, with no particular shades of grey between Good and Evil, Neophytos was not bothered with fine distinctions between the heretic and the infidel; and for a long time he did not care to distinguish either between the heretic, the infidel and the Orthodox sinner.

The Orthodox faith is, for Neophytos, a prerequisite for salvation, but it is not a guarantee of it. Those who sin, even if they are Orthodox, will end up in hell together with 'those of the wrong faith' and the 'infidel nations'. No particular differentiation will be made between the 'faithful sinner', the 'abhorrent Gentile (*ethnikos*)' and the 'utterly infidel' on the Day of Judgment.[11] The only distinction made will be simply the one between the 'faithful' and the 'unfaithful'.[12] Thus, heretics, infidels and Orthodox sinners, all appear together in a list of those who will go to hell;[13] in the second *Panegyric* for the Holy Cross the Cross is described as the 'fall of those of evil faith' 'the fall of the Jews', 'the loss of the Hellenes'; and infidels, pagans,

---

[7] E.g., *Cod. Paris. Gr. 1189*, fol. 26α (*Panegyric 6*); *Cod. Paris. Gr. 1317*, fol. 9α; and see, e.g., Egglezakes (1979–80: 47).
[8] *Cod. Lesb. Leim. 2, Homily 3*, 151.392–6.   [9] Theognōstos, 53.25–54.29.
[10] Patlagean (1978). On dualist heresies in Byzantium see Obolensky (1948; 1971: 121–7 and *passim*); Runciman (1947).
[11] E.g., *Cod. Coisl. Gr. 287*, fols. 126β–128α, 129β.
[12] E.g., *Cod. Coisl. Gr. 287*, fols. 126β–128α, 129β.   [13] *Cod. Paris. Gr. 1317*, fol. 139α.

heretics and those 'of evil faith' are all again indiscriminately herded in a list of the doomed.[14] Writing his *Panegyric* against the Jews, Neophytos clarifies that it is not only addressed to the Jews but also to all like-minded people.[15]

The identification of all the non-Orthodox as the dreaded and threatening outsiders is so indiscriminate that at times characterisations usually employed for one such group of outsiders are interchanged with those of another without any sense of inconsistency on Neophytos' part. Thus, the Arabs (Hagarenes) who pursued the Saint in Neophytos' story of St Polychronios are described as people 'of the wrong faith', a term usually reserved for non-Orthodox Christians;[16] the Jews are called 'infidel';[17] those Christians who do not believe that the Holy Ghost is God are also on one occasion called 'infidel';[18] and the predominantly Christian raiders of Cyprus led by Renaud de Châtillon are called 'barbarians'.[19]

Neophytos' apparent confusion of terminology was one which he shared with the Byzantines in general. The term *ethnē* was more polite than that of *barbaroi*. Both were used to describe foreigners, the second term being usually (though not always, as we have seen) reserved for pagans, infidels and 'backward' races rather than for Christians. All these terms were contrasted to that of *Romaios*, the Byzantine citizen of whatever race. (Though, again, the earlier apparent disregard for the particular ethnic identity of the Byzantine citizen appears seriously undermined and confused by the twelfth century: we saw earlier a striking example of this, in Skylitzēs' reference to the *ethnos* of the Cypriots.)[20] Just as the Byzantines never clearly defined their categories of classification for the non-Byzantines, so too the distinction between the *barbaroi* and the *ethnē* was never clearly made. Dēmētrios Chōmatianos and George Akropolitēs called the Bulgarians 'barbarians', and the patriarch of Constantinople in Nicaea also used the same term for the Orthodox inhabitants of Ochrid.[21] Anna Komnēna called the Norman leader Robert Guiscard a 'barbarian' and

---

[14] *Cod. Paris. Gr. 1189*, fol. 52α, 53α (*Panegyric 8*). Neophytos never came to use the word *Hellēnes* in the nationistic way in which it had started being used by the Byzantines. See e.g., Angold (1975: 64–8); Nicol (1967: 317–18).

[15] *Cod. Paris. Gr. 1189*, fol. 207β (*Panegyric 27*).

[16] *Panegyric 10*, 178.12.

[17] *Cod. Lesb. Leim. 2, Homily 3*, 148.297.

[18] *Cod. Paris. Gr. 1317*, fols. 215α–β.

[19] *Cod. Athen. 522*, fols. 75α–β, 45.3. On this raid see earlier, pp. 51–2, 187–8.

[20] See earlier, p. 221.

[21] Respectively, Dēmētrios Chōmatianos, LXXXI, col. 361: LIX, col. 264; Akropolitēs, 34.8–12; *Letter of Patriarch Manuel*, 269.9–22.

heavily hinted that the Franks were also barbarians, while she described the Christian Paulicians as 'savages'.[22] The *Opusculum Contra Francos*, a pamphlet which appeared soon after the events of 1054 (between the papal legatee, cardinal Hubert, and the patriarch Michael Kēroullarios, and which events have been traditionally seen as marking the date of the Schism) attributes to the Latins characteristics usually defining the Byzantines' 'barbarian' – for instance, that the Latins ate wolves, or that they baptised with saliva.[23] The same appears in later Byzantine polemical writings, for example in Theodore Balsamōn's commentaries on the Canons, and in the letter of Dēmētrios Tornikēs to the bishop of Esztergorn.[24] In Neophytos' early writings, the crucial difference was one and one only: that between the 'faithful' (meaning the Orthodox Christians) and the 'unfaithful' (the sinning Orthodox, as well as the non-Orthodox Christians and people of other religions: pagans, Jews, Muslims), between those of 'pious mind' and those of 'unpious mind'.[25]

Neophytos is virulent against all the non-Orthodox, but he becomes particularly so whenever any such group is perceived by him as a force threatening the Orthodox Church, whether from the inside (through heresy) or from the outside (through political–military expansion and persecution of the Orthodox faith). In this respect, three groups are attacked by the Recluse: the Muslims, the heretics and the Latins (as the westerners were collectively called by the Byzantines); though, as we shall see, Neophytos came to treat the last two as indistinguishable.

Neophytos' polemic against the Muslims is carried out in the most abusive language possible. He frequently calls the Muslims 'dogs', likens them to other beasts, describes them as 'barbarians' and 'infidel nations'. Their leader and conqueror of Jerusalem, Saladin, is characterised as 'wretched'; while in his *Interpretation* of the *Apocalypse* Neophytos hurls abuse on

[22] *Alexiad*, I, 51.26–61.12 (esp. 54.17); III, 39.8–40.6; II, 206.24–220.14. See also Patlagean (1978), Nicol (1957 *passim*); Kazhdan and Wharton Epstein (1985: 166–70).
[23] See *Opusculam contra Francos* for the tract wrongly attributed to Phōtios and dating from at least the eleventh century (according to Runciman dated to soon after the 1054 events between Kēroullarios and cardinal Hubert). See Runciman (1955: 50–2); on the date and nature of the Schism see *ibid.* (esp. 159–70); on the theological aspects of the Schism see Meyendorff (1975: 91–102); see also generally Patlagean (1978).
[24] See respectively Ralles and Potles (1852–9, II: 463); George and Dēmētrios Tornikēs, 190–201; Tornikēs' letter is dated between 1184 and 1204: see Nicol (1967: 317–18; 1976: 23–4).
[25] *Cod. Lesb. Leim. 2, Homily 5*, 242.83–4; also *Cod. Paris. Gr. 1189*, fols. 36α (*Panegyric 7*), 56α (*Panegyric 8*); *Cod. Paris. Gr. 1189*, fol. 10β (*Panegyric 3*).

Mohammud: he is characterised as the apostle and pseudo-prophet of Satan; a servant of the devil and the Anti-Christ, whose teachings were repugnant also because of their morally degenerate emphasis on sexuality and generally on sensuality.[26] Neophytos' attitude represents but one expression of a continuing Byzantine polemical literary tradition against the Muslims. This appeared mainly in theological treatises and was revived in the twelfth century, producing works such as chapter 28 of the *Panoplia Dogmatikē* (*c.* 1100) of Euthymios Zigabēnos, or chapter 20 of the *Thesauros Orthodoxias* (*c.* 1200) of Nikētas Chōniatēs.[27] Byzantine polemic against the Muslims throughout the centuries reflects the changing Byzantine attitudes towards them: from considering Islam as a Christian heresy, up to the ninth century, to subsequently considering it as a different, false religion. Scholars have already observed that the Muslims' reverence for Jesus Christ contrasted sharply with the calumnies heaped upon Mohammud by the Christians. Neophytos' writings formed no exception to this general Christian attitude.[28]

Neophytos' attacks against the 'heretics' are more frequent. In his circular letter concerning the breaking of the fasting rules by the people of the district of Paphos Neophytos defines as heresy any transgression of the Canons of the Orthodox Church: the Orthodox who do not keep the rules of fasting are characterised by the Recluse as committing an act of heresy.[29] There is no end to the abusive terms used by Neophytos against the transgressors of Orthodoxy. Apart from 'heretics', they are also characterised as 'holding beliefs foreign to God', 'blasphemous', 'treacherous', 'blind', 'corrupt', 'of the wrong beliefs', 'malicious', 'possessed by

[26] 'Dogs': *Letter 4*, 10.10; *Panegyric 5*, 172.18, 173.7; *Panegyric 17*, 213.34, 214.4, 214.13; other beasts: *Cod. Athen. 522*, fol. 76β, 45.30–2. 'Barbarians': *Cod. Athen. 522*, fol. 77α, p. 46.9, 46.20; *Panegyric 15*, 53.172, 54.175; *Panegyric 5*, 173.24. 'Infidel nations': *Cod. Lesb. Leim. 2, Homily 1*, 226.288–9. Saladin abused: *Letter 4*, 10.5. Mohammud abused: *Panegyric 9*, 105.51–72, 109.19–24, 102.14–24.

[27] Zigabēnos, *Panoplia Dogmatikē*, cols. 1332–60; Chōniatēs, *Thesauros*, ch. 20, cols. 105–36; and see van Dieten (1970: 55.12–15).

[28] Compare, though, the respect with which the Arabs are treated in the Grottaferrata *Digenēs Akritēs*, a work marked by absence of dogma, ecclesiastical or political. See Galatariotou (1987b: 37–40, 44–51, note 77); Mavrogordato, *Digenēs Akritēs*, lxvi, lxviii; also, Beaton (1980: 79–80); Herzfeld (1980: esp. 63, 79). On the changing Byzantine attitudes towards Islam through the centuries see Waardenburg (1978); Vryonis (1971b); for the twelfth century, Kazhdan and Wharton Epstein (1985: 186–7); on western attitudes towards Islam see Daniel (1960); Southern (1962); for the role of religion in Arab–Byzantine relations see generally Canard (1973); for a survey of Byzantine views of Islam see Meyendorff (1964); for a survey of Byzantine polemical literature see Khoury (1969, 1972). On the presence of Muslims in Cyprus in Neophytos' times see earlier, ch. 3, pp. 62–3.

[29] *Letter 5*, 63–4.

demons', 'of the wrong faith', 'unholy', 'foreigners'.[30] Their dogmas are 'abominable to God', 'shameful', 'perverse'; their teachings are 'impure', 'frivolous', 'blasphemous'; their very names 'stink'; they are the wolves threatening Christ's sheep, the parasites on the sower's land, the darkness of impiety, the waves threatening the ship of Orthodoxy.[31]

It must be remembered that by the time of the Fourth Crusade the Schism between the Churches had been established. Indeed, a crucial factor in the consolidation of the rift was the growth of dislike and mistrust between the Byzantines and the Crusader nations. The encounter between Byzantium and the west during the Second and the Third Crusade caused such negative feelings to become even more entrenched.[32] By the time of the Fourth Crusade there can be no doubt that the Byzantines had come to regard the Latins as heretics.[33] We have already seen how seriously the Byzantines of the eleventh and twelfth centuries were preoccupied and worried with heresy in any shape or form.[34] The inclusion of *anathemas* against Constantine of Corfu and John Eirenikos (condemned in 1169 and 1170) in the twelfth century *Synodikon* of Cyprus shows that the Constantinopolitan climate against deviations from Orthodox dogma had also enveloped the island.[35] Concerning the Latins' classification as heretics, it must also be remembered that there was a difference between the definition of heresy in east and west. The westerners knew their heretics clearly, because the pope defined them – and by 1054 he had indeed launched the first 'official' accusation of heresy against the Orthodox.[36] The Byzantine definition of heresy, however, required the ruling of an Oecumenical Council,

---

[30] *Hairetikoi: Cod. Lesb. Leim. 2*, fols. 264β–265α (*Homily 2*); *Cod. Paris. Gr. 1317*, fols. 22β, 141α; *Cod. Coisl. Gr. 287*, fol. 17β; also *Panegyric 16*, 208.15; *Cod. Paris. Gr. 1189*, fol. 53α (*Panegyric 8*). *Allotriophrones: Cod. Paris. Gr. 1317*, fol. 215α. *Blasphēmoi: Cod. Paris. Gr. 1317*, fols. 215α–β; also *Cod. Lesb. Leim. 2*, *Homily 3*, 151.392–6. *Doleroi: Cod. Paris. Gr. 1317*, fols. 215α–β. *Typhloi: Cod. Lesb. Leim. 2*, *Homily 3*, 152.431–8. *Dieptharmenoi: ibid.*, 152.438. *Kakodoxoi: Cod. Paris. Gr. 1189*, fol. 26α, p. 46.4; *Cod. Paris. Gr. 1189*, fol. 53α (*Panegyric 8*); *Cod. Paris. Gr. 1317*, fol. 183β. *Kakophrones: Cod. Paris. Gr. 1189*, fol. 27α (*Panegyric 6*); *Panegyric 16*, 208.15. *Kakodaimones: Panegyric 25*, 9.10. *Kakopistoi: Cod. Paris. Gr. 1189*, fol. 27α (*Panegyric 6*). *Asebois: Cod. Paris. Gr. 1189*, fols. 28α–β (*Panegyric 6*), 53α (*Panegyric 8*). *Othneioi:* the characterisation of *othneios* is one commonly used by the Byzantines to describe the Latins. See, e.g., Theognōstos, 54.35.

[31] *Theostyga: Cod. Paris. Gr. 1189*, fol. 26β (*Panegyric 6*). *Aischra: Cod. Paris. Gr. 1189*, fol. 9α (*Panegyric 6*). *Diephtharmena: Panegyric 16*, 208.16. *Mysara, lērodē, blasphēma, ozōde: Cod. Paris. Gr. 1317*, folss. 81β–81α.

[32] Runciman (1955: 145–58).

[33] Nicol (1964: 162, 167, 171–2). On Byzantine anti-Latin polemics in this period see generally Kazhdan and Wharton Epstein (1985: 187–91).

[34] See earlier, ch. 6, p. 165.

[35] Cappuyns (1935: 492–3, 502–3).

[36] The first open accusation on the part of the Latins that the Orthodox were heretical appeared in the Bull of 16 July 1054, which accused the Orthodox of prozymite heresy. See Runciman (1955: 47–8).

and the Latins were never actually condemned as heretical by any such Council. Therefore, even though it is clear that the Latins were, in the Byzantines' mind, heretics, there was uncertainty as to how they should be treated. For instance, Theodore Balsamōn thought that they should be refused communion in Orthodox churches, but Dēmētrios Chōmatianos disagreed because of the absence of a Synodical condemnation of the Latins as heretics. Perhaps the general Byzantine – intellectual – feeling was best expressed by the *chartophylax* John Bekkos, who said that the Latins were in a position of being, but not being called, heretics.[37]

Anti-Latinism, already present in the eleventh century, reached its peak in Constantinople in the twelfth century. Already by the reign of Manuel I Komnēnos, patriarch Michael III of Anchialos preferred submission to the Muslim than to the Latin: 'Let the Muslim be my material master', he wrote to Manuel shortly after 1169, 'rather than the Latin my spiritual master. If I am subject to the former, at least he will not force me to share his faith. But if I have to be united in religion to the latter, under his control, I may have to separate myself from God.'[38] Even before 1204, anti-Latinism in Constantinople grew fast and strong, exploding in such acts as the massacre of the Latin residents of Constantinople in 1182. In that year it was partly the same wave of anti-Latin feeling that brought Andronikos I Komnēnos to the throne.

Subsequently, the events of the Fourth Crusade made the gap between the Byzantines and the Latins unbridgeable. The well-known words of Nikētas Chōniatēs at the close of the twelfth century expressed a feeling which was shared by more than the circle of intelligentsia, Court and high Church in Constantinople; it was a feeling certainly shared by Neophytos: 'Between us and the Latins is set the widest gulf. We are poles apart. We have not a single thought in common.' Thus wrote Chōniatēs, expressing a marked shift in attitudes from Anna Komnēna's time, when she had seen the Latins as simply gross and uncultured and even, maybe, heretical.[39] The Norman sack of Thessalonikē in 1185 and the fall and sack of Constantinople in 1204 proved the Byzantines' worst fears right. Byzantine attitudes towards foreigners were hardened in a way amounting, according to one scholar, to 'nationalism' and 'xenophobia' or, according to another, to

---

[37] For Dēmētrios Chōmatianos on the Latins see Ralles and Potles (1952–9, V: 434–6); for John Bekkos see Pachymerēs (1835, I: 376.6–17). See also Nicol (1964: 171–2).

[38] This was an attitude which persisted until the very end of Byzantium. On the eve of the Turkish conquest of Constantinople in 1453 the Grand *doux* Luke Notaras announced that he preferred the sultan's turban to the cardinal's hat. See Runciman (1955: 121–2). Concerning the *Dialogue* of Michael III referred to in the text, we must note that its date appears to be uncertain, at least two eminent scholars suggesting that it is a thirteenth-century work: Laurent and Darrouzès (1976: 49–52).

[39] Chōniatēs, *Historia*, 301.27–9. For references in the *Alexiad*, see note 22, above.

'aggressive nationalism'. This caused a further, stricter drawing of the cultural boundaries between 'us' and 'them'; expressed, for instance, in such developments as the post-1204 spread of the term *Hellēnes*, to distinguish the Byzantines from the rest of the world and to give them a national identity and cohesion.[40]

Interestingly, for Neophytos the heretic as well as the complete infidel stands in the position of one who has lost his mind. Those who do not believe that the Holy Ghost is God are 'out of their senses' and 'devoid of understanding'.[41] The heretics are characterised by 'want of understanding';[42] the 'heresiarch' Noētos (meaning 'one perceptible to the mind') is instead called by Neophytos the very opposite ('Anoētos');[43] and the pagan Alexander the Recluse calls 'deranged'.[44] By contrast, the Orthodox are 'sensible' and 'godly-minded'.[45] Further, the non-Orthodox are perceived by Neophytos as linked with the devil, while the Orthodox are close to God. Mohammud is the 'apostle and prophet of the devil' and the 'servant of the devil'; while the heretics preach 'devilish' dogmas.[46] It is Satan who, envious of the goodness of Orthodoxy, spread the seeds of heresy, so that many would be gained by him, writes Neophytos repeatedly, reiterating a belief widely held by the Byzantines.[47] In two other passages Neophytos lists some of the heretics, classifying them as non-Christians.[48] He reminds his reader or listener that the Church fought heretics by its Councils, and he often presents Saints, Church Fathers, preachers and emperors as having fought for the Orthodox faith and against heresy.[49]

[40] On the growth of anti-Latin feeling in eleventh- and twelfth-century Byzantium see Brand (1968: *passim*); also, Nicol (1967: 327–30; 1962); Bryer (1973: 87–8); Runciman (1955: 116, 139). On the rise of nationalism and the use of the term *Hellēnes* see Nicol (1967: 318–19); Angold (1975: 64–8 (66 for 'xenophobia')); Bryer (1973: 88); Browning (1966: 16 and note 56).

[41] *Alogoi: Cod. Lesb. Leim. 2, Homily 3*, 152.431–4. *Asynetoi: Cod. Paris. Gr. 1317*, fols. 215α–β.

[42] *Anoia: Cod. Paris. Gr. 1189*, fol. 27α *(Panegyric 6)*.

[43] *Cod. Lesb. Leim. 2, Homily 3*, 151.409–152.2.

[44] *Paraphrōn: Panegyric 2*, 137.12–14.

[45] *Echephrones: Cod. Paris. Gr. 1189*, fol. 44β *(Panegyric 8)*. *Theophrones: Panegyric 2*, 137.13.

[46] Respectively, *Panegyric 9*, 102.14–16, p. 109.19–20; *Cod. Lesb. Leim. 2, Homily 3*, 152.432.

[47] *Cod. Paris. Gr. 1317*, fols. 81α, 87α (p. 58.9–15); *Cod. Lesb. Leim. 2*, fol. 292α *(Homily 4)*. The same link is made by Neophytos also in respect of the Muslims: *Cod. Lesb. Leim. 2, Homily 1*, 226.287–9. See also, e.g., Theognōstos, 54.18–19. Theognōstos also relates the didactic story of a monk on Sina who was pushed by the devil into embracing Judaism: *ibid.*, 51–2, para. 9; and see also 71.284–5.

[48] *Cod. Paris. Gr. 1317*, fols. 81α, 87α (p. 58.9–15); *Cod. Lesb. Leim. 2*, fol. 292α *(Homily 4)*.

[49] References to Church Councils: *Cod. Paris. Gr. 1317*, fols. 81β–81α; *Cod. Paris. Gr. 1189*, fol. 46α *(Panegyric 8)*. References to Saints: *Cod. Lesb. Leim. 2*, fols. 264β–265α *(Homily 2)*; *Cod. Paris. Gr. 1317*, fols. 22β, 141α; *Cod. Coisl. Gr. 287*, fol. 17β; also *Panegyric 16*, 208.15; *Cod. Paris. Gr. 1189*, fol. 53α *(Panegyric 8)*. References to Church Fathers: *Cod. Paris. Gr. 1317*, fol. 80α; to preachers: *Cod. Coisl. Gr. 287*, fol. 17β; also *Cod. Paris. Gr. 1317*, fol. 183β; to emperors: *Cod. Paris. Gr. 1317*, fols. 81β–81α.

There is no doubt that Neophytos' polemic against the non-Orthodox after 1191 was not an expression of a desire to educate his audience in Church history, but a way of fighting what he saw as a contemporary threat to the Byzantine Church and state. More specifically, most of Neophytos' polemic was aimed at the 'heretics' who took Constantinople in 1204, and those who took Cyprus in 1191. We know from his writings that in Neophytos' mind heretics had caused earthquakes during the reign of Theodosios, just as the homosexuals had done during the reign of Leo;[50] but in 1191 heretics had divorced Cyprus from Byzantium, and in 1204 they conquered and sacked the Queen of Cities.

Neophytos had indeed many reasons for being violently hostile to the Latins, not just because of the general Byzantine hostility against the Latin Church and states, but further because of specific developments in ecclesiastical politics in Cyprus. It is true that the years immediately following the Latin occupation of Cyprus brought no change to the status of the Cypriot Orthodox Church or of the Orthodox monasteries. On the contrary (as we saw earlier) the first Latin king of Cyprus, Guy de Lusignan, even tried to befriend the Cypriots during his brief reign (1192–4). They, however, already suspected that their immunity would be short lived. Their suspicions, fired by the examples of the treatment of other Orthodox in Latin-occupied territories, made the Cypriots deeply resentful and defensive towards the Latin Church. In the words of the historian of the Church of Cyprus, J. Hackett, 'they were resolved, so long as they were able, to defend their Church and ancestral faith from the attacks of enemies, whom bitter experience soon taught them to regard with the greatest hatred and aversion'.[51]

The first solid indications of the impending persecution of the Cypriot Church came during the reign of Aimery de Lusignan (1194–1205). He applied to pope Celestine III for permission to establish Latin dioceses in Cyprus, in order to give roots to the Latin Church in Cyprus, but also – and more importantly for us – in order to convert the 'schismatic Greeks' to Catholicism. Aimery's aims are clearly stated as such in Celestine's Bull of 20 February 1196. By this, the pope appointed two commissioners (the archdeacons of Laodicea and Lydda) with full power to carry out the king's wishes. As a result, a Latin metropolitan was established in Lefkōsia with suffragans in Nemesos, Paphos and Ammochōstos. The endowment of

---

[50] *Panegyric 16*, 208.10–22, 209.14–210.2. On Neophytos' conception of sexuality see Galatariotou (1989).

[51] Hackett (1901: 74). The Latin ecclesiastical policy concerning the Orthodox in Cyprus over the following few centuries was not uniformly aggressive: it vacillated between treating the Greek Orthodox as heretics to be subjected to persecution, and considering them at other times as schismatics to be treated with moderation and tolerance. See Efthimiou (1987: 31ff., 40ff.).

these sees involved the diminution of the property of the Cypriot Orthodox Church.[52] The native Church reacted with charges against the Latin Church. They accused them of depriving them of the patrimony of their Church and with harbouring designs against their flock. The Latin Church answered with counter-accusations of simony and encouragement of disloyal sentiments amongst the Orthodox. Tension had reached such high levels by 1198 that, before leaving Cyprus for the Holy Land to assume the crown of Jerusalem, king Aimery de Lusignan summoned the heads of both Churches and ordered them, under the severest of penalties, to live in peace with each other during his absence. He also declared that all ecclesiastical property in Cyprus was under his exclusive prerogative power, which he would exercise in any way that appeared to him to be the most satisfactory for both parties.[53]

Neophytos most probably did not live long enough to know of the rules passed by a meeting of the Latin clergy on 20 October 1220, aimed at curbing the growing stream of Cypriots who became priests in the Orthodox Church or joined monasteries probably in an effort to avoid the feudal burdens imposed on them.[54] Nor did Neophytos witness the expulsions of the Cypriot bishops, including two successive archbishops (Ēsaias and Neophytos) between 1218 and 1222, because of their refusal to make a formal submission to the pope.[55] He did not know, either, of the martyrdom of thirteen monks from the Kantariōtissa monastery, who were tortured to death in 1231 because of their refusal to accept the Latin version in the dispute concerning the *azyma*.[56] Whether the Latins during Neophytos' lifetime were prepared to go to the lengths they did go to in 1231 is doubtful, but the events of 1231 must, of course, have been only a culmination of an attitude and feeling already present during Neophytos' lifetime. Certainly, Neophytos had lived long enough to have sufficient evidence in his hands to fear the worst from the Latins, to resent and to hate them. In the years between 1191 and the end of his life, he used his writings to carry out a propaganda war against the Latins, which was as camouflaged as it was effective.

An examination of Neophytos' pre-1191 references to the westerners

[52] The whole proceedings have been characterised as 'one of the most unwarrantable examples of ecclesiastical intrusion on record' and 'a most glaring breach of canon law': Hackett (1901: 74–6). This may be a rhetorical way of putting it (Cyprus formed no exception for the Latins) but it certainly seems to reflect the way the Orthodox Cypriot Church saw it.
[53] Hackett (1901: 74–6).
[54] *Ibid.*, 81–3.
[55] Faced with this problem the Cypriots sought the advice of Patriarch Germanos II in Nicaea, as to the stance to be adopted to the Latin demands. See the bibliography in ch. 9, note 83 above. On the boundaries of the Latin dioceses in Cyprus see Edbury (1975).
[56] See generally Hackett (1901: 74–7, 81–95). Also Hill (1972, II: 41, 45–7); and above, note 83, in ch. 9, for bibliography.

helps clarify the later shift in his attitude towards them. The anti-Latin feeling which existed in Constantinople well before 1204 was undoubtedly also present beyond the walls of the Queen City. It seems that – especially, perhaps, in provinces in which westerners had settled – at least occasional Orthodox polemics against the Latins were *de rigueur*. Thus Neophytos too felt that he had to concern himself with the westerners. He did so, referring specifically to 'the Latins' (as opposed to unnamed 'heretics') twice before 1191. On one such occasion he pointed out that the Latins committed the 'error' of using unleavened bread (*azyma*) in the Eucharist – a Latin ritual practice which Michael Kēroullarios had listed amongst the Latin 'heretical' practices. Echoing the usual Byzantine view on the matter, the Recluse wrote that this Latin practice was related to the Old Testament and the Exodus rather than to the New Testament and Christ's Passion. The relevant passage is short, and is found in a work in which Neophytos is dealing with a number of religious issues, the remaining of which are unrelated to the Latins.[57] In another pre-1191 work Neophytos explores the beginnings of the Schism. Helped by 'one of the chronographers' books' (probably Theophanēs), he locates the beginning of the Schism at the coronation of Charlemagne by pope Leo III.[58] Subsequently, he lists ten Latin 'errors'. The *azyma* are at the top of his list; followed by the accusations that the Latin priests are beardless, and live licentious lives; that the Latins cross themselves using five fingers instead of 'two fingers and the thumb'; that they bend one knee instead of both when praying; that they eat meat on the Sunday of the Tyrophagos and do not on Saturdays; that they venerate the earth, but most of them refuse to venerate icons; that they are wrong in their view concerning the Holy Ghost.[59] It is interesting to note

[57] *Panegyric* in *Cod. Paris. Gr. 395*, 344.17–345.35. See Egglezakes (1979–80: 51–2); and Appendix, below, pp. 266–7.

[58] *Cod. 13, Andros, Panegyric 3*, 355.95–126. This part of Neophytos' work belongs to the *opuscula de origine schismatis*, which appeared in great numbers after Phōtios' and Kēroullarios' own contributions to the *genre*. See Egglezakes (1979–80: 53–6, esp. 54, 55); and Appendix, below, pp. 267–8.

[59] *Cod. 13, Andros, Panegyric 3*, 355.127–356.144, completed by Egglezakes (1979–80: 54). For an analysis of Neophytos' ten accusations against the Latins see Egglezakes (1979–80: 54–6, 68–72). As Egglezakes points out, the list of accusations which Neophytos had consulted was probably an eleventh-century one: such lists tended to contain about twenty-eight accusations, while the lists produced in the twelfth century included up to thirty-two, and in the thirteenth century up to 104 accusations: see Darrouzès (1963). Neophytos' argument against the use of unleavened bread was the standard – since the eleventh century – argument that the *azyma* imply that the body of the Logos is soulless and mindless. On the *azyma* dispute see Runciman (1955: 47–8, 108–10, 114–23); Meyendorff (1975: 95–6). The dispute concerning the beardless western priests was an old one, being already under way in the ninth century. Concerning the accusation that the Latin clergy led immoral lives, it is interesting to note that the Papal Legate confirmed the point in 1223, when he issued a series of rulings aimed at curbing the Latin clergy's licentious way of life on the island: Hackett (1901: 510). Neophytos appears to be the first witness of the Greeks' use of three fingers (instead of two fingers, which was the custom since the eighth or ninth century) for making the sign of the cross. His evidence thus precedes that of the *Dialogue between Panayiotēs and*

that Neophytos had before him a list of twenty-seven accusations against the Latins when he wrote this piece, for which he selected all, or most, of the ten accusations referred to above. Both this and the passage referred to earlier are characterised by a certain detachment, a lack of passion. There is a definite sense of difference and superiority on the part of the Orthodox; but not one of urgent and bitter hostility towards the Latins. The fact itself that Neophytos lacked the motivation necessary to quote all the accusations he knew of, is indicative of his mood at this stage. Equally telling is the fact that he uses none of the abusive epithets which he came to employ after 1191 in respect of the Latins; and that at this point (before 1191) he perceived the Latins as foolish rather than as actually and immediately threatening.[60] It was only after 1191 that the Recluse's mood changed, as dramatically as did the situation in Cyprus, and – in 1204 – in Constantinople.

Perhaps the most interesting aspect of Neophytos' post-1191 polemic against the Latins is that it never became open and explicit. First, because he was afraid, and with good reason: after all, the monk in Cyprus who had become so openly anti-English as to join the rebellion against them in 1191, had been hanged.[61] Second, because Neophytos' own monastery, just like all other Cypriot monasteries during his lifetime, was actually left intact by the Latin rulers: perhaps it was therefore wiser not to be too openly hateful towards them. Third, because the Recluse did not need to be explicit in his references against the current Latin regime in Cyprus: he could simply reutilise long-established phraseology, well-known *topoi* and clichés referring generally to 'heretics'; for he knew that after 1191 such references could not fail to be instantly reinterpreted by his audience within the context of the current situation on the island. Thus, on a superficial level there was nothing startlingly different in Neophytos' religious polemic after 1191: short of a greater frequency of such references and a sharper focus on the non-Orthodox, the manifest content of his preachings remained the same, and formed part of the general cultural Byzantine heritage. The twist in the tale concerned not the manifest but the *latent* content of Neophytos' religious polemic – a latent and very powerful politico-religious content

---

an *Azymite*, which, written between 1274 and 1282, is usually considered to contain the earliest reference to the Greeks' use of three fingers for crossing themselves: see Argyriou (1972: 21–3). The accusation that the Latins bend only one instead of two knees when praying may have been Neophytos' own contribution to the list of accusations – and is, actually, factually incorrect. The reference to the Latins being wrong about the Holy Ghost is our only direct piece of evidence that Neophytos knew of a dispute between the east and the west concerning the *filioque*. See note 79, below. On all these points see Egglezakes (1979–80: 54–6, 68–72).

[60] For example, when he says that instead of turning to the Orthodox Church for guidance, the Latins 'rather rebuke us for not using *azyma* in our liturgy': *Cod. 13, Andros, Panegyric 3,* 356.147–52; and see also Appendix, below, pp. 267–8.

[61] Benedict of Peterborough, II, 172–3, translated in Cobham (1908: 9); Roger of Hoveden, III, 116. See Hackett (1901: 64–5); Hill (1972, II: 34).

with which the changed circumstances automatically endowed his otherwise standard phraseology. The Recluse thus used established forms of expression to devise a strategy of attacking the Latins in ways which were clear enough for his Orthodox audience to know exactly what he was talking about, but also covert enough for Neophytos to protect himself against the Latins, who would not have found his words immediately and openly hostile to them.

The evidence for this comes from internal comparative examination of the Recluse's writings which contain passages of a polemical religious nature. Out of some forty-six such passages, twenty definitely post-date 1191; eighteen are of uncertain date, of which, however, ten contain elements pointing to a post-1191 date; and only two appear to, and six definitely, date from before 1191. It is true that most of Neophytos' surviving dated or datable writings are of post-1911, but it would be wrong to assume that his increasing preoccupation with polemical writing against the non-Orthodox simply went hand in hand with his increasing preoccupation with writing in general. Rather, we should consider the reason for this increase in Neophytos' activity as a writer. This appears to have been caused by a combination of factors: certainly, the more his conviction in his own holiness increased, the more he was motivated to put into writing what he believed to be God's words; and we must also not disregard the simple fact that in 1197 Neophytos created better working conditions for himself as a writer: he must, indeed, have found, as he had hoped he would, more time and quiet once he removed himself to his upper cell. But Neophytos' activity as a writer intensified after 1191 also because he had more to write about – in the sense that he now had more to fight against. We have already discussed his involvement with social and more strictly secular political matters. The Latin occupation of Cyprus also caused Neophytos to become passionately involved in Church politics.

Let us compare two writings of Neophytos, one of a (conclusive) pre-1191 and one of a post-1911 date, with specific reference to their exclamations on religious matters: Neophytos' *Interpretation of the Commandment*, of 1176, and his *Catecheseis* of about 1214.

In his 1176 writings Neophytos was already referring to the Orthodox struggle against the heretics; but he did so only fleetingly, and only in order to illustrate passages from the writings of Church Fathers. For example, in one passage Neophytos defines the Church as 'the organisation of the faithful which demons, kings of the wrong faith and a multitude of demons failed to destroy'.[62] The vagueness of the phrase is worth taking note of: demons, kings of the wrong faith and heretics are all mixed together. Also noticeable is Neophytos' reference to past attacks against the Orthodox

[62] *Cod. Coisl. Gr. 287*, fols. 91α–β.

Church (as opposed to present ones). The same lack of sharpness is found later in the same work, in reference to righteous people living in poverty and misery, while unjust ones are seen to thrive and prosper. Neophytos states that this is not very surprising, when one considers that many of the nations of the wrong faith and the infidel ones – let alone single persons – also live in wealth and health and glory. The Recluse explains that the whole world is divided between good and evil people, and that sinning Orthodox Christians will meet the same fate as the infidels.[63] He then proceeds to castigate the rich in Cyprus for their oppression of the poor.[64] Neophytos' commentary thus moves on the general lines of siding with the righteous and speaking up for the poor while castigating the unjust, the rich and all sinners – Orthodox and non-Orthodox.

By contrast to Neophytos' 1176 writings, his *Catecheseis* contain comments on ecclesiastical matters which are focused with sharpness and precision around what now appears to be a very clear distinction between the Orthodox and the non-Orthodox. Now, at around 1214, Neophytos stresses the uniqueness of the Orthodox faith, the only correct one, according to him, over and above every other.[65] Neophytos' list of 'heretics', sharply differentiating them from the 'Christians', ends in invitingly open terms: 'Arians and Nestorians and Bedonians and Jacobites and this one and that one'. Anyone, especially including a Latin, can fit in the last 'group'. The Orthodox faith as defined by the Canons of the Oecumenical Synods is upheld as the one and only true faith, and any transgression from it is rejected as heresy in a torrent of abuse.[66] The link between heretics and the devil is repeatedly made.[67] The fight of the Orthodox Church against heresy is also repeatedly alluded to;[68] while, significantly, a call is made to the Orthodox to gather together and show solidarity.[69] Amongst those who fought 'the dogmas of those of the wrong faith' Neophytos mentions a number of Orthodox bishops, including Sts John Chrysostom, Basil, Gregory and Athanasios.[70] It is illuminating to juxtapose this list with another one, given earlier in the same work, where suffering as a Christian is sharply differentiated from suffering as a murderer, a thief, a fornicator, an adulterer, some other evil-doer, or 'as a foreign bishop'.[71] This is a clear and telling – if very brief – reference to the recently installed Latin bishops in Cyprus and to Neophytos' level of esteem for them.

---

[63] *Cod. Coisl. Gr. 287*, fols. 126α–128α, 126β–127β, 129β.
[64] *Cod. Coisl. Gr. 287*, fols. 130α–132α.
[65] *Cod. Paris. Gr. 1317*, fols. 12α, 82α.   [66] *Cod. Paris. Gr. 1317*, fols. 81α–β.
[67] E.g., *Cod. Paris. Gr. 1317*, fols. 81α, 87α (p. 58.9–15). See also *Cod. Lesb. Leim. 2*, fol. 292α (*Homily 4*), whose date is uncertain.
[68] *Cod. Paris. Gr. 1317*, fols. 80α, 81α–82β, 22β, 141α; also *Cod. Lesb. Leim. 2*, fols. 264β–265α (*Homily 2*), which is probably – but not certainly – of post-1191 date. (For pre-1191 references see *Cod. Coisl. Gr. 287*, fol. 17β; *Panegyric 16*, 208.15.)
[69] *Cod. Paris. Gr. 1317*, fol. 87β, p. 58.1–18.
[70] *Cod. Paris. Gr. 1317*, fol. 183β.   [71] *Cod. Paris. Gr. 1317*, fol. 106β.

There can be no doubt, too, that Neophytos' circular letter to the people of Paphos (written some time between 1191 and 1209) must be seen within the context of his anti-Latin polemical writings.[72] Neophytos was partly motivated by the absence of a bishop in Paphos, but above all he was concerned with the building up of the defences within the Orthodox camp and against the Latins. Faced with the Latins' stated intention to bring the 'schismatic Greeks' back to the fold, Neophytos draws the lines between the Orthodox and the rest with fervour: Canons of Church Synods are invoked, the Orthodox faith is upheld, any transgression of its rules is characterised as heresy.

It is important to remember that this circular letter had an intended audience of all the inhabitants – lay and ecclesiastical – of the district. But in other writings (which, as we saw earlier, were also expected to be heard by the general public and not just by the Enkleistra's monks) Neophytos also communicated to the people information which can only be interpreted as part of a polemic against the Latins. In his post-1191 writings we find a concentration of comments against heretics and for the Orthodox which is largely absent from his pre-1191 works. In his very late *Homily* for the Presentation of the Virgin Neophytos tells his public that even virginity is coloured by creed: 'virgins of the heretics' will be refused entry in the Kingdom of Heaven.[73] In his *Panegyric* for the Consecration of a Church he repeatedly refers to the 'one, holy, catholic and apostolic Church' which 'the gates of the devil and the tyranny of those of evil faith' shall not defeat.[74] Since, Neophytos argues, the Orthodox Church is founded on 'pure faith' a flood of dangers will not destroy it. In the same *Panegyric* Neophytos angrily addresses – without actually naming – persons who were obviously not expected to be present in his audience. The hints which he gives as to the identity of these people are many: he calls them 'people of the wrong belief' and 'of the wrong faith', and exclaims at their 'folly and evil thinking'. He is amazed that they are not ashamed 'to believe in stone idols'. He follows his angry rebuke of such persons by a statement to the effect that Christ clears away the 'tares of heresies'.[75] He calls the Orthodox Church the only 'pious' one, which dissolves the darkness of impiety. Finally, stating again that the only true Church is the Orthodox one, he sternly warns those who became obstacles to the union of all peoples under this one Church of the fate of damnation that awaits them.[76]

---

[72] *Letter 5*, 63–4; for a discussion of which see earlier, pp. 170, 184.

[73] *Cod. Lesb. Leim. 2, Homily 1*, 228.323–7.

[74] *Cod. Paris. Gr. 1189*, fol. 26α (p. 46.1–4), 28α–β (*Panegyric 6*).

[75] 'For the sake of whom, o people of the wrong belief and of the wrong faith, are you ashamed to confess that Christ is God? ... And you, who are stonier than the worst stone, are not ashamed to believe in stone idols; and yet you are ashamed to believe in the one whom God called His stone, making up false excuses – that He called him a stone and not a son?!' (*Cod. Paris. Gr. 1189*, fol. 27α (*Panagyric 6*)).

[76] *Cod. Paris. Gr. 1189*, fols. 28α–β (*Panegyric 6*).

Our evidence leads us to conclude that Neophytos is again referring to the Latins in this passage. We have seen how the accusations of being 'of the wrong faith' and of 'the wrong belief' were commonly hurled against the Latins by the Byzantines, including Neophytos. His insistence on the uniqueness of the Orthodox Church and its difference from other, non-Orthodox creeds, follows a pattern in his writings comparable to his identification of the Latins as heretics. Those who became obstacles to the union of all peoples under the One Church can (within the context of non-Orthodox Christianity which Neophytos is clearly referring to) be none other than the non-Orthodox Latins. Finally, the reference to these people as worshipping stone idols can only be an expression of cultural difference and disapproval on the part of the provincial Orthodox Cypriots, faced with a manifestation of Christian worship which was different from theirs: namely, the Latins' adornment of their churches with statues rather than icons. Neophytos, immobile in his cell, never saw these, but some of his visitors must have done. The whole passage is revealing in its manifestation of the way in which Neophytos carried out his post-1191 polemic against the Latins. Just as he does in his references to his own sanctity (where he also treads on dangerous ground) Neophytos protects himself by using hint and evocation rather than direct statement.

In two other *Panegyrics* of late date Neophytos again differentiates between 'the faithful' and the rest, stating that even virginity will not save a heretic on the Day of Judgment.[77] In his *Panegyric* for the Holy Cross the Recluse talks of the salvation of the faithful and the eternal loss of the unfaithful, and of the might of 'Christ-loving *basileis*'.[78] Neophytos' second *Panegyric* for the Holy Cross should be dated to the post-1191 period on the basis of its internal evidence concerning Church politics. It is a *Panegyric* which revolves almost entirely around one theme, that of the Trinity. Neophytos was no highly educated theologian, but the dispute between the Orthodox and the Catholics over the *filioque* (the westerners' addition of 'and from the Son' to the Creed) was certainly known to him, as we saw earlier.[79] Throughout, Neophytos stresses the Orthodox conception of one consubstantial (*omoousia*) Trinity, whereby Father, Son and the Holy Ghost are of one and the same importance in the Trinity, God not being greater than Christ.[80] This is what the faithful believe in, Neophytos says, invoking

[77] See, e.g., *Cod. Lesb. Leim. 2, Homily 1*, 228.322–7.
[78] *Cod. Paris. Gr. 1189*, fols. 36α, 38α (*Panegyric 7*).
[79] When Neophytos included the Latins' 'great error' concerning the Holy Ghost in a list of accusations against them: *Cod. 13, Andros, Panegyric 3*, 355.17–356.141; completed by Egglezakes (1979–80: 54); and see note 59 above. On the dispute between the Church of Rome and the Eastern Orthodox Churches concerning the *filioque* see Runciman (1955: 29–34ff., 108–10, 114–23, and *passim*); Meyendorff (1975: 91–4); Kazhdan and Wharton Epstein (1985: 187–91); Herrin (1987: 439–44, 462–4).
[80] *Cod. Paris. Gr. 1189*, fols. 39α, 43β, 44α, 44β, 45β, 46α (*Panegyric 8*).

the Creed formulated at the Nicaean Synod.[81] Some people, Neophytos says, did not know and did not respect the Son and the Holy Ghost, and they ended up ignoring the Father, too, and paying their respects to the demons instead.[82]

The gist of Neophytos' argument bears a striking resemblance to passages found in other Byzantine works which are openly and clearly concerned with the Orthodox position in the *filioque* dispute.[83] Most of Neophytos' comments could also be interpreted as referring to the dispute amongst the Orthodox concerning Christ's 'the Father is greater than I';[84] but the closing passages at the end of the *Panegyric* contain unmistakable indications that at least part of Neophytos' commentary was aimed at the Latins: the Cross is described as 'the pride of the Orthodox and the fall of those of the wrong faith';[85] as giving strength to the faithful against every 'wrong faith' until the former are proved victorious against an enemy who is defined as 'ruling in the wrong faith', 'heretical' and 'infidel', who 'dogmatised evil' and 'brought evil to the peoples'. The military tone is carried over in another passage where the 'rulers of the wrong faith', above, can be contrasted with the 'faithful *basileis*', for whom the Cross is the 'most holy sceptre' and, more to the point, their 'undefeatable trophy'. The Cross is 'the victory of *basileis* ... and the fall of the adversaries'; the 'wall and fortification' of 'all the towns of the most faithful people'; the 'tower of strength in the face of the enemy and the guardian of the righteous'; the 'unbetrayed wall' of 'all the Orthodox'; the destruction of 'infidel nations'; the 'weapon of peace, with which the *basileis* are armed for salvation, and hoards of enemies are quickly destroyed'.[86]

There can be no doubt that Neophytos is referring to a conflict between the Orthodox and the non-Orthodox, a conflict which had assumed military proportions. As such, the Recluse could only be referring to the conflict

---

[81] *Cod. Paris. Gr. 1189*, fols. 39α, 46α (*Panegyric 8*).

[82] *Cod. Paris. Gr. 1189*, fol. 44α (*Panegyric 8*).

[83] E.g., Theognōstos, 60.227–61.230; and see also 61.231–5.

[84] *John*, 14: 28. This passage vexed theologians from the times of Arianism until the end of the twelfth century. In the twelfth century the dispute over its interpretation culminated in a Synod called in 1170 when Michael III of Anchialos was patriarch in Constantinople and Manuel I Komnēnos emperor. The archbishop of Cyprus, John, took part in the Synod which deposed and anathematised Constantine, the bishop of Corfu. This followed the dispute which had taken place in 1165 concerning the same passage. In 1156 emperor Manuel I Komnēnos called a Synod which accepted four of the seven current interpretations of this passage; and the Synod of 1170 was called to deal with those who persisted on the three rejected interpretations: see Mango (1963); Sakkos (1967). In Cyprus the dispute was remembered not only by Neophytos but also by the official Church: *anathemas* against Constantine of Corfu and all those who agreed with him are found in the twelfth century *Synodikon* of Cyprus: Neophytos' *Panegyric 25*; and for the *Synodikon* of Cyprus see Cappuyns (1935: 491, 493); Sakkos (1967).

[85] *Cod. Paris. Gr. 1189*, fol. 52α (*Panegyric 8*).

[86] *Cod. Paris. Gr. 1189*, fols. 52α, 52β, 53α, 54α (*Panegyric 8*).

between the Orthodox and the Latins. His message in the passage above is one of hope and encouragement for the Orthodox Cypriots beleaguered by Latin domination. The references to the heretics and the Byzantine *basileis* could only act, under the circumstances, as a reminder to his Orthodox audience of the difference between the Byzantines and the westerners – between 'us' and 'them'.

In this again Neophytos was representative of a general attitude prevailing in Byzantium. The polarisation between the Byzantines and the rest of the world was deeply felt by the Byzantines, and it became only more so after 1204. He who was not part of the Byzantine *oikoumenē* was 'an enemy of God and a foreigner'.[87] To a state shocked by 1204, 'the outsider' inevitably came to be synonymous with 'the enemy', and as Byzantium desperately tried to retain the identity of its now fragmented, exiled self, the boundaries between 'us' and 'them' were drawn high and hermetic, reaching the proportions of xenophobia. Orthodoxy became the one focal point of unity of this world, 'Byzantinism' (or 'Hellenism'), the other.[88] Neophytos' war againt Latin non-Orthodoxy and his resistance to a Latin-imposed reality was typical of a general Byzantine attitude. The Recluse, in common with other Byzantines, remained hostile and rebellious to the Latin structures, which seemed to them, in the words of patriarch Germanos II, 'transplantations which failed to take root'.[89] The anti-Latin sentiment assumed proportions of nationist as well as religious exigency. The Orthodox faith came to signify the unconditional attachment to the notion of the Byzantine *oikoumenē* so emphatically that, as Hélène Ahrweiler put it, 'the ideological basis of the Nicaean Empire was the holy war against the Latins'.[90] It was such a war that Neophytos, in his own way, carried out after 1191 and until the end of his life.[91]

---

[87] Theognōstos, 61.235.   [88] See Angold (1975: 55–6, 63ff.); Nicol (1967: 316–18).
[89] Patriarch Germanos, *Contra Bogomilos*, 641.
[90] Ahrweiler (1975b: esp. 24–5). See also Ahrweiler (1975a: 103–4); Nicol (1967: 338–9).
[91] A confirmation that Neophytos' anti-Latin polemic was clearly recognised and remembered by the Orthodox as such comes from the subsequent inclusion of some of his polemical works in manuscripts containing texts of anti-Latin character. Thus, the fourteenth-century *Cod. Paris. 1335* includes a list of Cypriot Orthodox episcopal sees, an account of the martyrdom of the thirteen Kantariōtissa monks, and Neophytos' letter concerning the misfortunes of Cyprus: see Darrouzès (1950: 186). The fifteenth-century *Cod. Paris. Gr. 395*, which contains Neophytos' *Panegyric* on the Schism, also contains the polemical-satirical '*Dialogue between Panayiotēs and an Azymite*': see Argyriou (1972: 21–3); Egglezakes (1979–80: 52). Curiously at first sight, Neophytos' status as a monk may have helped him in his anti-Latin war. Monks and priests after Neophytos persisted in carrying out such a war, in various and different ways, throughout the long years of foreign domination of Cyprus whether by Latin, Ottoman or British. Thus, for example, the village priest in modern rural Cyprus before the declaration of the island's independence in 1960 was considered by the villagers to be the only legitimate political and religious authority, and was deemed to be responsible for keeping alive their Greek-Orthodox identity: Peristiany (1965: 175–6; 1968: 80–2).

Part 4

Saint Neophytos the Recluse

11   Sanctification

Out of Neophytos' surviving writings emerges the picture of a society. In otherwise unconnected passages, strewn throughout his manuscripts and reinforced by the paintings in his caves, the Recluse in effect described in considerable detail the most important aspects of the material and symbolic universe of his society.

According to this picture, this was a society whose system of cosmology rested on four equally indispensable cornerstones: God, the emperor, the Orthodox Church and the notion of the Byzantine *oikoumenē*. These four fundamental tenets of the Byzantine universe were inseparable. Each closely reflected the other; the existence of each validated and helped perpetuate the existence of the other; and the material and symbolic capital invested in each was, as always, perfectly interconvertible. For instance, it was through a ritual ceremony in the Orthdox Church that a man became emperor, thus becoming at once a representative (*ekprosōpos*) of God on earth and the supreme human authority in the Byzantine *oikoumenē*. Again, Byzantium was perceived as being unlike any other state: it was unique, since it was God's own state on earth, His *oikoumenē*. Thus when enemies attacked the empire they committed not just a political offence but a sin against God; and when the emperor's life was in danger, the existence of the Orthodox Church, of the entire Byzantine *oikoumenē* and therefore the authority of God, were all at once in danger of being subverted.

Neophytos frequently reminds us that the citizens of the empire lived in a society possessed of a system of social stratification which was complex and intensely hierarchical. Its taxonomies were multiple, and the difference between them (in terms of the material and symbolic power associated with each) were pronounced and clearly defined. Yet this divided people were held together in strong union, woven into a web of material and especially ideological significance which their system – that is to say, they themselves – had spun. Paradoxically at first sight, the taxonomies of the system at once divided and unified it. Byzantium legitimised its unity in its division: that is to say, it legitimised its unity through adhering closely to its hierarchical system. It resorted, in this respect, to the ultimate legitimisation of hierarchy: it sacralised its institutions, by linking directly its empire, its Church and its emperor to God. We saw this in Neophytos' own attitude towards the Byzantine emperor, Church and empire; as well as in his attempt to turn himself into an institution (a Saint) partly through the sacralisation of his own *enkleistra*.

In the society which Neophytos described, the other side of the coin of the sacralisation of institutions was inscribed by their 'naturalisation'. All systems of ideology have the tendency to present themselves and their products as 'natural', to create (as Gramsci was the first to note) 'the belief about everything that exists that it is "natural", that it should exist, that it could not do otherwise than exist'.[1] On occasions of ultimate triumph, the totality of a society's network of ideologies succeeds in naturalising the fundamental tenets of its own culture to such an extent, that for its members to question them becomes unthinkable.[2] And indeed, to the citizens of the Byzantine Empire the fundamental assumptions of their culture appeared as commonsensical, as self-evident, as indisputable, eternal and 'given', as was the presence of mountains and rivers, the existence of beasts, the interchange of night and day. The fundamental tenets of the culture were experienced by its members as forming part of the Natural Order (the ultimate *taxis*) of the universe; as being not cultural assumptions but axiomatic propositions – and therefore as unquestionable as Nature was.

Neophytos described a society that was silent about the fundamental characteristics of its own culture, because it was incapable of thinking critically about them on a conscious level: what was most essential 'went without saying, because it came without saying', to use Pierre Bourdieu's words. Thus Neophytos could, and did, criticise the symptomatic manifestations of the inherent inequalities of the social system (evidenced, for instance, in the Recluse's passionate condemnation of the treatment of the poor by the representatives of authority on the island); and for a brief minute he even became critical of the emperor immediately after the disaster of 1204. But he never challenged the fundamental assumptions of his culture: he never questioned the need to have an emperor at all; he never considered that the Orthodox Church might not possess the exclusive rights over the totality of God's Truth; he never imagined that the Byzantine *oikoumenē* could be anything other than God's own. To question any of these fundamental assumptions was to him as inconceivable (at least, on a conscious level) as it was to question the existence of God. The society

---

[1] Gramsci (1971: quote from 157; see also 206–76, 348–51). Gramsci was referring to industrial societies but the gist of the argument referred to above is equally applicable to pre-industrial societies.

[2] For a relevant discussion see Bourdieu (1977: esp. 165, 167, 188).

which Neophytos described had developed a complex but stable social system – stable enough to be capable of ensuring the perpetuation of its fundamental tenets, which appeared to survive unquestioned and unaltered both external attacks and internal upheavals. The latter were perceived as representing merely temporary upsets in the order of the *oikoumenē*: since this was God's own *oikoumenē*, it followed that in good time order would certainly be restored.

The naturalisation of the culture, its ability to unify its members by creating strong material and especially symbolic bonds between them, their institutions and God and the conception of God as just, but also wrathful, all together concurred in a conception of a fundamentally just universe, in which pain and suffering were explicable only as constituting rightful punishments of God for individual human misdeeds. A causative link thus existed between individual acts and collective fate: the effect of one person's virtue (the presence and the prayers, for instance, of a holy man) was considered to have beneficial effects on the whole of society; while individual moral failings were likewise charged to the community. Thus it was that this society rationalised disasters: whether enemy victories, earthquakes or famines, all disasters were explained as constituting deserved punishments of a justly wrathful God for people's sins. In this aspect the system described closely resembles the Durkheimian system, in which God is Society and Society is God; and where all moral failings are at once sins against God and against the community.[3]

The characteristics discussed so far themselves bear witness to another aspect of the culture Neophytos described: the clarity with which it formulated its definition of what was pure and what impure; the rigour with which it drew the boundaries between them. Simply put, the totality of its own rules *was* purity; everything else was impurity. To this characteristic was related another attitude, whose imprints we also find in Neophytos' writings: the aversion to the stranger and the outsider, whom the Recluse amongst many other Byzantine writers so consistently equated with the enemy. For the Byzantines as Neophytos described them, beyond the borders of the *oikoumenē* lay a vast wasteland, peopled by un-Godly enemies – the unenlightened at best, the barbarians at worst. To the members and agents of Neophytos' society the notion that there may be a different social universe, the whole or aspects of whose culture might be equally legitimate to theirs, was non-existent.

Further, the strangers were not only those who existed outside the physical borders of the empire. Equally foreign – and even more hated – were those who lived within the physical borders of the *oikoumenē* but had placed themselves beyond its cultural boundaries by committing acts which

3 Durkheim (1976).

dared challenge its rules. This was a society which afforded no place for plurality of opinion as liberal ideologies understand it. A difference of opinion in respect of the system's fundamental tenets was seen as abnormal, impure, unnatural and in need of ritual cleansing. A dissent from the social rules laid down by the representatives of authority was *ipso facto* a sin against God. Dissent was seen as threatening the integrity of the cosmos, and as such it was treated with extreme intolerance. In Neophytos' writings the existence of strictly defined boundaries between purity and impurity is particularly obvious in his pronouncements concerning the Orthodox in relation to the non-Orthodox, the Byzantine to the non-Byzantine.[4] He attacked with equal vehemence and absolutism whoever trespassed the laws of the culture, the boundaries of Byzantine purity: from the inhabitants of Paphos who failed to observe the fasting rules of Lent to the rebel Isaac Komnēnos; from the dreaded heretic and the infidel to the practising homosexual.[5]

To conclude, Neophytos presented us with a picture of a Byzantine society whose major characteristics were as follows: a stable and self-perpetuating social system; a complex, intensely hierarchical system of social order; closely knit and highly structured social relations; causative links between individual acts and collective fate; sacralisation of institutions; extreme naturalisation of the fundamental tenets of the culture; strong boundaries between purity and impurity; intolerance; abhorrence of dissent. Its mood was one of introversion but not (when it came to the essentials of the culture) of introspection. It was xenophobic, narcissistic, self-congratulatory and highly defensive, having proclaimed its symbolic universe and itself perfect, totally self-sufficient and inseparable from God. This universe was not of Neophytos' own creation. As we have repeatedly seen throughout this book, it was consistently upheld by contemporary Byzantine representatives of authority; and the fact that Neophytos' society heeded his words clearly shows it to have been a universe also inhabited by the common people.

Neophytos, who so absolutely believed in the uniqueness of Byzantium, would have found it extremely difficult to believe that it was only in the specific expressions of its culture that Orthodox Byzantium was, like any other society, unique. In fact, when abstracted from the specificity of their expression (as in the preceding paragraph), the basic characteristics of that culture are commonly manifested by a number of pre-industrial societies. As work in the field of social anthropology clearly suggests, such societies form a recognisable 'type.' In describing and analysing such societies, each

---

[4] They are also very obvious in Neophytos' conception of gender and sexuality: see Galatariotou (1984–5, 1989).

[5] For the latter example see Galatariotou (1989: 117–24).

social anthropologist has tended to develop and use his or her own terminology; but it is essentially the same social type which, for instance, Mary Douglas referred to in detail and with respect to a number of societies when she wrote of her 'strong Group and strong Grid social type'; which Meyer Fortes gave us in his account of the Tallensi of the Volta region in Ghana; which Pierre Bourdieu described when, drawing on his fieldwork in Kabylia (Algeria), he spoke of the society which relates to the totality of its culture in a 'doxic mode'.[6] It would not be out of place in this context to call this same type of society in its Byzantine expression the 'divine imperial' type.

Comparison with other societies thus shows that the type of society which Neophytos described was historically not unique. But further, and perhaps more significantly, internal examination of that society instantly puts into question the extent to which Neophytos' description of the Byzantine 'divine imperial' society actually represented the commonly perceived – let alone the factual – reality of twelfth-century Byzantine society. Some aspects of the evidence contained in the Recluse's description conflict with other pieces of information which we possess about Byzantium during this period. We had occasion to refer to some of them earlier: the administration of the provinces in the eleventh and the twelfth centuries, for instance, which had slid into a spiralling pattern of corruption, fiscal oppression and military inefficiency; the darker side of the economic expansion of these centuries, which was the widening gap and greater polarisation between classes, with ever-increasing numbers of independent peasants being reduced to the pitiful status of the *paroikos*; the revolts caused by excessive taxation, to whom were added increasingly successful separatist revolts, especially in the period of the Angeloi. The separatist revolts instigated by Greek Orthodox subjects of the empire, which so clearly rejected the notion of the divine unity and integrity of Byzantium, were a new phenomenon in the empire. Their very novelty showed above all that by the end of the twelfth century the Byzantine Empire was breaking apart both materially and symbolically, for the empire's physical disintegration would have been impossible without the disintegration of aspects of its symbolic universe which had in the past helped to hold it together.

Further, in his reference to his immediate social environment of Cyprus, the Recluse himself provided abundant evidence which is contrary to his own description of the Byzantine 'divine imperial' society. In examining this evidence in detail earlier, we saw how, while Cyprus was still a part of the Byzantine empire, Neophytos acted as a critic of society. He did not act simply as an institutionalised renouncer, the monk or holy man for whom

6 Douglas (1973: esp. ch. 4, 77 ff., and 91, 169, 175 ff.); Fortes (1959); Bourdieu (1977: esp. 164–9 and *passim*).

renouncing the world and the vanity of its ways was a socially accepted and even expected act. Moving far beyond the general renunciations which formed part of the accoutrements of the ascetic, the Recluse's castigations of the rich and of the secular and even ecclesiastical representatives of authority on the island were specific, passionate and highly topical. They had the urgency which only conditions of intense adversity generate.

Through such critical passages Neophytos spoke of a social universe some of whose aspects were far removed from the stable and ordered world of the 'divine imperial' society. He spoke of a society whose internal structure was seriously deteriorating, whose members lived in a hostile and dangerous universe, where leadership was precarious, and traditional roles had become ambiguous and undefined. He spoke of a people that stood frightened and confused, lost in their uncertainty as to what further calamity, oppression and injustice the future might bring. He described them as living in a cosmos endangered by agents of evil who infiltrated society from outside, or sprang from within to impose on it unacceptable – but also uncontrollable – deviance. Intensely insecure, this was a society which was preoccupied with rituals of cleansing, by the identification and expulsion of spies and witches within it, by the need for constant redrawing of its crumbling cultural boundaries. In social anthropological terms, this society is recognisably different from, though not entirely dissimilar to, the one represented by Neophytos' 'divine imperial' model.[7]

This was, in fact, the Orthodox Cypriot society in which Neophytos actually lived. When the Recluse described a 'divine imperial' society, he was describing not the society in which he lived, but that which he aspired to. He was describing the image of such a society as the rules of the Byzantine system of social, political and religious ideologies formulated. All the citizens of the Byzantine *oikoumenē* subscribed, in varying degrees of commitment, to aspects at least of the 'divine imperial' society. Neophytos represents those Byzantines whose degree of commitment to the entirety of the 'divine imperial' model was absolute: they did not recognise the 'divine imperial' society as representing an idealistic and unrealistic abstraction; to them it represented the Truth, it represented a reality which co-existed with and transcended in importance the factual reality of their current situation.

The Recluse's pre-1191 social commentary already bespeaks an internally deteriorating social system. The Cypriots' exploitation in the hands of Constantinople's representatives, and the corresponding undermining of aspects of their symbolic universe, caused them much pain, frustrated anger and bitterness. But infinitely more bitter times lay ahead.

---

[7] It corresponds very substantially with the societies which Mary Douglas characterised as of a 'strong Group and low Grid' type: Douglas (1973: esp. 77 ff., 169, 193).

Already in crisis during the closing decades of Byzantine rule, the Orthodox Cypriot society was further assailed by Isaac Komnēnos and then savagely attacked by the westerners. After 1184, and far more after 1191, the social system was felt by its members to be threatened to the point of extinction. All its symbols and authorities, all that gave it unity and cohesion, was assailed. Physically removed from the Byzantine *oikoumenē* and turned into a Latin fee, Orthodox Cyprus was devastated politically, socially, economically: its civil administrative system was destroyed at a stroke; its ruling class fled away; the rest of its people were reduced to unprecedented levels of poverty and social worthlessness, their religious institutions and beliefs (the only survivors of the onslaught) menaced by a foreign Church that threatened to turn them all into something non-Orthodox. No recognisable authority was left to give rules and laws with which the Orthodox Cypriots could, albeit grudgingly, identify. The situation was one of societal breakdown, or, to use Durkheim's term, of *anomie* (rulelessness, the extinction or eradication of laws). And it is in such instances that more and more people tend to feel helpless, alienated, disorientated, and tend to feel that the society in which they live, and hence the universe, has become meaningless and normless.

Already under Byzantine rule there was a chasm between what Neophytos and his society perceived as a real, factual situation, the factual reality of their everyday lives, and what they perceived and preferred as an ideal but equally true and tangible situation: the 'divine imperial' society. The chasm between the two realities became greater under Isaac Komnēnos, and far greater still under the Latins.

My suggestion is that the greater this chasm the more clearly it indicates a correspondingly severe dislocation of society's material and symbolic universe, and an equally great vacuum of authority within that society. The need to fill that vacuum is as great, if that society is culturally to survive. Precisely in order to do so, such a society would, under certain circumstances, both produce and accept a charismatic leader.

Charisma was described by Max Weber as

a certain quality of an individual personality by virtue of which he is considered extraordinary and treated as endowed with supernatural, superhuman, or at least specifically exceptional powers or qualities. These are such as are not accessible to the ordinary person, but are regarded as of divine origin or as exemplary, and on the basis of them the individual concerned is treated as a 'leader'.[8]

This is Weber's most frequently cited reference to charisma, but neither on this nor on any other occasion does he analyse explicitly the appeal of charisma. He appears to take it for granted, and concentrates not so much

---

[8] Weber (1968: 241).

on the charismatic leader as, rather, on the charismatic group or band which grows around the leader; and on the 'routinisation' of charisma: that is to say, the process by which the charismatic characteristics are transferred from the unique personality or the unstructured group to an orderly institutionalised reality. Weber does not analyse, either, the precise nature of the charismatic leader's personality, that 'certain quality', to use his words.[9]

Other sociologists of religion subsequently undertook the difficult task of defining and analysing the characteristics of the charismatic personality. Edward Shils' was an important contribution to this effort: he described the charismatic quality of an individual as perceived by others, or by himself or herself, as lying in what is thought to be his or her connection with (including possession by, or lodgement of) some very central feature of man's existence and the cosmos in which he lives. The centrality, coupled with an intensity, is what makes such an individual extraordinary. That central power has often been conceived of as God, the ruling power or creator of the universe, or some divine or other transcendent power controlling or markedly influencing human life and the cosmos within which it exists. Thus, in Shils' understanding, all forms of genius, in the original sense of the word as permeation by 'the spirit', are as much instances of charismatic things as is religious prophecy.[10]

This is precisely the picture that Neophytos had created for himself, and the one he presented his society with, as we saw in our discussion of his process of self-sanctification. That process helped Neophytos develop the external characteristics which could easily be perceived by society as signifying charisma, since he so closely fashioned his behaviour and his life's story on the model of those of Saints and Old Testament prophets. Concurrently and more importantly, there is no doubt that the genuine belief in his own sanctity helped Neophytos not only to manifest external behaviouristic patterns, but also to develop out of his personal idiom internal personality traits which were characteristic of the charismatic personality. The 'intensity' of the charismatic personality referred to earlier was, in Neophytos' case, the outcome of the combination of a number of his attitudes and personality traits which we have encountered in the course of this book. It stemmed both from his uncompromising stands on secular and ecclesiastical politics, above and against factual reality itself and revitalising the

[9] For general introductions to Weber's work on charisma see B. Wilson (1975); Theobald (1980). Weber's lack of systematic analysis and his ambiguous and even contradictory references to charisma have led to endless debate and controversy over the nature of charisma and Weber's understanding of it. See generally Miyahara (1983); also Wallis and Bruce (1986: 83 ff.).

[10] E. A. Shils, *Charisma, Order and Status* (199ff.), quoted in Eisenstadt (1968: xxv). See also *ibid.* (xviii–xxvi).

alternative reality of the 'divine imperial' society; and from Neophytos' conflicting personality. 'Conflicting', since he professed Christian humility and yet went to astonishing lengths to propagate his own sanctification; since he spoke up for the poor, at the same time being a spiritual father to the rich; since he was a recluse, and yet in touch with a public far removed from the confines of his cell; a humble hermit, and yet a snob about class and intellect; a loner, and yet as much in touch with the society from which he had fled as any passionate secular or ecclesiastical leader would be. Since, in other words – and to paraphrase Peter Brown – he was both in this world and yet not of it.[11]

The development of charismatic characteristics in an individual and the acceptance of this by society are, of course, interdependent. In this sense, as Roy Wallis and Steve Bruce point out, 'charisma is essentially a relationship born out of interaction between a leader and his followers'.[12] An individual's personal idiom may be possessed of an inherent predisposition towards charisma; but it is a specific set of social circumstances that tends to encourage the development of charisma in an individual, and which at the same time also tends to predispose society into accepting that individual as charismatic. In this respect, for someone who so longed to be a Saint, Neophytos could not have chosen a more propitious time and place in which to live. Max Weber suggested that it is 'in times of physical, ethical, religious, political distress' that charisma appears; and that its development 'may involve a subjective or internal reorientation born out of suffering, conflicts or enthusiasm'.[13] These suggestions have been interpreted by subsequent commentators as referring to the creation of societal predisposition to acceptance of charismatic leadership.

Other sociologists elaborate on Weber's ideas, frequently differing in their estimation of the most important factor in this process. The 'deprivation' theorists, for instance, argue that religion is a response to strain or deprivation which is felt by individuals and which is caused by events in society. Thus, when a society is stable, it employs all its efforts and energy in maintaining its equilibrium; but when stability is threatened – by internal dissent, external force or both – society may attempt to revitalise itself by various means. This revitalisation may be achieved by way of creating a new cult, sect or even religion, centred around a charismatic individual. One school of thought thus argues that deprivation is the cause of stress which generates new religious movements.[14]

Other theorists argue that the threat of societal breakdown forces people

---

[11] Brown (1971b).
[12] Wallis and Bruce (1986: 130ff.); my agreement with whom ends here: see below, and especially note 18. For an analysis of the charismatic relationship between leader and followers based on psychoanalytical premises, see Downton (1973).
[13] Weber (1947: 333).   [14] See, e.g. Aberle (1971: 528–31).

to examine new ways in order (socially) to survive; and that it is the hope that people gain from examining and implementing these new ways, and not the deprivation, that lies at the core of the desire to revitalise their society, perhaps by way of religious revivalism. This becomes thus one way in which people try to save a culture by infusing it with new purpose and new life, and it is one of the consequences which may arise from disruption of a culture by contact with a dominant society. According, for instance, to Anthony Wallace, religious beliefs and practices always originate in situations of cultural stress, and represent an effort on the part of the stress-laden to construct systems of dogma, myth and ritual which are internally coherent as well as true descriptions of a world system, and which will thus serve as guides to efficient actions.[15] Wallace gives the example of the Seneca Indians, an Iroquois tribe, who were faced with such a situation in the aftermath of the American Revolution. They had lost their lands and were confined to isolated reservations amidst an alien and dominant people. They were in a state of despondency when a member of their tribe, a man called Handsome Lake, claimed – and undoubtedly believed – that he had re-ceived a vision from God which led him to preach a new religion. This the Seneca Indians absorbed fully and quickly because, Wallace argues, they needed it to revitalise their badly shaken society.[16]

The social situation which Wallace describes is, in its gist, and particu-larly in its emotional content, strikingly similar to that which the Orthodox Cypriot society found itself in, especially after 1191. Wallace refers, of course, to a charismatic leader who founded a new religion, but the same dynamics could be at work in the case of the charismatic man who acts as a renewer rather than a founder, and around whose person a new cult is created. There is no radical difference between the two charismatic person-alities at the centre of such instances, as a number of sociologists – including Weber – point out.[17] Indeed, Neophytos preached nothing new.[18] His

---

[15] Wallace (1966: 30).   [16] *Ibid.* (31–4).   [17] Weber (1965: 46).

[18] For some sociologists this fact would preclude Neophytos from being described as a charismatic leader. Such sociologists might concede that Neophytos developed charismatic characteristics, but not that he became a charismatic leader, because they consider the presence of innovation to be essential in the message of the charismatic personality. See Wallis and Bruce (1986: esp. chs. 4, 6). Their view is, of course, only one of many. Their basic objection to Weber's formulation – that it is far too wide – is well taken, but their proposed alternative solution is marred by three inherent flaws. First, it leads to the even more complicated task of defining the degree of novelty required, for there is obviously no 'new' message that has nothing whatsoever to do with the past. Second, it leads to far too narrow an interpretation of charisma, which perforce excludes all political and religious revivalists on the reductive grounds that they are not founders of a new religion or exponents of a radically novel political credo (they thus accept Jesus and Adolf Hitler as charismatic, but consider the status of the Old Testament prophets to be at least problematic). Third, they overlook the possibility that what makes a message 'new' and perhaps charismatic might not lie exclusively in the message itself, but in the combination of that message and the social circumstances under which it is delivered: Gandhi, whose message was essentially one of return to, or revivalism of, traditional values, is a case in point; Neophytos is another.

words were neither meant nor taken to signify a change in the Orthodox Cypriots' cosmology. They were, rather, simply a clear, tightly drawn and uncompromising reaffirmation of what the Cypriots already knew to be their universe, but which a series of social, political and economic catastrophes had shaken badly. What made Neophytos' old words 'new', what infused them with current and urgent relevance, were the changed social circumstances under which he uttered them.

Neophytos' belief in the 'divine imperial' model was always absolute. During Byzantine rule this commitment was shared by the members of Cypriot society outside his cell, though in all probability less intensely (not least because of their maltreatment by Constantinople's agents). Subsequently, the more the conditions of the Cypriots' factual reality worsened and the greater the blows delivered to their material and symbolic universe, the more normless the world appeared to them; and accordingly the more urgent grew their need for order to be imposed on the chaos that threatened to engulf them. Clearly, the Orthodox Cypriots could not relate to the new order imposed by the hated Latins, who had wrought havoc on their material and symbolic universe and who collectively displaced and confined them to the very bottom of the social scale. The one and only order to which the Cypriots could instantly relate was naturally the one they recognised as their own culture's, and in whose scheme of things a place was definitely reserved for them, the otherwise displaced and dispossessed. The time was thus ripe for the 'divine imperial' model, which represented the purest expression of their culture's system of world order, to become more relevant and more necessary than ever before: for on the strong commitment to the preservation of its ordered and purposeful cosmos now depended the survival of the Orthodox Cypriots' cultural identity – and on the latter depended their very existence as social beings. Thus, paradoxically at first sight, the demise of Byzantine rule and its aftermath had the effect not of lessening the relevance of the 'divine imperial' model for the Orthodox Cypriots, but of increasing it. Concurrently, equally great became their need for one authority powerful enough to appear, reclaim this alternative cosmos and reassert their place in it.

Neophytos was the one who filled that need. He was the one who articulated the cosmology of the perfect, 'divine imperial' society; and in so doing, he infused it with new life. What he thus offered to the Orthodox Cypriots was more than a bridge between two realities; more than a temporary emotional escape from the miserable factual reality of their everyday lives: in propagating the reality of the 'divine imperial' society, he effectively gave the Cypriots a cultural 'survival kit', as complete as it could be under the circumstances. Especially after 1191, Neophytos' society listened to him and revered him because he was the one who redrew with vigour the lines of a seemingly broken-down social universe. In a time of threatened *anomie*, Neophytos reiterated and gave the rules and laws. His uncompromising redrawing of cultural boundaries at a time of vacant bishops' thrones, social – and looming religious – persecution, fleeing economic figureheads and extinction of the only civil authorities which society could recognise and identify with, turned Neophytos himself into an authority, a law-giver. He became the charismatic leader who, undaunted by factual reality, was desperately needed to fill the vacuum of authority in what the Orthodox Cypriots knew to be their society.

It is, thus, impossible to divorce Neophytos' rise to sanctity from his society's changing social, economic, political and religious circumstances, on the one hand, and his own response to them, on the other. It is easy to imagine that, had Neophytos never been a hermit, but had he involved himself directly with lay or ecclesiastical politics, he would have become a political or Church leader, for the driving ambition, the conflicting personality with the charismatic tendencies, the surrounding circumstances, would all still be there and would in all likelihood have been adapted to the circumstances in different ways; but he would not have become a Saint. Again, had Neophytos been more openly direct and more overtly violent in the way in which he did concern himself with politics, then he would probably have ended up in the way of the Cypriot 'emperor'–monk of 1191: hanged, in the aftermath of a quickly suppressed rebellion.

The fact is that Neophytos, sometimes purposefully and sometimes without consciously meaning to, conducted himself in the most prudent and appropriate way possible under the changing circumstances in order to survive the process of turning from man to holy man, from holy man to Saint. He thus carried out his polemic in a way which could not be missed by any Orthodox Cypriot, but which would not be noticed by a Latin. He changed his polemic through the years, reacting to what was at every given time the Cypriot society's main cause for anxiety: in the early days the social conditions and the oppression of poor man by rich man, in the later days the oppression of Orthodox Cypriot by Latin. The aura of his seclusion and his self-taught education already raised him above the level of the ordinary member of society. But further, he used his writings to promote his self-image of sanctity, to spread his fame all over Cyprus and to establish a relationship with the widest possible Cypriot public, over and above the small but influential circle of his secular aristocratic and ecclesiastical devotees. It is this ability to reach out to the wider audience from the seclusion of his *enkleistra*, that gave Neophytos the public which then turned venerator.

Neophytos' process of self-sanctification, with all its surrounding social circumstances, certainly helped him to develop out of his personal idiom traits characteristic of a charismatic personality; and it also helped his society to accept him as a charismatic leader. But the tale of Neophytos' sanctification (including the development and acceptance of charisma) was, above all, spun out of his ongoing response to society's needs, and out of society's equally ongoing reaction to his response. This was the basis of the relationship that developed between the Recluse and his society, within the context of the changing circumstances brought about by the succession of the social, economic, religious and political traumas which marked Cypriot society – materially and symbolically – during Neophytos' lifetime.

Whether because of their relative deprivation or because of their need to hope, the Cypriots heeded Neophytos' words because they provided a powerful confirmation of the rules and laws of a society – their society – which they saw threatened with extinction. The 'commodity' which Neophytos offered to the Cypriot Orthodox was the unconditional reaffirmation of the reality, current validity and superiority of their own culture in its purest form: that of the 'divine imperial' society. Neophytos offered hope in projecting not simply the possibility of a 'divine imperial' society, but in projecting the image of such a society as a real, tangible and (when time took its course and God's wrath ended) inescapable eventuality. To the members of a society on the verge of complete breakdown, overcome by disasters, subjected to foreign domination and threatened with total cultural extinction, what Neophytos had to offer became a very precious and rare commodity indeed. In harnessing their faith in the Byzantine 'divine imperial' cosmos, he gave them the way in which they could keep their cultural identity intact, their cultural selves in one piece.

Thus it was that to the Orthodox Cypriots the need to revitalise their society, to keep it alive by infusing it with life, came by way of creating a new cult; and thus it was that this new cult centred around the charismatic man who had become the very focus of that cultural revitalisation. Dispossessed of most of the material aspects of their society, the Orthodox Cypriots still possessed the treasures of its symbolic universe; and Neophytos had indeed both reminded them of the existence of these treasures and showed them how to keep them in the safety of their hearts and minds, from which they could not be looted, spoiled or burned to a cinder by any human agent. The members of the beleaguered Cypriot Orthodox society dipped into those same treasures and out of them they gave Neophytos, in grateful return and recognition, the most precious gift he and they knew of: sanctity.

Appendix

The writings of Neophytos: a guide

Neophytos gave the following descriptive list of his works in his *Typikon* of 1214:

There are also, so help me God, the writings of the recluse: sixteen books, small as well as big ones, which are the following. The three major *Books of Panegyrics*; and two other books, containing many *Letters*, of benefice to the soul of everyone [who reads them], as well as four hundred *Ascetic Chapters* and twenty-four *Telōnia*; and a *Book of Fifty Chapters*, which also contains an *Interpretation of the Song of Songs*; and another, the book of the *Sign of God*; and another, an *Interpretation of the Hexaēmeros* in sixteen parts; and another, an *Interpretation of the Psalms* in twelve parts; and another, the *Interpretation of the Canons* of the twelve divine feasts; and another, of twelve parts, the *Log-book* of the recluse, in which reference is made to forty and fifty years, and to physiology; and another, of twenty parts, containing comprehensive *Interpretations* of the divine law laid down in the Old and the New Testament; and another, the *Book of Catecheseis*; and another, a small *Book of Poems* of devout concentration; and another, the present *Typikon*; and yet another, the so-called *Last Book*. All of which add up to sixteen, which the lovers of virtue and of God must not snub simply because they are not ancient writings; but having perceived that they were produced not out of human wisdom or craftmanship but through the grace of the Holy Ghost, let them glorify God. Amen.[1]

There follows a basic guide to Neophytos' writings, cited as and in the order in which they appear in his *Typikon*. It is a fivefold guide, referring to: (1) the surviving manuscripts of Neophytos' works; (2) the way each work has been cited in this book; (3) a brief description of each work whenever its title is not descriptive enough; (4) existing editions of Neophytos' manuscripts or of extracts thereof; (5) dating, whenever possible, of each work. A number of dates are established or suggested here for the first time on the basis of internal textual evidence. A list of Neophytos' works in the chronological order resulting appears at the end of this Appendix. No mention of edition or date signifies, respectively, that the text is unedited and the date unknown.

I Αἱ μειζότεραι τρεῖς πανηγυρικαί.[2]
Three books containing *Panegyrics* to be delivered on particular feast-days of the Orthodox ecclesiastical year. The titles appear below in an abbreviated form.

[1] *Typikon*, 83.16–31.   [2] *Typikon*, 83.16.

I(a) *First book of Panegyrics*
MS: *Cod. Paris. Gr. 1189*.
The manuscript, comprised of 235 folios and containing Neophytos' autograph notes, contains thirty of his *Panegyrics*. These were written at various times, to celebrate feast-days of the first four-month period (September to December) of the Orthodox ecclesiastical year.[3]

(i) Cited: *Panegyric 1* (fols. 1α–3α).
Title: Εἰς τὴν ἀρχὴν τῆς ἰνδίκτου.
According to the Orthodox ecclesiastical year, the beginning of the indiction is 1 September.
Edn: Tsiknopoulos (1950a: 3–7).

(ii) Cited: *Panegyric 2* (fols. 3α–7β).
Title: Εἰς τὸν ἅγιον μεγαλομάρτυρα Μάμαντα.
Edn: Tsiknopoulos (1966: 133–7).

(iii) Cited: *Panegyric 3* (fols. 7β–12α).
Title: Εἰς τὸν θεῖον ἀρχάγγελον Μιχαήλ.

(iv) Cited: *Panegyric 4* (fols. 12β–15α).
Title: Εἰς τὸ γενέθλιον τῆς Θεοτόκου.
Edn: Jugie (1922: 528[104]–532[108]).
Date: Neophytos states his intention to write a *Homily* on the Presentation of the Virgin to the Temple, when the time for that feast-day approached.[4] In his undoubtedly very late *Homily* for the Presentation of the Virgin Neophytos writes that he had completed a *Homily* seventy-three days earlier, celebrating the Birth of the Virgin. The same date for the *Homily* for the Presentation – of about 1214 – must therefore also be accepted for Neophytos' *Panegyric 4*.[5]

(v) Cited: *Panegyric 5* (fols. 15α–24β).
Title: Περί τινος μοναχοῦ ἐν τῇ Παλαιστίνῃ παρὰ δαιμόνων ἀπατηθέντος καὶ ἐκπεπτωκότος δεινῶς.
Neophytos narrates the contemporary story of a stylite in Palestine who was pushed into sin by demons.
Edn: Delehaye (1907: 162–75); repr. Chatziioannou (1914). I use Delehaye's edition.
Date: 1187 or shortly thereafter.[6]

(vi) Cited: *Panegyric 6* (fols. 24β–29α).
Title: Εἰς τὰ ἐγκαίνεια τοῦ ναοῦ τῆς ᾿Αναστάσεως καὶ περὶ πάντος ἱεροῦ ἐγκαινιαζομένου ναοῦ.
For the feast-day of the consecration of the church of the Anastasis in Jerusalem and of any other church.
Edn: Extracts, Egglezakes (1979–80: 45, 46).
Date: Between 1191 and 1204, possibly 1197.[7]

---

[3] For an introduction to this first book of *Panegyrics* see Delehaye (1907: 279–97); Stiernon (1981: 110); Tsiknopoulos (1958: 101); Petit (1898–9).
[4] *Panegyric 4*, 531 [107].11–15.   [5] *Cod. Lesb. Leim. 2, Homily 1*; see below, p. 278.
[6] Delehaye (1907: 280–2).   [7] Egglezakes (1979–80: 48–9).

(vii) Cited: *Panegyric 7* (fols. 29β–38β).
Title: Εἰς τὸν τίμιον καὶ ζωοποιὸν σταυρόν.
For the feast-day of the exaltation of the Holy Cross.
Edn: Extracts, Egglezakes (1979–80: 48).
Date: 1196.[8]

(viii) Cited: *Panegyric 8* (fols. 38β–57β).
Title: Εἰς τὸν σταυρόν.
For the same feast-day as *Panegyric 7*.
Edn: Extracts, Tsiknopoulos (1954f: 258–62).
Date: Internal evidence suggests a post-1191 date.[9]

(ix) Cited: *Panegyric 9* (fols. 57β–77β).
Title: Περὶ τῆς ᾽Αποκαλύψεως τοῦ ἁγίου ᾽Ιωάννου.
Interpretation of the *Apocalypse*.
Edn: Egglezakes (1975–7: 87–112).
Date: Shortly after the 1204 fall of Constantinople.[10]

(x) Cited: *Panegyric 10* (fols. 77β–81α).
Title: Εἰς τὸν ἅγιον ἱερομάρτυρα Πολυχρόνιον.
Edn: Delehaye (1907: 175–8); repr. Chatziioannou (1914). I use Delehaye's edition.

(xi) Cited: *Panegyric 11* (fols. 81α–86β).
Title: Εἰς τὸν ἅγιον ᾽Ανδρόνικον καὶ τὴν ὁσίαν ᾽Αθανασίαν.
Edn: Large extracts, Delehaye (1907: 178–80); repr. Chatziioannou (1914). I use Delehaye's edition.

(xii) Cited: *Panegyric 12* (fols. 86β–105α).
Title: Εἰς τὸν βίον τοῦ ὁσίου Θεοσεβίου τοῦ ᾽Αρσινοΐτου
Edn: Delehaye (1907: 181–97); repr. Chatziioannou (1914). I use Delehaye's edition.

(xiii) Cited: *Panegyric 13* (fols. 105β–114β).
Title: Εἰς τὸν ὅσιον ᾽Ιλαρίωνα.
Edn: Tsiknopoulos (1966: 138–47).
Date: A reference to the fall of Constantinople makes 1204 a *terminus post quem*.[11]

(xiv) Cited: *Panegyric 14* (fols. 114β–122α).
Title: Εἰς τὸν βίον τοῦ ἁγίου ᾽Αρκαδίου ἐπισκόπου ᾽Αρσινόης.
Edn: Delehaye (1907: 197–207); repr. Chatziioannou (1914). I use Delehaye's edition.

(xv) Cited: *Panegyric 15* (fols: 122β–129α).
Title: Εἰς τὸν ἅγιον Δημήτριον.
Edn: Laourdas (1955–60: 49–55, 122–5).
Date: The *Panegyric* contains a reference to a defeat of the Byzantine armies;[12] and the most likely case is that it refers to the battle at Myriokephalon.[13] The *Panegyric* may thus be dated to 1176 or shortly thereafter.

---

[8] *Ibid.* (44, 48).   [9] See ch. 10, pp. 241–2.   [10] See Egglezakes (1975–7: 75–6, B(i)).
[11] See Egglezakes (1979–80: 50, 2iv); Delahaye (1907: 286); Tsiknopoulos (1958: 90).
[12] *Panegyric 15*, 54.198–203.   [13] See ch. 9, p. 214, note 41.

(xvi) Cited: *Panegyric 16* (fols. 129α–134α).
Title: Περὶ σεισμῶν διαφόρων.
26 October is the Orthodox Church's principle commemoration day of great earthquakes.
Edn: Delehaye (1907: 207–12); repr. Chatziioannou (1914). I use Delehaye's edition.
Date: The *Panegyric* contains a reference to a great contemporary earthquake in Antioch, which occurred a short time after Neophytos' seclusion. This almost certainly refers to the earthquake of 1170,[14] which gives the *Panegyric* a *terminus post quem* of 1170.

(xvii) Cited: *Panegyric 17* (fols. 134α–139β).
Title: Εἰς τὸν ὅσιον Διομήδην τὸν Νέον.
Edn: Delehaye (1907: 212–20); repr. Chatziioannou (1914). I use Delehaye's edition.
Date: Neophytos writes that he had already produced a number of works – *Panegyrics*, *enkōmia*, Saints' stories; and, defending his writing activities, he refers to works which elucidate passages 'difficult to comprehend' in the Gospels. This seems to refer to his *Interpretation of the Commandments*, of 1176, as a recent work (fols. 137β–138α).[15] The *Panegyric* can be dated, therefore, to 1176 or shortly thereafter.

(xviii) Cited: *Panegyric 18* (fols. 139β–141α).
Title: Περὶ τῶν ἁγίων Κοσμᾶ καὶ Δαμιανοῦ.

(xix) Cited: *Panegyric 19* (fols 141α–152β).
Title: Εἰς τὴν σύναξιν τῶν ἀσωμάτων.

(xx) Cited: *Panegyric 20* (fols. 153α–164α).
Title: Εἰς τὸν μέγαν ἱεράρχην Χρυσόστομον.
Edn: Dyovouniotes (1926: 8–19).[16]
Date: The *Panegyric* must be dated to the pre-1191 period, because of Neophytos' favourable references to 'king Onorios' of Rome and 'pope Innocent', who, according to the Recluse, rebuked emperor Arkadios and empress Eudoxia for their behaviour towards St John Chrysostom.[17] Judging from Neophytos' virulent post-1191 anti-Latinism, it is reasonable to assume that he would have avoided such references after 1191.[18]

(xxi) Cited: *Panegyric 21* (fols. 164β–169α).
Title: Περὶ Μαρίας τῆς Θεόπαιδος.
Edn: Jugie (1922) 533[109]–538[114].
Date: Neophytos' reference to his 'recently built' cell of the upper *enkleistra*[19] dates this *Panegyric* to 1197 or soon thereafter.

---

14 See Rochricht (1898: 348).   15 *Panegyric 17*, 217.32–218.29.
16 An extract is also edited by Delehaye (1907: 291; from fols. 153α–β).
17 *Panegyric 20*, 16.4–10.
18 See, generally, ch. 10, pp. 230ff.   19 *Panegyric 21*, 538 [114].23–5.

(xxii) Cited: *Panegyric 22* (fols. 169β–172β).
Title: Εἰς τὸν βίον τοῦ ὁσίου ᾽Αλυπίου.
Edn: Delehaye (1923: 188–94).

(xxiii) Cited: *Panegyric 23* (fols. 173α–180α).
Title: Εἰς τὸν θεῖον πατέραν ἡμῶν Σάβαν.
Edn: Extracts, Tsiknopoulos (1951b).
Date: A reference to Palestine's recent fall to Saladin (fols. 179β–180α) dates the
Panegyric to 1187 or soon thereafter.

(xxiv) Cited: *Panegyric 24* (fols. 180α–199α).
According to Tsiknopoulos, this *Panegyric* also survives in the seventeenth-century
Cod. 6 of Argyrokastron (fols. ΜΔα–ΝΣΤβ).[20]
Title: Εἰς τὸν ἅγιον Νικόλαον.
Edn: Anrich (1913: 392–417).
Date: Most probably an early work: Neophytos' reference to people who die
unjustly because their opponents bribe others (fol. 199α) is strongly reminiscent of
Neophytos' commentary on social conditions, which is very characteristic of his
early writings and which disappears in his post–1184 works.[21]

(xxv) Cited: *Panegyric 25* (fols. 199β–200α).
According to Tsiknopoulos, this *Panegyric* also survives in *Cod. Marcian. 575* (fols.
396β–397α) and in *Cod. Paris Gr. 1335* (fols. 7α–β) under the title: Περὶ τῶν θείων
καὶ φρικτῶν μυστηρίων.[22]
Title: Παρεξέτασις περὶ νεοφανοῦς διχονοίας.
The *Panegyric* refers to the theological controversy at the end of the twelfth century
over the corruptibility of the body and blood of Christ in the Eucharist.
Edn: Jugie (1949: 7–9).
Date: *c.* 1200. Neophytos refers to the dispute as a 'newly appeared' one. The
dispute culminated in a Synod held in 1199–1200, and Neophytos was possibly
informed of it by the bishop of Paphos Bakchos, who was involved in the dispute and
who also ratified Neophytos' *Typikon* in 1214.[23]

(xxvi) Cited: *Panegyric 26* (fols. 200β–206β).
Title: Εἰς τὸ γενέθλιον τοῦ σωτῆρος Χριστοῦ.
Edn: Extracts, Tsiknopoulos (1950d: 451–6).

(xxvii) Cited: *Panegyric 27* (fols. 206β–218α).
Title: Λόγος ἀντιρρητικὸς πρὸς ᾽Ιουδαίους.
Commentary on Biblical texts.
Date: A veiled reference to Isaac Komnēnos' rule (fol. 209α) places this *Panegyric* in
the period between 1184 and 1191.[24] More precisely, in a paper given at the Seminar
in Jewish and Hebrew Studies at the University of Cambridge (in November 1989)
B. Egglezakes dated this *Panegyric* to 1186 on the basis of three considerations: first,
Neophytos' reference to the Jews not being allowed to live in Jerusalem (fol. 212β)

---

[20] Tsiknopoulos (1958: 86).
[21] See ch. 8, esp. pp. 199ff.   [22] Tsiknopoulos (1958: 86).
[23] See *Typikon*, 92.7–12; Jugie (1949: 1–7); earlier, p. 39.   [24] See ch. 9, pp. 199–200.

indicates a pre-1189/90 date, since in that year Saladin did permit the Jews to return to the city; second, it is highly unlikely that Neophytos would have referred to Jerusalem just after its fall to Saladin (2 October 1187) without commenting on that event; and, third, the *Panegyric* was written for Christmas. It must, therefore, have been written at the end of 1186.

(xxviii) Cited: *Panegyric 28* (fols. 218α–219β).
Title: Εἰς τὸν πρωτοδιάκονον Στέφανον.

(ixxx) Cited: *Panegyric 29* (fols. 220α–230β).
Title: Εἰς τὸν ἅγιον ᾿Ιωάννην τὸν ᾿Ελεήμονα.
Edn: Tsiknopoulos (1966: 148–59).
Date: A reference to the fall of Constantinople makes 1204 a *terminus post quem*.

(xxx) Cited: *Panegyric 30* (fols. 230β–235β).
Title: Εἰς τὸν ἐν ἁγίοις πατέρα Γεννάδιον.
Edn: Delehaye (1907: 221–8); repr. Chatziioannou (1914). I use Delehaye's edition.

I(b) *Second book of Panegyrics*
MS: lost.
According to Tsiknopoulos three *Panegyrics* from this book survive: two in *Cod. 13* of the monastery of Hagias in Andros (*Cod. Adrien. monast. Hagias* 13, fols. 75β–81β and 82α–87β), and one in *Cod. Paris. Gr. 395* (fols. 122α–126α). The two *Homilies* in the Andros manuscript are both on the Adoration of the Cross.[25] The *Panegyric* in *Cod. Paris. Gr. 395* is on the *azyma*. Tsiknopoulos believed that this work belonged to Neophytos' *Second Book of Panegyrics*; while Petit thought that it belonged to the *Interpretation of the Commandments (Cod. Coisl. 287)*. Note however that Darrouzès thought that this *Homily* cannot be ascribed to Neophytos with any certainty (a view in which Darrouzès was alone).[26]

Cited: *Cod. 13, Andros, Panegyric 1*.
Title: ᾿Εν τῇ τρίτῃ Κυριακῇ τῆς ἀμώμου νηστείας λόγος περὶ τοῦ Σταυροῦ.
Edn: Tsiknopoulos (1969b: 321–4).

Cited: *Cod. 13, Andros, Panegyric 2*.
Title: ᾿Εν τῇ τετράδι τῆς μεσονηστίμου, ὁμιλία εἰς τὴν προσκύνησιν τοῦ Σταυροῦ.
Edn: Tsiknopoulos (1969b: 330–3).

Cited: *Panegyric in Cod. Paris. Gr. 395*.
Title: Περὶ τῆς ἱεραρχίας Χριστοῦ καὶ τῶν ἀζύμων.
Edn: Tsiknopoulos (1969b: 344–8).
Date: Neophytos' reference to 'the Latins' who 'commit the error of using unleavened bread [*azyma*] in their liturgy', and the lack of any reference to Constantinople's fall in 1204, have led scholars to suggest that this work was written after 1191 and before 1204.[27] I disagree. An interest in the *azyma* (a dispute which had already

---

[25] See Tsiknopoulos (1969b: 321–35; 1965: 88); Petit (1898–9: 266). For the MS see Lampros (1898: 151).
[26] Tsiknopoulos (1969b: 348–9); Petit (1898–9); Darrouzès (1950: 175).
[27] *Panegyric in Cod. Paris. Gr. 395*, 344.17–345.35. See Tsiknopoulos (1969b: 349); Egglezakes (1979–80: 52).

peaked in the eleventh century) is not in itself indicative of a post-1191 date. At any rate, this work is only partly concerned with the *azyma*: only slightly more than one folio is devoted to this matter, while the rest of the work discusses in far greater detail other matters, which are irrelevant to the Latins. Further, Neophytos refers to the westerners as 'the Latins', which contrasts very sharply with his veiled post-1191 references to them.[28] Finally, the references have an unmistakably informative and educational character, and lack the urgency and bitterness of Neophytos' post-1191 references: he simply points out that the Latins 'commit the error [*planontai*]' of using unleavened bread, which (he says, echoing a well-established Orthodox polemical view) relate to the Old Testament and the Exodus rather than to the New Testament and Christ's Passion. There is not one of the many extremely abusive words which Neophytos habitually used to characterise the Latins after 1191; and no trace either of the passion which informs his post-1191 polemics. In the light of the above, I suggest that this is a pre-1191 work.

I(c) *Third book of Panegyrics*
MS: lost
As Tsiknopoulos has shown, the third *Homily* by Neophytos in *Cod. 13* of the monastery of Hagias in Andros belonged to his *Third Book of Panegyrics*.[29]

Cited: *Cod. 13, Andros, Panegyric 3.*
MS: *Cod. Adrien. monast. Hagias*, 13, fols. 255α–266α.
Title: Περὶ τῶν ἑπτὰ οἰκουμενικῶν συνόδων, καὶ ὅτου χάριν καὶ πότε ἡ πρεσβυτέρα Ῥώμη καὶ ἡ νέα Ῥώμη διεστήκασιν ἀπ' ἀλλήλων.
Edn: Tsiknopoulos (1969b: 352–7); completed by Egglezakes (1979–80: 54).
Date: Tsiknopoulos suggests a post-1191 date because of Neophytos' concern with the *azyma* and the Schism; Egglezakes agrees, and considers 1204 to be a *terminus ante quem* because of the lack of references to the fall of Constantinople to the Latins in that year.[30] Yet, just as with Neophytos' *Panegyric in Cod. Paris. Gr. 395*, there are a number of internal indicators pointing at a pre-1191 date. Neophytos describes his work as a 'brief commemorative work concerning the Seven Oecumenical and great holy Councils; and concerning why and when the first Rome and the New Rome became distanced from each other'.[31] And indeed, about half of this *Panegyric* is devoted to a description of the Oecumenical Councils, their principal decisions and protagonists.[32] Neophytos opens his *Panegyric* by explaining that he had frequently wondered over a certain matter and had 'just found what I had been looking for; and, because it is of use, I wished to make it known to many people'.[33] He then proceeds to discuss the Councils, to return later to his initial statement. The matter in question, he says, 'is, for those who will pay attention, very valuable'. He had wondered, he says, when and why 'Rome distance[d] herself from New Rome, and [now] uses unleavened bread in the liturgy ... And having just found the answer in

---

[28] I am excluding the Recluse's references in *Letter 4*, which was meant to be read outside Cyprus; and in his *Typikon*, which was meant to be read to the monks inside the Enkleistra and not to the general public: *Typikon*, 81.12–19, 82.24–7.
[29] Tsiknopoulos (1969b: 358); and see also Lampros (1898: 159).
[30] Tsiknopoulos (1969b: 358); Egglezakes (1979–80: 52, 56).
[31] *Cod. 13, Andros, Panegyric 3*, 352.4–6.
[32] *Ibid.*, 352.11–354.94, 357.182–204. [33] *Ibid.*, 352.8–10.

one of the chronographers' books, . . . I shall summarily narrate it for the benefit of those who wish to know.'[34] The Recluse's main aim is thus clearly an educational one, and one which explicitly addresses his and his audience's intellectual curiosity. This is dramatically different from his usual post-1191 aim (which became directly and urgently political and polemical); and he closely links the present work to an accidental occurrence (of having just come across the relevant information) rather than to any political event. Further, despite the subject-matter, the 'Latins' as he openly calls them (by contrast again to his veiled post-1191 references to them), are comparatively only mildly attacked. For instance, Neophytos lists ten accusations against them, all or most of which he reproduced from a much longer list of twenty-seven accusations which he had before him.[35] Considering his virulent post-1191 anti-Latin propaganda, it is extremely unlikely that after 1191 Neophytos would have restrained himself to reproducing only some of a list of accusations against the westerners. It is equally unlikely that he would have referred to westerners with respect, as he does in the case of the western church leaders who took part in the Oecumenical Synods. In the light of the above considerations, I conclude that this *Panegyric* was written before 1191.

II . . . καὶ ἕτερα δύο βιβλία πλείστων ἐπιστολῶν ψυχοφελῶν πάνυ, ἐν οἷς καὶ ἀσκητικὰ κεφάλαια τετρακόσια καὶ τελώνια κδ' . . .[36]
MS: for both books, lost.
A few of Neophytos' letters survive:

(i) Cited: *Letter 1.*
Title: Περὶ τῆς Θεοσημείας ἀντίγραμμα πρὸς τὸν ἴδιον ἀδελφὸν Χρυσοστομίτην κῦρ 'Ιωάννην.
MS: lost.
Edn: Kyprianos (1779); repr. Chatziioannou (1914: 150–2). I use the Chatziioannou reprint.
Date: 1197 (as for *Sign of God*, below).

(ii) Cited: *Letter 2.*
Title: Πρὸς τινὰ προεστῶτα.
MS: *Cod. Coisl. Gr. 287* (fols. 201β–202β).
A letter about goodness, addressed to an unnamed abbot.
Edn: Extract, Eustratiades (1934: 215); also in Chatziioannou (1914).

(iii) Cited: *Letter 3.*
Title: Πρὸς Εὐθύμιον μοναχὸν καὶ ἱερέαν τὸν Χρυσοστομίτην.
MS: *Cod. Coisl. Gr. 287* (fols. 202β–207β).
A letter to a monk at the monastery of St John Chrysostom at Koutsovendēs, advising him on the building of a cell.
Edn: Eustratiades (1934: 215–18).

---

[34] *Ibid.*, 354.95–355.106.
[35] *Ibid.*, 355.127–356.144; completed by Egglezakes (1979–80: 54).
[36] *Typikon*, 83.14–15.

Cited: *Letter 4*.
Title: Περὶ τῶν κατὰ χώραν Κύπρον σκαιῶν.
MS: *Cod. Marcian. 575* (fols. 395β–396β) (fifteenth-century MS); *Cod. Paris. Gr. 1335* (fols. 6α–β) (fourteenth-century MS).
Neophytos' letter lamenting the misfortunes of Cyprus under Isaac Komnēnos and subsequently under the westerners.
Edn: Cobham (1908: 10–13); Cotelerius (1681, II: 457–62); Sathas (1873, II: 1–4); *MPG*, 135, 495–502; Tsiknopoulos (1969b: 336–43). This list is not exhaustive; I give only the most accessible editions. I use Cobham's edition.
Date: Securely dated to 1196, despite earlier disagreement amongst scholars.[37]

(v) Cited: *Letter 5*.
Title: Πρὸς τοὺς ἀτακτοῦντας καὶ λύοντας τὰ τῆς νηστείας προοίμια.
Neophytos' circular letter to all the people of the district of Paphos, concerning their breach of the rules of fasting during Lent.
MS: *Cod. Marcian Gr. 111, 4* (fols. 367β–368β); *B.M. Burney 54* (fols. 212α–214α); *B.M. Addit. 34060* (fol. 444α).
Edn: Tsiknopoulos (1951a: 61–4); also Tsiknopoulos (1969b: 404–7).
Date: During the years when the see of Paphos remained vacant, between bishop Bakchos (?–1194–8–?) and bishop Sabas (?–1209–?).[38]

(vi) Cited: *Bibliographical Note*.
Title: Βιβλιογραφικὸν σημείωμα.
MS: *Cod. Phil. Gr. 330*, fol. 132β (National Library, Vienna).
A bibliographical note accompanying a report of two Synodical acts.
Edn: Chatzipsaltes (1972–3: 125–6).
Date: After 1206, most possibly c. 1214.[39]

III ... καὶ βιβλίον πεντηκοντακέφαλον, ἐν ᾧ καὶ τὸ ᾆσμα τῶν ἀσμάτων ἑρμηνεύεται ...[40]
Cited: *Book of Fifty Chapters*.
MS: *Cod. 522*, National Library, Athens (fols. 8α–91β, 377α–424β) (this sixteenth-century MS contains the entire work); *Cod. 4285*, Monastery of Iberōn, Athos (contains only the *Song of Songs*). The following MSs contain only Neophytos' Prologue to the *Song of Songs*: *GR. 155/Mutin. 155*, Bibl. Estense, Modena (fifteenth-century MS); *Phil. 1411*, Berlin (fifteenth-century MS); *Matrit. 018*, National Library, Madrid (of 1556); *Matrit. 063*, National Library, Madrid (sixteenth-century MS); *Cod. Gr. Mon. 131*, Munich (sixteenth-century MS).
A book divided into fifty chapters which also contains the *Song of Songs* and a commentary on it. The fifty chapters contain commentary on a wide variety of subjects, ranging from Biblical texts to the human condition, contemporary events (earthquakes, droughts, battles), commentary on social conditions. The following is a description of *Cod. 522* of the National Library in Athens. The titles have been abbreviated.

---

[37] See Egglezakes (1979–80: 44).
[38] See Tsiknopoulos (1969b: 408–9) and Egglezakes (1979–80: 52–3).
[39] Chatzipsaltes (1972–3: 128).   [40] *Typikon*, 83.19.

270   *Appendix*

Title: (Index) (fols. 8α–10α).
Edn: Dyovouniotes (1937: 41–3).[41]

(i) Title: Ἐν ποίαις ἀνάγκαις ἀδελφοὶ χρήσιμοι ἔστωσαν (fols. 11α–12α).
Edn: Dyovouniotes (1937: 43–4).

(ii) Title: περὶ τοῦ ποῖον ἄρα καλὸν πάντων πρωτεύει τῶν καλῶν (fols. 12α–β).

(iii) Title: Περὶ τοῦ διατὶ ὁ Θεὸς ἀπήρτισε τὸν κόσμον ἐν ἓξ ἡμέραις (fol. 12β).

Chapters iv–ix are lost.

(x) Title: Περὶ τοῦ τὶ ἐστὶν ὁ σκόλοψ ἐν τῇ σαρκί (fols. 13α–β).

(xi) Title: Περὶ τοῦ Ἰὼβ καὶ περὶ ὑπομονῆς (fols. 13β–24α).
Edn: Extracts (from fols. 15α–16β), Tsiknopoulos (1954a: 47–8).

(xii) Title: Περὶ τοῦ πῶς οἱ ἅγιοι τὰς θλίψεις γενναίως ὑπέφερον καὶ περὶ ὑπομονῆς καὶ διακονίας (fols. 24α–28β).
Edn: Extracts (from fols. 25β–26α and 28α–β), Tsiknopoulos (1954a: 48–9).

(xiii) Title: Περὶ μωσαϊκῶν μαρτυριῶν (fols. 28β–30α).

(xiv) Title: Περὶ τοῦ ἐν ἀρχῇ ἐποίησεν ὁ Θεὸς τὸν οὐρανὸν καὶ τὴν γῆν (fols. 30α–32β).

(xv) Title: Περὶ τοῦ ὅσοι κτηνώδη βίον διανύουσι (fols. 32β–34β).

(xvi) Title: Ὑπόδειγμα τῆς ἀνθρωπίνης φύσεως (fols. 34β–35β).
Edn: Tsiknopoulos (1954b: 76–7).

(xvii) Title: Περὶ τοῦ ἐν ποίῳ τὶς τρόπῳ πρὸς κλαυθμὸν καὶ δάκρυον κατανύγεται (fols. 36α–β).
Edn: Extract (from fols. 36α–β), Tsiknopoulos (1958: 131).

(xviii) Title: Ὅτι ἐξ ὧν τις ἀποφθέγγεται ἢ σιωπᾶ (fols. 36β–37β).

(xix) Title: Περὶ διαφόρων θεωριῶν καὶ λόγων καὶ μνημῶν (fols. 37β–40β).

(xx) Title: Περὶ μνήμης καὶ θείου πάθους (fols. 40β–41α).

(xxi) Title: Περὶ μνήμης μαρτύρων (fols. 41α–42β).
Edn: Extract (from fols. 41α–β), Tsiknopoulos (1958: 131).

(xxii) Title: Περὶ τοῦ παραδείσου τὸ φυτόν (fols. 42β–44α).

(xxiii) Title: Περὶ τοῦ πῶς μελωδοῦσιν ἢ θρηνωδοῦσί τινες, τῆς ἰδίας ἕκαστος μνημονεύων πατρίδος, εἴτε τῆς νῦν εἴτε τῆς πάλαι (fols. 44α–46α).

(xxiv) Title: Περὶ τοῦ Ἀδάμ (fols. 46α–52β).
Edn: Extracts (from fols. 46α–49β and 51α), Tsiknopoulos (1954c: 146–8).

---

[41] Also by Tsiknopoulos (1953b: 73–4).

(xxv) Title: Περὶ τοῦ φθόνου τοῦ Κάϊν κατὰ τοῦ ἀδελφοῦ αὐτοῦ (fols. 52β–55β).
Edn: Extract (from fols. 53β–54α), Tsiknopoulos (1958: 131).

(xxvi) Title: Περὶ τοῦ πῶς αὐθαιρέτως ὁ Λάμεχ τὴν τοῦ φόνου πεποίηκεν ἐξαγόρευσιν (fols. 55β–56β).

(xxvii) Title: Περὶ τοῦ ἐμπεσόντος εἰς τοὺς ληστάς (fols. 56β–58β).
Edn: Tsiknopoulos (1954d: 173–4).

(xxviii) Title: Περὶ μετανοίας (fols. 58β–61β).
Ed: Extracts (from fols. 58β–60β, 60β and 61β).
Tsiknopoulos (1954g: 292–3; 1954d: 174).

(xxix) Title: Περὶ τοῦ ὅτι πλῆθος θυσιῶν ἐκ κακουργούντων ὁ Θεὸς οὐ προσδέχεται (fols. 61β–73α).
Edn: Extracts (from fols. 66α, 66β–67α, 67α–β, 67β–68β, 69α, 70α, 70β, 70β–71α, 71β, 71β–72α, 73α), Tsiknopoulos (1954b: 77–8; 1954d: 174, 175; 1958: 131–2).

(xxx) Title: Περὶ τῶν ἀκουόντων τῶν θείων προσταγμάτων (fols. 73α–75β).

(xxxi) Title: Περὶ τοῦ εὐσεβεστάτου βασιλέως ἡμῶν κυροῦ Μανουὴλ τοῦ Κομνηνοῦ (fols. 75β–77β).
Edn: Dyovouniotes (1937: 45–6).

(xxxii) Title: Περὶ τῆς γενομένης ἀνομβρίας καὶ ἀφορίας καὶ δυσχερείας τοῦ ἔτους (fols. 77β–78α).
Edn: Extract (from fol. 78α), Tsiknopoulos (1945e: 213).

(xxxiii) Title: Περὶ τῆς νέας Κυριακῆς, ὅτε ἐγένετο σκότος (fols. 78α–β).
Edn: Extract (from fols. 78α–β and 78β), Tsiknopoulos (1954e: 213–14).

(xxxiv) Title: Περὶ τοῦ ἡλίου ὁ σκοτασμός (fols. 78β–79α).
Edn: Extract (from fol. 79α), Tsiknopoulos (1954e: 214).

(xxxv) Title: Περὶ τοῦ γῇ ἐάν ἁμάρτῃ μοι (fols. 79β–81α).

(xxxvi) Title: Εἰς τὴν παραβολὴν τοῦ δεσπότου, τὴν φάσκουσαν ἄνθρωπός τις ἐποίησε δεῖπνον (fols. 81α–82α).

(xxxvii) Title: Περὶ ὑπακοῆς ἁγίων πρὸς Θεὸν (fols. 82α–83α).

(xxxviii) Title: Ὅτι ἡ ὑπακοὴ ὠφέλιμος (fols. 83α–β).

(ixl) Title: Περὶ τοῦ μαργονίου παραβολή (fols. 83β–88α).

(xl) Title: Περὶ τοῦ τίνες οἱ Θεοί (fols. 88α–91β, 377α–β).

(xli) Title: Περὶ τοῦ διατὶ ἀπεσταλμένον ἑαυτὸν λέγει ὁ Χριστός (fols. 377β–378α).

(xlii) Title: Παροιμία πρὸς τοὺς δοκοῦντας τιμᾶν τὸν πατέρα (fols. 378α–379α).

(xliii) Title: Περὶ τῆς τοῦ βίου ματαιότητος (fols. 379β–383α).

(xliv) Title: Περὶ θανάτου αἰφνιδίου (fols. 383α–386β).
Edn: Extract (from fols. 386α–β). Tsiknopoulos (1954e: 214).

(xlv) Title: *Περὶ ταφῆς* (fols. 386β–389α).
Edn: Extracts (from fols. 387α–β), Tsiknopoulos (1954e: 215).

(xlvi) Title: *Περὶ ἀναστάσεως* (fols. 389β–394α).

(xlvii) Title: *Περὶ τῆς δευτέρας τοῦ Χριστοῦ παρουσίας* (fols. 394β–396β).

(xlviii) Title: *Περὶ τοῦ ἐν ποίῳ τρόπῳ καινωθήσεται ἡ γῆ* (fols. 396β–400β).
Edn: Extract (from fols. 398α–β), Tsiknopoulos (1958: 132).

(xlix) Title: *Περὶ κρίσεως* (fols. 400β–405α).
Edn: Extract (from fols. 403β–404α and from 404β–405α), Tsiknopoulos (1958: 132; 1954g: 293).

(l) Title: *Περὶ τοῦ νυμφίου* (fols. 405α–412β).
Edn: Extracts (from fols. 405α–406β and 412α–β), Tsiknopoulos (1954g: 293–4) and Dyovouniotes (1937: 44–5).

Title: *Πρόλογος εἰς τὸ ᾆσμα τῶν ᾀσμάτων* (fols. 412β–414β).
Edn: Dyovouniotes (1937: 47–8).

Title: *Τὸ ᾆσμα τῶν ᾀσμάτων* (fols. 414β–421α).

Title: *Συνοπτικὴ ἑρμηνεία* (fols. 421β–424β).
Edn: Extract (from fols. 421β–424β), Dyovouniotes (1937: 48–9).

Date: the *Book of Fifty Chapters* has been dated by scholars to the years between 1176 and 1181.[42] Egglezakes dates the work to 'about 1179'.[43] The precise year of 1179, however, can be deduced as the date of this work from internal textual evidence: Neophytos refers to a partial sun eclipse as having occurred 'in the previous year' (fol. 78β). According to Grumel an 86 per cent sun eclipse occurred on 13 September 1178 at 1.30 p.m.[44] Neophytos' references to other events, vaguely referred to in chronological terms, link well with this date: another, total sun eclipse which Neophytos describes as having occurred 'a few years ago' (fol. 78α) must be the one which, according to Grumel, occurred on 11 April 1176; while the battle of Myriokephalon of 1176 is also described as having taken place 'in these years' (fol. 75β).

IV ... *καὶ ἕτερον τῆς Θεοσημείας*...[45]
Cited: *Sign of God*.
MS: lost.
Edn: Kyprianos (1779); repr. Chatziioannou (1914: 137–50), together with Neophytos' letter to his brother John (*Letter 1*), the liturgy and the poem which the Recluse composed after his survival from a fall: Chatziioannou (1914: 153–6). I use Chatziioannou's reprint.
Date: Neophytos' fall dates to 1197, despite earlier disagreement amongst scholars.[46] The work undoubtedly dates from the same year.

42 Tsiknopoulos (1958: 121–2; 1967: 351).
43 Egglezakes (1979–80: 39).   44 Grumel (1958: 466).
45 *Typikon*, 83.20.   46 Petit (1898–9: 261); Mango and Hawkins (1966: 124).

V ... καὶ ἕτερον ἑρμηνεία τῆς ἐξαημέρου ἐν λόγοις ιστ' ...⁴⁷
Cited: *Hexaēmeros*.
MS: lost. Seven folios from a MS containing this work were discovered in recent years in the monastery of the Enkleistra. They are in very poor condition.
Edn: Kyprianos (1779); repr. Chatziioannou (1914: 157–231). I use Chatziioannou's reprint.
Date: Neophytos refers to his recent move to the upper *enkleistra*, the date for which is 1197. The *Hexaēmeros* must therefore be dated to 1197 or very shortly after.⁴⁸

VI ... καὶ ἕτερον ἑρμηνεία τῶν ψαλμῶν ἐν λόγοις ιβ' ...⁴⁹
Cited: *Psalms*.
MS: *Cod. 3628–94*, monastery of Dionysiou, Athos (of 1322); *Cod. 551*, monastery of St Sabas, now in the Patriarchal Library at Jerusalem (of 1321); *Cod. 4182–62*, monastery of Ibērōn, Athos (fourteenth-century MS); *Cod. 6280–773*, monastery of Panteleēmonos, Athos (sixteenth-century MS); *Cod. 533*, monastery of Batopediou, Athos (of 1664).
The book contains ten interpretative *Homilies* on the Psalms and two *Homilies* interpreting the *Odes*.
Edn: Chatziioannou (1935) (from *Cod. 3628–94*, monastery of Dionysiou).
Date: References to Neophytos' fall while digging in 1197 indicate that this work was written in or very shortly after 1197.⁵⁰

VII ... καὶ ἕτερον ἑρμηνεία κανόνων τῶν δώδεκα δεσποτικῶν ἑορτῶν ...⁵¹
MS: lost.
The *Cod. Lesb. Leim. 2* had for long been regarded by scholars as containing nine of these twelve *Homilies*; though Ehrhard disagreed, believing that the *Homilies* belong to the two lost books of *Panegyrics*.⁵² It now seems clear that the *Homilies* in the Lesbian manuscript do not belong to the Ἑρμηνεία Κανόνων.⁵³

VIII ... καὶ ἕτερον δωδεκάλογον, τὸ πρόχειρον τοῦ ἐγκλείστου, ἐν ᾧ τεσσαρακονταετίας καὶ πεντηκονταετίας καὶ φυσιολογίας ἀναφορά ...⁵⁴
MS: lost.

IX ... καὶ ἕτερον δισδεκάλογογον, καινῆς καὶ παλαιᾶς νομοθεσίας εὐσύνοπτοι ἑρμηνεῖαι δεσποτικῶν ἐντολῶν ...⁵⁵
Cited: *Interpretation of the Commandments*.
MS: *Cod. Coisl. Gr. 287* (thirteenth-century MS).

---

⁴⁷ *Typikon*, 83.21.   ⁴⁸ *Hexaēmeros*, 169.17–170.16.   ⁴⁹ *Typikon*, 83.22.
⁵⁰ *Psalms*, 60.   ⁵¹ *Typikon*, 83.23.
⁵² Petit (1898–9: 265); Delehaye (1907: 278); Tsiknopoulos (1958: 147–51; 1967: 366ff.); Ehrhard (1943: 683–4).
⁵³ Egglezakes (1978); Congourdeau (1975–7: 120–32); Toniolo (1974: 189ff.).
⁵⁴ *Typikon*, 83.24–5.   ⁵⁵ *Ibid.*, 83.26–7.

The first and part of the second *Homily* are lost. The end of the second and the further eight *Homilies* survive, bearing Neophytos' autograph corrections (fols. 1α–197β). These are followed by another *Homily* (fols. 198α–201β) and two letters of Neophytos' (fols. 201β–207β).[56] H. Delehaye believed that the remaining *Homilies* are contained in the *Cod. Paris. Gr. 395.*[57]

Edn: The titles of the *Homilies* have been edited, amongst others, by Montfaucon (1715: 404, no. 282; 1739: 1062); Delisle (1871–4); Devreese (1945: 271–2).[58]

The surviving *Homilies* are as follows (the titles have been abbreviated):

(ii) Title: Ἐκ τῶν προσκαίρων τὰ αἰώνια καθορᾶν (fols. 1α–4α).
Edn: Extract (from fol. 2β), Tsiknopoulos (1958: 114).

(iii) Title: Περὶ τοῦ θείου βαπτίσματος καὶ τῆς ἁγίας ἀγάπης (fols. 4α–16α).
Edn: Extracts (from fols. 5β, 9β, 11β), Tsiknopoulos (1958: 115).

(iv) Title: Λόγος ἀπολογητικός (fols. 16α–35α).
Edn: Extracts (from fols. 28β–29α and 29β–30α), Tsiknopoulos (1958: 115).

(v) Title: Γενικὰ περὶ τῶν πέντε αἰσθήσεων (fols. 35β–65α).
Edn: Extracts (from fols. 62α–β), Egglezakes (1979–80: 36); and (from fols. 41α, 42β, 63β, 61β–63α, 57β–60α, 60α–β, 61α), Tsiknopoulos (1958: 116; 1955b: 145–7).

(vi) Title: Ἐρευνᾶτε τὰς Γραφάς (fols. 65α–83α).
Edn: Extracts (from fols. 66β–69α, 80α–β, 81α–83β, 71α–β, 77α–β), Tsiknopoulos (1955a: 47–9; 1958: 116).

(vii) Title: Λύχνος τοῦ σώματος ὁ ὀφθαλμός (fols. 83β–117α).
Edn: Extracts (from fols. 89α–β, 95α, 96β), Tsiknopoulos (1958: 116).

(viii) Title: Μὴ κρίνετε καὶ οὐ μὴ κριθῆτε (fols. 117α–144β).
Edn: Extract (from fols. 139β, 140α), Tsiknopoulos (1958: 116–17).

(ix) Title: Τὰ ἐπίλοιπα τοῦ μὴ κρίνετε καὶ οὐ μὴ κριθῆτε (fols. 145α–171β).
Edn: Extracts (from fols. 146α–β, 147β), Egglezakes (1979–1980: 38 and 37, respectively); and (from fols. 153α–β, 154α, 154β, 155α, 155β–157β, 157α–β), Tsiknopoulos (1956a: 180–2; 1958: 117).

(x) Title: Μάθετε ἀπ' ἐμοῦ ὅτι πρᾶός εἰμι καὶ ταπεινὸς τῇ καρδίᾳ (fols. 172α–197β).
Edn: Extracts (from fols. 182α–β, 197α). Tsiknopoulos (1958: 117).

Date: Comparison of passages from the *Interpretation of the Commandments* with the *Book of Fifty Chapters* of 1179 allows us to date the former with precision. In the *Book of Fifty Chapters* Neophytos wrote that the current year was the second of a drought. These two years of drought had been preceded by one of rain, which had succeeded yet another dry year (*Cod. 522*, National Library, Athens, fols. 77β–78α). It is thus obvious that the winter months of 1175–6 brought no rain; that rain fell in 1176–7; and did not in 1177–8 and 1178–9. In the *Interpretation of the Commandments* Neophytos refers to a year of drought which rain had just brought to

---

[56] For the letters see earlier, p. 268.
[57] Delehaye (1907: 278). See earlier, p. 266.
[58] See also Sophronios of Leontopolis (1934).

an end (*Cod. Coisl. Gr. 287*, fols 188β–189α). This could refer to no other but the rainy season of 1176–7, and Neophytos' characterisation of the first rain as 'late in the season' helps us date the *Interpretation of the Commandments* to late winter or the spring of 1176.

Following the *Interpretation of the Commandments, Cod. Coisl. Gr. 287* contains a *Homily* of Neophytos'.
Cited: *Homily* in *Cod. Coisl. Gr. 287.*
Title: Παραινετικὴ ὁμιλία *(fols. 198α–201β).*
The manuscript further contains two letters of Neophytos (*Letter 2, Letter 3*).

X . . . καὶ ἑτέρα ἡ τῶν κατηχήσεων βίβλος . . .[59]
Cited: *Catecheseis.*
MS: *Cod. Paris. Suppl. Gr. 1317* (thirteenth-century MS). Its 222 folios contain Neophytos' autograph corrections.[60]
The MS contains fifty-six *Catecheseis* divided in two 'books' of twenty-four and thirty-two *Catecheseis* respectively. The titles of the *Catecheseis* appear below in an abbreviated form.

X(a) *First book of Catecheseis*

Title: Πίναξ (fols. 2α–5β).
Edn: Ehrhard (1941: 684–6); Tsiknopoulos (1958: 161–5).

Title: Πρόλογος (fols. 6α–10α).
Edn: Tsiknopoulos (1952b: 268–70).

(i) Title: Εἰς τὴν Κυριακὴν πρὸ τῆς Χριστοῦ γεννήσεως (fols. 10α–13α).

(ii) Title: Περὶ τοῦ Χριστοῦ γενεθλίων (fols. 13α–18α).

(iii) Title: Περὶ τῆς ἁγίας περιτομῆς (fols. 18α–25β).

(iv) Title: Εἰς τὴν ἁγίαν Ὑπαπαντήν (fols. 26α–34β).
Edn: Toniolo (1974: 304–14).

Title: Περὶ τῶν Εὐαγγελίων τῆς Θεομήτορος (fols. 35α–40β).
Edn: Toniolo (1974: 284–90).

(vi) Title: Κυριακὴ πρώτη τῶν νηστειῶν (fols. 41α–46β).

(vii) Title: Κυριακὴ δεύτερη τῶν νηστειῶν (fols. 46β–48β).
Edn: Extract (from fol. 48α), Tsiknopoulos (1958: 168).

(viii) Title: Κυριακὴ γ' τῶν νηστειῶν (fols. 49α–51β).

(ix) Title: Κυριακὴ δ' τῶν νηστειῶν (fols. 52α–57β).
Edn: Extracts (from fols. 52β–53α and 56α–57β), Tsiknopoulos (1958: 169).

(x) Title: Περὶ ἑβδομάδος τῶν Βαΐων (fols. 57β–63β).

(xi) Title: Εἰς τὴν Κυριακὴν τῶν Βαΐων (fols. 63β–67β).

[59] *Typikon*, 83.28.
[60] On the MS see Astruc and Concasty (1960: 602–8); Darrouzès (1950: 185–6); Toniolo (1974: 191).

(xii) Title: *Εἰς τὸν περὶ Ἀναστάσεως λόγον* (fols. 67β–71α).
Edn: Extract (from fols. 69α–β), Tsiknopoulos (1958: 169).

(xiii) Title: *Περὶ ταπεινοφροσύνης* (fols. 71α–75β).

(xiv) Title: *Περὶ τῆς Ἀναλήψεως* (fols. 75β–80α).

(xv) Title: *Περὶ τῶν ἐν Νικαίᾳ ἁγίων πατέρων* (fols. 80α–84α).
Edn: Extract (from fols. 83α–84α), Egglezakes (1979–80: 56–7).

(xvi) Title: *Περὶ τοῦ ἁγίου Πνεύματος* (fols. 213α–220β).
Edn: Extract (from fols. 214α, 214β, 215α), Tsiknopoulos (1958: 170).

(xvii) Title: *Περὶ τῆς ἁγίας Τριάδος* (fols. 84α–88β).
Edn: Extracts (from fols. 86β–87β), Egglezakes (1979–80: 57–8).

(xviii) Title: *Εἰς τοὺς ἀποστόλους* (fols. 88β–93α).

(xix) Title: *Εἰς τὴν ἁγίαν Μαρῖναν* (fols. 93α–98α).
Edn: Extracts, Tsiknopoulos (1966: 160–1); extracts also in Tsiknopoulos (1955c: 326–9).

(xx) Title: *Περὶ τῆς Μεταμορφώσεως* (fols 98α–100β).
Edn: Egglezakes (1973).

(xxi) Title: *Περὶ τῆς κοιμήσεως τῆς Θεοτόκου* (fols. 100β–103β).
Edn: Toniolo (1974: 292–4).

(xxii) Title: *Εἰς τὴν ἀποτομὴν τῆς κάρας τοῦ Ἰωάννου* (fols. 104α–107β).

(xxiii) Title: *Εἰς τὸ γενέθλιον τῆς Θεομήτορος* (fols. 107β–109β).
Edn: Toniolo (1974: 296–8).

(xxiv) Title: *Εἰς τὴν εἴσοδον τὴν ἐν τῷ ναῷ τῆς Θεομήτορος* (fols. 109β–112α).
Edn: Toniolo (1974: 300–2).

X(b) *Second book of Catecheseis*

(i) Title: *Κυριακὴ αʹ* (fols. 112β–117α).

(ii) Title: *Κυριακὴ βʹ* (fols. 117α–120β).

(iii) Title: *Κυριακὴ γʹ* (fols. 120β–124α).

(iv) Title: *Κυριακὴ δʹ* (fols. 124α–128α).

(v) Title: *Κυριακὴ εʹ* (fols. 128α–131α).

(vi) Title: *Κυριακὴ στʹ* (fols. 131α–135α).

(vii) Title: *Κυριακὴ ζʹ* (fols. 135α–138β).

(viii) Title: *Κυριακὴ ηʹ* (fols 138a–142a).

(ix) Title: *Κυριακὴ θʹ* (fols. 142α–145β).

(x) Title: *Κυριακὴ ιʹ* (fols. 145β–148β).

(xi) Title: *Κυριακὴ ιαʹ* (fols. 148β–151β).

(xii) Title: *Κυριακὴ ιβʹ* (fols. 151β–155α).
Edn: Extract (from fol. 154α), Egglezakes (1979–80: 39, note 31).

(xiii) Title: *Κυριακὴ ιγ'* (fols. 155α–157α).

(xiv) Title: *Κυριακὴ ιδ'* (fols. 157α–160β).

(xv, xvi) Lost.

(xvii) Title: *Κυριακὴ ιζ'* (fols. 161α–162β).

(xviii) Title: *Κυριακὴ ιη'* (fols. 162β–165β).

(xix) Title: *Κυριακὴ ιθ'* (fols. 165β–168β).

(xx) Title: *Κυριακὴ κ'* (fols. 168β–172β).
Edn: Extract (from fol. 171α), Tsiknopoulos (1958: 169–70).

(xxi) Title: *Κυριακὴ κα'* (fols. 172β–176α).

(xxii) Title: *Κυριακὴ κβ'* (fols. 176α–179α).
Edn: Extracts (from fols. 177β, 178α), Tsiknopoulos (1958: 170).

(xxiii) Title: *Κυριακὴ κγ'* (fols. 179α–182α).

(xxiv) Title: *Κυριακὴ κδ'* (fols. 182α–185α).
Edn: Extracts (from all folios), Tsiknopoulos (1953c: 111–12).

(xxv) Title: *Κυριακὴ κε'* (fols. 185α–188α).

(xxvi) Title: *Κυριακὴ κστ'* (fols. 188α–191β).

(xxvii) Title: *Κυριακὴ κζ'* (fols. 191β–194β).

(xxviii) Title: *Κυριακὴ κη'* (fols. 194β–196β).

(xxix) Title: *Κυριακὴ κθ'* (fols. 196β–200α).

(xxx) Title: *Κυριακὴ λ'* (fols. 200α–205α).
Edn: Extract (from fols. 200α–β), Tsiknopoulos (1958: 170).

(xxxi) Title: *Κυριακὴ λα'* (fols. 205α–208α).

(xxxii) Title: *Κυριακὴ λβ' του 'Ασώτου* (fols. 208α–212β).

Date: a late work, of *c.* 1214.[61]

Following the *Catecheiseis* the manuscript contains part of a tract of Neophytos' on the Pentecost (fols. 213α–220β).
Date: The tract contains a reference to Neophytos' *Catecheisis* on the Holy Trinity (fols. 84α–88β) on fol. 213β. It appears, therefore, that it was written shortly after the *Catecheiseis, c.* 1214.

XI ... *καὶ ἄλλο μικρὸν κατανυκτικῶν στιχηρῶν* ...[62]
MS: Lost.

XII ... *καὶ ἄλλο ἡ παροῦσα τυπικὴ διάταξις* ...[63]
Cited: *Typikon.*

---

[61] See Egglezakes (1979–80: 56).   [62] *Typikon*, 83.29.   [63] *Ibid.*, 83.30.

MS: *Laing III 811*, Bibl. Univers. 224, University of Edinburgh.[64]
Edn: Kyprianos (1779), repr. Chatziioannou (1914); Warren (1882); Tsiknopoulos (1969a: 69–104). I use the Tsiknopoulos edition.
Date: 1214.[65]

XIII ... καὶ ἄλλο πάλιν, τὸ καλούμενον τελευταῖον ...[66]
MS: lost.

XIV A special problem is presented by the *Cod. Lesb. Leim. 2*. This manuscript contains nine *Homilies* of Neophytos', which scholars have not been able to ascribe with certainty to any of the works mentioned by him in his *Typikon*.[67] The nine *Homilies* are the following (the titles have been abbreviated):

(i) Cited: *Cod. Lesb. Leim 2, Homily 1*.
Title: Εἰς τὰ Εἰσόδια τῆς Θεοτόκου (fols 248α–260α).
Edn: Toniolo (1974: 210–36).
Date: Undoubtedly very late in Neophytos' life: he refers to his very advanced age and approaching death.[68] Therefore, dated *c.* 1214.

(ii) Cited: *Cod. Lesb. Leim. 2, Homily 2*.
Title: Εἰς τὴν γέννησιν τοῦ Χριστοῦ (fols. 260α–273β).
Edn: Extracts (from fols. 260α–β, 260β–261β, 262α, 262β–263β, 273β), Tsiknopoulos (1956b: 205–8).
Date: According to Marie-Hélène Congourdeau, all these surviving *Homilies* except the first one were written before 1170; according to Egglezakes the last eight *Homilies* date from about 1176; according to Toniolo this is a very late *Homily*.[69] None of these views is conclusive, but there is some internal evidence to support the view that this *Homily* is of late date: Neophytos refers to a *logos* of his concerning the Holy Cross (*Cod. Lesb. Leim. 2*, fol. 262α). If this refers either to *Panegyric 7* or to *Panegyric 8*, then this *Homily* is at least a post-1191 one; and if it refers to *Panegyric 7*, then it was written in or after 1196.

(iii) Cited: *Cod. Lesb. Leim. 2, Homily 3*.
Title: Εἰς τὰ ἅγια φῶτα (fols. 273β–285α).
Edn: Congourdeau (1975–7: 113–85).
Date: Unknown. (Congourdeau and Egglezakes as in *Homily 2* above.)

(iv) Cited: *Cod. Lesb. Leim. 2, Homily 4*.
Title: Εἰς τὴν Ὑπαπαντήν (fols. 285β–297β).
Date: Unknown. (Congourdeau and Egglezakes as in *Homily 2* above.)

(v) Cited: *Cod. Lesb. Leim. 2, Homily 5*.
Title: Εἰς τὸν Εὐαγγελισμὸν τῆς Θεοτόκου (fols. 298α–306β).
Edn: Toniolo (1974: 238–62).

[64] On the MS see Darrouzès (1957: 143).
[65] See Laurent (1949b).   [66] *Typikon*, 83.31.
[67] See also earlier, Appendix, VII, *Interpretation of the Canons*.
[68] See Toniolo (1974); Congourdeau (1975–7: 129, 132); Egglezakes (1978).
[69] Congourdeau (1975–7: 130–2); Egglezakes (1978); Toniolo (1974).

Date: Congourdeau and Egglezakes as in *Homily 2* above; while Toniolo believes this to be the earliest of Neophytos' *Homilies*.[70] There is, however, an indication that it was written in the closing years of the twelfth century: in *Panegyric 21* (dated to 1197 or shortly thereafter) Neophytos says that he would be presenting a *Homily* on the Annunciation when its feast-day came.[71] The meaning is, admittedly, unclear: Neophytos could be referring to the reading out rather than the writing of a *Homily*; or he may well have written more than one work for the same feast-day (cf., e.g., *Panegyric 7* and *Panegyric 8*). The date of this *Homily* remains uncertain, though there is a possibility that it is a late work.

(vi) Cited: *Cod. Lesb. Leim. 2, Homily 6.*
Title: Εἰς τὴν γέννησιν τοῦ Ἰωάννου τοῦ Προδρόμου (fols. 307α–312α).
Date: Unknown. (Congourdeau and Egglezakes as in *Homily 2* above.)

(vii) Cited: *Cod. Lesb. Leim. 2, Homily 7.*
Title: Εἰς τοὺς ἀποστόλους Πέτρον καὶ Παῦλον καὶ εἰς τοὺς λοιποὺς ἀποστόλους (fols. 312α–318β).
Date: Unknown. (Congourdeau and Egglezakes as in *Homily 2* above.)

(viii) Cited: *Cod. Lesb. Leim. 2, Homily 8.*
Title: Εἰς τὴν μεταμόρφωσιν τοῦ Ἰησοῦ Χριστοῦ (fols. 318β–325β).
Date: Unknown. (Congourdeau and Egglezakes as in *Homily 2* above.)

(ix) Cited: *Homily 9* in *Cod. Lesb. Leim. 2.*
Title: Εἰς τὴν κοίμησιν τῆς Θεοτόκου (fols. 325β–333β).
Edn: Toniolo (1974: 264–82).
Date: Congourdeau and Egglezakes as in *Homily 2* above. Internal evidence suggests a late date for this *Homily*: in his very late *Panegyric 4*, Neophytos states that he will speak of the Dormition when that feast-day arrives.[72] As in *Homily 5*, above, Neophytos' meaning is unclear (as to whether he would write or read out a *Homily*, or whether the *Homily* he refers to is the one in question here). However, another possible indication of a late, post-1191 date, is the *Panegyric*'s polemical anti-Latin content.[73] On the balance of this internal evidence I would suggest a post-1191 date.

CONCLUSION ON DATES

WORKS OF KNOWN OR SUGGESTED DATE

Work (MS)	*Date*
Panegyric 16 (Cod. Paris. Gr. 1189)	1170 *terminus post quem*
Interpretation of the Commandments (Cod. Coisl. Gr. 287)	1176
Panegyric 17 (Cod. Paris. Gr. 1189)	1176 or soon thereafter
Panegyric 15 (Cod. Paris. Gr. 1189)	1176 or soon thereafter
Book of Fifty Chapters (Cod. Athen. 522)	1179
Panegyric 24 (Cod. Paris. Gr. 1189)	1185 *terminus ante quem*
Panegyric 27 (Cod. Paris. Gr. 1189)	1186
Panegyric 5 (Cod. Paris. Gr. 1189)	1187 or very soon thereafter

[70] Toniolo (1974: 190).   [71] *Panegyric 21*, 537 [113].1–3.
[72] *Panegyric 4*, 529 [105].4–6.   [73] See ch. 10, pp. 230ff.

Panegyric 23 (Cod. Paris. Gr. 1189)	1187 or very soon thereafter
Panegyric 20 (Cod. Paris. Gr. 1189)	1191 *terminus ante quem*
Panegyric in Cod. Paris. Gr. 395	1191 *terminus ante quem*
Cod. 13, Andros, Panegyric 3	1191 *terminus ante quem*
Panegyric 8 (Cod. Paris. Gr. 1189)	1191 *terminus post quem*
Cod. Lesb. Leim. 2, Homily 9	1191 *terminus post quem*
Panegyric 7 (Cod. Paris. Gr. 1189)	1196
Letter 4 (Cod. Marcian. 575, i.a.)	1196
Panegyric 6 (Cod. Paris. Gr. 1189)	between 1191 and 1204, possibly 1197
Letter 1	1197
Sign of God	1197
Hexaēmeros	1197 or very soon thereafter
Psalms (Cod. 3628–94, Monē Dionysiou, i.a.)	1197 or soon thereafter
Panegyric 21 (Cod. Paris. Gr. 1189)	1197 or very soon thereafter
Letter 5 (Cod. Marcian. Gr. 111 i.a.)	between 1198 and 1209
Panegyric 25 (Cod. Paris. Gr. 1189)	*c.* 1200
Panegyric 9 (Cod. Paris. Gr. 1189)	1204 or very soon thereafter
Panegyric 13 (Cod. Paris. Gr. 1189)	1204 *terminus post quem*
Panegyric 29 (Cod. Paris. Gr. 1189)	1204 *terminus post quem*
Panegyric 4 (Cod. Paris. Gr. 1189)	*c.* 1214
Bibliographical Note (Cod. Phil. Gr. 330, Vienna)	*c.* 1214
Cod. Lesb. Leim. 2, Homily 1	*c.* 1214
Catecheseis (Cod. Paris. Suppl. Gr. 1317)	*c.* 1214
Typikon (Laing III 811, Bibl. Univers. 224, Edinburgh)	1214

WORKS OF UNKNOWN DATE

(*c.* 1170 *terminus post quem*; 1214 *terminus ante quem*)

Panegyric 1 (Cod. Paris. Gr. 1189)
Panegyric 2 (Cod. Paris. Gr. 1189)
Panegyric 3 (Cod. Paris. Gr. 1189)
Panegyric 10 (Cod. Paris. Gr. 1189)
Panegyric 11 (Cod. Paris. Gr. 1189)
Panegyric 12 (Cod. Paris. Gr. 1189)
Panegyric 14 (Cod. Paris. Gr. 1189)
Panegyric 18 (Cod. Paris. Gr. 1189)
Panegyric 19 (Cod. Paris. Gr. 1189)
Panegyric 22 (Cod. Paris. Gr. 1189)
Panegyric 26 (Cod. Paris. Gr. 1189)
Panegyric 28 (Cod. Paris. Gr. 1189)
Panegyric 30 (Cod. Paris. Gr. 1189)
Cod. 13, Andros, *Panegyric 1*

Cod. 13, Andros, *Panegyric 2*
Letter 2 (Cod. Coisl. Gr. 287)
Letter 3 (Cod. Coisl. Gr. 287)
Homily in *Cod. Coisl. Gr. 287*
Cod. Lesb. Leim. 2, Homily 2 (1191 possible *terminus post quem*)
Cod. Lesb. Leim. 2, Homily 3
Cod. Lesb. Leim. 2, Homily 4
Cod. Lesb. Leim. 2, Homily 5 (possibly *c.* 1200)
Cod. Lesb. Leim. 2, Homily 6
Cod. Lesb. Leim. 2, Homily 7
Cod. Lesb. Leim. 2, Homily 8

Bibliography

Any attempt to present a bibliographical list of the sources used was bound to be less than fully satisfactory because of the problems of transliteration, the use of more than one language, the varied nature of the source material, the overlap between sources (e.g. the publication of a source within a book or article which also contains secondary-source material, or which contains an edition of a Neophytic passage together with passages from other medieval authors). In the end the Bibliography's shape depended on its intended uses, which are two: first, to present a list of the sources to which reference has been made in this study (I have omitted works which were not directly referred to in the text or in the notes); second, to enable the reader to convert, in the easiest and quickest way possible, the short-hand citations in the footnotes to the full references given in the Bibliography.

I have therefore listed all works in the way in which they are cited in the book (e.g. the *Mousai* ascribed to Alexios I Komnēnos is introduced as 'Alexios, *Mousai*', followed by the full reference of the work, because it is cited thus in the notes; while the twelfth-century *Synodikon* of Cyprus appears under the name of its editor, 'Cappuyns, N.', for the same reason); and I have divided the Bibliography in only two parts, for primary and secondary sources, respectively. I decided to keep all the primary sources in one list rather than sub-divide them into several, hoping that the practical needs thus served outweigh the inelegance of the inevitable inconsistencies which ensued. The Bibliography of primary sources thus includes collections of sources, hagiographies, and books and articles which are very substantially based on or include publication or reprints of particular sources.

I have listed hagiographies according to the Saint's (first) name; while Byzantine and other authors who have a 'surname' are listed according to that. Thus, the various *Lives* of St John the Almsgiver are listed under J; while the *History* of John Kantakouzēnos is under K.

References to several works are followed by [N]. This indicates that they contain editions or reprints thereof of works by Neophytos; further details of which can be found in the Appendix.

PRIMARY SOURCES

Akropolitēs: Akropolitēs, George, 'Historia', ed. A. Heisenberg, in *Georgii Acropolitae Opera* (2 vols., Leipzig, 1903), I, 1–189.
Alberti Aquensis, *Historia*: Alberti Aquensis, 'Historia Hierosolymitana', *RHC, Occ.*, IV, 265–713.

Alexiad: Komnēna, Anna, *Alexiad*, ed. B. Leib (3 vols., Paris, 1937, 1943, 1945); Index by P. Gautier (Paris, 1976).

Alexios, *Mousai*: P. Maas (ed.), 'Die Musen des Kaisers Alexios I', *BZ*, 22 (1913), 348–69.

Ancient *Life* of St Alypios: 'Sancti Alypii Stylitae Vita prior', in H. Delehaye (ed.), *Les Saints stylites* (Brussels and Paris, 1923), 148–69.

Metaphrastic *Life* of St Alypios: 'Sancti Alypii Stylitae Vita altera', in H. Delehaye (ed.), *Les Saints stylites* (Brussels and Paris, 1923), 170–87.

Anrich, G., *Der heilige Nikolaos in der griechischen Kirche*, vol. I: *Die Texte* (Leipzig and Berlin, 1913). [N]

Michael Autorianos: 'Cinq actes inédits du Patriarche Michel Autoreianos', N. Oikonomides (ed.), *REB*, 25 (1967), 113–45.

Baldrici, *Historia*: Baldrici, episcopi Dolensis, 'Historia Jerosolimitana', *RHC, Occ.*, IV, 1–111.

Banescu, N. (ed.), *Deux poètes byzantins inédits du XIIIe siècle* (Bucharest, 1913).

Bar Hebraeus: *The Chronography of Gregory Abu'l Faraj ... commonly known as Bar Hebraeus*, E. A. W. Budge, transl. from the Syriac (2 vols., London, 1932).

St Basil: *Basil, Aux Jeunes Gens sur la manière de tirer profit des lettres helléniques*, ed. F. Boulanger (Paris, 1952).

Benedict of Peterborough: 'Gesta Regis Henrici Secundi', in W. Stubbs (ed.), *Rerum brittanicarum medii aevi scriptores* (2 vols., London, 1867).

Benjamin of Tudela: *Benjamin ben Jonah, of Tudela. Itinerary*, ed. and transl. M. N. Adler (London, 1907).

Life of Nikēphoros Blemmydēs: *Nicephori Blemmydae Autobiographia sive Curriculum Vitae, Epistula Universalior* (Corpus Christianorum, Series Graeca, 13), ed. J. Munitiz (Turnhout-Brepols, 1984).

Boilas: 'Le Testament d'Eustathios Boilas (Avril 1059)', in P. Lemerle (ed.), *Cinq études sur le XIe siècle byzantin* (Paris, 1977), 13–63.

Boines, K., Ἀκολουθία τοῦ ὁσίου Χριστοδούλου, ... ἡ Ὑποτύπωσις, ὁ Βίος, δύο Ἐγκώμια καὶ Διήγησις θαύματος αὐτοῦ (Athens, 1884).

Bryennios: Ἰωσὴφ μοναχοῦ τοῦ Βρυεννίου τὰ εὑρεθέντα, ed. E. Boulgaris (Leipzig, 1768).

Cappuyns, N. (ed.), 'Le Synodicon de Chypre au XIIe siècle', *B*, 10 (1935), 489–504.

Chatziioannou, I. Ch., Ἱστορία καί ἔργα Νεοφύτου Πρεσβυτέρου, Μοναχοῦ καί Ἐγκλείστου (Alexandria, 1914). [N]
Νεοφύτου Πρεσβυτέρου, Μοναχοῦ καί Ἐγκλείστου Ἑρμηνεία εἰς τούς Ψαλμούς (repr. Athens, 1935). [N]

Chatzipsaltes, K. (ed.), Νεοφύτου Πρεσβυτέρου, Μοναχοῦ καί Ἐγκλείστου Βιβλιογραφικόν Σημείωμα, *EKEE*, 6 (1972–3), 125–32. [N]

Dēmētrios Chōmatianos: in J. B. Pitra (ed.), *Analecta sacra et classica spicilegio solesmensi parata*, VI (Rome, 1891).

Michael Chōniatēs: Μιχαὴλ Ἀκομινάτου τοῦ Χωνιάτου τὰ σωζόμενα, ed. S. Lampros (2 vols., Athens, 1879–80; repr. Groningen, 1968).

Chōniatēs, *Historia*: *Nicetae Choniatae, Historia*, ed. J.-L. van Dieten (2 vols., Berlin and New York, 1975).

Chōniatēs, *Thesauros*: Chōniatēs, Nikētas, Θησαυρὸς Ὀρθοδοξίας, *MPG* 139, cols. 1004–1444; 140, cols. 9–280.

Enkōmion of Athanasios for St Christodoulos of Patmos: in Boines (1884: 134–62).

Enkōmion of Theodosios for St Christodoulos of Patmos: in Boines (1884: 163–208).

Life of St Christodoulos of Patmos: in Boines (1884: 109–33).

Clugnet, L. (ed.), 'Vie et récits de l'abbé Daniel, de Sceté', *ROC*, 5 (1900), 370–406.

Cobham, C. D. (ed., transl.), *Excerpta Cypria* (Cambridge, 1908; repr. New York, 1969). [N]

Cobham, C. D. (transl.), *Travels in the Island of Cyprus* (Cambridge, 1909).

Congourdeau, M.-H. (ed.), 'Discours sur les saintes lumières de Neophyte le Reclus', *EKEE*, 8 (1975–7), 113–85. [N]

Life of St Constantine of Synnada: *AASS*, Nov., IV, 657–69.

Cotelerius, J. B. (ed.), *Ecclesiae graecae monumenta*, II (Paris, 1681). [N]

Life of St Cyprian of Calabria: *BHG*³ 2089.

Life of St Cyril Phileotes: *La Vie de Saint Cyrille le Philéote, moine byzantin (+1110)*, ed. É. Sargologos (Subsidia Hagiographica, 39) (Brussels, 1964).

Cyril of Skythopolis: *Kyrillos von Skythopolis*, ed. E. Schwartz, *TU* 49/2 (Leipzig, 1939).

Life of St Daniel: 'Sancti Danielis stylitae vita antiquior', in H. Delehaye (ed.), *Les Saints stylites* (Brussels and Paris, 1923), 1–147.

Les Saints stylites (Subsidia Hagiographica, 14). (Brussels, 1923). [N]

Delehaye, H. (ed.), 'Saints de Chypre', *AB*, 26 (1907), 161–297. [N]

—— (ed.), 'Une Vie inédite de Saint Jean l'Aumônier', *AB*, 45 (1927), 5–74.

Martyrion of St Dēmētrios: 'S. Demetrii martyris acta', *MPG* 116, 1173–84 (Anonymous), 1185–1202 (Metaphrastēs).

Digenes Akrites: Digenes Akrites, ed. and trans. I. N. Mavrogordato (Oxford, 1956).

Dölger, F., *Regesten der Kaiserurkunden des oströmischen Reiches von 565–1453* (5 vols., Munich and Berlin, 1924–65).

Dyovouniotes, K. (ed.), Νεοφύτου 'Εγκλείστου 'Ανέκδοτον 'Εγκώμιον είς 'Ιωάννην τόν Χρυσόστομον, *EEBS*, 1 (1926), 3–19. [N]

—— (ed.), Νεοφύτου 'Εγκλείστου 'Ανέκδοτα "Εργα, *EEBS*, 13 (1937), 40–9. [N]

Edrisi: *Geography*, P. A. Jaubert (transl.), *Géographie d'Edrisi traduite de l'arabe en français* (2 vols., Paris 1836, 1840).

Egglezakes, B. (ed.), 'Ανέκδοτος Κατήχησις τοῦ ὁσίου Νεοφύτου τοῦ 'Εγλείστου είς τήν ἀγίαν Μεταμόρφωσιν (Athens, 1973). [N]

—— (ed.), 'Ανέκδοτον 'Υπόμνημα τοῦ ὁσίου Νεοφύτου τοῦ 'Εγκλείστου είς τήν 'Αποκάλυψιν, *EKEE*, 8 (1975–7), 73–112. [N]

EIE: 'Εθνικόν "Ιδρυμα 'Ερευνῶν – Κέντρον Βυζαντινῶν 'Ερευνῶν, *Παράλιος Κυπριακός Χῶρος. 'Αποδελτίωση πηγῶν καί καταγραφή μνημείων (μέσα 11ου – τέλη 13ου αί.)* (Athens, 1982).

Epiphanios: Epiphanios Monachos, Λόγος περί τοῦ βίου τῆς ὑπεραγίας Θεοτόκου, *MPG*, 120, 185–216.

Eracles: L'Estoire de Eracles empereur et la conqueste de la terre d'outremer, *RHC*, *Occ.*, II, 1–481.

Eustathios, *Opuscula: Eustathii Metropolitae Thessalonicensis Opuscula*, ed. G. L. F. Tafel (Frankfurt-am-Main, 1832; repr. Amsterdam, 1964).

Eustathios, *Orationes*: Eustathius, 'Orationes Politicae', eds. W. Regel and N. Novossadsky, in W. Regel, *Fontes rerum byzantinarum sumptibus Academie Caesareae Scientarum*, I, 1 (Petrograd, 1892), 1–131.

Life of St Euthymios the Younger: 'Vie de Saint Euthyme le jeune', ed. L. Petit, *ROC*, 8 (1903), 168–205.

Germanos II, *Letters*: 'Επιστολὴ πρὸς Κυπρίους, 1 and 2, *MPG* 140, cols. 601–13 and 613–21; also in Sathas (1872–94, II: 5–14 and 14–19).

Germanos II, Contra Bogomilos, *MPG* 140, 621–43.

Glykas: Glykas, Michael, *Annales*, ed. I. Bekker, *CB* (Bonn, 1836).

Glykas, *Aporiai*: Μιχαὴλ τοῦ Γλυκᾶ, Εἰς τὰς ἀπορίας τῆς θείας Γραφῆς κεφάλαια, ed. S. Eustratiades (2 vols., Athens, 1906, Alexandria, 1912).

Life of St Gregory: Βίος τοῦ ὁσίου Γρηγορίου, in D. G. Tsames (ed.), 'Ιωσὴφ Καλοθέτου Συγγράμματα (Thessalonikē, 1980), 503–22. (Also in 'Επιστημονικὴ 'Επετηρὶς Θεολογικῆς Σχολῆς Πανεπιστημίου Θεσσαλονίκης, 19 (1974), 47–129.)

Life of Gregory of Assos: 'Saint Grégoire d'Assos. Vie et synaxaire inédits', ed. F. Halkin, *AB*, 102 (1984), 5–34.

Gregory: St Gregory the Theologian, 'Επιστολὴ 'Επιφανίῳ, *MPG*, 37, 381.

Guiberti, *Gesta*: 'Guiberto, Domno, Historia quae dicitur Gesta Dei per Francos', *RHC Occ.*, IV.

Life of St Hilariōn of Moglena: E. Kaluzniacki (ed.), *Werke des Patriarchen von Bulgarien Euthymius* (Vienna, 1901), 27–58.

Histoire Anonyme: *Histoire anonyme de la première croisade. Les Classiques de l'histoire de France au moyen age*, fasc. 4, ed. and transl. (in French) L. Bréhier (Paris, 1924).

Itinerarium: 'Itinerarium regis Ricardi', ed. E. Stubbs, in *Rerum brittanicarum medii aevi scriptores* (London, 1864), 3–450.

Anonymous *Life* of St John the Almsgiver: 'Une Vie inédite de S. Jean l'Aumônier', ed. H. Delehaye, *AB*, 45 (1927), 19–74.

Leontios' *Life* of St John the Almsgiver: 'Vie de Jean de Chypre', ed. A. J. Festugière in collab. with L. Rydèn, in *Leontios de Neapolis, Vie de Syméon le Fou et de Jean de Chypre* (Paris, 1974), 343–409.

Metaphrastic *Life* of St John the Almsgiver: 'Bruchstuck aus dem von Iohannes Moschos und dem Sophisten Sophronios verfassten Leben des heiligen Iohannes des Barmherzigen von Alexandria', in H. Gelzer (ed.) *Leontios' von Neapolis Leben des Heiligen Johannes des Barmherzigen Erzbischofs von Alexandrien* (Freiburg and Leipzig, 1893), 108–12.

John of Damascus: *Contra imaginum calumniatores orationes tres, die Schriften des Johannes von Damaskos*, III (Berlin, 1975).

Jugie, M. (ed.), 'Homilies Mariales Byzantines', *PO*, 16, fasc. 3 (1922), 526[102]–538[114]. [N]

(ed.), 'Un Opuscule inédit de Néophyte le Reclus sur l'incorruptibilité du corps du Christ dans l'Eucharistie', *REB*, 7 (1949), 1–11. [N]

Kantakozēnos: Kantakozenos, John, *Historiarum Libri IV*, ed. L. Schopen (3 vols., Bonn, 1828, 1831, 1832).

Karagiannopoulos, I. E., 'Η Βυζαντινὴ 'Ιστορία ἀπό τάς πηγάς (Thessalonikē, 1974).

Kedrēnos-Skylitzēs: Kedrenos, George, *Historiarum compendium*, ed. I. Bekker, *CB* (2 vols., Bonn, 1838, 1839); and *Skylitzēs, John* (printed in the second volume of Kedrēnos, 639–744).

Kekaumenos, *Strategikon*: *Cecaumeni consilia et narrationes*, ed. G. G. Litavrin,

(Moscow, 1972); *Cecaumeni strategicon*, eds. B. Wassiliewski and V. Jernstedt (St Petersburg, 1896; repr. Amsterdam, 1965).

Kekaumenos, *Logos Nouthetētikos*: Λόγος Νουθετητικὸς πρὸς βασιλέα, eds. B. Wassiliewski and V. Jernstedt (St Petersburg, 1896; repr. Amsterdam, 1965), in Kekaumenos, *Strategicon*, 91–104.

Kemal-ed-Din: 'Extraits de la chronique d'Alep par Kemal ed Din', *RHC Or.*, III, 571–690.

Kinnamos: Kinnamos, John, *Epitome*, ed. A. Meineke, *CB* (Bonn, 1836).

Kyprianos, Archimandrite (ed.), Τυπικὴ σὺν Θεῷ διάταξις καὶ λόγοι εἰς τὴν Ἑξαήμερον τοῦ ὁσίου πατρὸς ἡμῶν Νεοφύτου τοῦ ἐγκλείστου (Venice, 1779). [N]

Lameere, W., *La tradition manuscrite de la correspondance de Grégoire de Chypre, patriarche de Constantinople (1283–1289)* (Brussels and Rome, 1937).

Lanfranchi, L. (ed.), *S. Giorgio Maggiore, II, documenti 982–1159* (Venice, 1968).

Laourdas, B. (ed.) Νεοφύτου πρεσβυτέρου, μοναχοῦ καί ἐγκλείστου, ἐγκώμιον εἰς τόν ἅγιον Δημήτριον, *Μακεδονικά*, 4 (1955–60), 49–55, 122–5. [N]

Life of St Lazaros: 'Vita S. Lazari auctore Gregorico monacho', *AASS*, Nov., III, 508–88.

Life of St Leontios of Jerusalem: Βίος τοῦ ὁσίου Λεοντίου Πατριάρχου Ἱεροσολύμων, συγγραφεὶς παρὰ Θεοδοσίου μοναχοῦ τοῦ Κωνσταντινουπολίτου, in *Λόγοι Πανηγυρικοὶ ΙΔ' τοῦ Μακαρίου Χρυσοκεφάλου* (Vienna, 1793), 380–434.

Loredano: Loredano, G. F., *Historie de' re' Lusignani, publicate da Henrico Giblet Cavalier* (Bologna, 1647).

Life of St Luke the Younger: 'Vita Lucae Iunioris', *MPG* III, 441–80; completed by E. Martini (ed.), *AB*, 13 (1894), 81–121.

Lusignan, *Chorograffia*: Lusignan, Estienne de, *Chorograffia et breve historia universale dell'isola de Cipro per in sino al 1572* (Bologna, 1573; repr. Famagusta, 1973).

Lusignan, *Description*: Lusignan, Estienne de, *Description de toute l'isle de Chypre, et des roys, princes et seigneurs, jusques en l'an 1572* (Paris, 1580).

Machairas: Leontios Machairas, *Recital Concerning the Sweet Land of Cyprus entitled 'Chronicle'*, ed. and transl. R. M. Dawkins (2 vols., Oxford, 1932).

Magoulias, H. J. (transl.), *O City of Byzantium. Annals of Niketas Choniates* (Detroit, 1984).

Manassēs: 'Das Hodoiporikon des Konstantin Manasses', ed. K. Horna, *BZ*, 13 (1904), 313–55.

Mansi, G. D. (ed.), *Sacrorum conciliorum nova et amplissima collectio* (31 vols., Florence, 1759–98; repr. Graz, 1960).

Letter of Patriarch Manuel: Ἐπιστολὴ πατριάρχου κῦρ Μανουὴλ πρὸς τὸν μητροπολίτην Ναυπάκτου καὶ τὸν ἀρχιεπίσκοπον Γαρδικίου, ed. B. Basilievsky, *VV*, 3 (1896), 268–9.

Manuel II Palaiologos, *Hypothēkai*: Ὑποθῆκαι βασιλικῆς ἀγωγῆς, *MPG*, 156, 313–84.

Mariti, G., *Viaggi per l'isola di Cipro, e per la Soria e Palestina*, I (Lucca, 1769).

Martyrion Kypriōn: Διήγησις τῶν ἁγίων τριῶν καὶ δέκα ὁσίων μαρτύρων τῶν διὰ πυρὸς τελειωθέντων παρὰ τῶν Λατίνων ἐν τῇ νήσῳ Κύπρῳ ἐν τῷ

‚ϛψλθ’ ἔτει, in Th. Papadopoulos (ed.), *Μαρτύριον Κυπρίων* (Nicosia, 1975). Also in Sathas (1872–94, II: 20–39).

Mas Latrie, M. L. de, *Histoire de l’isle de Chypre sous le règne des princes de la Maison de Lusignan* (3 vols., Paris, 1861, 1852, 1855; repr. Famagusta, 1970).

Life of St Meletios the Confessor: Βίος Μελετίου τοῦ ‘Ομολογητοῦ, ed. S. Lauriotes, *Γρηγόριος ὁ Παλαμᾶς*, 5 (1921), 582–4, 609–24.

Life of St Meletios the Younger: Νικολάου ἐκ Μεθώνης καὶ Θεοδώρου τοῦ Προδρόμου βίοι Μελετίου τοῦ Νέου, in V. G. Vasiljevskij (ed.), *Pravoslavnii Palestinskii Sbornik*, 17 (St Petersburg, 1886), 1–39, 40–69, respectively.

Life of St Michael Maleinos: ‘Vie de Saint Michel Maléinos’, ed. L. Petit, *ROC*, 7 (1902), 543–94.

Miklosich, F., and J. Müller (eds.), *Acta et diplomata graeca medii aevi sacra et profana* (6 vols., Vienna, 1860–90).

Mogabgab, Th. A. H. (transl.), *Supplementary Excerpts on Cyprus* (2 vols., Nicosia, 1941, 1943).

Morozzo della Rocca, R., and A. Lombardo, *Documenti del commercio veneziano nei secoli XI–XIII* (2 vols., Turin, 1940).

Mouzalōn: ‘Η παραίτησις τοῦ Νικολάου τοῦ Μουζάλωνος ἀπὸ τῆς ’Αρχιεπισκοπῆς Κύπρου. ’Ανέκδοτον ἀπολογητικὸν ποίημα, ed. S. Doanidou, *‘Ελληνικά*, 7 (1934), 109–50.

Mukaddasi: *Description of Syria*, transl. G. Le Strange (London, 1886).

Diataxis of Neilos: ed. I. P. Tsiknopoulos, in *Κυπριακά Τυπικά* (Nicosia, 1969), 1–65.

Nicolas of Thingeyrar: ‘Annotations géographiques dues à l’abbé Nicolas de Thingeyrar’, in C. C. Rafn (ed.), *Antiquités russes d’ après les monuments des Islandais et des Scandinaves* (2 vols., Copenhagen, 1850, 1852), II, 394–415.

Life of St Nikēphoros of Medikion: ‘La Vie de Saint Nicéphore, fondateur de Medikion en Bithynie (+813)’, ed. F. Halkin, *AB*, 78, I–II (1960), 396–430.

Oldfather, W. A. (ed.), *Studies in the Text Tradition of St. Jerome’s Vitae Patrum* (Urbana, 1943).

Opusculum contra Francos: J. Hergenrother (ed.), *Monumenta Graeca ed Photium eiusque historian pertinentia* (Ratisbonne, 1869), 62–71.

Pachymerēs: Pachymeres, George, ‘De Michaele et Andronico Palaeologis’, ed. I. Bekker, *CB* (2 vols., Bonn, 1835).

Papachryssanthou, D., *Actes du Prôtaton. Archives de l’Athos*, VII (Paris, 1975).

Ch. Papadopoulos (ed.), ‘Ο ὅσιος Μελέτιος ὁ Νέος (Athens, 1949); and in *Θεολογία*, 13 (1935), 97ff.

Papadopoulos – Kerameus, A. (ed.), *Noctes Petropolitanae* (St Petersburg, 1913).
(ed.), Συνοδικὰ γράμματα ’Ιωάννου τοῦ ’Αποκαύκου, *Βυζαντίς*, 1 (1904), 14.

Life of St Paul the Younger: ‘Vita S. Pauli Iunioris in monte Latro’, ed. H. Delehaye, in T. Wiegand (ed.) *Der Latmos* (Milet Ergebnisse der Ausgrabungen und Untersuchungen seit dem Jahre 1899) III, 1 (Berlin, 1913), 105–35. (Repr., *AB*, 11 (1892), 5–74, 136–82.)

Life of St Paul of Latros: ‘Vita S. Pauli’, *BHG*[3] 1474, 13.

Life of St Peter of Atroa: *La Vie marveilleuse de saint Pierre d’Atroa (+837)*, (Subsidia Hagiographica, 29), ed. and transl. V. Laurent (Brussels, 1956).

Life of St Philaretos: ‘La Vie de Saint Philarète le Miséricordieux’, eds. M.-H. Fourmy and M. Leroy, *B*, 9 (1934), 85–170.

Philip the Monk, *Dioptra*: ed. S. Lauriotes, '*O* "*Αθως*, 1 (1920), 9–264.
Homilies of Phōtios: *The Homilies of Photios, Patriarch of Constantinople*, transl. C. Mango (Cambridge, Mass., 1958).
Letters of Phōtios: *Φωτίου 'Επιστολαί*, ed. I. N. Balettas (London, 1864).
Pitra, J. B. (ed.), *Iuris ecclesiastici Graecorum historia et monumenta* (2 vols., Rome, 1864, 1868).
Theodoros Prodromos, Historische Gedichte, ed. W. Horändner (Vienna, 1974).
Ralles, G. A., and M. Potles, *Σύνταγμα τῶν θείων καὶ ιερῶν κανόνων* (6 vols., Athens, 1852, 1853, 1854, 1855, 1859).
Raymond of Aguilers: 'Historia Francorum qui ceperunt Iherusalem', *RHC, Occ.*, III (Paris, 1866), 231–309.
Rodinos: Rodinos, Neophytos, *Περὶ ἡρώων, στρατηγῶν, ἁγίων, καὶ ἄλλων ὀνομαστῶν ἀνθρώπων, ὅπου εὐγήκασιν ἀπὸ τὸ νησὶ τῆς Κύπρου* (Rome, 1659). (Repr. in *KX*, 3 (1925), 1–48.)
Roger of Hoveden: Roger of Hoveden, 'Chronica', ed. W. Stubbs, *Rerum Brittanicarum medii aevi scriptores* (4 vols., London, 1868, 1869, 1870, 1871).
Life of St Sabas: in *Kyrillos von Skythopolis*, ed. E. Schwartz, *TU*, 49, 2 (Leipzig, 1939), 85–200.
Sathas, K. N. *Μεσαιωνικὴ Βιβλιοθήκη / Bibliotheca Graeca medii aevi* (7 vols., Venice and Paris, 1872, 1873, 1874, 1876, 1877, 1894).
Life of St Stephen the Younger: 'Vita S. Stephani Iunioris', *MPG*, 100, 1069–1185.
Life of St Symeōn the New Theologian: 'Vie de Syméon le Nouveau Théologien (949–1022) par Nicétas Stethatos', ed. I. Hausherr, *OC*, 12, 45 (Rome, 1928), 3–228.
Life of St Symeōn the Stylite: *Das Leben des heiligen Symeon Stylites*, ed. M. Lietzmann (Leipzig, 1908).
Life of St Symeōn the Stylite the Younger: 'Vita Symeonis stylitae iunioris', *BHG*[3] 1689–9/c.
Tafel, G. L. F., and G. M. Thomas (eds.), *Urkunden zur älteren Handels- und Staatsgeschichte der Republik Venedig*, I (3 vols., Vienna, 1856, 1857).
Gesta Tancredi: 'Gesta Tancredi in expeditione Hierosolymitana auctore Radulfo Cadomensi', *RHC Occ.*, III, 587–716.
Life of St Theodore of Sykeon: *Vie de Théodore de Sykéôn* (Subsidia Hagiographica, 48), ed. and transl. A.-J. Festugière (2 vols., Brussels, 1970).
Theognōstos: *Theognosti Thesaurus*, ed. J. Munitiz (Brepols and Turnhout, 1979).
Theophanēs: Theophanis, *Chronographia*, ed. C. de Boor (2 vols., Leipzig, 1883, 1885).
Toniolo, E. (ed.), 'Omilie e catechesi mariane inediti di Neofito il recluso', *Marianum*, 36 (1974), 184–315. [N]
Euthymios Tornikēs: 'Les discours d'Euthyme Tornikes (1200–1205)', ed. J. Darrouzès, *REB*, 26 (1968), 49–121.
George and Dēmētrios Tornikēs: *Georges et Demetrios Tornikes, Lettres et Discours*, ed. J. Darrouzès (Paris, 1970).
Tsiknopoulos, I. P. (ed.), *Βίος καὶ αἱ δύο ἀκολουθίαι τοῦ ἁγίου Νεοφύτου* (Larnaka, 1953). (1953a) [N]
(ed.), *Κυπριακά Τυπικά* (Nicosia, 1969). (1969a) [N]
Αἱ Δύο 'Ακολουθίαι τοῦ 'Αγίου Νεοφύτου (τῆς 24ης 'Ιανουαρίου καὶ τῆς 28ης Σεπτεμβρίου (Paphos, 1976). [N]

(ed.), Νεοφύτου πρεσβυτέρου, μοναχοῦ καὶ ἐγκλείστου, λόγος εἰς τὴν ἀρχὴν τῆς ἰνδίκτου, *ABar*, 11 (1950), 3–7. (1950a) [N]

(ed.), Νεοφύτου πρεσβυτέρου, μοναχοῦ καὶ ἐγκλείστου, λόγος εἰς τὸ (...) γενέθλιον τοῦ (...) Ἰησοῦ Χριστοῦ *ABar*, 11 (1950), 451–6. (1950b) [N]

(ed.), Νεοφύτου πρεσβυτέρου, μοναχοῦ καὶ ἐγκλείστου, πρὸς τοὺς ἀτακτοῦντας καὶ λύοντας τὰ τῆς νηστείας προοίμια, *ABar*, 12 (1951), 61–4. (1951a) [N]

(ed.), Νεοφύτου πρεσβυτέρου, μοναχοῦ καὶ ἐγκλείστου, εἰς τὸν ἅγιον Σάβαν, *Νέα Σιών* (1951). (1951b) [N]

(ed.), Νεοφύτου πρεσβυτέρου, μοναχοῦ καὶ ἐγκλείστου, λόγος εἰς τὸν Εὐαγγελισμὸν τῆς (...) Θεοτόκου, *ABar*, 13 (1952), 67–71. (1952a) [N]

(ed.), Νεοφύτου πρεσβυτέρου, μοναχοῦ καὶ ἐγκλείστου, πρόλογος εἰς τὴν βίβλον τῶν κατηχήσεων, *ABar*, 13, (1952), 267–72. (1952b) [N]

(ed.), Νεοφύτου πρεσβυτέρου, μοναχοῦ καὶ ἐγκλείστου, περὶ τοῦ εὐσεβεστάτου βασιλέως κυροῦ Μανουήλ, *ABar*, 14 (1953), 72–5. (1953b) [N]

(ed.), Νεοφύτου πρεσβυτέρου, μοναχοῦ καὶ ἐγκλείστου, περί ἀνδρείας διττῆς, *ABar*, 14 (1953) 111–14. (1953c) [N]

(ed.), Νεοφύτου πρεσβυτέρου, μοναχοῦ καὶ ἐγκλείστου, ἐγκώμιον εἰς τὸν (...) Μάμαντα, *ABar*, 14 (1953), 250–5, 279–82. (1953d) [N]

(ed.), Νεοφύτου πρεσβυτέρου, μοναχοῦ καὶ ἐγκλείστου, περὶ σεισμῶν, *ABar*, 14 (1953), 312–15. (1953e) [N]

(ed.), Νεοφύτου πρεσβυτέρου, μοναχοῦ καὶ ἐγκλείστου, περὶ ὑπομονῆς, *ABar*, 15 (1954), 47–52. (1954a) [N]

(ed.), Νεοφύτου πρεσβυτέρου, μοναχοῦ καὶ ἐγκλείστου, τὰ αἴτια τῶν θλίψεων, *ABar*, 15 (1954), 76–81. (1954b) [N]

(ed.), Νεοφύτου πρεσβυτέρου, μοναχοῦ καὶ ἐγκλείστου, ἐξαγόρευσις καὶ μετάνοια, *ABar*, 15 (1954), 146–51. (1954c) [N]

(ed.), Νεοφύτου πρεσβυτέρου, μοναχοῦ καὶ ἐγκλείστου, ὁ καλὸς Σαμαρείτης, *ABar*, 15 (1954), 173–8. (1954d) [N]

(ed.), Νεοφύτου πρεσβυτέρου, μοναχοῦ καὶ ἐγκλείστου, δύο ἐκλείψεις ἡλίου, *ABar*, 15 (1954), 213–17. (1954e) [N]

(ed.), Νεοφύτου πρεσβυτέρου, μοναχοῦ καὶ ἐγκλείστου, ἐγκωμιαστικὸς λόγος εἰς τὴν ὕψωσιν τοῦ Τιμίου Σταυροῦ, *ABar*, 15 (1954), 258–62. (1954f) [N]

(ed.), Νεοφύτου πρεσβυτέρου, μοναχοῦ καὶ ἐγκλείστου, οὐκ ἔχει ὅρον ἡ τοῦ ἀνθρώπου ζωή, *ABar*, 15 (1954), 292–7. (1954g) [N]

(ed.), Παράβασις καὶ τήρησις τῶν ἐντολῶν, *ABar*, 16 (1955), 47–53. (1955a) [N]

(ed.), Νεοφύτου πρεσβυτέρου, μοναχοῦ καὶ ἐγκλείστου, οἱ Γραμματεῖς καὶ Φαρισαῖοι ..., *ABar*, 16 (1955), 145–50. (1955b) [N]

(ed.), Νεοφύτου πρεσβυτέρου, μοναχοῦ καὶ ἐγκλείστου, ἐγκώμιον εἰς Μαρῖναν, *ABar*, 16 (1955), 326–32. (1955c) [N]

(ed.), Νεοφύτου πρεσβυτέρου, μοναχοῦ καὶ ἐγκλείστου, ὁ πολύτιμος μαργαρίτης, *ABar*, 17 (1956), 180–4. (1956a) [N]

(ed.), Νεοφύτου πρεσβυτέρου, μοναχοῦ καὶ ἐγκλείστου, λόγος εἰς τὴν τοῦ Ἰησοῦ Χριστοῦ γέννησιν, *ABar*, 17 (1956), 205–15. (1956b) [N] (ed.), Νεοφύτου πρεσβυτέρου, μοναχοῦ καὶ ἐγκλείστου, ἐγκώμιον εἰς τὴν Παναγίαν, *ABar*, 21 (1960), 215–22. [N]

(ed.), Τρία ἀνώνυμα βυζαντινὰ ποιήματα ἐπανευρίσκουν τὸν ποιητὴν των ἅγιον Νεόφυτον, *ΚΣ*, 27 (1963), 75–117. [N]

(ed.), ''Αγιοι τῆς Κύπρου, *ΚΣ*, 30 (1966), 132–61. [N]

(ed.), Τὰ ἐλάσσονα τοῦ Νεοφύτου, *B*, 39 (1969), 318–419. (1969b) [N]

Tzetzēs: *Ioannes Tzetzae Epistulae*, ed. P. A. M. Leone (Leipzig, 1972).

Van Dieten, J. L. (ed.), *Zur Uberlieferung und Veroffentlichung der Panoplia Dogmatike des Niketas Choniates* (Amsterdam, 1970).

Van den Ven, M. P., S. *Jérome et la Vie du moine Malchus le Captif* (Louvain, 1901).

Warren, F. E. (ed.), 'The "Ritual Ordinance" of Neophytos', *Archaeologia*, 47 (1882), 1ff. [N]

Wilbrand of Oldenburg: 'Wilbrandi de Oldenborg Peregrinatio', ed. J. C. M. Laurent, in *Peregrinatores medii aevi quatuor*, 2nd edn (Leipzig, 1873).

William of Tyre: 'Historia rerum in partibus transmarinis gestarum a tempore successorum Mahumeth usque ad annum domini MCLXXXIV', *RHC, Occ.*, I, 1; I, 2.

Cont. of William of Tyre: 'Extraits inédits d'une continuation de Guillaume de Tyre', and 'extraits d'une nouvelle continuation de Guillaume de Tyr', ed. M. L. de Mas Latrie, II, 1–19, and III, 591–7, respectively.

Zigabēnos: Zigabenos, Euthymios, Πανοπλία Δογματική, *MPG*, 130, cols. 20–1362.

Zonaras: Zonaras, John, *Epitome Historiarum*, ed. L. Dindorf (6 vols., Leipzig, 1848, 1849, 1870, 1871, 1874, 1875); *Annales*, ed. M. Pinder, *CB* (3 vols., Bonn, 1841, 1844, 1897).

SECONDARY SOURCES

Aberle, D. 1971. 'A Note on Relative Deprivation Theory as Applied to Millenarian and Other Cult Movements', in W. A. Lessa and E. Z. Vogt (eds.), *Reader in Comparative Religion*. New York.

Ahrweiler, H. (Glykatzi) 1960a. 'Recherches sur l'administration de l'empire byzantin aux IXᵉ–XIᵉ siècles', *BCH*, 84: 1–111.

1960b. 'Les Fortresses construites en Asie Mineure face a l'invasion seljoucide', *Akten des XI. Internationalen Byzantinistenkongress*, 182–9. Munich.

1961. 'L'Administration militaire de la Crète byzantine', *B*, 31: 217–28.

1966a. *Byzance et la mer. La Marine de guerre, la politique, et les institutions maritimes de byzance aux VIIᵉ–XVᵉ siècles*. Paris.

1966b. 'Le Sébaste, Chef de groupes ethniques', in P. Wirth (ed.), *Polychronion. Festschrift F. Dölger*, 34–8. Heidelberg.

1967. 'Charisticariat et autres formes d'attribution de fondations pieuses aux Xᵉ–XIᵉ siècles', *ZRVI*, 10: 1–27.

1975a. *L'Ideologie politique de l'empire byzantin*. Paris.

1975b. 'L'Expérience Nicéene', *DOP*, 29: 21–40.

1976. 'Erosion sociale et comportements exentriques à Byzance aux XIᵉ–XIIIᵉ siècles', *XVᵉ Congrès International d'Etudes Byzantines*, I, 1, 3–21. Athens.

1977. 'The Geography of the Iconoclast World', in A. A. M. Bryer and J. Herrin (eds.) *Iconoclasm*, 21–7. Birmingham.

Alexander, P. J. 1962. 'The Strength of Empire and Capital as seen through Byzantine Eyes', *Speculum*, 37: 339–57.

Alexiou, M. 1986. 'The Poverty of Écriture and the Craft of Writing: towards a Reappraisal of the Prodromic Poems', *BMGS*, 10: 1–40.

Alibizatos, A. 1941–8. Ἡ Ἀναγνώρισις τῶν ἁγίων ἐν τῇ Ὀρθοδόξῳ Ἐκκλησία, Θεολογία, 19: 18–52.

Allatius, L. 1664. *De Symeonum scriptis diatriba*. Paris.

Angold, M. 1972. 'The problem of the Unity of the Byzantine World after 1204: The Empire of Nicaea and Cyprus (1204–1261)', *ΠΚΣ* 2: 1–6.

1974. *A Byzantine Government in Exile. Government and Society under the Lascarids of Nicaea (1204–1261)*. Oxford.

1975. 'Byzantine "Nationalism" and the Nicaean Empire', *BMGS*, 1: 49–70.

1984a. *The Byzantine Empire (1205–1204). A Political History*. London and New York.

(ed.) 1984b. *The Byzantine Aristocracy. IX to XIII Centuries* (BAR, 221). Oxford.

1984c. 'Archons and Dynasts: Local Aristocracies and the Cities of the Late Byzantine Empire', in M. Angold (ed.) *The Byzantine Aristocracy. IX to XIII Centuries* (BAR, 221), 236–53. Oxford.

Argyriou, A. 1972. 'Remarques sur quelques listes grecques enumérant les heresies latines', *BF*, 4: 9–30.

Aristeidou, Ai. 1980. Ἡ καλλιέργεια ζαχαροκάλαμου καί ἡ παραγωγή ζάχαρης στήν Κύπρο ἀπό τό 10ο μέχρι τό 16ο αἰώνα, *Κυπριακός Λόγος*, 69–72: 281–6.

1982. Ὁ Τεκκές τῆς Χαλᾶ Σουλτάν. Nicosia.

1983. *Kolossi Castle*. Nicosia.

1984. Ἡ καλλιέργεια ζαχαροκάλαμου καί ἡ παραγωγή ζάχαρης στήν Κύπρο κατά τό Μεσαίωνα, *Πρακτικά Συμποσίου Κυπριακῆς Ἱστορίας*, 63–9. Ioannina.

Assemani, S. E. 1759. *Bibliothecae apostolicae Vaticanae codicum manuscriptorum catalogus*. Rome.

Astruc, Ch., and M.-L. Concasty 1960. *Le Supplément grec*, III. Paris.

Baynes, N. H. 1955. 'The Icons before Iconoclasm', in his *Byzantine Studies and Other Essays*, 226–39.

Beard, M. 1980. 'The Sexual Status of the Vestal Virgins', *JRS*, 70: 12–27.

Beaton, R. 1980. *Folk Poetry in Modern Greece*. Cambridge.

1986. 'Byzantine Historiography and Modern Greek Oral Poetry: the Case of Rapsomates', *BMGS*, 10: 41–50.

Beck, H. G. 1959. *Kirche und Theologische Literatur im byzantinischen Reich*. Munich.

1974. *Das literarische Schaffen der Byzantiner. Weger zu seinem Verstandnis* (Österreichische Akademie der Wissenschaften, philosophisch–historische Klasse, Sitzungsberichte 294/4). Vienna.

Berger, P., and T. Luckmann. 1967. *The Social Construction of Reality. A Treatise in the Sociology of Knowledge*. Harmondsworth.

Blum, R., and E. Blum. 1970. *The Dangerous Hour. The Lore and Culture of Crisis and Mystery in Rural Greece*. London.

Bollas, Ch. 1989. *Forces of Destiny. Psychoanalysis and Human Idiom*. London.

Bon, A. 1952. *Le Péloponnèse byzantin jusqu'en 1204*. Paris.

Bourdieu, P. 1977. *Outline of a Theory of Practise*, transl. R. Nice. Cambridge.

Boyd, S. 1974. 'The Church of the Panagia Amasgou, Monagri, Cyprus, and its Wall Paintings', *DOP*, 28: 277–327.

Brand, C. M. 1968. *Byzantium Confronts the West, 1180–1204*. Cambridge, Mass.

E. Branouse (ed.) 1966. *Τά ἁγιολογικά κείμενα τοῦ 'Οσίου Χριστοδούλου*. Athens.

Breckenridge, J. D. 1974. 'Apocrypha of Early Christian Portraiture', *BZ*, 67: 101–9.

Brown, P. 1971a. *The World of Late Antiquity*. London.

(1971b) 'The Rise and Function of the Holy Man in Late Antiquity', *JRS*, 61: 80–101.

1973. 'A Dark Age Crisis: Aspects of the Iconoclastic Controversy', *EHR*, 88: 1–34.

1976. 'Eastern and Western Christendom in Late Antiquity: a Parting of the Ways', *Studies in Church History*, 13: 1–24.

1981. *The Cult of the Saints. Its Rise and Function in Latin Christianity*. London.

1982. *Society and the Holy in Late Antiquity*. London.

Browning, R. 1962, 1963. 'The Patriarchal School at Constantinople in the Twelfth-Century', *B*, 32: 167–201; 33: 11–40.

1964. 'Byzantine Scholarship', *PP*, 28: 3–20.

1966. *Greece, Ancient and Medieval*. London.

1975. 'Enlightenment and Repression in Byzantium in the Eleventh and Twelfth Centuries, *PP*, 69: 3–23.

1978a. 'Literacy in the Byzantine World', *BMGS*, 4: 39–54.

1978b. 'The Language of Byzantine Literature', *Byzantina and Metabyzantina*, 1 103–33.

1989. 'Notes on Greek Manuscripts of Cypriot Provenance or Connection in the Libraries of Great Britain', *EKEE*, 17: 113–22.

Bryer, A. A. M. 1973. 'Cultural Relations between East and West in the Twelfth Century', in D. Baker (ed.), *Relations between East and West in the Middle Ages*, 77–94. Edinburgh.

1981. 'The First Encounter with the West', in P. Whitting (ed.), *Byzantium. An Introduction*, 83–110. Oxford.

1986. 'Eclipses and Epithalamy in Fourteenth-Century Trebizond', *B*, *Tribute to Andreas Stratos*, 347–52.

Bryer, A. A. M., and J. Herrin (eds.) 1977. *Iconoclasm*. Birmingham.

Buckler, G. 1948. 'Byzantine Education', in N. H. Baynes and H. S. L. B. Moss (eds.), *Byzantium. An Introduction to East Roman Civilisation*, 200–20. Oxford.

Bulmer, R. 1967. 'Why the Cassowary is not a Bird', *Man*, 2, 1: 5–25; repr. in M. Douglas (ed.), *Rules and Meanings: the Anthropology of Everyday Knowledge*, 167–93. Harmondsworh, 1973.

Camera, M. 1836. *Istoria della citta e costiera di Amalfi*. Naples.

Cameron, A. 1978. 'The Theotokos in Sixth-Century Constantinople. A City Finds its Symbol', *JTS*, 29, 1: 79–108.

1979. 'Images of Authority: Elites and Icons in Sixth-century Byzantium', *PP*, 84: 3–35.

Campbell, J. K. 1964. *Honour, Family and Patronage. A Study of Institutions and Moral Values in a Greek Mountain Community*. Oxford.

Canard, M. 1973. *Byzance et les musulmans du Proche Orient*. London.

1981. 'Les Ecritures livresques chypriotes du milieu du XIᵉ siècle au milieu du XIIIᵉ siècle et le style palestino-chypriote "epsilon"', *Scrittura e civilta*, 5: 17–76.

Chalandon, F. 1900. *Essai sur le règne d' Alexis I Comnène*. Paris.

1912. *Jean II Comnène (1118–1143) et Manuel II Comnène (1143–1180). Les Comnénes. Études sur l'empire byzantin au XIᵉ et au XIIᵉ siècles*, II. Paris.

Charanis, P. 1948. 'The Monastic Properties and the State in the Byzantine Empire', *DOP*, 4: 53–118.

1951. 'On the Social Structure and Economic Organisation of the Byzantine Empire in the Thirteenth-Century and Later', *BS*, 12: 94–153.

1972. 'Armenians and Greeks in the Byzantine Empire', *The Armenian Review*, 25: 25–32.

Chatzipsaltes, K. 1951. Σχέσεις τῆς Κύπρου πρός τό ἐν Νικαίᾳ Βυζαντινόν Κράτος, *ΚΣ*, 15: 65–82.

1955. Συμβολαί εἰς τήν ἱστορίαν τῆς Ἐκκλησίας τῆς Κύπρου κατά τήν βυζαντινήν περίοδον. (α) Ὁ ἀρχιεπίσκοπος Ἰωάννης ὁ Κρητικός, *ΚΣ*, 18: κζ'ff.

1964. Ἡ Ἐκκλησία Κύπρου καί τό ἐν Νικαίᾳ Οἰκουμενικόν Πατριαρχεῖον ἀρχομένου τοῦ ΙΓ' μ.Χ. αἰῶνος, *ΚΣ*, 28: 135–68.

1988. Σημειώσεις ἀναφερόμεναι εἰς τήν ἱστορίαν τῆς βυζαντινῆς Κύπρου, in J. Chrysostomides (ed.), *Καθηγήτρια. Essays Presented to Joan Hussey*, 345–51. Camberley.

Chitty, D. J. 1928. 'Two Monasteries in the Wilderness of Judaea', *PEF*: 134–52.

1977. *The Desert a City*. Oxford.

Clucas, L. 1981. *The Trial of John Italos and the Crisis of Intellectual Values in Byzantium in the Eleventh Century* (Miscellanea Byzantina Monacensia, 26). Munich.

Constantine, Metropolitan of Serres, 1956. Περί ἀναγνωρίσεως τῶν ἁγίων ἐν τῇ Ὀρθοδόξῳ Ἐκκλησίᾳ, *Θεολογία*, 27: 609–15.

Constantinides, C. N. 1982. *Higher Education in Byzantium in the Thirteenth and Early Fourteenth Centuries (1204–c.1310)*. Nicosia.

Cormack, R. 1984. 'Aristocratic Patronage of the Arts in 11th and 12th Century Byzantium', in M. Angold (ed.), *The Byzantine Aristocracy. IX to XIII Centuries* (BAR 221), 158–72. Oxford.

1985. *Writing in Gold. Byzantine Society and its Icons*. London.

1986. '"New Art History" vs. "Old History": Writing Art History', *BMGS*, 10: 223–31.

Crabbe, A. 1981. 'St. Polychronios and his Companions – but which Polychronios?', in S. Hackel (ed.), *The Byzantine Saint*, 141–54. London.

Daniel, M. 1960. *Islam and the West. The Making of an Image*. Edinburgh.

Darrouzès, J. 1949. 'Les Catalogues récents de manuscripts Grecs', *REB*, 7: 56–68.

1950. 'Manuscripts originaires de Chypre à la Bibliothèque National de Paris', *REB*, 8: 162–96.

1957. 'Autres manuscripts originaires de Chypre', *REB*, 15: 131–75.

1963. 'Le Mémoire de Constantine Stilbés contre les Latins', *REB*, 21: 50–100.

Dawes, E., and N. H. Baynes. 1948. *Three Byzantine Saints*. Oxford.

Dawkins, R. M. 1953. *Modern Greek Folktales*. Oxford.

Delehaye, H. 1906. *Les Légendes hagiographiques*. Brussels. (Repr. Subsidia Hagiographica, 18. Brussels, 1927.)

Delisle, L. 1868–74. *Le Cabinet des manuscripts de la Bibliothèque Impériale*. 3 vols., Paris. [N]

Delooz, P. 1969 *Sociologie et canonisation*. Paris and The Hague.

1983. 'Towards a Sociological study of Canonised Sainthood in the Catholic Church', in S. Wilson (ed.), *Saints and their Cults. Studies in Religious Sociology, Folklore and History*, 189–216. Cambridge.

Devreese, R. 1945. *Catalogue des manuscripts Grecs*, vol. II: *Le Fonds Coislin*. Paris. [N]

Dikigoropoulos, A. I. 1956. 'A Contribution to the Chronology of Events in Cyprus from the Seventh to the Tenth Century', Πεπραγμένα τοῦ Θ' Διεθνοῦς Βυζαντινολογικοῦ Συνεδρίου, II, 366ff. Thessalonikē.

1958. 'The Political Status of Cyprus A.D. 648–965', *RDAC*, 1940–8: 94–114.

1965–6. 'The Church of Cyprus during the period of the Arab Wars, A.D. 649–965', *The Greek Orthodox Theological Review* 11, 2: 237–79.

Djobadze, W. 1984. 'Observations on the Georgian Monastery of Yalia (Galia) in Cyprus', *OC*, 68: 196–209.

Doanidou, S. 1934. Ἡ παραίτησις τοῦ Νικολάου Μουζάλωνος ἀπό τῆς Ἀρχιεπισκοπῆς Κύπρου, *Ἑλληνικά*, 7: 109–50.

Dölger, F. 1935. 'Zu dem Abdankungsgedicht des Nikolaos Muzalon', *BZ*, 35: 8–14.

Douglas, M. 1969. *Purity and Danger*. London, Boston and Henley.

1973. *Natural Symbols*. Harmondsworth.

Downton, J. 1973. *Rebel Leadership*. London.

Durkheim, E. 1976. *The Elementary Forms of the Religious Life*, transl. J. W. Swain. London.

Edbury, P. W. 1975. 'Latin Dioceses and Peristerona. A Contribution to the Topography of Lusignan Cyprus', *EKEE*, 8: 45–51.

Efthimiou, M. 1987. *Greeks and Latins on Cyprus in the Thirteenth Century*. Brookline, Mass.

Egglezakes, B. 1976. 'La Question de "Commentaire sur les canons des douzes fêtes du Seigneur" par Néophyte le Reclus', *Actes du XVᵉ Congrès International d' Études Byzantines, Rapports et co-rapports*, V/5 Athens.

1978. Ἡ εἰς τούς κανόνας τῶν δεσποτικῶν ἑορτῶν ἑρμηνεία τοῦ ὁσίου Νεοφύτου τοῦ Ἐγκλείστου, *ABar*, 39: 367–75.

1979–80. Ὁ ὅσιος Νεόφυτος ὁ Ἔγκλειστος καί αἱ ἀρχαί τῆς ἐν Κύπρω Φραγκοκρατίας, *EKEE*, 10: 31–83. [N]

Ehrhard, A. 1943. *Überlieferung und Bestand der hagiographischen und homiletischen Literatur der griechischen Kirche* (TU, III, 4) (Leipzig 1968).

Eisenstadt, S. N. 1968. *Max Weber. On Charisma and Institution Building*. Chicago and London.

Enlart, E. 1899. *L'Art gothique et la Renaissance en Chypre*, 2 vols., Paris.

Eustratiades, S. 1933, 1934. Κυπριακοὶ Κώδικες ἐν τῇ Ἐθνικῇ Βιβλιοθήκῃ Παρισίων, *ABar*, 3, 4. [N]

Festugière, A. J., in collab. with L. Rydèn, 1974. *Leontios de Neapolis, vie de Syméon le Fou et vie de Jean de Chypre*. Paris.

Fiey, J. M. 1966. 'Notes d'hagiographie syriaque', *OS*, 11: 133–45.

Fischer, E. 1963. *The Necessity of Art. A Marxist Approach*, transl. A. Bostock. London; repr. 1984.

Fortes, M. 1959. *Oedipus and Job in West African Religion*. Cambridge.

Frangiskos, A. 1989. *Ἱστορία καί Λαογραφία Μαρωνιτῶν Κύπρου*. Nicosia.

Freud, S. 1966–74. *The Standard Edition of the Complete Psychological Works of Sigmund Freud*, ed. and transl., J. Strachey in collab. with A. Freud. 24 vols., London.

Galatariotou, C. 1984–5. 'Holy Women and Witches: Aspects of Byzantine Conceptions of Gender', *BMGS*, 9: 55–94.

— 1987a. 'Byzantine Ktetorika Typika: a Comparative Study', *REB*, 45: 77–138.

— 1987b. 'Structural Oppositions in the Grottaferrata Digenes Akrites', *BMGS*, 11: 29–68.

— 1988. 'Byzantine Women's Monastic Communities: the Evidence of the Typika', *JÖBG*, 38: 263–90.

— 1989. '*Eros* and *Thanatos*: a Byzantine Hermit's Conception of Sexuality', *BMGS*, 13: 95–137.

— forthcoming a. 'The Bishop and the Hermit: Church Patronage in Action in Twelfth-Century Cyprus', *EKEE*, 18 (1991).

— forthcoming b. 'Travel and Perception in Byzantium', in J. Shepard and S. Franklin (eds.), *Byzantine Diplomacy*.

Gamillscheg, E. 1987. 'Fragen zur Lokalisierung der Handschriften der Gruppe 2400', *JÖB*, 37: 313–21.

Gautier, P. 1971. 'Le Synode de Blachernes (fin 1094)', *REB*, 29; 213–84.

Gedeon, M. 1899. *Βυζαντινόν Ἑορτολόγιον*. Constantinople.

Geertz, C. 1975. *The Interpretation of Cultures*. London.

Gelzer, H. (ed.) 1893. *Leontios' von Neapolis Leben des Heiligen Johannes des Barmherzigen Erzbischofs von Alexandrien*. Freiburg and Leipzig.

Goodich, M. 1975. 'The Politics of Canonisation in the Thirteenth Century: Lay and Mendicant Saints', *CH*, 44: 294–307.

Gramsci, A. 1971. *Selections from the Prison Notebooks*, ed. and transl. Q. Hoare and G. Nowell-Smith. London.

Grumel, V. 1958. *Traité d'études byzantines*, vol. I: *La Chronologie*. Paris.

Guilland, R. 1957. 'Etudes de titulature et de prosopographie byzantines. Les chefs de la marine byzantine', *BZ*, 44: 214–40.

Hackett, J. 1901. *History of the Orthodox Church of Cyprus* London.

Haldon, J. F. 1981. 'On the Structuralist Approach to the Social History of Byzantium'. *BS*, 42, 2: 203–11.

— 1984–5. '"Jargon" vs. "the Facts"? Byzantine History-writing and Contemporary Debates', *BMGS*, 9: 95–132.

— 1986. 'Ideology and Social Change in the Seventh Century: Military Discontent as a Barometer', *Klio*, 66: 139–90.

Harvey, A. 1982–3. 'Economic Expansion in Central Greece in the Eleventh Century', *BMGS*, 8: 21–8.

— 1989. *Economic Expansion in the Byzantine Empire, 900–1200*. Cambridge.

Hatfield Young, S. 1978. 'The Iconography and Date of the Wall Paintings at Ayia Solomoni, Paphos, Cyprus', *B*, 48: 91–111.

Hauscherr, I. 1955. 'Direction spirituelle en orient autrefois', *OCA*, 144.

Hendy, M. F. 1969. *Coinage and Money in the Byzantine Empire, 1081–1261* (DOS, 12). Washington, DC.

1970. 'Byzantium 1081–1204: an Economic Reappraisal', *Transactions of the Royal Historical Society*, 20, 5: 31–52; repr. in Hendy (1989) II.

1981. 'Seventeen Twelfth- and Thirteenth-century Byzantine Hoards', *Coin Hoards*, 6: 61–72.

1985. *Studies in the Byzantine Monetary Economy, c. 300–1450.* Cambridge.

1989. *The Economy, Fiscal Administration and Coinage of Byzantium* (Variorum Reprints). Northampton.

Herrin, J. 1975 'Realties of Byzantine Provincial Government: Hellas and Peloponnesos, 1180–1205', *DOP*, 29: 253–86.

1982. 'Women and the Faith in Icons in Early Christianity', R. Samuel and G. Stedman Jones (eds.), *History Workshop. Culture, Ideology and Politics*, 56–83. London.

1987. *The Formation of Christendom.* Oxford.

Herzfeld, M. 1980. 'Social Borderers: Themes of Conflict and Ambiguity in Greek Folk Song', *BMGS*, 6: 61–80.

Hill, G. 1948–52, repr. 1972. *A History of Cyprus.* 4 vols., Cambridge.

Horna, K. (ed.) 1904. 'Das Hodoiporikon des Konstantin Manasses', *BZ* 13: 313–55.

Hunger, H. 1964. *Prooimion. Elemente der byzantinischen Kaiser idee in den Arengen der Urkunden.* Vienna.

1968. *Die byzantinische Literatur der Komnenenzeit: Versuch einer Neubewertung* (Österreichische Akademie der Wissenschaften, philosophische-historische Klasse, 105). Vienna.

Hunt, D. (transl.) 1987. *Gothic Art and the Renaissance in Cyprus* (transl. of Enlart 1899). London.

Hussey, J. M. 1986. *The Orthodox Church in the Byzantine Empire.* Oxford.

Indianos, A. C., and G. H. Thomson 1940. 'Wall Paintings at St. Neophytos Monastery', *KΣ*, 3: 155–224.

Jacoby, D. 1974. 'Catalans, Turcs et Vénitiens en Romanie (1305–1332): un nouveau témoignage de Marino Sanudo Torsello', *Studi Medievali*, 3rd series, 15: 217–61; repr. in Jacoby, *Recherches sue la Méditeranée orientale du XIIe au XVe siècle. Peuples, sociétés, économies* (Variorum Reprints). London, 1979: V.

1977. 'Citoyens, sujets et protégés de Venise et de Gênes en Chypre du XIIIe au XVe siècle', *BF*, 5: 159–88; repr. in Jacoby, *Recherches sur la Méditeranée orientale du XIIe au XVe siècle. Peuples, sociétés, économies* (Variorum Reprints). London, 1979: VI.

Janin, R. 1964. 'Le Monachisme byzantin au Moyen Âge. Commende et Typica (Xe–XIVe siècles), *REB*, 22: 5–44.

Jeffreys, M. J. 1974. 'The nature and origins of the Political Verse', *DOP*, 28: 141–95; repr. in E. M. Jeffreys and M. J. Jeffreys, *Popular Literature in Late Byzantium* (Variorum Reprints). London, 1983: IV.

Jenkins, R. J. 1953. 'Cyprus between Byzantium and Islam A.D. 688–965', *Studies Presented to D. Robinson*, II: 1006–14. St Louis.

Kazhdan, A. P., and G. Constable. 1982. *People and Power in Byzantium. An Introduction to Modern Byzantine Studies.* Washington, DC.

Kazhdan, A. P., in collab. with S. Franklin. 1984. *Studies in Byzantine Literature of the Eleventh and Twelfth Centuries*. Cambridge.

Kazhdan, A. P. and A. Wharton Epstein. 1985. *Change in Byzantine Culture in the Eleventh and Twelfth Centuries*. Berkeley, Los Angeles, and London.

Khoury, A. Th. 1969. *Les Théologiens byzantins et l'Islam. Textes et Auteurs (VIIIᵉ–XIIIᵉs.)*. Paris and Louvain.

1972. *Polémique byzantine contre l'Islam (VIIIᵉ–XIIIᵉs.)*. Leiden.

Konidares, G. 1934. Αἱ μητροπόλεις καὶ ἀρχιεπισκοπαὶ τοῦ Οἰκουμενικοῦ Πατριαρχείου καὶ ἡ "τάξις" αὐτῶν, *Text und Forschungen*, 13.

1943. Ἡ θέσις τοῦ αὐτοκεφάλου Ἐκκλησίας τῆς Κύπρου ἔναντι τοῦ Οἰκουμενικοῦ Πατριαρχείου κατὰ τὸν Θ' καὶ Ι' αἰῶνα, *Text und Forschungen*, 18: 135–46.

1972. Ἡ θέσις τῆς Ἐκκλησίας τῆς Κύπρου εἰς τὰ Ἐκκλησιαστικὰ Τακτικὰ (Notitia Episcopatum) ἀπὸ τοῦ Η' μέχρι τοῦ ΙΒ' αἰῶνος, *ΠΚΣ*, 2: 81–120.

Konidares, I. M. 1984. *Νομικὴ Θεώρηση τῶν Μοναστηριακῶν Τυπικῶν*. Athens.

Koukoules, Ph. 1948–55. *Βυζαντινῶν Βίος καὶ Πολιτισμός*. 6 vols., Athens.

Krikos-Davis, K. 1982. 'Moira at Birth in Greek Tradition', *Folia Neohellenica*, 4: 106–34.

Krumbacher, K. 1970. *Geschichte der Byzantinischen Litteratur*. 2 vols., New York.

Kyrris, C. 1970. 'Military Colonies in Cyprus in the Byzantine Period: their Character, Purpose and Extent', *BS*, 31: 157–81.

Laiou-Thomadakis, A., 'Saints and Society in the Late Byzantine Empire', in A. Laiou-Thomadakis (ed.), *Charanis Studies. Essays in Honor of Peter Charanis*, 84–114. New Brunswick, N.J.

Lampros, S. 1898. Περὶ τῶν χειρογράφων τῶν ἀποκειμένων ἐν τῇ ἐν "Ανδρῳ μονῇ τῆς 'Αγίας, *'Επετηρὶς τοῦ Παρνασσοῦ*, 2.

1917. Κυπριακὰ καὶ ἄλλα ἔγγραφα ἐκ τοῦ Παλατινοῦ κώδικος 367 τῆς βιβλιοθήκης τοῦ Βατικανοῦ, *ΝΕ*, 14: 14–50.

Larrain, J. 1979. *The Concept of Ideology*. London.

1983. *Marxism and Ideology*. London.

Laurent, V. 1931a 'Bulletin de sigillographie byzantine', *B*, 6: 771–829.

1931b 'Les Bulles métriques dans la sigillographie byzantine', *'Ελληνικά*, 4: 321–60.

1932. *Les Bulles métriques dans la sigillographie byzantine*. Athens.

1949a. 'La Succession épiscopal des derniers archevêques de Chypre, de Jean le Crétois (1152) a Germain Pésimandros (1260)', *REB*, 7: 33–41.

1949b. 'Le Typikon monastique de Néophyte le Reclus. Nombre et dates de ses recensions', *REB*, 7: 52–5.

1951. 'Les Monnaies tricéphales de Jean Comnéne. Notes de numismatique byzantine et d'histoire chypriote', *Revue Numismatique*, 5: 97–107.

1962. *Les sceaux byzantins du Medailler Vatican*. Vatican.

1963–72. *Le corpus des sceaux de l'empire byzantin, vol V: L'église*, I/1.2 Suppl. Paris.

Laurent, V., and J. Darrouzés 1976. *Dossier grec de l'Union de Lyon (1273–1277)*. Paris.

Lemerle, P. 1971. *Le Premier Humanisme byzantine. Notes et remarques sur l'enseignement et culture à Byzance des origines aux Xᵉ siècle*. Paris.

1972. 'Séance de la clôture de la section médiévale', *ΠΚΣ*, 2: 151–6.

1977. *Cinq études sur le XIᵉ siècle byzantin*. Paris.

1979. *The Agrarian History of Byzantium. From the Origins to the Twelfth Century*. Galway.

Leroy, J. 1964. *Les Manuscripts syriaques à peintures*. Paris.

Lévi-Strauss, C. 1949. *Structures élémentaires de la parenté*. R. Needham (ed.), Paris. (J. H. Bell and J. R. von Sturmer (transl.), *The Elementary Structures of Kinship*, London, 1969.)

1965. 'Le Triangle culinaire', *L'Arc*, 26/1: 19–29.

1972, 1978. *Structural Anthropology*, transl. C. Jacobson and B. Grundfest Schoepf (vol. I), M. Layton (vol. II). 2 vols., Harmondsworth.

Loizos, P. 1981. *The Heart Grown Bitter. A Chronicle of Cypriot War Refugees*. Cambridge.

Lovell, T. 1980. *Pictures of Reality. Aesthetics, Politics, Pleasure*. London.

McCormick, M. 1986. *Eternal Victory. Triumphal Rulership in Late Antiquity, Byzantium and the Early Medieval West*. Cambridge.

Macrides, R. 1981. 'Saints and Sainthood in the Early Palaiologan Period', in S. Hackel (ed.), *The Byzantine Saint*, 67–87. London.

Magdalino, P. 1981. 'The Byzantine Holy Man in the Twelfth Century', in S. Hackel (ed.), *The Byzantine Saint*, 51–66. London.

1983. 'Aspects of Twelfth-Century Byzantine *Kaiserkritik*', *Speculum*, 58, 2: 326–46.

1984. 'Byzantine Snobbery', in M. Angold (ed.), *The Byzantine Aristocracy. IX to XIII Centuries* (BAR, 221), 58–78. Oxford.

1987. 'The Literary Perception of Everyday Life in Byzantium. Some General Considerations and the Case of John Apokaukos', *BS*, 57/1: 28–38.

Makarios III, Archbishop of Cyprus, *Κύπρος, ή 'Αγία Νῆσος* (Athens 1968).

Mango, C. 1963 'The Conciliar Edict of 1166', *DOP*, 17: 315–30.

1975a. 'The Availability of Books in the Byzantine Empire, A.D. 750–850', in *Byzantine Books and Bookmen. A Dumbarton Oaks Colloquium*, 29–45. Washington, DC. (Repr. in Mango (1984) VII.)

1975b. *Byzantine Literature as a Distorting Mirror*. Oxford. (Repr. in Mango (1984) II.)

1976a. 'Chypre, Carrefour du Monde Byzantine', *XVᵉ Congrès International d' Etudes Byzantines, Rapports et co-rapports*, V, 5. Athens. (Repr. in Mango (1984) XVII.)

1976b. 'Les Monuments de l'architecture du XIᵉ siècle et leur signification historique et sociale', *TM*, 6: 351–65.

1977. 'Historical Introduction', in A. A. M. Bryer and J. Herrin (eds.), *Iconoclasm*, 1–6. Birmingham.

1980. *Byzantium. The Empire of New Rome*. London.

1984. *Byzantium and its Image* (Variorum Reprints). London.

Mango, C., and E. J. Hawkins 1964. 'Report on Field Work in Istanbul and Cyprus, 1962–1963', *DOP*, 18: 333–9.

1966. 'The Hermitage of Saint Neophytos and its Wall Paintings', *DOP*, 20: 120–206.

Mango, C., and I. Ševčenko 1973. 'Some Churches and Monasteries in the Southern Shores of the Sea of Marmara', *DOP*, 27: 235–79.

Marinatos, S. 1930. Εὐμάθιος ὁ Φιλοκάλης, τελευταῖος στρατηγὸς τοῦ θέματος τῆς Κρήτης, *EEBS*, 7: 388–93.

Mas Latrie, M. L. de 1871–4. *Nouvelles preuves de l'histoire de Chypre sous le règne des princes de la Maison de Lusignan* (Bibliothèque de l'École des Chartes, XXXII, XXXIV, XXXV). Paris.

Megaw, A. H. S. 1954. 'Archaeology in Cyprus, 1953', *JHS*, 74: 172–6.

1961. *A Brief History and Description of Cyrenia Castle*. Nicosia.

1964. 'Twelfth Century Frescoes in Cyprus', *Actes du XIIe Congrès International d'Etudes Byzantines*, 257–66. Belgrade.

1972a. 'Supplementary Excavations on a Castle Site at Paphos, Cyprus, 1970– 1971', *DOP*, 26: 322–43.

1972b. 'Background Architecture in the Lagoudera Frescoes', *JÖB*, 21: 195–202.

1974. 'Byzantine Art and Architecture in Cyprus: Metropolitan or Provincial?', *DOP*, 28: 57–88.

1988. 'Reflections on Byzantine Paphos', in J. Chrysostomides (ed.), *Καθηγήτρια*. *Essays Presented to Joan Hussey*, 135–50. Camberley.

Megaw, A. H. S., and E. J. Hawkins. 1977. *The Church of Panagia Kanakaria at Lythrankomi in Cyprus. Its Mosaics and Frescoes* (DOS, 14). Washington, D.C.

Menardos, S. 1907. Τοπωνυμικόν τῆς Κύπρου, *Athena*, 18: 315–421.

1929. Ἡ ἐν Κύπρῳ ἱερά μονὴ τῆς Παναγίας τοῦ Μαχαιρᾶ. Peiraias.

Merakles, A. Ch. 1976. Ὁ Βίος καί τά ''Εργα τοῦ Ἁγίου Νεοφύτου καί σύντομος ἱστορία τῆς ἱερᾶς Μονῆς του. Nicosia.

Meyendorff, J. 1964. 'Byzantine Views of Islam', *DOP*, 18: 113–32.

1974. *Byzantine Hesychasm* (Variorum Reprints). London.

1975. *Byzantine Theology. Historical Trends and Doctrinal Themes*. Oxford.

Mitsides, A. 1973. Αἱ κατά καιρούς γενόμεναι καθαιρέσεις 'Αρχιεπισκόπων καί 'Επισκόπων τῆς Κύπρου. Nicosia.

1976. Τό αὐτοκέφαλον τῆς 'Εκκλησίας τῆς Κύπρου, *XVe Congrès International d'Etudes Byzantines*, V, 2. Athens.

Miyahara, K. 1983. 'Charisma: from Weber to Contemporary Sociology', *Sociological Inquiry*, 53, 4: 368–88.

Moffat, A. 1977. 'Schooling in the Iconoclastic Centuries', in A. A. M. Bryer and J. Herrin (eds.), *Iconoclasm*, 85–92. Birmingham.

Montfaucon, B. de 1715. *Bibliotheca Coissliniana*. Paris. [N]

1739. *Bibliotheca Bibliothecarum Nova*. Paris. [N]

Morris, R. 1976. 'The Powerful and the Poor in Tenth-Century Byzantium', *PP*, 73: 3–27.

1978. 'The Byzantine Church and the Land in the Tenth and Eleventh Centuries', unpublished D.Phil. Thesis, University of Oxford.

1981. 'The Political Saint of the Eleventh Century', in S. Hackel (ed.), *The Byzantine Saint*, 43–50. London.

1984. 'The Byzantine Aristocracy and the Monasteries', in M. Angold (ed.), *The Byzantine Aristocracy. IX to XIII Centuries* (BAR, 221), 112–37. Oxford.

1985. 'Monasteries and their Patrons in the Tenth and Eleventh Centuries', *BF*, 10: 185–232.

Mouriki, D. 1980–1. 'Stylistic Trends in Monumental Paintings of Greece during the Eleventh and Twelfth Centuries', *DOP*, 34–5; 77–124.

1984. 'The Wall Paintings of the Church of the Panagia at Moutoullas, Cyprus', in I. Hutter (ed.), *Byzanz und der Westen: Studien zur Kunst des europäischen Mittelalters* (Österreichische Akademie der Wissenschaften, philosophisch-historische Klasse, 432), 171–213. Vienna.

1985–6. 'Thirteenth-century Icon Painting in Cyprus', *The Griffon*, 1–2: 9–112.

Mullett, M. 1981. 'The Classical Tradition in the Byzantine Letter', in M. Mullett and R. Scott (eds.), *Byzantium and the Classical Tradition*, 75–93. Birmingham.

1984. 'Aristocracy and Patronage in the Literary Circles of Comnenian Constantinople', in M. Angold (ed.), *The Byzantine Aristocracy. IX to XIII Centuries* (BAR, 221), 173–201. Oxford.

J. Munitiz 1981. 'Self-canonisation: the "Partial Account" of Nicephoros Blemmydes', in S. Hackel (ed.), *The Byzantine Saint*, 164–8. London.

Nicol, D. M. 1957. *The Despotate of Epirus*, I. Oxford.

1962. 'Byzantium and the Papacy in the Eleventh-Century', *JEH*, 13: 1–20.

1964. 'Mixed Marriages in Byzantium in the Thirteenth Century', in C. W. Dugmore and C. Duggan (eds.), *Studies in Church History*, I, 160–72. London and Edinburgh.

1966. 'The Fourth Crusade and the Greek and Latin Empires, 1204–1261', in J. M. Hussey (ed.), *Cambridge Medieval History*, IV, 1, 275–330. Cambridge.

1967. 'The Byzantine View of Western Europe', *GRBS*, 8 (1967) 315–39.

1969. 'The Byzantine Church and Hellenic Learning in the Fourteenth-Century', in G. J. Cuming (ed.), *Studies in Church History*, V, 23–57. Leiden.

1975. *Meteora. The Rock Monasteries of Thessaly*. London.

1976. 'Refugees, Mixed Population and Local Patriotism in Epirus and Western Macedonia after the Fourth Crusade', *XVᵉ Congrès International d'Etudes Byzantins*, I, 2. Athens.

1980. Πρόσφατες ἔρευνες γιά τίς ἀπαρχές τοῦ Δεσποτάτου τῆς ᾿Ηπείρου ᾿Ηπειρωτικά Χρονικά, 22.

1988. *Byzantium and Venice. A Study in Diplomatic and Cultural Relations.* Cambridge.

Obolensky, D. 1948. *The Bogomils. A Study in Balkan Neo-Manichaeism.* Cambridge.

1971. *The Byzantine Commonwealth. Eastern Europe, 500–1453.* London.

Oikonomakes, N. 1972. ῾Η ἐν Κύπρῳ ἀραβοκρατία κατά τάς ἀραβικάς πηγάς, ΠΚΣ, 2: 193–200.

1984. ῾Η Κύπρος καί οἱ ῎Αραβες (622–925 μ.Χ.), *Μελέται καί ῾Υπομνήματα*, 1: 218–374.

Omont, H. 1896. *Catalogus codicorum hagiograficorum bibliothecae nationalis Parisensis.* Brussels and Paris.

Ostrogorsky, G. 1956. 'The Byzantine Empire and the Hierarchical World Order', *Slavonic and East European Review*, 35, 84: 1–14.

1968. *History of the Byzantine State*, transl. J. Hussey. Oxford.

Panagiotakos, P. 1959. Τὸ Αὐτοκέφαλον τῆς ῾Αγιωτάτης ᾿Αποστολικῆς ᾿Εκκλησίας τῆς Κύπρου. Athens.

Papachryssanthou, D. 1973. 'La Vie monastique dans les campagnes byzantines du VIIIᵉ au XIᵉ siècles', *REB*, 43: 158–82.

Papadopoulos, Ch. 1934. Περί τῆς ἀνακυρήξεως ἁγίων ἐν τῇ ᾿Ορθοδόξῳ ᾿Εκκλησία. Athens.

Papadopoulos, Th. 1976. 'Chypre: frontière ethnique et socio-culturelle du monde byzantin', *Rapports, XVᵉ Congrès International d' Etudes Byzantines*. Athens.

Papadopoulou, E. 1983. Οἱ Πρῶτες 'Εγκαταστάσεις Βενετῶν στήν Κύπρο, Σύμμεικτα, 5: 303–32.

Papageorgiou, A. 1964. 'Les Premières Incursions arabes à Chypre et leur conséquences', in 'Αφιέρωμα εἰς Κ. Σπυριδάκην, Nicosia, 152–8.

1972. ''Ιδιάζουσαι βυζαντιναί τοιχογραφίαι τοῦ 13ου αἰώνος ἐν Κύπρῳ', ΠΚΣ, 2: 201–12.

1974. 'Recently discovered wall-paintings in 10th–11th Century churches of Cyprus', M. Berza and E. Stănescu (eds), *Actes du XIVᵉ Congrès International d'Etudes Byzantines*, III, 411–14. Bucharest.

1975. 'Οἱ ξυλόστεγοι ναοί τῆς Κύπρου', *ABar*: 47–52.

Patlagean, E. 1968. 'Ancienne hagiographie byzantine et histoire sociale', *Annales. Economies, Sociétés, Civilisations*, 1: 106–26. (Repr. in Patlagean 1981a, V.).

1976. 'L'histoire de la femme déguisée en moine et l'évolution de la sainteté féminine à Byzance', *Studi Medievali*, 3ᵉ ser., 17. Spoleto, 597–623. (Repr. in Patlagean 1981a, XI.)

1977. *Pauvreté économique et pauvreté sociale à Byzance, 4ᵉ–7ᵉ siècles*. Paris.

1978. 'Byzance, le barbare, l' hérétique et la loi universelle', in *Ni Juif ni Grec. Entretiens sur le racisme, sous la direction de Leon Poliakov. Ecole des Hautes Etudes en Sciences Sociales*, 81–90. Paris. (Repr. in Patlagean 1981a, XV.)

1981a. *Structure sociale, famille, Chrétienté à Byzance* (Variorum Reprints) London.

1981b. 'Sainteté et Pouvoir', in S. Hackel (ed.), *The Byzantine Saint*, 88–105. London.

1987. 'Byzantium in the Tenth and Eleventh Centuries', in P. Veyne (ed.), A. Goldhammer, (transl.), *A History of Private Life*, I, 550–641. Cambridge, Mass., and London.

Peristiany, J. G. 1965. 'Honour and Shame in a Cypriot Highland Village', in J. G. Peristiany (ed.), *Honour and Shame. The Values of Mediterranean Society*, 171–90. London.

1968. 'Introduction to a Cyprus Highland Village', in J. G. Peristiany (ed.), *Contributions to Mediterranean Sociology. Mediterranean Rural Communities and Social Change*, 75–91. Paris.

Petit, L. 1898–9. 'Vie et ouvrages de Néophyte le Reclus', *EO*, 2: 257–68, 372.

Petropoulos, D. 1954. 'Οἱ ποιητάρηδες στήν Κρήτη καί στήν Κύπρο', Λαογραφία, 15: 374–400.

Philippou, L. 1935. 'Η ἱερὰ μονὴ Χρυσορογιατίσσης. Paphos.

Polemis, D. I. 1968. *The Doukai*. London.

Prawer, J. 1988. *The History of the Jews in the Latin Kingdom of Jerusalem*. Oxford.

Reynolds L. D., and N. G. Wilson. 1974. *Scribes and Scholars*. Oxford.

Ringrose, K. M. 1979. 'Monks and Society in Iconoclastic Byzantium', *EB*, 6: 135ff.

Rochricht 1898. *Geschichte des Koningreichs Jerusalem*. Innsbruck.

Rodley, L. 1985. *Cave Monasteries of Byzantine Cappadocia*. Cambridge.

Rosser, J. 1985. 'Excavations at Saranda Kolones, Paphos, Cyprus, 1981–1983', *DOP*, 39: 81–97.

Rudt de Collenberg, W. H. 1968. 'L'Empereur Isaac de Chypre et sa fille (1155–1207), *B*, 38: 123–79.

Runciman, S. 1947. *The Medieval Manichee*. Cambridge.

1955. *The Eastern Schism. A Study of the Papacy and the Eastern Churches during the XI and the XII Centuries*. Oxford.

1978. *A History of the Crusades*. 3 vols., Harmondsworth.

Sacopoulo, M. 1975. *La Theotokos à la Mandorle de Lythrankomi*. Paris.

Sakkos, S. N. 1967. Ἡ ἐν Κωνσταντινουπόλει Σύνοδος τοῦ 1170, in *Σπουδαστήριον 'Εκκλησιαστικῆς Γραμματολογίας, Θεολογικόν Συμπόσιον, Χαριστήριον εἰς τόν Καθηγητήν Παναγιώτην Κ. Χρήστου*, 311–52. Thessalonikē.

Schiemenz, G. P. 1969. 'Die Kapelle des Styliten Niketas in den Weinbergen von Ortahisar', *JÖB*, 18: 239–58.

Schlumberger, G. 1884a. *Sigillographie de l'empire byzantin*. Paris.

1884b. 'Sigillographie byzantine des ducs et catépans d'Antioche, des patriarches d'Antioche et des ducs et catépans de Chypre', *AOL*, 2: 423–38.

Setton, K. M. (ed.) 1969–85. *A History of the Crusades*. 6 vols., Madison, Milwaukee and London.

Ševčenko, I. 1979–80. 'Constantinople Viewed from the Eastern Provinces in the Middle Byzantine Period', in *Eucharisterion: Essays presented to Omeljan Pritsak, Harvard Ukrainian Studies, III–IV, Part 2*, 712–47. Cambridge, Mass. (Repr. in Ševčenko, *Ideology, Letters and Culture in the Byzantine World* (Variorum Reprints). London, 1982: VI.)

Sharf, A. 1971. *Byzantine Jewry from Justinian to the Fourth Crusade*. London.

Sophronios (Eustratiades) of Leontopolis 1932–4. 'Κυπριακοί Κώδικες ἐν τῇ 'Εθνικῇ Βιβλιοθήκῃ Παρισίων", *ABar* 4, 5, 6. [N]

Southern, R. W. 1962. *Western Views of Islam in the Middle Ages*. Cambridge, Mass.

Sperber, D. 1975. *Rethinking Symbolism*. Cambridge.

Stiernon, D. 1960. 'Démétrios Chomatianos', in A. Baudrillart, A. Vogt, U. Rouziès (eds.), *Dictionnaire d'histoire et de géographie ecclésiastiques*, XIV, 199–205, Paris.

1981. 'Néophyte le Reclus', in *Dictionnaire de spiritualité*, fasc. LXXII–LXXIII, 99–110. Paris.

Stylianou, A., and J. Stylianou 1985. *The Painted Churches of Cyprus. Treasures of Byzantine Art*. London.

Talbot, A.-M. 1983. *Faith Healing in Late Byzantium. The Posthumous Miracles of the Patriarch Athanasios I of Constantinople by Theoktistos the Stoudite*. Brookline, Mass.

Tambiah, S. J. 1969. 'Animals are Good to Think and Good to Prohibit', *Ethnology*, 8, 4: 423–59.

Theobald, R. 1980. 'The role of charisma in the development of social movements', *Archives de sciences sociales de religions*, 49, 1: 83–100.

Thomas, G. M. 1878. 'Ein Bericht uber die altesten Besitzungen der Venezianer auf Cypern', *Sitzungsberichte der Philosophisch-philologischen Classe der K. bayer. Akademie der Wissenschaften*, 1, 2: 143–57.

Tsiknopoulos, I. R. 1950a, 1950b: see Primary sources.

1950c. 'Ο "Άγιος Νεόφυτος, *ABar*, 11 (1950) 49–56, 83–92.

1954a–g: see Primary sources.

1954h. Κίνητρα καὶ πηγαὶ τοῦ συγγραφικοῦ ἔργου τοῦ ʽΑγίου Νεοφύτου. ʽΗ ʽΑγία Βιβλιοθήκη, *ΚΣ*, 18 (1954) ογ΄–β΄.

1955a–c: see Primary sources.

1955d. ʽΟ ″Αγιος Νεόφυτος καὶ ἡ ʽΙερὰ αὐτοῦ Μονή. Ktema.

1955e. ʽΗ ὀρθογραφικὴ ἰδιομορφία τῶν συγγραφῶν τοῦ ʼΕγκλείστου ἁγίου Νεοφύτου, *ΚΣ*, 19 (1955). [N]

1958. Τὸ συγγραφικὸν ἔργον τοῦ ἁγίου Νεοφύτου, *ΚΣ*, 22 (1958) 67–214. [N]

1959. ʽΗ ʽΙερὰ Μονὴ τοῦ Χρυσοστόμου τοῦ Κουτσουβέντη. Nicosia.

1964–5. ʽΗ Παναγία ἡ Χρυσορρωγιάτισσα. Nicosia. [N]

1965. *The Enkleistra and St. Neophytos*. Nicosia.

1967. ʽΗ θαυμασία προσωπικότης τοῦ Νεοφύτου, *Β*, 37 (1967) 311–413.

1968. ʽΗ ʽΙερὰ Μονὴ τῆς ʽΥπεραγίας Θεοτόκου τοῦ Μαχαιρᾶ. Nicosia.

Turdeanu, E. 1947. *La Littérature bulgare du XIV* siècle et sa diffusion dans les pays roumains*. Paris.

Turner, H. J. M. 1985. ʼSt Symeon the New Theologian. A Study of his Experience and Teaching Concerning Spiritual Fatherhood', unpublished Ph.D. thesis, University of Manchester.

Turyn, A. 1964. *Codices Vaticani saeculus XIII*–XIV* scripti*. Vatican.

Van Bruyn: *Cornelis van Bruyn*, ed. G. Cavalier (Paris 1714).

Vasiliev, A. A. 1929–30. ʼManuel Comnenos and Henry Plantagenet', *BZ*, 29, 233–44.

Vryonis, S. 1957. ʼThe Will of a Provincial Magnate, Eustathios Boilas (1059)', *DOP*, 9: 263–77.

1971a. *The Decline of Medieval Hellenism in Asia Minor and the Process of Islamization from the Eleventh through the Fifteenth Century* (Berkeley, Los Angeles, London 1971).

1971b. ʼByzantine Attitudes towards Islam during the Late Middle Ages', *GRBS*, 12, 2: 263–86.

1981. The *Panegyris* of the Byzantine Saint: a Study in the Nature of a Medieval Institution, its Origins and Fate', in S. Hackel (ed.), *The Byzantine Saint*, 196–226. London.

Waardenburg, J. D. J. 1978. ʼTwo Lights Perceived: Medieval Islam and Christianity', *Nederlands Theologisch Tijdschrift*, 31, 4: 267–89.

Ward, B., and N. Russell 1981. *The Lives of the Desert Fathers*. Oxford.

Wallace, A. 1966. *Religion. An Anthropological View*. New York.

Wallis, R., and S. Bruce 1986. *Sociological Theory, Religion and Collective Action*. Belfast.

Ware T. (K.) 1980. *The Orthodox Church*. Harmondsworth.

1982. ʼIntroduction', in *John Climacus, The Ladder of Divine Ascent*, 1–70. London.

Weber, M. 1947. *Theory of Social and Economic Organisation*, ed. T. Parsons, transl. R. A. Henderson and T. Parsons. New York.

1965. *The Sociology of Religion*. London.

1968. *Economy and Society*. New York.

Weyl Carr, A. 1982. ʼA Group of Provincial Manuscripts from the Twelfth Century', *DOP*, 36: 39–81.

1989. ʼCyprus and the "Decorative Style"', *EKEE*, 17: 123–67.

Wharton, A. J. 1988. *Art of Empire. Painting and Architecture of the Byzantine Periphery*. London.

Wiegand, T. 1913. *Der Latmos (Milet. Ergebnisse der Ausgrabungen und Untersuchungen seit dem Jahre 1899)*. Berlin.

Wilson, B. 1975. *The Noble Savages: the Primitive Origins of Charisma and its Contemporary Survival*. Berkeley.

Wilson, N. 1975. 'Books and Readers in Byzantium', in *Byzantine Books and Bookmen. A Dumbarton Oaks Colloquium*, 2–15. Washington, DC.

Winfield, D. C. 1971a. 'Reports on Work at Monagri, Lagoudera, and Hagios Neophytos, Cyprus, 1969/1970', *DOP*, 25: 259–64.

1971b. 'Dumbarton Oaks (Harvard University) Work at Lagoudera and Monagri, 1970', *RDAC*.

1972. 'Hagios Chrysostomos, Trikomo, Asinou. Byzantine Painters at Work', *ΠΚΣ*, 2: 285–91.

Winfield, D. C., and E. J. Hawkins 1967. 'The Church of Our Lady at Asinou, Cyprus. A Report on the seasons of 1965 and 1966', *DOP*, 21: 261–6.

Zakyntinos, D. 1941. Μελέται περὶ τῆς διοικητικῆς διαιρέσεως καὶ τῆς ἐπαρχιακῆς διοικήσεως ἐν τῷ Βυζαντινῷ κράτει, *EEBS*, 17: 208–74.

Index

305